This book is dedicated to the citizens of West Des Moines as they celebrate the 125th anniversary of their fine community.

Copyright © 2018 by the Historic Valley Junction Foundation
137 5th Street
West Des Moines, IA 50265

All rights reserved, including the right to reproduce this work in any form whatsoever without permission in writing from the publisher, except for brief passages in connection with a review. For information, please contact Historic Valley Junction Foundation.

Cover Photo: Courtesy of West Des Moines Historical Society
The plaid on the cover is a Cunningham plaid from Scotland.

The Donning Company Publishers
731 S. Brunswick
Brookfield, MO 64628

THE
DONNING COMPANY
PUBLISHERS

Lex Cavanah, General Manager
Nathan Stufflebean, Donning Production Supervisor
Richard A. Horwege and Anne Burns, Editors
Jeremy Glanville, Graphic Designer
Alyssa Neimeier, Project Research Coordinator
Katie Gardner, Marketing and Production Coordinator
Barry Haire, Project Director

ISBN: 978-1-68184-176-2

Cataloguing-in-Publication Data available from the Library of Congress

Printed in the United States of America at Walsworth

PURSUIT OF A DREAM
JAMES JORDAN
HIS LIFE AND HIS LEGACY

By M. Louise Gately
with Jan Davison

"You can have anything you want if you want it badly enough. You can be anything you want to be, do anything you set out to accomplish, if you hold to that desire with singleness of purpose."
—Abraham Lincoln

TABLE OF CONTENTS

Foreword by Michael Swanger 6
Acknowledgments 7
Introduction—"Pursuit of a Dream" 8
Part One–Genesis of the Dream 10
    Chapter 1—The Jordan and Cunningham Ancestry 12
    Chapter 2—Coming into the Valley 13
        Insert: What Was an Indian Old Field? 15
    Chapter 3—The French and Indian War 19
    Chapter 4—Peace in South Branch Valley 23
    Chapter 5—After the Revolutionary War 26
    Chapter 6—One Family—Different Directions 29
    Chapter 7—The Beginning of the End of Slavery 31
    Chapter 8—The War of 1812 34
    Chapter 9—James Jordan's Childhood 36
        Insert: How the Presbyterian Church Influenced the Lives of the Cunninghams and the Jordans 40
    Chapter 10—The Second Great Awakening 41
    Chapter 11—A Visit to Cunningham Plantation 44
    Chapter 12—Slavery in the Virginia Highlands 47
    Chapter 13—The Jordan Family Decides to Leave Western Virginia 51
Part Two–Pursuing a Destiny 54
    Chapter 14—A New life in Michigan 56
    Chapter 15—Platte County, Missouri 63
        Insert: Humphrey "Yankee" Smith and "Little Dixie" 65
    Chapter 16—"Discovering" Iowa 68
        Insert: What is a "Dragoon"? 70
Part Three–Settling in the "Land of Milk and Honey" 74
    Chapter 17—Staking a Claim in Iowa 76
        Insert: What Happened to the Indians in Iowa? 79
    Chapter 18—A Cabin in the Woods 85
    Chapter 19—Making the Farm 88
    Chapter 20—Making Friends in Town 91
    Chapter 21—Building a Community 94
    Chapter 22—James Jordan, Methodist 98
    Chapter 23—Uncle Jimmy's New House 102

Part Four–Becoming a Legend 104
    Chapter 24—"Honorable" James C. Jordan 106
    Chapter 25—". . . and her loss was keenly felt." 111
    Chapter 26—Uncle Jimmy Meets a Yankee 114
    Chapter 27—The Capital Comes to Des Moines 118
    Chapter 28—Further Changes in the Iowa Constitution 122
        Insert: The Methodist Church's Position on Temperance 122
    Chapter 29—James Jordan, Republican 126
        Insert: The Methodist Church's Official Position on Slavery Prior to the Civil War 127
    Chapter 30—The Underground Railroad 133
        Insert: Reflections on the Treatment of Slaves 134
        Insert: Some "Known" Members of the Polk County URR 135
        Insert: James Jordan, A Friend to John Brown 144
    Chapter 31—The Civil War Years 145
    Chapter 32—Supporting the War Effort 149

Part Five–Attaining the Dream 152
    Chapter 33—The Coming of the Railroad 154
        Insert: Crossing the Mississippi River 155
    Chapter 34—Uncle Jimmy, "Good Old Boy" 160
    Chapter 35—James Jordan, Cattle Baron 163
    Chapter 36—The Farmhouse Becomes a Mansion 167
    Chapter 37—The Jordan Cemetery 172
    Chapter 38—The Victorian Lifestyle 174
    Chapter 39—A Beloved Son-in-Law 179
    Chapter 40—The Junction in the Valley 185

Part Six–Leaving a Legacy 188
    Chapter 41—The Later Years 190
    Chapter 42—Valley Junction, Iowa 194
    Chapter 43—Home Sweet Home 197
    Chapter 44—The Jordan Fortune 201
        Insert: James Jordan's Last Will and Testament 202
    Chapter 45—James Cunningham Jordan's Impressive Legacy 208

Family Tree 211
Family Photo Collage 215
James Jordan Descendents 216
Bibliography 218
Index 228
About the Author and Editor 232

FOREWORD
By Michael Swanger

Pursuit of a Dream is much more than a biography of James Cunningham Jordan, the founding father of West Des Moines. While this book tells the story of James Jordan and the odyssey of his life, it also describes the lives of the men, women, and children who settled in the United States and later in central Iowa. Many readers will discover not only the story of the Jordan family but also the history of their own forebears.

What made James Jordan stand out from other Iowa pioneer settlers was his strength of character, forged by his experiences as a youth and his commitment to his religious faith. This strength transformed him from a backwoods boy to an influential political leader, a successful livestock businessman, and an advocate for social causes locally, statewide, and nationally.

Born in western Virginia, James Cunningham Jordan was a descendant of Scots-Irish and German immigrants. While Jordan's Virginia cousins owned plantations and slaves, *his* branch of the family eschewed that lifestyle and eventually left the state, journeying across the United States in search of a new life. Their journey ended when the Jordan family chose to settle five miles west of Fort Des Moines (No. 2) on the northern bank of the Raccoon River in 1846—the same year Iowa became the twenty-ninth state.

Jordan could be called the first citizen of what is now known as the Greater Des Moines area. Although he established his farm in western Polk County, Fort Des Moines was the nearest town, and he embraced it as his own. His election to Fort Des Moines' first town council catapulted him into politics, where he served as a member of the Iowa Senate, a member of the Iowa House of Representatives, and a Polk County supervisor. Over the years, Jordan played a vital role in central Iowa, heading up the effort to relocate Iowa's capital to Fort Des Moines and leading the Underground Railroad in Polk County. He collaborated with leaders in Iowa and the Midwest to launch the Republican Party, establish the State Bank of Iowa, and create Iowa's insurance industry. He helped bring the first railroad to Des Moines and eventually negotiated with the railroad to build tracks closer to his farm. This was the genesis of a railroad junction village he platted. From this tiny town—Valley Junction—the community of West Des Moines emerged and eventually became one of Iowa's premier cities.

The publication of this book in 2018 coincides with the celebration of West Des Moines' 125th anniversary of incorporation and the eightieth anniversary of its moniker. Today, Jordan's enduring legacy remains omnipresent. By name, he is commemorated by the Jordan House, Jordan Creek, Jordan Cemetery, Jordan Creek Elementary School, Jordan Creek Park, Jordan Creek Town Center, and Jordan Creek Parkway.

Those who have visited the Jordan House—the former Jordan family home, now a museum listed on the National Register of Historic Places and the National Underground Railroad Network to Freedom—have had the opportunity to learn Jordan's fascinating story. But to most, Jordan's story is largely unknown. That is, until now. Thanks to the painstaking, devoted work of long-time West Des Moines resident Louise Gately, Jordan's fascinating life and historical contributions to Iowa are revealed for all to acknowledge and appreciate.

Gately's decision to donate the publishing rights and proceeds from the sale of this book to the nonprofit Historic Valley Junction Foundation mirrors the spirit in which Jordan led his life—to enhance the lives of the people of Iowa—past, present, and future.

Michael Swanger
Owner and Publisher
Iowa History Journal
West Des Moines, Iowa

ACKNOWLEDGMENTS

When you do something for the sake of doing it, your expectations of yourself adjust accordingly and you can relax into the very fulfilling process of learning.
—Author unknown

The origin of this quote is unknown, but the words perfectly express my thoughts when writing this book. I learned a lot from writing it and I hope it becomes a basis for knowledge for those who read it.

There is no way this book would have seen the light of day without the encouragement of my family and friends. Indeed, my completion of this book was on my *husband's* bucket list; I started writing it twenty-five years ago and he didn't want it to sit on the shelf any longer. So my personal thanks to my beloved husband, Gary Gately.

I also received gentle encouragement from my children. From the very beginning they were proud that I was working on this project, and now it really has become a book! Thanks and love to my two incredible children, Robert Dunster Julius Cook and Susannah Ruth Wattson Morris.

That said, my book team gave me the confidence to get the job done: Barry Haire of Donning Company Publishers who persevered for years, patiently nudging me to move forward; Jim Miller, executive director of the Historic Valley Junction Foundation, who was in charge of the business and finance details of publishing the book; Michael Swanger, editor/publisher of the *Iowa History Journal*, who made me feel that this book would have historical credibility; and most importantly, Jan Davison, my editor, who made the book readable and kept me on track throughout the editing process.

The visuals are an integral part of this book, and my friend Scott Little, a professional photographer, knows everything about how pictures go onto the page and assisted with talent, humor, and perseverance.

Along the way I added a reader to the team who became much more: Katie Getting, Drake University, BA in history, summa cum laude, who, along with Scott Little, organized the hundreds of visuals in the book as well as provided technical support in her very own millennial style.

Thanks also to Vicki Baker, an early president of the West Des Moines Historical Society, who introduced me to "Uncle Jimmy Jordan" when we started writing grants together to renovate the Jordan House 'way back in the early 1980s. In order to write the grants, we needed to tell the story—and what a story it is! In doing research and writing about James Jordan, I have "lived with" this man for decades. I will never get to personally meet him, but I feel that I got to know him well, and I can say he positively influenced my life.

From the moment I started writing it, this book was to be a gift to my adopted "home town," Valley Junction. The Historic Valley Junction Foundation holds the copyright on the book, the proceeds from which will be administered by them to use as they see fit to improve our community. I think James Jordan would be proud a book about him is doing that, and so am I.
—Louise Gately

INTRODUCTION
"Pursuit of a Dream"

After an eleven-year odyssey, Walnut Township, Iowa, became the final destination for pioneer settler James Cunningham Jordan. He set out on his journey from western Virginia at the age of nineteen, stopping for several years in southwestern Michigan and then moving on to northwestern Missouri. Poised to continue on to the West Coast via the Oregon Trail, he was instead drawn north to an area he heard might be opening up for pioneer settlement.

Compelled to explore this new land, Jordan saw rich soil, numerous streams, rivers, woodlands, and verdant prairies. A friendly man himself, he discovered like-minded folks at a fort that had been built at the confluence of two rivers—the Raccoon and the Des Moines. The name of this place was "Iowa," and he decided to give it a try.

The story of James Jordan is not unlike that of many pioneers who settled the midwestern states during the first half of the nineteenth century. Moving ever westward, new territory was being claimed by the US government, many times in contentious battles with the people indigenous to the land.

Once secured, the land could be bought cheaply. The fertile heartland of America became attractive not only to folks living in the eastern part of the United States, but also to people as far away as Europe.

In addition to the lucrative economic opportunities in the newly opened territories, pioneers may have had other reasons to move. The issue of slavery prompted some families to leave places where owning slaves was the accepted and legal practice. Religious and political freedom was another factor, while many, struck by "frontier fever," were in it purely for the adventure.

It was a time of great migration. Thousands of families were moving west. It was not at all unusual for them to leave their established homes and towns settled generations earlier by their ancestors and go in search of a new life.

Pioneer settlement had begun in the Iowa Territory along the Mississippi River in 1824. Two decades later, in 1846, the western Iowa territory, newly purchased from the Indians, was opened by the US government to homesteaders. By 1850 almost 2.5 million settlers from the East and South had settled in newly opened territory spanning from eastern Ohio west to the Missouri River. Over ninety thousand trailblazers had migrated even further west in wagon trains following the Oregon Trail to the Northwest and California.

James Jordan could have chosen to be a part of the wave of adventurers in the early years of the California migration, but Iowa beckoned. As soon as he explored it, he knew Iowa would be the perfect place to pursue his boyhood dream of raising and selling livestock. By the time Iowa had been admitted to the Union, 116,295 pioneers were living in the new state, and James Jordan had begun to establish a livestock enterprise a few miles west of Fort Des Moines. He was on his way to becoming one of the most prominent stockmen in the region, buying and selling thousands of head of hogs and cattle that were raised on the lush grasslands of Iowa prairie. Jordan had turned his dream into reality.

Jordan's business success catapulted him into the role of leader—locally in Walnut Township, in the larger arena of the city of Des Moines, and in the state of Iowa. However, his business success was only one element that made the man.

Jordan was intensely committed to the principles in which he believed and which formed the foundation that guided his life. These were based upon his devoted attachment to the Methodist religion and the extraordinary influence of the Second Great Awakening he had experienced as a young man. His faith shaped his character—he was devoted to his family, his community, and their welfare, building schools, churches, and a fine home for his eleven children.

James Jordan's religious beliefs were the source of his moral stand against slavery. His strong abolitionist feelings influenced his involvement in the Underground Railroad prior to the Civil War and he became its chief conductor in Polk County, Iowa. Not only did he personally provide refuge to slaves escaping along the secret routes of the Underground Railroad, he quietly helped lead it, along with his many influential friends involved in Iowa politics and government.

Jordan's Methodist faith and abolitionist stance helped link him to the newly emerging Republican Party, in which he played an active role locally and in the state of Iowa. A man of vision, James Jordan embraced the challenge of bringing Iowa's capital to Des Moines, guiding the establishment of the State Bank of Iowa, introducing prohibition to the state, and helping to start the Polk County Poor Farm after the Civil War years.

Jordan is credited as playing a significant role in leading the intense effort to bring the railroad to Des Moines, thus assuring the city a successful economic future. Later, he started a little railroad town of his own out in Walnut Township, which was renamed Valley Junction and eventually West Des Moines. His reputation as a successful and prosperous stockman led him, along with other top-ranking Des Moines business leaders, to support the establishment of Iowa's insurance industry. He did not do all this alone. His name has been closely linked with the most prominent early Iowa leaders: James Harlan, Samuel Kirkwood, James Grimes, Hoyt Sherman, Phineas Casady, and F. M. Hubbell, to name a few.

At James Jordan's funeral in 1891, he was eulogized as being "strong in the defense of right," and remembered as being a "man of superior intelligence, great force of character and sterling worth." Characterized as having "indefatigable energy, enterprise and sagacious business foresight," he was described as "a man of gruff speech" but also as a "tender man of charity and love, which constantly cropped up and made his friends feel that in him they could place utmost confidence."

James Jordan was a man who lived what he believed. This was undoubtedly why he accomplished so much in his lifetime and was so highly regarded by those who knew him. His legend has been remembered for over a century. His legacy touches lives daily and will continue to touch the lives of future generations.

Part One

Genesis of the Dream

    To better understand the strong, visionary, and principled man James Cunningham Jordan came to be, a look into his family roots sheds light on important historical events that influenced and shaped his grandparents, his parents, and even James Jordan himself.

    For this story we will trace James Jordan's heritage and family history back to his family roots on the other side of the Atlantic Ocean and then proceed from the mid-1700s when his ancestors arrived in America.

CHAPTER 1
The Jordan and Cunningham Ancestry

Settling in the Valley of Virginia

James Jordan's great-grandparents were colonial pioneers who came to the British Colony of Virginia around 1740. They settled in the western Virginia highlands in the Valley of Virginia. This area is a series of extraordinarily beautiful mountain valleys laced with streams and rivers located between the Blue Ridge Mountains on the east and the Allegheny Mountains on the west.

The Colony of Virginia was geographically divided into two distinct sectors—the eastern Tidewater and Piedmont along the shore leading up into the mountains and the western Highlands, most of which is now known as the state of West Virginia. The Blue Ridge Mountains stood firmly in between these two areas. There were no easy access routes from eastern Virginia over the mountains. The colonial pioneers who settled in the western Virginia Highlands entered the area from the north—Pennsylvania—following rivers upstream or traversing the mountain ridges down into the fertile bottomlands of the Valley of Virginia.

James Cunningham Jordan's maternal great-great-grandfather, William Cunningham, and his great-grandfather, John Cunningham, together followed this route into western Virginia around 1747. About the same time, his paternal great-grandfather, George Jordan, also arrived. The stories of these men, their wives and families and how they made their homes in the western Virginia Highland valleys are very different, but both illustrate how family history influenced James Cunningham Jordan, his values, and his beliefs.

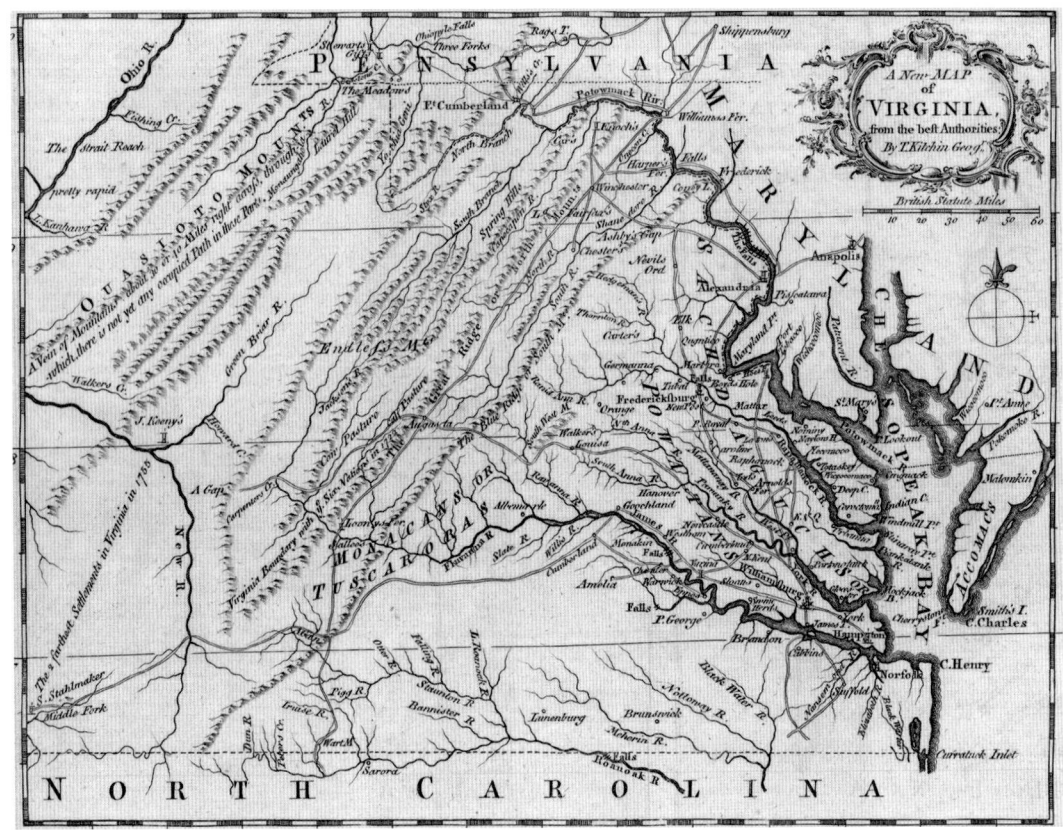

A map of Virginia around the time the Jordan and Cunningham ancestors arrived. Library of Congress

12 Pursuit of a Dream

CHAPTER 2
Coming into the Valley

The Cunningham Men Arrive in South Fork Valley

James Cunningham Jordan's great-great-grandfather, William Cunningham, was born around 1690 in Ayrshire, a county in southwestern Scotland. The Cunningham clan, like many of the other clans in Scotland, raised and traded cattle for their livelihood.

About the time William was born, there was a great famine in Scotland. William's family left their home in northern Ayrshire County and emigrated across the Northern Channel to Armagh, a county in the northern part of Ireland. They followed other Protestant Presbyterians who were granted land in the 1600s as a "spoil" of the war between the Irish Catholics and James I of England. The British had won; the Irish Roman Catholic nobility lost their estates in the north and had fled to southern Ireland, and the Presbyterian Scots replaced them. This area of Ireland had been renamed "The Ulster Plantation," and the Scots who settled there were known as "Ulster Scots."

William's family made their home in Armagh, and it was there where he reached adulthood, married, and had a son, John, born sometime after 1710. John (referred to in later years as "Lord John"), like his father, grew up in Armagh, but after he and his wife Elizabeth were married, they relocated to Dublin where their son, William II, was born. William II, who would be nicknamed "Irish Billy," was born about 1733. About 1735, Irish Billy was joined by a brother, John Jr.

Benjamin Van Meter, a descendant of the Cunningham family, reminisced about his ancestors in 1901, recounting a family legend about John and Elizabeth's son William II, "Irish Billy:" "It is said this William has been known more than once to give the lineal descent of the family back to an unbroken line to Scotch title ancestry. . . ."

About three years after John Jr.'s birth, John and Elizabeth, along with John's father, William, now a widower, left Ireland. Tired of the ongoing contentious political battles between the Irish and the British, they joined an estimated two hundred thousand Scots-Irish emigrants, who traveled across the Atlantic Ocean between 1717 and 1775 to launch a new life in America.

When the Cunningham family arrived in Philadelphia, Old William was close to fifty years of age. The group resided initially in Bucks County in the colony of Pennsylvania, where Elizabeth gave birth to a third son, Robert, around 1740.

Although they lived in Pennsylvania, it was the Cunningham family's desire to settle in the western Virginia highlands where they had heard from other immigrants they could purchase excellent farmland, and where many Scots-Irish families had already settled. Their chance came in 1747.

During the previous century, King Charles II of England had granted Thomas, Lord Fairfax's ancestors (the Culpepers) five million acres in colonial Virginia, encompassing all the lands bounded by the Potomac and Rappahannock Rivers. This land became known as the Northern Neck Proprietary. When the Virginia House of Burgesses voted to open up Virginia's western highlands to pioneer settlement in the 1730s, Lord Fairfax, an owner of a substantial amount of Virginia land, wanted to be a player in this massive real estate venture. Because his holdings had been a grant from England's king, he needed permission to sell patents on his land from Britain's Privy Council. Official permission was granted around 1747, although Fairfax had already preemptively opened his Northern Neck Proprietary to settlement years before, selling pioneers patents on parcels of the land without "official" permission. Fairfax realized significant income from this venture: he collected annual quitrents from the many hundreds of owners of the patents.

The area of the Northern Neck Proprietary where the Cunninghams wanted to settle was located on the South Branch Potomac, a tributary of the Potomac River. This area was referred to as South Branch Valley and was considered a prime area for settlement due to its rich limestone soil.

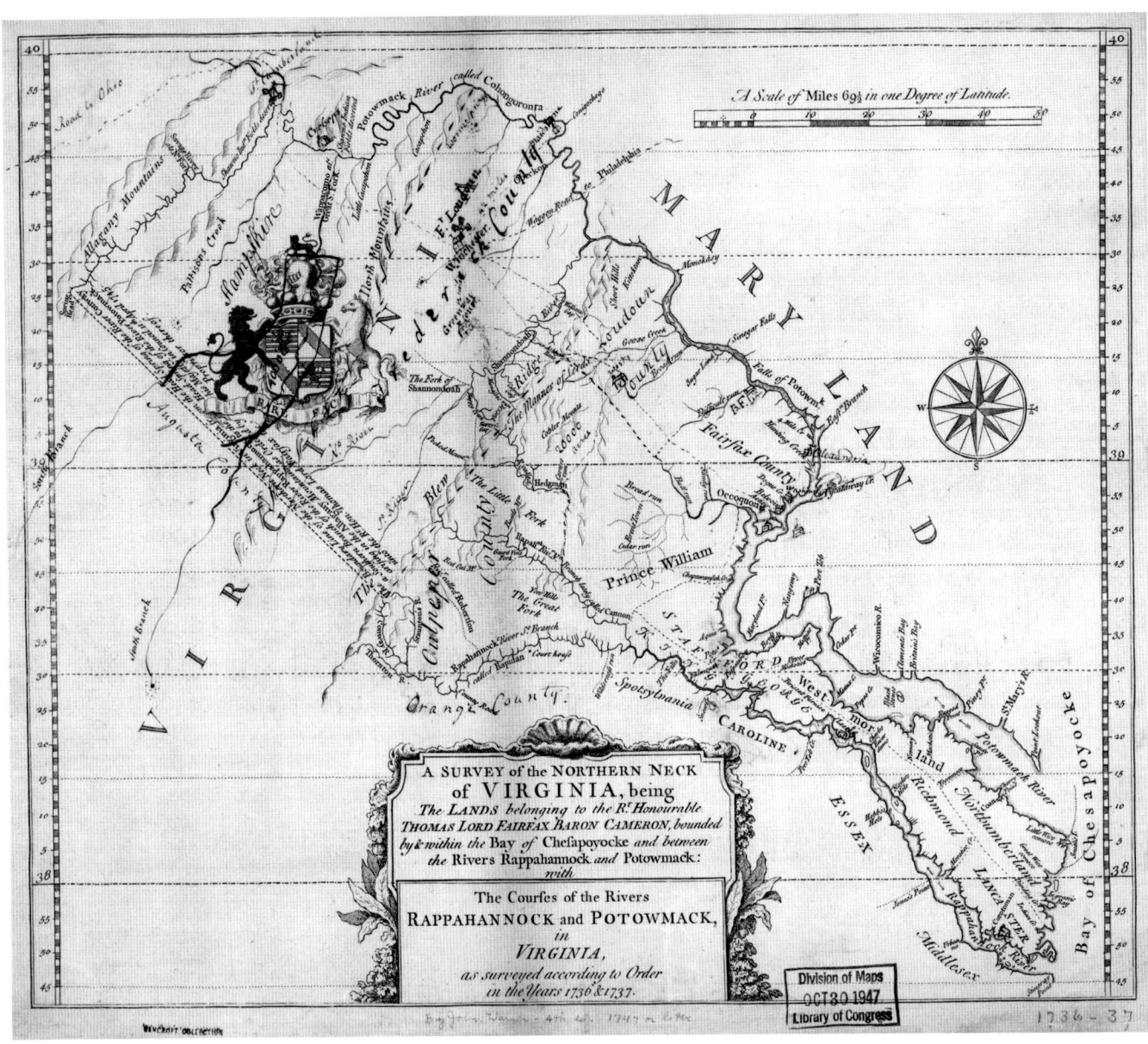

Map of the Northern Neck Proprietary in Western Virginia. Library of Congress

Journeying south from what would be their temporary home in Bucks County, Pennsylvania, into the Valley of Virginia, the Cunningham clan stopped for a short time in Lancaster County. It may have been at this time that John's wife, Elizabeth, died. Afterwards, Old William, his son John, and John's three sons forged on, joining the procession of settlers making their way into the Valley of Virginia.

Because there were no roads—only a few rugged Indian trails—the very early settlers had traveled into western Virginia from Pennsylvania on foot or horseback. The pioneers' few personal possessions came in on the backs of horses or other beasts of burden. By the time the Cunninghams arrived, access to the area had improved with more useable roadways.

When they finally arrived in South Branch Valley, Old William, John, and the boys chose a parcel of land upon which to permanently build their new life in America. The original Cunningham stake, referred to as "The Homestead," was at the upper end of the valley of the South Branch Potomac River, a few miles south and east of the Indian "old field" that comprised a part of the significant holdings (ten thousand acres) claimed over a decade earlier by Isaac and Annetje (Hannah) Van Meter, wealthy

14   Pursuit of a Dream

landowners of Dutch descent. Isaac, a former fur trader, had happened upon the property and then purchased it because of its location on a spectacularly beautiful plunging "trough" in the river that ran along the Indian old field. At the south end of the Trough, he built a fortified cabin he named Fort Pleasant, and at the north end he constructed a fort he named Fort Van Meter.

According to the recollections of Cunningham/Van Meter descendant Benjamin Van Meter: "Three sons and their aged father came from Ireland and settled in the upper end of the valley of the South Branch of the Potomac about 1750 to 1755 . . . There was a Lord John Cunningham of Ireland, who lived there . . . and probably (they) are living there now, who descended from an old Scotch family."

"Cunningham, Virginia"

The Cunninghams arrived in South Branch Valley in 1747 and eventually secured legal patents on the land. According to western Virginia historian Charles Morrison:

> The settlers who rented land from Lord Fairfax or were squatters on the land in the early 1750s had farms that averaged between 370 and 400 acres. . . . Lord Fairfax offered a good deal for a man of small means. A tenant could lease as much land as he could pay for.

Fort Van Meter located at the northern end of "The Trough." National Park Service, US Department of the Interior

He leased his land under two types of patents. The first type was for 21 years at one shilling a year per each hundred acres. The second type was a "three lives" lease (the lifetime of usually the husband, wife and youngest son). No quitrents were due the first year and thereafter the annual fee was minimal with Fairfax's agent collecting the annual quitrent fees on St. Michaelmas Day, the 29th of September.

What Was an Indian Old Field?

An Indian old field was a large area of flat land the Indians had prepared for short-term settlement and hunting grounds. The Indians chopped down all the trees and created a spacious grassy meadowland. These fields held temporary Indian camps or were places they could easily hunt animals that came to graze. Typically, these old fields were located along major Indian trails used by the numerous tribes coming and going through an area.

Indian old fields were a preferred location of colonial settlers to situate their holdings, especially at that early stage of settlement. There were no roads in western Virginia at the time, only Indian trails. The old fields, linked by Indian trails, provided a rudimentary transportation network. The pioneers used the Indian trails as much as the Indians did until they built actual roads through the wilderness, many of which followed the old Indian trails. The old fields provided the settlers with another advantage: they were already cleared so pioneers did not have to remove trees and clear land for their farms and dwellings.

Problems occurred, of course, when the pioneers settled on these old fields, which had been quite significant to the traditional Indian way of life. The settlers were displacing people who had occupied these lands for hundreds of generations. Treaties and agreements had been executed, with the Indians forced into agreeing to colonial settlement. The area was supposed to have been vacated by the Indians, but they had been roaming there for thousands of years and many did not leave. In fact, the ones who stayed were quite unhappy that they could not continue to inhabit the region and live their lives as they always had.

The patent required the leaseholder to build a cabin that measured at least 16 x 20 feet, with a brick or stone chimney, fence and cultivate land and maintain his fences and plant a fenced orchard of at least 100 fruit trees.

The following is the first land patent registered to "Lord John" Cunningham in South Branch Valley:
John Cunningham
- 430 acres, Lot #38, Wappacomo or Great South Branch, occupied 1747/49, recorded in 1757.

The land's location was originally described as "on the Wappacomo or great South branch of Potowmack . . . Lord Fairfax to John Cunningham, Lot thirty-eight. South branch, 1757." This would be the property the Cunninghams referred to as "The Homestead."

Even though they occupied the land in the late 1740s, the patent was not on file in Hampshire County until 1757, ten years after John Cunningham had settled on the land. At that time the Virginia colonial government functioned poorly in the wilderness; it took a great amount of time for land patents to be surveyed, proven, and legally recorded. In addition, leases with Fairfax were considered private transactions and were often not immediately recorded in county deed books.

The county of record for South Branch Valley at the time the Cunninghams settled was Augusta County, whose county seat was one hundred miles away in Staunton. In order to travel to Staunton one had to ford rivers and cross over mountains. By the time their deed was filed, Augusta County had been divided and their property was in newly named Hampshire County, with the county seat only twenty-five miles away in Romney.

Once they staked their land, Old William, "Lord John," and John's three teenaged sons, William II ("Irish Billy"), John Jr., and Robert, immediately set about building a crude log structure, using the trees on the property. In time, they constructed a more stable cabin and built outbuildings which would be the beginning of their farm.

One feature of pioneer cabins at the time was the absence of windows. Instead there were small cutouts in the logs on all sides of the cabin at about shoulder height. This was not so much to let in light as to provide a space for those inside the cabin to peer outside, position a musket, and shoot at the Indians.

Within a year the Cunningham men had established their residence on their Great South Branch property, and "Lord John," a forty-five-year-old widower, remarried. His new wife was Mary Ursula Biedert Peterson, the daughter of Swiss immigrants Hans Joggi Biedert Peterson and his wife, Sarah Mohlerin Peterson. Not long after their marriage, John and Mary's son, James, was born, around 1748 (James Cunningham Jordan would be his grandson and namesake). Old William, now over sixty years old, passed on. According to Benjamin Van Meter: "The aged father died and was buried in the garden at the homestead not many years after they settled there."

Other parcels of land in the proximity of "The Homestead" were purchased as the family could afford them. The parcels were put in the Cunningham sons' names:
William Cunningham
- 68 acres, Lot No. 57w, South Branch Manor, occupied about 1750.
- 242 acres, Lot No. 42, South Branch Manor, occupied about 1750.
- 248 acres on Mill's Branch, patent recorded on November 24, 1757, in Hampshire County.

Robert Cunningham
- 338 acres, Lot No. 43, South Branch Manor, occupied about 1750.
- 318 acres beginning and below the mouth of a spring where it runs into Mill Creek on the south side of said creek, occupied in 1751.

John Cunningham Jr.
- 150 acres on the North Fork of the South Branch of Potomack part of Walnut Bottom. Patent registered in 1756 and recorded 1762 in Hampshire County.

James Cunningham
- 150 acres, South Branch Manor, Lot No. 24 (adjoining Simon and Samuel Hornback), occupied in 1747/49, recorded in 1758 in Hampshire County.
- 225 acres in South Branch Manor, North Fork of the South Branch of Potomowmack, called Walnut Bottom and bounded as follows to wit beginning at two Lynnes (Linden trees) on the southeast side of the river and running thence north thirty-nine degrees east forty-nine poles

to a White Oak and Sugar Tree at the head of a spring thence north ten degrees east one hundred and forty poles to a Hickory and White Oak north forty degrees east one hundred and thirty-six poles to a Birch tree on a spur of a mountain and north forty degrees west one hundred and twenty poles to a Sugar Tree and Hickory on an island in the river thence up the several courses of the river. (Patent No. 34 1756–1762—registered in 1756 in Augusta County recorded July 12, 1762).

By 1758, counting John's original 430 acres, members of the Cunningham family were the collective owners of patents on over two thousand acres of land. In less than a decade after their arrival in South Branch Valley the Cunningham family would make their homestead farm into a prosperous plantation, and the area where they lived and farmed would eventually be shown on maps as Cunningham, West Virginia.

George Jordan Arrives in South Branch Valley

George Jordan came to America as a German "Redemptionist" on a Dutch ship sailing out of Rotterdam, Holland. A poor refugee from the Palatinate region of southern Germany, young George longed to flee the strife and certain poverty he would soon face as an adult in Germany and travel to a better life in America. He may have been trying to join his older brother, John Jordan, who had come to America earlier. John, born in 1709 in Germany, had settled in Duchess County, New York, where he worked as a weaver.

Journeying down the Rhine River from southern Germany to Rotterdam, George Jordan booked free passage to America. The ship was bound for Philadelphia. Perhaps he didn't know that in order for his brother to meet him, the ship would have had to land in New York City. It is unlikely George ever saw his brother during the rest of their lives in America.

Immediately upon George's disembarkation in Philadelphia, he was under obligation to pay his fare, and there was no brother there to meet his ship. Instead, a contract for his indentured service was negotiated with a Welshman named David Evans by the ship's dock agent. Evans, who was looking for a strong young man to work for him, met the ship and paid (redeemed) George's fare to the dock agent.

This would have been a quick and confusing transaction—the ship's agent was eager to obtain George's fare and did not care a whit if George, a German, could understand the English being spoken by Evans while negotiating his indenture price and passage fare.

Upon becoming "master and servant," the language barrier between English-speaking Evans and German-speaking Jordan was challenging, the amount of work requested of George was probably unreasonable, and his living conditions deplorable. However, he had no choice; he was under contract to David Evans. Evans eventually took him to Augusta County in the Virginia highlands.

After a time in Virginia, George made the acquaintance of Fred Carlock, the son of David Carlock, who, like George, had been a German immigrant from the Palatinate. In 1741, David Carlock had resettled his family from Upstate New York, where they had all served their indenture, to a new homestead in South Branch Valley in Augusta County, Virginia.

Meeting Fred Carlock was a fortuitous experience in the life of young George Jordan. On November 20, 1746, George Jordan's contractual relationship with David Evans was severed by the Augusta County Court and Fred Carlock, probably now a friend, purchased George's indenture contract from the court. George Jordan had a few more years on his seven-year contract but was very happy to finish it out with people from his homeland with whom he was more compatible and with whom he could more easily communicate.

A clue as to why George changed his service contract may be evident in the following entry in the court records of Augusta County four years later in 1750: "Letter to vestry, Feb. 20, 1750 'David Evans is so leasey (lazy) that he will not work and provide for his family, for they are almost starved with cold and hunger, and they have no other example but cursing, swearing, lying and the like bad vice. We think it our duty to acquaint you of this condition.'"

In the early 1750s, after seven long years, George was finally finished with his indentured servitude. He had enough money saved up to purchase land. Most likely, George participated in the "head rent" system. The parcel he could afford to buy was small and in the

James Jordan: His Life and His Legacy   17

upland area of the valley; he initially bought fifty acres with the promise to pay an annual one-shilling quitrent, build a cabin, and improve the land within three years.

George augmented the income he derived from farming his own land by working for established landowners. The larger and more established of those, like Isaac Van Meter, the Cunningham family, and the Carlocks, would be likely employers. At that time there were few slaves in the area, and work opportunities for a strong young man like George Jordan were plentiful.

George's indenture contract had stipulated he was not allowed to marry while in service. With his indenture completed, land in his name, and money in his pocket, he was finally able to take a wife. On January 26, 1754, George and his wife welcomed the arrival of their son, George Jr., whose birth they recorded in the Augusta County Courthouse.

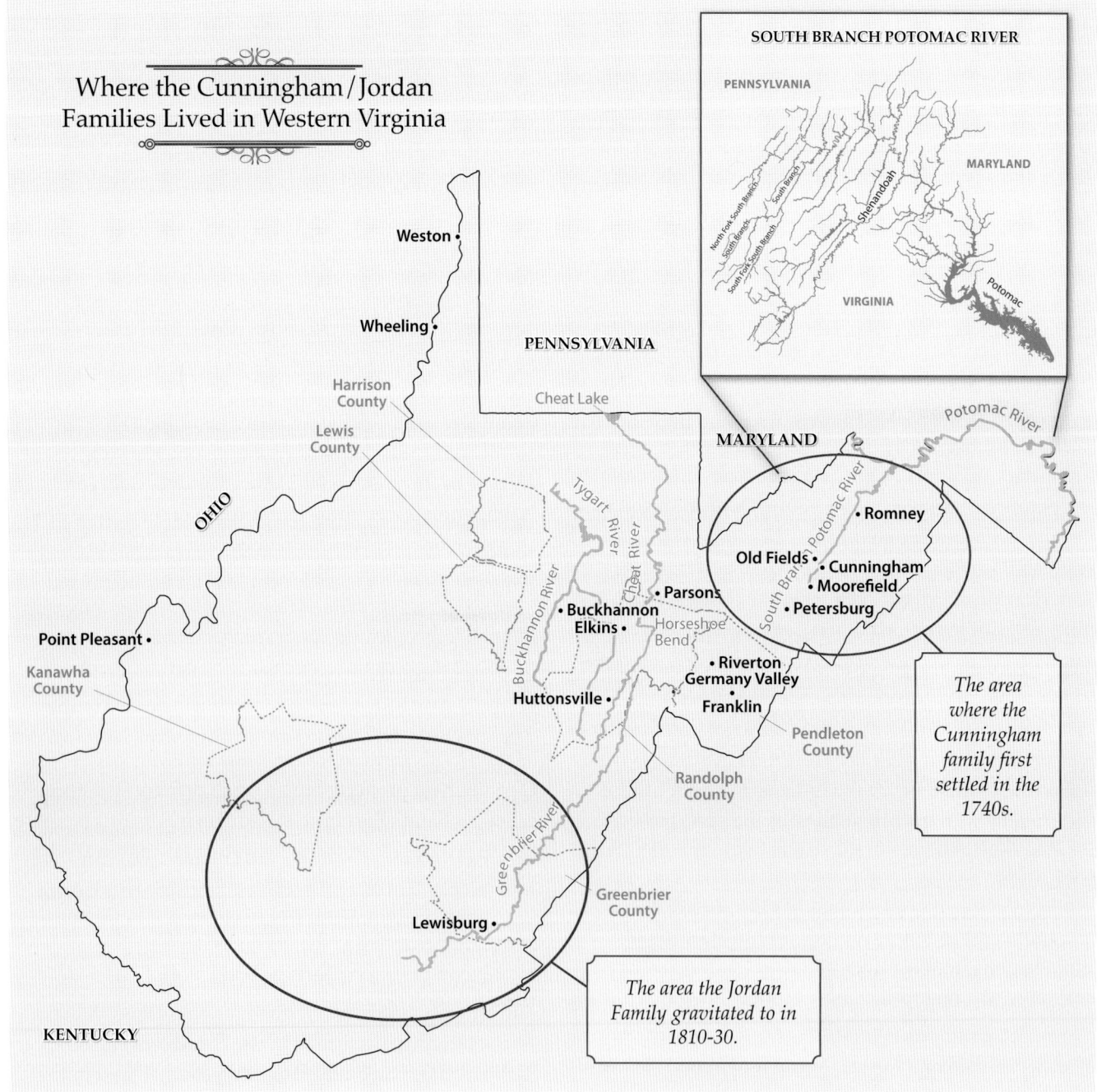

18   Pursuit of a Dream

CHAPTER 3
The French and Indian War

It was a frightening time for George Jordan Jr. to be born. For years Indians had been on an angry rampage of killing, kidnapping, and scalping, with the colonists fighting back in ugly, bloody skirmishes. Finally, the colonists had had enough. Four months after George Jr.'s birth, the French and Indian War officially began on May 28, 1754.

Before the French and Indian War, treaties had been agreed upon: in 1737–38 Virginia's Governor William Gooch hired a negotiator to broker peace between the Six (Indian) Nations to end the warfare in the western highlands between the Iroquois Tribes and their enemies. This enabled armistice and allowed Gooch to authorize settlement of a "peaceful" Shenandoah Valley. Later, in the 1744 Treaty of Lancaster (Pennsylvania), the Indians relinquished their claim to all the lands between the Blue Ridge Mountains and the Ohio River, resulting in the first conveyance by the Indians of title to lands in that region. However, Indians continued to hunt and live in and around the areas that were being settled, as they had for over ten thousand years.

During the time George Jordan and the Cunningham family were acquiring their property, in the 1740s and 1750s, the western Virginia land rush was at a fever pitch. With each parcel settled, more and more Indians were being displaced. Their hunting lands were disappearing, their trails were being converted to improved roadways, and their old fields deeded, fenced, and turned into pasture or cropland. Their way of life was being destroyed by settlers occupying territory in which the Indians were still trying to exist. While the Indians had been helpful and friendly with the first settlers, as the years passed they became increasingly angry and began to fight against those taking ownership of their land.

Stories were told and retold in gory detail, even one hundred years after the gruesome events took place, about how the Indians attacked settlers and their families: Indians stabbed them, scalped them, and, if they didn't kill them, took them prisoner. There were just as many stories of settlers—men *and* women—who fought back, some fending off the Indians and some not. When working on their farmland—or anywhere on their property—farmers, their wives, and their older children always carried a musket, so constant was the Indian threat.

Many settlers were so terrified by the ominous presence and aggressive actions of the Indians, and the back and forth slaughter that occurred between them, that they abandoned the cabins they had built in the western Virginia highlands and retreated to more civilized areas in Pennsylvania on the Eastern Seaboard. Those who stayed were in constant, mortal danger.

The desertion of settlers from western Virginia encouraged the possibility of French and Indian land reclamation, which was not a popular prospect in the colonial Virginia legislature. They wanted the highlands occupied. The highland settlers who stayed wanted more protection. The Virginia House of Burgesses responded by funding increased military presence in the area. They eventually would declare war on the Indians.

To assist the Virginia legislature in protecting its citizens in the western highlands, Colonel George Washington issued orders for a chain of forts to be built along the frontier of the Allegheny Mountains to provide a barricade against the Indians. These forts, some large, some small, made local settlers feel safer, especially when they were traveling or out farming in their fields.

The local folks also pitched in to defend themselves. On March 22, 1753, John Cunningham Jr. became a lieutenant in the militia under Captain Foote. Two years later, in 1755, farmers in the immediate area of the Cunningham property built a small defense structure called Holland's Fort (also called Town Fort). Its purpose was to provide close, local access to a safe haven from the Indians, and a place from which the Virginia Militia could provide protection and defend the settlers and their families living in the immediate area.

One of the largest forts ordered by Colonel Washington was constructed in 1756 in South Branch Valley, not far from the Cunningham homestead on part of the Indian old field next to Isaac Van Meter's massive fortified cabin. Washington ordered that the South Branch fort was to be a quadrangular shape with ninety-foot-long walls, bastions in the corners, barracks, and a magazine. It was to have a palisaded defense wall enclosing a blockhouse and log houses. When it was completed, with Washington's permission, the Van Meters called this structure "Fort Pleasant," the same name they had given their commodious homestead.

The building of Fort Pleasant was accomplished in two years, and during the French and Indian War it served as the local headquarters for a detachment of Colonel Washington's Virginia Regiment. Along with the enlisted soldiers assigned to Fort Pleasant, many of the local men volunteered to serve as well. George Jordan joined the Augusta County Militia in 1758, serving under Colonel John Buchanan. The two Cunningham brothers, William and Robert, also served. William, the oldest Cunningham son, was a lieutenant.

Fort Pleasant had been built as a post for military defense, and from 1759 to 1761 the fort also served in a civil function as the seat of the Hampshire (previously part of Augusta) County Courthouse. It was chosen because it was the main fort in that part of the county, and the area around the fort held the majority of the county's population.

Indian warrior holding a scalp. Library of Congress

20   Pursuit of a Dream

A community had emerged in the fort's shadow referred to as "Old Fields." With the constant Indian threat, Fort Pleasant in Old Fields had been the safest place to conduct county business—court cases, business agreements, tax collection, orders for new roads, and so on, as well as keeping the records of the proceedings in the fort.

The Hampshire County Court documents were eventually moved, in December 1761, to Pearsall's Flats, twenty miles to the north. Lord Fairfax renamed Pearsall's Flats "Romney," after a town in England, the following year. Romney eventually became the county seat for Hampshire County, where the Cunningham family homestead had been established.

Scalped! Kidnapped!

Most of Fort Pleasant's military activities involved detachments of soldiers pursuing Indians who had kidnapped settlers. Usually the soldiers were not successful, and the settlers were never seen again. Settlers under attack were first scalped and then killed with tomahawks or stabbed to death with knives. Those who weren't killed were kidnapped and taken to Indian settlements in the west, at that time in Ohio.

The settlers who were fortunate enough to be alerted to approaching Indians would rush to safe refuge in one of the nearby forts. Upon returning to their property, they would find their hastily abandoned cabins and out buildings a smoldering pile of rubble, burned down by the Indians. Their livestock would have been released or slaughtered.

The protection offered by Fort Pleasant did not help the (now elderly) Van Meters, living on their homestead next to the Cunningham land. In 1757, while Isaac and his wife, Hannah, were working unprotected in farm fields adjacent to their Fort Pleasant home, they were both scalped and then killed by Indians of the Delaware and Shawnee Tribes. A year later the same thing happened at the Cunningham homestead.

On March 19, 1758, at a time when John's older sons William, John Jr., and Robert were away fighting in the French and Indian War, members of the Shawnee Tribe raided the Cunningham cabin, scalped, and then slaughtered John. John's wife, Mary, pregnant with their second child, and their nine-year-old son, James, could not get to safe sanctuary at Holland's Fort near their home. Instead they were captured and taken as prisoners to a Shawnee Indian village in Chillicothe, Ohio.

Mary's baby daughter, whom she named Mary, was born in captivity while at the Indian village. The next year mother and baby daughter were allowed to return to their home in South Branch Valley. Her son, James, was not so fortunate. He remained a prisoner of the Indian tribe.

After their return, Mary Cunningham and her daughter lived at the Cunningham homestead in the cabin she had shared with her now deceased husband. Despite her horrific experiences, Mary persevered and built a life for herself and her daughter. Local farmers James and Sarah Trimble were selling land adjacent to other Cunningham property, this time on the North Fork of the South Branch Potomac, and, in 1761, Mary Cunningham purchased the property. This may have been intended for her baby daughter, Mary, as it had been the custom of Mary's husband, "Lord John," to put parcels of land in his children's names:

Mary Cunningham
- 17/18 August 1761—160 acres on North Fork of South Branch Potomack, above John Cunningham's Walnut Bottom (from James and Sarah Trimble).

In 1762 Mary Cunningham was remarried—to Sylvester Ward, a neighboring landowner and friend who had been in the militia with Mary's stepsons. Mary did not know if her older son, James, was still alive; nevertheless, she and Sylvester decided they needed to move on with their lives. They, along with Mary's daughter, Mary, moved west to a new life in Germany Valley in Randolph County. They chose this area so they could be near Mary's parents, who had made their home there with other former Redemptionist families of Swiss and German origin. Mary and Sylvester Ward's family eventually grew to include not only her son and daughter, James and Mary Cunningham, but also seven more children whom Mary had with Sylvester.

Two Cunningham Sons Get Married

About 1758, during the time he was fighting the Indians in the French and Indian War, Lord John's oldest son, William II ("Irish Billy"), married Phoebe Scott. Phoebe and her family were early settlers to South

Branch Valley. William and Phoebe settled in at the Cunningham homestead, now a plantation, and Phoebe soon gave birth to a son, whom they named William III.

John Cunningham Jr. also married when he came back from the war. His bride was Rebecca Harness, whose family, like George Jordan and Mary Cunningham Ward's, had been German Redemptionists who settled in South Branch after serving their indenture. The Harness family had come to South Branch by way of Schotarie Valley in New York. The prosperous Harness family would, like the Cunninghams, become substantial landholders in western Virginia.

John Jr. and Rebecca lived on Harness family land in South Fork Valley not far from Cunningham Plantation. It was the custom at that time in the Shenandoah Valley to select a portion of the land owned by their parents and build a house there, to be occupied by the newlyweds. In this case, they chose to live near Rebecca's parents. There is no record of John Jr. acquiring more land. Rebecca and John had no children, and when they died, probably at a young age, it is likely they were buried in the Harness family cemetery.

Making a Business Plan for the Plantation

The parcels of property constituting the Cunningham Plantation were owned separately by "Lord John" Cunningham's offspring: William, Robert, John Jr., James, and little Mary. Any property where the now-deceased "Lord John" Cunningham had been the sole owner was transferred, per the Virginia laws of primogeniture, to the oldest son—William II. "Lord John's" other children: John Jr., Robert, James, and Mary, would not have any rights to this property, other than the deeds to the parcels of land that they might have in their own names.

In the early 1760s Robert and William II consolidated their original Cunningham properties as they instituted a sound business plan for sustaining the Cunningham Plantation. Since there were so many acres, it is probable that a good share of Cunningham land was devoted to a livestock operation rather than putting it all into crops. A livestock production industry in South Branch Valley was in its infancy; the neighboring Van Meters were in the process of developing one on their plantation and the Cunninghams followed their example.

John Jr. was not involved—he had cast his lot with his wife's family enterprises—and James was still in captivity; the family didn't know if he was still alive. Mary Cunningham Ward retained her son James' and her daughter Mary's property for them even though she now lived some distance away in Germany Valley. In doing so, James' and Mary's properties were kept intact and the door was kept open for James and Mary to feel a part of their father's South Branch Valley "empire." Their land was managed by William, and profits were split between William and his half-siblings.

As William II directed the Cunningham Plantation business, his younger brother Robert was becoming a wealthy man in his own right. As the third son, Robert knew he would *not* be in line to be the legal heir to Cunningham Plantation so he focused on his own business affairs, continuing to acquire prime farmland in the south and western parts of South Branch Valley:

Robert Cunningham:
- 300 acres Crab Apple Bottom on a branch south of the Potowmack, recorded 18th August 1761, Hampshire County.
- 240 acres in South Branch Manor called the West Meadows, recorded July 12, 1762, Hampshire County.

The land provided the means for a good income from livestock or crop production. However, Robert knew full well that in the future, the branch of the family line of Cunninghams who would prevail in the plantation land and business would be the offspring of his older brother William II. When they became old enough, Robert encouraged his older sons to venture away from South Branch Valley, and he purchased land for them so they could settle in Kentucky. Moving west would be the trend for the future generations of the early pioneer settlers of western Virginia.

CHAPTER 4
Peace in South Branch Valley

By 1764 the American colonists had been victorious in the French and Indian War, and the Indians had vacated to territory to the west—primarily inhabiting what is now Kentucky and Ohio. South Branch Valley, where the Cunningham Plantation was located, was peaceful and stable. The families who had left the valley in fear of the Indians returned to their South Branch Valley properties, ending their self-imposed exile in Pennsylvania and other eastern locations.

The Indian Hostage Returns with a Bride

The Cunningham family was elated when, in 1764, James Cunningham appeared in South Branch Valley—and with him was a wife! James had finally escaped from the Shawnee Indian Tribe in Ohio where he had been held captive for six long years. He had become nearly blind as a result of starvation while in captivity.

As he slowly made his way back to his family in South Branch Valley, he traveled through Pennsylvania where he met a young woman named Agnes Slater. They were married, and afterwards James brought his new bride to the Cunningham homestead, which, in his absence, had become a plantation.

In honor of her marriage to James, the Cunningham brothers presented Agnes with a generous wedding present—two hundred acres of prime South Branch Valley land:

Agnes Cunningham
- September 16, 1765—200 acres, Crab Apple Bottom, South Branch, recorded in Augusta County.

The land had been surveyed in 1761 and was patented to Agnes on September 16, 1765, a year after her marriage. With the 375 acres that already belonged to James, the young couple began married life with 575 acres of highly productive South Branch Valley farmland in their names.

James and Agnes resided briefly at Cunningham Plantation and then settled for a short time on Agnes' new property in Crab Apple Bottom. They then moved on, about ninety miles west, over the mountains and on the east side of the Tygart Valley in the area of Randolph County (that became Lewis County and Harrison County) where they staked out 142 acres, settled the land, and started their family. Randolph County historian Dr. A. S. Bosworth related in the 1800s: "James Cunningham, the pioneer, was captured by the Indians in 1758. He was kept a prisoner for nearly six years and became nearly blind as a result of starvation while in captivity. After his release and return to his people he moved to Randolph."

Another historian, Edward Conrad Smith, speculates on why people like James would want to leave what was now the more settled and civilized area of South Branch Valley and move to a less developed region:

> Besides those who felt more comfortable on the western side of the wilderness there were three other principal classes. The first was made up mostly of younger men who were attracted by the magnificent hunting. To such as these, existence for a long time in one place was unthinkable. The second class was composed of home seekers who had been unable to buy farms further east, and who came west where good land was to be had for little or nothing. According to Adam O'Brien, it was necessary only to cut his initials, A.O.B. on some trees, cut down a few saplings and plant a handful of corn, and he had secured the right to four hundred acres of land, "though it afterwards cost him a great deal of hard swearing." The third class were men of initiative and energy who came west to secure large tracts of land and to make their fortunes.

It is probable that James, who had spent much of his youth living an Indian lifestyle, wanted to be in an area less civilized than South Branch Valley. The affluent plantation lifestyle that was beginning to emerge there was not as agreeable to him as being in wilder territory to the west, doing some farming but also being able to hunt for his food like he did when living with the

Indians. In time, and with the birth of his children, he probably settled into a more conventional lifestyle, and, as years went by, the area where he and Agnes lived became more populated, which forced him to adapt to a more normal life of a pioneer settler.

Country life in the early years of Lewis County (carved from Randolph County) is described by Captain Michael Egan in his memoir and provides a picture of what it was like for young James and Agnes:

> In such places, above all others, are happiness and godliness sure to be found; person and property were alike safe in the keeping of those kind-hearted, industrious, and religious people. They were like one happy family in their daily intercourse, cheering and helping each other along the steep, stony path of life.
>
> During the summer months it was customary for the young people of both sexes to attend camp-meetings, revivals, geography singing schools, and other religious or instructive gatherings. In winter the male portion of the population engaged in the exciting pleasures of the chase, hunting deer, bear, and smaller game.

Robert Cunningham's Adventure

The last of the four Cunningham brothers to marry was James' half-brother, Robert, in 1766. His wife, Prudence Parsons, like Robert, was a member of one of the first pioneer families that had come to the South Branch Valley. The Parsons family, however, had roots going back to the thirteen colonies—one of Prudence's mother's ancestors came to America in 1635.

Parsons Plantation, the home of Prudence's father, Thomas Sr., and her mother, Parthenia, was south of the confluence of the South Branch Potomac River and the South Fork South Branch Potomac River. It was in the area of what would become the village of Moorefield, which the Parsons would help to develop.

Prudence's pioneer father had a reputation as having been a fierce Indian fighter and was hated so much by them he asked (in jest) that when he died and was buried, he not be buried in the cemetery but in the basement of his home near Moorefield "so the Indians wouldn't desecrate his grave."

As newlyweds, following Shenandoah Valley tradition, Prudence and Robert probably began married life residing on Parson Plantation land located about seven or eight miles south of Cunningham Plantation. Living nearby were Prudence's brothers, Tom and James, with whom they became very close. All of Robert and Prudence's seven children were born in this area between the years 1767 and 1782.

In 1770, four years after their marriage and at the time of Prudence's father's death, Robert and Prudence followed the trend and moved west. They purchased land over the mountain in a beautiful area in the Cheat River Valley at Horseshoe Bend, sixty-five miles west of Parsons Plantation.

Prior to that, Prudence's father had claimed a sizable

Pioneer log cabin. Library of Congress

amount of land along the Cheat and gave it to his two sons, Tom Jr. and James, who had built a cabin there as a second home. Prudence and Robert decided to build a home there as well and purchased land on the Big Yough (then called Right Hand Fork), about a mile from the Parsons brothers' cabin and nearby to a dozen of their friends who were doing the same thing.

As they prepared to take up residence in their new place that summer, Prudence and Robert bought two cows, calves, sixteen shoats, carpenter tools, furniture, and other items in March of 1773. Looking forward to an idyllic summer with their friends, they moved into their Horseshoe Bend cabin.

Robert and Prudence's life went according to plan during their first year there. The situation would soon change, however, and their dream to live peacefully in the Cheat River Valley would *not* be realized.

The ending of the French and Indian War, marked by treaties where the Indians agreed to move further west, had created a feeling of safety for the people of the western wilds of Virginia. That proved to be a false perception. Lord Dunmore's War broke out in May 1774 not far from their settlement.

Lord Dunmore's War was a "last gasp" by the Indians for ownership of territory south of the Ohio River, in far western Virginia, and southwestern Pennsylvania. The Indians and settlers fought over the land, each claiming it as their own.

Fearing for their lives, the Parsons, Cunninghams, and other families hurriedly deserted their Cheat River Valley cabins, rushing back to South Branch Valley. Upon his family's return to safety, Robert immediately joined the Virginia militia to go back west and help fight the Indians.

The militia engaged in battle in (now) Mason County/Hancock County, West Virginia, for five months. On October 10, 1774, during the Battle of Point Pleasant, the "grand finale" of Lord Dunmore's War, Robert was taken prisoner by the Indians. The Indians lost the battle and the war, and, unlike his brother James, Robert's captivity was short-lived.

Still worried about the Indians, the Cheat River families waited a couple of years to move back, in about 1776. Robert and Prudence may or may not have returned with them, but if they did they were there only until 1780 when they sold their Cheat River stake. Prudence's brothers kept their land and expanded their holdings to thousands of acres. This region is known today as Parsons, West Virginia.

"Two Families"

With the passage of time, two branches of "Lord John" Cunningham's family now existed: Family #1—the three sons of Lord John and his first wife, Elizabeth, who had remained in South Branch Valley; and Family #2—James and Mary, the son and daughter of Lord John and his second wife, Mary Cunningham Ward, who had moved west, James to Randolph County and Mary, south of there to Germany Valley in Pendleton County.

Though the two branches of "Lord John's" family lived very different lives in two separate mountain valleys, they remained connected to one another. A total of twenty-eight children were born to the four sons and one daughter of "Lord John" Cunningham:

- William II ("Irish Billy") and Phebe Scott Cunningham, married about 1758, had one child: William III (born 1760).
- Robert and Prudence Parsons Cunningham, married in 1766, had seven children; Nancy (born 1767), Robert (born 1769) Jemima "Mimey or "Mindy" (born 1770), Elizabeth (born 1771), (Captain) Isaac Cunningham (born 1778), Mary (born 1780), and Francis "Frankey" (born 1782).
- John Cunningham Jr. and Rebecca Harness had no children of record.
- James and Agnes Slater Cunningham, married in 1764, had eleven children: William (born 1766), John (born 1767), James (born 1773), Margaret (born 1774), Phoebe (born 1776), Nancy (born 1777), Agnes (born 1778), Susanna (born about 1789), Stephen (born 1790), Catherine (born 1799), and Mary (born 1801).
- Mary Cunningham and Captain Isaac Hinkle/Henkel, married on December 13, 1781, in Pendleton County, Virginia, nine children: Adam, Catherine Hinkle Judy, Hannah, Mary Cunningham, John, William, (Colonel) Jesse, Phoebe Hinkle Dice Harper, and Solomon.

CHAPTER 5
After the Revolutionary War

Lord Fairfax lost his Great Neck Proprietary after the Revolutionary War. When the British lost the War in 1783, the king of England no longer had dominion over Virginia land. All of the land in the Great Neck Proprietary that had been granted to Lord Fairfax's ancestors would become the property of the new American citizens who owned the patents. The Cunningham family finally had clear titles to their properties.

Times were changing. Life took on greater stability and the people in South Branch Valley looked forward to improving their lives free from war and British sovereignty.

South Branch Valley Develops Regional Agriculture Enterprise

During the French and Indian War, the soldiers of the Virginia Regiment at Fort Pleasant had been assigned there to protect the settlers living in the area and carry out military operations in the region. To fill in their idle hours when not performing military duties, they helped the local farmers plant and harvest their crops. The extra labor from the soldiers resulted in a surplus of crops. The farmers kept what they needed for themselves and sold their surplus to the military. The income from the surplus provided extra capital to the farmers, which enabled them to grow more crops the next planting season and again sell the excess to the army. This evolved over the years into a regional crop-and-livestock production industry for the area, in which the Van Meters, as the largest landowners in the area, played a leading role.

After the death of his parents, Garrett Van Meter, the oldest son and heir of Isaac Van Meter, inherited ten thousand acres of prime South Branch Valley farmland adjacent to their Fort Pleasant home. Garrett continued to build the agricultural business he and his father had initiated during wartime.

Always keen businessmen, the Van Meters—along with all the other farmers in the area, including their friends and neighbors the Cunninghams—continued this profitable regional agricultural enterprise into the Revolutionary War and beyond. In doing so, they transformed the former Indian oil field at Fort Pleasant and South Branch Valley into a food producing area, raising and marketing crops, horses, and premium grain-fed cattle. According to Virginia historian Lyman Chalkley, "Garrett pioneered the way for cattle barons of the early nineteenth century who made South Branch Valley beef so famous that even young Queen Victoria was reported to have preferred it 'above all other.'"

At his death in 1788, Garrett Van Meter was one of the wealthiest men in the region. In addition to all of his land, he had transformed the original, large, fortified homestead into an impressive plantation "big house," and he owned 114 head of cattle, forty-five horses, twelve slaves, and a profitable whiskey still.

His children, born and raised in Old Fields, South Branch Valley, became friends and schoolmates of William Cunningham II's (Irish Billy's) son. Down the line, William II's grandson, William IV, married Garret's granddaughter, Sally Van Meter.

The seeds of this agricultural enterprise would eventually be planted in James Cunningham Jordan's mind as he heard stories about and personally observed the very profitable production of premium livestock in the valley settled by his forebears. Those seeds planted during his youth and nurtured by his Cunningham and Van Meter uncles, aunts, and cousins, bloomed in his adulthood when he became one of the largest producers of cattle and hogs in central Iowa.

New Design

James Cunningham Jordan's grandfather, George Jordan Jr. grew into adulthood and became a husband and father. He and his wife welcomed their son John, who was born in Augusta County on January 14, 1775, three months before the onset of the Revolutionary War.

In 1778, as little John Jordan was turning three, George Jr. joined the militia as one of the many soldiers who participated in the successful effort of freeing the American colonies from British rule. It was probably around this time that George Jordan Sr. passed away.

The Revolutionary War ended on January 14, 1784, on the exact date of little John Jordan's ninth birthday. His father came back from the war and rejoined his family. There had been changes in the area where they had lived. With increasing population, their part of Augusta County had been reallocated and reassigned to Harrison County, created by the Virginia legislature in 1784.

George and his family continued to farm and live in Harrison County for a couple of years but then decided to leave Virginia. Joining up with a group of John's Revolutionary War pals, he and his family moved near them in Hardy County. They were listed on the tax rolls there in 1786.

Preparing to leave, the group gathered supplies and their belongings and made their way to Pittsburg, Pennsylvania. There they all embarked on flatboats traveling down the Ohio River. They were heading to adventure—their destination the wild, rugged, and largely unsettled western frontier (now known as southern Illinois), along the Kaskaskia (now Okaw) River, not far from where Vandalia now stands.

Under the 1762 Treaty of Fontainebleau, which was signed after the defeat of the French at the close of the French and Indian War, France transferred all of its possessions east of the Mississippi to England. The southern Illinois section of the territory came under the jurisdiction of England's colony of Virginia. In order to secure the land, Virginia colonial governors encouraged pioneer settlement there and, after the Revolutionary War, a number of small permanent settlements of Virginians were established. Like George Jordan, many of the settlers had been soldiers who had fought in the Revolutionary War and were looking for a fresh beginning in new territory.

One of the settlements was called New Design, a community located south of Bellefontaine (now Waterloo, Illinois), east of the confluence of the Kaskaskia and Mississippi Rivers. Virginia soldiers had built a fort in Bellefontaine during the French and Indian War. A founding pioneer of New Design was Captain Joseph Ogle, a Revolutionary War veteran from Virginia who carried out the wishes of Virginia's governor by inviting young veterans and their families to the settlement. Arriving on flatboats traveling down the Ohio and Mississippi Rivers, the families were drawn to New Design by Ogle's descriptions of the incredible vista from the elevated (and fertile) land overlooking the Mississippi and Kaskaskia River Valleys—"beautiful country, then prairie, then timber." George Jordan and his wife and son were in the enthusiastic "first wave" of immigrant families to settle there in 1786.

The settlers, including Ogle, were also drawn there because of their unified commitment to the antislavery sentiment in that community. This attitude, pervasive throughout New Design, could not have been missed by George's young and impressionable son John, who would one day have a son named James Cunningham Jordan leading the abolitionist cause in Iowa.

Joseph Leman, the son-in-law of Captain Ogle and a Revolutionary War veteran, arrived after a harrowing flatboat journey down the Ohio River. He became the leader of the community and early on was converted to the Baptist faith by charismatic preacher James Smith, an abolitionist. The rest of the community came to embrace that religion, agreeing wholeheartedly with Smith's antislavery message. In later years, the Baptists of New Design shifted into the new and very popular Methodist faith, led by their founding father, Captain Ogle, who has been called "the first Methodist in Illinois."

The Jordan family lived in New Design for almost ten years, during which time George's wife died, leaving him a widower with a teenaged son. Father and son decided to return to Virginia with a group who were planning to go back and recruit a "second wave" of settlers for New Design.

On their way back east, while passing through Kentucky, George Jordan met a widow named Martha Lightfoot. Martha had been born and raised in Culpeper County, Virginia, a county just to the east of Hardy County where George, his wife, and son John had lived for a short time before they went to New Design. Martha's parents, Goodrich and Susanna Elizabeth Slaughter Lightfoot, had moved with their thirty-year-old daughter and her children to Kentucky after the Revolutionary War.

George stayed in Kentucky, married Martha Lightfoot, and had more children, raising them in the Bluegrass region of north central Kentucky between what would become the cities of Louisville and Lexington. George died on March 1, 1842, and Martha died the next month at the age of eighty-six. They are both buried in the George Jordan Family Cemetery in Anderson County.

John, now twenty-one, returned alone to Harrison County and either settled on the old homestead or found new property to farm in that county. In a short time, John found himself a wife: Agnes Cunningham. They were married at the home of her parents, James and Agnes Cunningham, in Pendleton County in 1796, and lived until 1816 on John's farm where the first nine children of their union were born.

John and Agnes Jordan welcomed eleven children into this world: Mary (born May 2, 1797), Susan (born July 12, 1799), Elizabeth (born September 2, 1802), Anna (born February 2, 1804), George Washington (born February 26, 1806), Phoebe (born April 20, 1808), Cynthia (born July 18, 1810), James Cunningham (born March 4, 1813), Margaret (born October 5, 1815), John Slater (born March 1, 1818), and Agnes (born August 2, 1821).

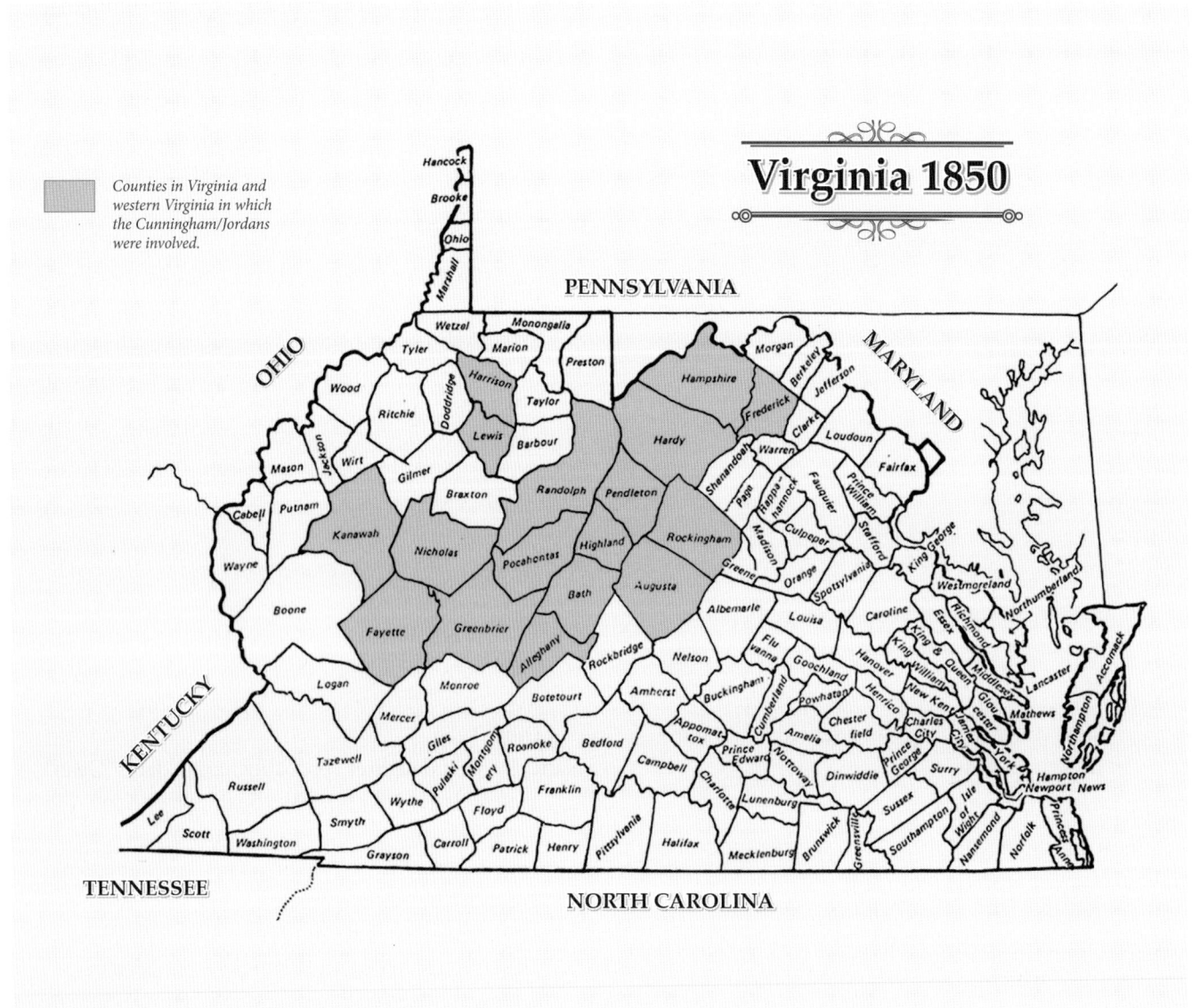

These are the counties in the Valley of Virginia where the Cunningham/Jordan family lived during the 1740s–1830s.

CHAPTER 6
One Family—Different Directions

When William "Irish Billy" Cunningham II died in 1790, the legal mandate of primogeniture again prevailed—property was transferred to the oldest living son. William III became the legal heir to all of his grandfather "Lord John's" property, which included Cunningham Plantation plus the many parcels William II and Robert had "joined together" thirty years earlier in the 1760s.

William III was the beginning of a succession of William Cunninghams that would be the primary owners of the Cunningham Plantation. In 1780, William III married Jemima Harness, the niece of Rebecca Harness Cunningham who had married John Jr.

William III and Jemima's son, William IV, would marry Sally Van Meter from the neighboring ten-thousand-acre South Branch Valley Farms Planation. In subsequent generations, Cunninghams and Van Meters would continue to intermarry, family lines and property ownership would blur, and the grandchildren and great-grandchildren of those families would inherit both the Cunningham and the Van Meter properties with primary ownership ultimately in the Van Meter name. Because they stayed in South Branch Valley on their plantations, many of them were buried in either the Cunningham or Van Meter family cemeteries or the Old Fields Church Cemetery.

Cunningham/Van Meter family historian Benjamin Van Meter recalls Irish Billy's grave ". . . is on the east side of the South Branch River and Valley, at the foot of a hill in the old Cunningham graveyard, marked by a plain stone slab, on the land where they settled when they came from Ireland to Virginia."

Robert Cunningham

Because his father's property was inherited by his older brother William II and would be transferred to his nephew William III, Robert Cunningham for decades had been building *his own* business enterprises, the foundation of which was real estate but which also included a mill, several buildings, homes, and slaves. In 1770, Robert and his brother-in-law, William Welton, inherited a half share of land from their father-in-law, Thomas Parsons.

- 290 acres on North Mill Creek, adjoining the upper land. From the estate of Thomas Parsons.

The gift of this property was an important factor in Robert and Prudence's decision to make their home in the Moorefield/Petersburg area. Though Robert was now completely severed from Cunningham Plantation, he continued to acquire premier land in the immediate vicinity of his old homestead:

- 254 acres on the South Branch Potomac. A patent purchased from Lord Fairfax. Recorded on May 11, 1779.

Three of his friends who witnessed the sale were Garret Van Meter, Abraham Hite, and James Parsons.

- 60 acres on South Branch from John Denham. Recorded in Hampshire County on May 11, 1784.

When Robert died about 1801 at the age of sixty-two, his will illustrates that he died a wealthy man. Robert's acquisition of even more property than that already described appears in the will, which was "proven" on April 16, 1802. His substantial assets were disbursed as follows:

Prudence (Robert's wife)
    One-third of his old place; two Negroes (Hannah and George); and one-third of his moveable assets.

Nancy (oldest daughter)
    The old home place; the Skillock Place in Randolph County in Tigers (probably Tygart) Valley and his Doly Place.

Nancy's oldest daughter (probably named Jane "Gean" Taaffe, Nancy may not have been married to Jane's father).
    The Mill; already having given her the Hanibelton Tract containing 445 acres.

Robert Jr. (his eldest son)
    The land he lives on in Kentucky (four hundred acres on the Green River; and five Negroes (Harry, Nan, Henry, Jane, and Peg).

Mindy (second daughter, "Jemima")
    His Mill place and two Negroes (Charles and Mage).
Elizabeth (third daughter)
    Robert's Upper Place on Patterson Creek; four Negroes (Jude, Dixie, Joe, and Jacob).
Isaac (youngest son)
    My home place; and four Negroes (Jos, Kate, Dol, and Mary); the proceeds from the sale of two parcels of land (upper and lower) on Patterson Creek.
Frankey (youngest daughter "Frances")
    My place in Petersburg and two other lots in Petersburg, Virginia; the tract by Minister Place and two Negroes (Peter and Win).

Robert did not free any of the nineteen slaves he owned. The phrase in his will that discussed the slaves he willed to his children stated, "I give (*the name of the slave/s*) to (*name of the son/daughter*) and his/her heirs forever."

His 1802 will shows he purchased property and a home on Dolly Ridge in Germany Valley, where his half-sister Mary grew up. He also owned property in the Tygart River Valley, where one of his children, Nancy, settled and where James and Agnes Cunningham resided in the early years of their marriage and many of their children were born.

Mary Cunningham Ward and Her Daughter, Mary

Mary Cunningham Ward, who had moved to Germany Valley in the 1760s with her husband, Sylvester, and young daughter, Mary, was probably acquainted with two of the area's original settlers, Jost and Maria Henkel/Hinkle, who had been living there since 1730. The Henkels had raised a large family, and one of their younger sons, Captain Isaac Hinkle, had been a commissioned officer in the Revolutionary War. In 1781 Mary Cunningham, age twenty-three, married Captain Hinkle.

James Cunningham

Mary Cunningham Ward's son, James Cunningham, and his wife, Agnes, had been living in Randolph County for almost fifteen years when on November 27, 1781, James received State Warrant No. 9409 for two thousand acres of land in Pendleton County. This land was probably not far from where his sister Mary and her new husband, Isaac Hinkle, were living. James received the land because of his visual disability (he was listed as blind on the land documents, having suffered poor eyesight since being held captive by the Indians in his youth). For many years he had been on a disability pension from the Commonwealth of Virginia, which would continue until his death.

Besides having the pleasure of being able to live closer to his sister and mother, receiving two thousand acres of free land was the impetus for James and Agnes to move their young family over to Pendleton County; he is listed in the Pendleton County deed book (1788–1813) as a taxpayer in 1782, 1784, and 1786, and he is listed in the census in 1790. In 1784, his name appears as the neighbor of Germany Valley residents George and Philip Teeter and Jost Henkel, among others. Most of James and Agnes' daughters were married in Pendleton County between the years 1786 and 1799, including the future parents of James Cunningham Jordan: their daughter Agnes married John Jordan in 1796.

James and Agnes Cunningham stayed in Pendleton County for about fifteen years, but eventually they sold their two thousand acres and brought their family back to Randolph County where they purchased ninety-five acres. James is listed in the Randolph County Land Book in 1802 as the purchaser of this property.

James still owned the property he had purchased in the mid-1760s—142 acres on the east side of the Tygart Valley in Randolph County. This land was near Huttonsville, where he spent the final years of his life. In his will, he designated one-third of this property for his wife, Agnes, to support her for the remainder of her life. The rest went to his male children and sons-in-law, including his daughter Agnes' husband, John Jordan.

By the early 1800s James Cunningham was almost totally blind. On September 28, 1810, he died in Huttonsville at the age of sixty-five. In three years his namesake would be born. James Cunningham Jordan would never know his grandfather nor his grandmother Agnes Cunningham. She passed shortly after James was born.

CHAPTER 7
The Beginning of the End of Slavery

The First Great Awakening

Besides introducing the unbelievable phenomenon of welcoming slaves into white worshipping communities, the First Great Awakening breathed new life into religion in America. The new style of delivering sermons caused people to "wake up." Wesley M. Gewehr, author of The Great Awakening in Virginia, 1740–1790, *stated:* "Before, they were sleeping in their pews. Now, they were inspired by an enthusiastic and passionate speaker. People attending religious services became emotionally engaged and involved in their religion rather than passively listening to intellectual discourse in a detached manner. This inspired new ways of thinking about that which was 'acceptable' in American society. The role of women and the role of slaves began to be questioned . . . and things began to change."

After negotiating itself through the Reformation (1517–1685), Protestant Europe during the next century was again poised to embark on a new evangelical religious movement known as the Great Awakening. By 1730 this revitalizing movement was beginning to spread across the Atlantic Ocean, first to the New England colonies and then to the Middle and Southern colonies, especially in the Presbyterian "back country" regions. The leaders of the movement led changes in many American people's understanding of God, themselves, the world around them, and religion in general. The result was a message of spiritual equality, including the spiritual equality of women and slaves.

The power of an immediate, personal religious experience was emphasized, as well as the idea that men and women were not predestined to damnation but could be saved by repenting their sins. Spiritual rebirth would grant them entrance to the "Promised Land." The movement featured itinerate preachers and deemphasized hierarchy and catechisms.

These ideas were appealing to people of all walks of life, from the richest to the poorest, from the educated to the illiterates. Those lowest on the social spectrum—women, English indentured servants,

George Whitefield painting by James Moore. National Gallery of Art

Jonathan Edwards. Public domain

German Redemptionists, Indians, and even slaves—were included and actually invited!

The movement began with Congregationalist pastor Jonathan Edwards of Northampton, Massachusetts—a man with Puritan roots but new ideas. In the mid-1730s he traveled throughout the northern colonies and preached in a dramatic and emotional style—a radical departure from the style of the traditional Puritan preacher.

Edwards was followed in 1740 by George Whitefield, an Anglican minister who had sailed from England to Georgia to bring American colonials his message. On his travels north and south through the colonies, Whitefield attracted large emotional crowds and elicited countless conversions of a full spectrum of the population, regardless of gender or ethnicity. According to religious scholar, Garrison J. Silor: "He developed a style of preaching that elicited emotional responses from his audiences. . . . Whitefield had charisma, and his loud voice, his small stature, and even his cross-eyed appearance (which some people took as a mark of divine favor) all served to help make him one of the first celebrities in the American colonies."

The very same attributes that attracted crowds to Whitefield were condemned by his critics. Silor

Jonathan Edward's most famous work. Library of Congress

continues, "His enthusiasm, his censoriousness, and his extemporaneous and itinerant preaching . . ." were deplored by the (largely Episcopalian) ecclesiastical establishment. In spite of their negative reaction, he became the prototype evangelist, and "his techniques were copied by numerous imitators, both lay and clerical." A movement was born.

Samuel Davies, a Presbyterian minister who later became the fourth president of Princeton University, was, like Whitefield, noted for preaching to African slaves. He converted great numbers and was credited with the first sustained "proselytization of slaves in Virginia." Active in the 1750s, by 1755 he had baptized about one hundred slaves, and approximately three hundred individuals regularly attended his meetings in Hanover County, Virginia.

Ironically, a slave owner himself, Davies wrote of an enslaved man whom he had encountered in 1757, representing *himself* as the slave and very effectively communicating his message of conversion: "I am a poor slave, brought into a strange country, where I never expect to enjoy my liberty. While I lived in my own country, I knew nothing of that Jesus I have heard you speak so much about. I lived quite careless what will become of me when I die; but I now see such a life will never do, and I come to you, Sir, that you may tell me some good things, concerning Jesus Christ, and my duty to GOD, for I am resolved not to live my life any more as I have done."

The Baptists Arrive in Virginia

By the 1750s the Presbyterian Church had become a grudgingly accepted presence within the Episcopalian-dominated Virginia Colony and were becoming a part of the Virginia establishment. The Presbyterian mode of worship was much more compatible to the Episcopalians than the new ideas and worshipping style set forth by the Great Awakening. In the next decade, however, Baptist preachers would soon cause many Presbyterians and those of other reformed denominations to question their religious traditions.

In the mid-1700s Baptist preachers were starting to travel from New England into Virginia. This denomination had a tradition of being Separatists: churches that had broken away from the Protestant establishment. The Separatist tradition began during the Reformation in Europe and spread to America, primarily in the Congregational strongholds of Connecticut and Massachusetts.

The Baptist church grew quickly in the American colonies, becoming firmly established in the coastal south, particularly in the Carolinas and Tidewater Virginia. Adhering to their centuries-old tradition of not asking for secular permission when practicing any and all aspects of their religion, Baptist preachers did not apply for licenses to preach in Virginia, as required by law. For that, the colonial authorities, most of whom were members of the Episcopalian establishment, aggressively persecuted them.

"In 1771 an Anglican minister disrupted a Baptist service by beating the preacher in the pulpit and dragging him outside, where the sheriff of Caroline County gave him twenty lashes with a bullwhip," according to Garrison Silor, who explains that during this time, thirty-four Baptist preachers were jailed for disturbing the peace and for holding unlawful assemblies. In Culpeper, Virginia, "Baptist preacher James Ireland was imprisoned, yet he continued to preach to his followers through a grate. His jailers retaliated by urinating on him and burning brimstone and pepper outside his cell to try to suffocate him." Silor further states: "The biggest controversy between the Baptists and the eastern Virginia colonial establishment was the Baptists' loose handling of conventional bounds of race and gender. . . . They always included African free men or slaves in their congregations, and some white Baptist leaders actually spoke out against slavery; unheard of in those days."

African and American Indian men occasionally served as exhorters, deacons, and even elders (the highest office of leadership among Baptists) in mixed race congregations. Women, too, found new positions of authority among Baptists as "deaconesses" and often received opportunities to publicly testify during religious gatherings about their experiences with God.

Out in New Design, this new way of looking at all people in a different light reinforced their abolitionist sentiment. The Baptist preacher John Smith had been greatly influenced by the First Great Awakening and throughout the 1780s and 1790s his flock heard his emphatic assertions that slavery should be abolished. George Jordan, his wife, and son John were all listening to this message, which they embraced and incorporated into their family mindset.

The Methodists

In 1735 John Wesley, an Episcopalian priest, came to General George Ogelthorpe's colony (now known as Georgia) to be a missionary. As an employee of the Anglican Society for the Gospel in Foreign Parts, his job was to serve as the parish priest for Georgia's diverse collection of settlers and to convert the Chickasaw Indians.

During the two years he was there, through trial and error he realized the most efficacious way to accomplish his task was through the introduction of intensive prayer meetings, resorting to female church officers, including the practice of hymn singing, instituting the concept of the itinerant preacher, preaching out of doors, and ministering to the poor and outcast, including slaves.

When John Wesley returned to England in 1737, he and his brother Charles founded the Methodist Movement and instituted a connection of itinerant preachers and a more fluid network of "united societies" to take the place of a collection of churches with preachers in each pulpit. By the end of the 1740s

John Wesley painting by William Hamilton. National Portrait Gallery, Smithsonian Institution

Methodism had spread throughout Great Britain and her colonies. This phenomenal growth was encouraged and maintained by increasing numbers of lay itinerants, by the Wesley brothers' massive literary output, and by John Wesley's lifelong charismatic leadership. In America, Methodism spread because the former Anglican minister George Whitefield, who had led the Great Awakening, embraced it.

Effects of the First Great Awakening

The First Great Awakening was a harbinger of the future. The genesis of a new way of thinking and behaving, its influence would ultimately impact the lives of every citizen in the United States, including the members of the Cunningham and Jordan families. It would force them to question their principles and ultimately divide them because of the disparity in the way they made their livings and conducted their lives.

CHAPTER 8
The War of 1812

In the years leading up to James Jordan's birth, the quality of life had improved in the highlands of western Virginia. The French and Indian War fifty years earlier had resulted in the successful removal of the Indians to western territories. Lord Dunmore's War had confirmed that the settlers were coming even further west, and the Indians would need to get out of the way.

The Revolutionary War against England had been won by the colonies, and the United States of America had been created. There were some ups and downs with regard to how the new federal government would function, with New England at times unhappy and threatening secession, but resolution was sought on issues, and the union of the states was maintained. However, international hostilities were on the increase, and war with Britain was again on the horizon.

The Revolutionary War had been fought to create a United States independent of England, yet in the early decades of the 1800s there was still ongoing friction between England and the Americans. England was once again at war with France. The United States announced their neutrality with regard to this war. However, Britain needed more recruits for their navy in order to fight France. They forced ten thousand US merchant marine sailors onto their battleships under the premise that US sailors were at one time British subjects and still owed Britain their loyalty and service. President Thomas Jefferson's angry response was the imposition of a trade embargo on Britain and France in 1807, a move which enraged the manufacturers and traders of New England who again threatened secession from the union.

The British were also in collusion with the Indians, with both Britain and the Indians trying to regain/retain western and southern territory on or adjacent to the US borders—from Canada to Detroit to New Orleans and Florida. The Indians, who had been banished from the Eastern Seaboard to Ohio, Kentucky, and Tennessee, were now being pushed even further west, partly because of the well-publicized results of the Lewis and Clark Expedition (1804–1806). Their explorations provided information about the territory the United States had acquired through President Thomas Jefferson's 1803 Louisiana Purchase from France. Lewis and Clark's reports of their exploration of the vast area between St. Louis and the Pacific Ocean inspired pioneer families to begin looking at settling on land farther west.

Understanding their displacement would continue as the pioneer settlers continued their westward march, the Indians realized if they had any chance to keep their lands, this was the time to stage a united opposition to the Americans. Consequently, they allied with Britain in an attempt to achieve their goal.

In the previous century, during the French and Indian War, the Indians and the French had fought Britain and the colonists. In the early decades of the new century, the English and Indians were allied with each other against the Americans. The endgame was the same in both centuries: acquisition and control of territory for all who were involved.

Most Americans reacted with an angry call to action to the many challenges they were now presented with from the Indians and Great Britain. This was especially true of young American men who had heard the stories about their fathers' and grandfathers' fight in the French and Indian War and the War of Independence from England. These young men wanted to show the country that their generation could defend the legacy they were now responsible for preserving.

"Game Chickens" and "War Hawks"

Family legend states that in confrontations with the Indians, James Cunningham Jordan's feisty Virginia Cunningham ancestors had played the role of "game chickens"—people fighting for a showdown where one must give in or both will be killed. This was especially true in the years prior to and during the French and Indian War, and Robert Cunningham had replayed that role during Lord Dunmore's War.

In later years, the Cunningham and Jordan men were probably supportive of the "War Hawks"—the name given to young congressmen (they were so young older congressmen called them "the boys"), primarily from the South and western frontier—western Virginia, South Carolina, Kentucky, Tennessee, and Ohio. These young men dominated the US Congress during the presidential term of James Madison (1808–1817). Led by thirty-three-year-old Henry Clay, Speaker of the House, and John C. Calhoun, the War Hawks adamantly insisted on a declaration of war on England.

Henry Clay. Public domain

John C. Calhoun. Public domain

The War Hawks prevailed when Henry Clay and his legislative colleagues passed legislation that directed President James Madison to declare war against the British. Madison did so on June 18, 1812, about nine months prior to James' birth on March 1, 1813.

Like his father, his uncles, and his two grandfathers before him, James Jordan was brought into a world filled with war and strife. One difference between the War of 1812 and the previous wars was that the army was not led by experienced military leaders like George Washington and his officers. Instead, a collection of largely untrained and inexperienced soldiers was entrusted with the responsibility of defending the new nation.

In September 1813, six months after James Jordan's birth, the Americans (surprisingly) overcame the British in the Battle of Lake Erie. That victory was a key factor in the failure of the British/Indian alliance, and it enabled the United States to gain control of the Great Lakes.

When James was one and a half, the British landed in Chesapeake Bay and from there entered the Potomac River. The British were alarmingly close to James' home—upriver on the south branch of the Potomac. Even more alarming was that the nation's capital city of Washington, DC, located on the Potomac River, was in dire jeopardy and rapidly being abandoned. On August 18, 1814, the British rampaged through the now-deserted city, burning down the Capitol, the White House, and much of the town. The destruction of their capital city further enraged the Americans and fully united the nation against the British, even bringing in support from the pro-British New Englanders who had been furious over Madison's trade embargo.

After their successful demolition of Washington, DC, the British advanced up the Chesapeake Bay to attack Baltimore, the third largest city in the United States. The determined American forces were able to defeat the British at Fort McHenry in Baltimore, inspiring a lawyer named Francis Scott Key to write the words to "The Star Spangled Banner," which later became the US national anthem.

In the meantime, Andrew Jackson wrested the Territory of Florida from Spain, eventually proceeding to New Orleans in late 1814. Two months before James' third birthday, Andrew Jackson and his men were successful in defeating the British Army in the Battle of New Orleans, thus retaining New Orleans, a major port as well as the entrance to the Mississippi River basin and the Louisiana Purchase, for the United States.

By the time he was three years old, the country in which James Jordan lived was free from international strife, national boundaries were established and enforced, and there was a dramatic increase of American pride, nationalism, and patriotism.

CHAPTER 9
James Jordan's Childhood

At the turn of the century, around 1800, John and Agnes Jordan moved their family from John's hill farm in Harrison County to homestead in a county to the south—Greenbrier County. They lived in the part of the county that evolved in 1818 into Nicholas County and then in 1831 (finally) became Fayette County.

They had chosen a wonderful place to farm and raise a family. The beauty of the area was unsurpassed. The mountainous terrain was crisscrossed by nine beautiful, plunging river valleys. One of the most spectacular was the breathtaking New River Gorge. Wooded mountainsides were bountiful with game; the valleys had good soil upon which to farm and verdant, grassy pastures for livestock to graze. Other than the two oldest daughters, all of the Jordan children would be born on that farm.

James Cunningham Jordan is Born

James Cunningham Jordan was born on March 4, 1813, on the Jordan family homestead in Greenbrier County, Virginia. He was the eighth of the eleven children born to John and Agnes Cunningham Jordan. He may have been so named because his grandmother Agnes Cunningham was on her death bed at the time of James' birth. It would have been a kind and reassuring gesture to Grandmother Agnes that the new baby boy was named for her deceased husband.

In the three years after his grandfather had died, until James was born, his family spent a good deal of time at Grandmother Agnes' house. Her farm needed attention and so did ailing Grandma Cunningham. Her children rallied around, including Grandma Agnes' namesake daughter, Agnes Cunningham Jordan, and son John Cunningham, both of whom had older teenaged children. John's son, Jesse, and Agnes' oldest daughter, Mary, first cousins with the same grandmother, fell in love with each other. They were married at Grandma Agnes' house in 1816. A few months after the nuptials, Grandmother Agnes died. Jesse and Mary Jordan Cunningham took over their grandmother's farm after her death. James Cunningham Jordan was three years old at the time.

Next came the 1819 wedding of James' second-oldest sister, Susan, to a local farmer, Abel Withrow. After their wedding, they settled on old Harrison County land that Susan's parents, John and Agnes, had owned for decades. Little James, now nicknamed "Jimmy," was six years old and all ready to start school.

School

According to West Virginia historian Edward C. Smith, "the people west of the Alleghenies were like the Puritans of New England in their belief in education as a factor in the development of democratic institutions. In general, they were an intelligent and enterprising class of people, many of whom could read and write. Most of them were passionately devoted to education, and they made tremendous sacrifices in order that the gift of learning which they had received should be passed on to their children."

James Jordan was educated in Virginia's "common schools." He was lucky to be born in 1813. Prior to 1810 there was no state provision for financial assistance for public education, no supervision of the schools by the state, no teachers' examinations, and no correlation of the curriculum among schools. It had been the responsibility of the families and/or the local communities to educate their children.

Furthermore, there had been notable discrepancies in education in Virginia. According to historian Edward C. Smith, "The people of the eastern part of the state had a fairly good system of private or parochial schools to which they might send their children. For most children in the west, there was no assurance of a school unless the parents of a community banded together and employed the services of such teachers as were available. The school term was sure to be short, the instruction was likely to be indifferent, and conditions were unsatisfactory all around."

After the Virginia state legislature passed the Literary Fund in 1810, parents throughout the Commonwealth of Virginia were required to pay the state $1.25 a month for each of their children to attend.

This fee provided for more educational supervision at the county and state levels and guaranteed that certain subjects would be taught.

Historian Edward C. Smith recalled: "The tuition charged by the teacher in the rural districts of the county was usually a dollar and a half per term for the simpler branches (the subjects of spelling, writing, reading, and a part or the whole of Pike's Arithmetic), and two dollars per term when geography and grammar were included in the program. All the schools were made up by subscription. Specific articles of agreement between the patrons and the teachers were drawn up showing what was to be taught."

The children of settlers living in isolated areas were likely to grow up illiterate. If James had a friend in school whose parents could not afford the $1.25 fee, the cost would be covered by the county/commonwealth; however, some parents were too proud to accept the subsidy for their children, and they were thus denied the opportunity to attend school.

The children living in the Commonwealth of Virginia who were *not* attending school were the sons and daughters of the slaves. In most places they were hardly considered human—just commodities to work for their owners. However, in a few of the small schoolhouses high up in the mountains, far away from the valley plantations, some children of emancipated and escaped slaves were allowed to attend school with the white children and learn how to read, write, and do math.

Down in Greenbrier County where the Jordan family lived, the countryside was dotted with small schoolhouses located in abandoned cabins, in newly constructed buildings on unproductive farm fields, or in buildings on former Indian old fields. John Strange Hall, superintendent of Free Schools in Lewis County, two counties north, described a typical schoolhouse during his tenure:

> The house was 16 x 18 feet; built of round logs, slightly scutched down on the inside. The door, loft, and roof were made of boards—the latter weighted down with poles. The cracks were chinked and daubed except one at the end and one at the side next to the door, which was near the corner. These were enlarged for windows. There was also a small window on the opposite side near the fire.

> Instead of glass for filling the windows, one of the patrons furnished a few copies of the Pittsburgh Christian Advocate for the purpose. These were cut into strips of suitable width and supported by upright slats, were pasted in the windows and greased to let in the light. My teacher told me it was to let the dark out.

> Broad poplar slabs were leveled with a broadax and closely jointed for a floor and others dressed more carefully were put up in front of the windows for writing desks. Chestnut saplings split, leveled and shaved, and supported by legs of suitable length, served for seats. Every pupil carried his own back, for the benches had none.

> Blackboards did not adorn the schoolhouses of that age. The chief glory of the edifice was its chimney. It was a half wooden concern liable to take fire whenever an armful of dry wood was thrown on. One-half the north end was cut out, and a rough, though substantial, stone chimney with a capacity to absorb a respectable log heap and roast an ox on the hearth completed the schoolhouse.

James and his brothers and sisters were educated together along with other children from neighboring farms, with the boys taking time off to help with planting and harvesting if needed. School began promptly at eight o'clock and ended at five. There was seldom a case of tardiness, though some of the children walked a distance of three or four miles from their homes.

The teacher, called the "master," was generally a young man in the local community who had stood at the head of his class. He may have gone on to another school or college where he received additional schooling. Standing at the front of the classroom, he would look like all the local men, wearing a flowing hunting shirt and buckskin moccasins.

Teaching was not regarded as a profession in pioneer days. With few exceptions teachers made it a stepping stone to some other position. If a local young man was not available, a traveling teacher would be employed. These "wandering pedagogues" settled wherever there were enough parents willing to pay them to teach their children. Occasionally schoolteachers from New England would come into Virginia, teach two or three years and then either settle there on a farm or return home. Most of the teachers were men, but there was the occasional woman.

West Virginia School Superintendent John Strange Hall remembers, "The minimum skills required of the teacher was that they understood the principles of elementary English, have good handwriting, be able to make goose quill pens, and to use the rod freely and with emphasis."

Books, ink, and pens were provided. The "Three Rs" were taught. By the time James Jordan began to attend school, teacher preparation was somewhat improved, and some teachers could give instruction in the classics and more advanced subjects, if requested to do so.

When not reciting, the pupils were kept constantly at their books, and no idleness was permitted. In many schools, *Pike's Arithmetic*, a speller, and a Testament were the only textbooks in use. After the War of 1812, textbooks that had been of British origin were replaced with textbooks authored and printed in the United States, thus ensuring the study of subjects with an American, not British, focus.

Spelling was the favorite accomplishment of the pupils, and, according to Superintendent John Hall, "there was no higher honor than to get the greatest number of head-marks or to stand up longest in the spelling match."

Discipline was maintained, "not with the classic birch of the north, but with a tough hickory switch from three to five feet in length." School Superintendent Hall recalled that the hickory switch "was used as an emblem of authority rather than as an instrument of torture, but it was convertible."

Both girls and boys attended school, and sometimes there was an opportunity to attend school in the summer. Summer schools were attended mainly by young women, as the boys were typically out in the fields helping on the farm. According to Charles E. Smith, the summer schools were located in communities where there was a "long line of especially distinguished teachers," and the schools where they taught evolved into respected education centers. In 1795 one such school in Randolph County evolved into Randolph Academy, the one permanent school in the area. It offered advanced education—primarily training men and women to become teachers and preparing men to go into the ministry. The presence of this school and the educational opportunities it offered their children and grandchildren might be one of the reasons Jimmy's grandparents, James and Agnes Cunningham, chose to move back to Randolph County in 1802.

Worshipping in the Virginia Highlands

In the early years in the Virginia highlands there were no churches and no ministers to lead formal worship services. Religious meetings, which were typically held in cabins, included Scripture readings and singing. In the Presbyterian gatherings, where early generations of the Jordan family worshipped, the singing was more a recitation of the Scriptures in a somewhat monotone "melody." The notes might vary somewhat, but they never strayed from one or two notes up or down. Oftentimes, a Scripture passage or Psalm would be sung to the congregation by a leader, and the congregation would sing it back. On the rare occasions when a minister came to visit a worshipping congregation of any denomination—maybe two to four times a year—the service would be much like what the parishioners experienced back in their home countries, as many of the preachers had been trained in Europe and were sent over the Atlantic to preach in America.

The Great Awakening in the late 1700s had brought changes. In Greenbrier County at the time James Jordan was growing up, life was probably saturated with religion. Baptist preachers and Methodist circuit riders braved all the perils of the wilderness to bring their message to the people on the frontier. Before the close of the Revolutionary War the Methodists established "classes" and "societies" at numerous places in the Valley of Virginia. Although these were regular gatherings, worship services continued to be held in settlers' cabins, in schoolhouses, or in summertime, on the banks of a stream or at an Indian old field.

Methodist preachers residing in a permanent place were eventually granted licenses from the Commonwealth of Virginia to perform marriages. The construction of permanent church buildings followed. Methodism, as well as other denominations, were absorbed into the highland communities and became part of the fabric of the lives of the people living there.

Popular preachers were followed by large congregations. In 1788 Bishop Asbury came to Clarksburg in nearby Randolph County to hold a quarterly meeting, where he preached to an audience of over seven hundred people. The number of Methodist societies in that county was so great it was easy for James Jordan's mother, Agnes, a practicing Scots-Irish Presbyterian, to be converted. Her husband, John, was already a Methodist, having embraced Methodism while living in New Design. No doubt, the pervasive influence of religion and the emotional support it offered had helped Agnes' father, James, heal after his captivity with the Indians. It also bound the settlers together into a close and supportive community and helped them adopt good values that served them well in their lives, as demonstrated later on by James Cunningham Jordan.

The letters and journals of some of the old circuit riders reveal interesting glimpses of pioneer settlements in the western Virginia highlands where the Jordan family lived. The Reverend Henry Smith came to the Clarksburg circuit in 1784 and held a meeting at the house of Joseph Bonnett. Of this congregation Smith says:

> The people came to this meeting from four or five miles around. They were all backwoods people and came to the meeting in backwoods style, all on foot, a considerable congregation. I looked around and saw an old man who had shoes on his feet. The preacher wore Indian moccasins. Every man, woman, and child besides was barefooted. The old women had on what we called then short gowns, and the rest had neither short nor long gowns. This was a novel sight for me for a Sunday congregation.
>
> I soon found if there were no shoes and fine dresses in the congregation there were attentive hearers and feeling hearts. In meeting the class I heard the same humble loving religious experience that I had often heard in better-dressed societies. If this scene did not make a backwoods man of me outright, it at least reconciled me to the problem and I felt happy among them.

Making a Living

The farmers living in the upcountry highlands had smaller farms with less fertile soil than those in the lowland valleys like South Branch Potomac, so they raised some crops (usually corn) but mostly grazed livestock, mainly cattle. Through the years, the principal source of wealth continued to be cattle, though the prices were low.

An appraisal bill of an estate in 1828 shows the following prices:

"Hiawatha," a famous Shorthorn bull. Author's personal collection.

1 pide (multicolored dairy) cow $7.00
1 red cow 1 year $8.00
1 brindle pide Heifer $5.00
1 2-year-old steer $8.00
1 red heifer with white back $3.00
1 small black bull $1.75

Cattle from this area were driven east to Baltimore. Helpers traveled on foot with their beasts and were given 25 cents a day. On their return they received one cent per mile, which they used to purchase food. In order to eliminate profiteering, the prices for the keeping of livestock were fixed by the county court in 1821:

For Horses per day—8 cents
For Slaves per day—20 cents
For cattle per day—6 cents
For sheep and hogs per day—4 cents

A significant event in the region was the introduction, in about 1840, of pure-bred Shorthorn Durham cattle. While some farmers, disliking innovation or ignorant of breeding principles, continued to keep scrub stock, the more progressive farmers appreciated this opportunity to improve their herds. The introduction of Shorthorn cattle to enhance herds would be a practice James Jordan would embrace as a premier cattle breeder in Iowa in future decades.

How the Presbyterian Church Influenced the Lives of the Cunninghams and the Jordans

During the Reformation the Presbyterian church was founded in Scotland by John Knox, a follower of John Calvin. The Presbyterian church was adopted by the Scottish government as the Church of Scotland and exerted a strong, pervasive, and lasting influence over the citizens of that country.

In 1696 Scotland's Parliament passed its "Act for Setting Schools," establishing a school in every parish in Scotland not already equipped with one. According to Arthur Herman, Scotland historian, "The reason behind all this was obvious to Presbyterians: boys and girls must know how to read holy scripture. John Knox's original 1650 *Book of Discipline* had called for a national system of education. Eighty years later the Scottish Parliament passed a law to this effect." If there was no teacher, the Presbyterian pastors of the churches offered reading instruction for all the children and any adults who had the desire to learn to read. In a relatively short time, Scotland became a highly literate society that greatly valued the tradition of learning. When possible, local schools also offered advanced classes in other subjects.

Within a generation nearly every parish school (not so many in the highlands) had some sort of school and a regular teacher. This had a profound effect on Scottish citizenry in the ensuing years; by the eighteenth century, Scotland's literacy rate was higher than any other country and Scotland became Europe's first literate society.

An English observer at the time noted that "in the low country of Scotland, the poorest are in general taught to read." By 1750 male literacy was estimated to be at 75 percent, whereas in England it was only about 53 percent.

Many Presbyterian churches throughout Scotland contained libraries offering the Bible *plus* a variety of other books. This tradition continues today in Presbyterian churches all over the world. The presence of libraries in the Presbyterian churches inspired the creation of libraries in Scottish towns. Herman states, "Even a person of relatively modest means had his own collection of books, and what he couldn't afford he could get at the local lending library, which by 1750 every town of any size enjoyed."

The city of Glasgow, northeast of the Cunningham clan's homeland, was a seat of bookselling, printing, paper, and ink industries that reached back to the Middle Ages and had supplied Scottish universities with educational materials.

The Scots took this tradition of literacy with them wherever they went—to Ireland when they settled the Ulster Plantation in the 1600s and to America when they emigrated there in the 1600s and 1700s. In western Virginia the Scots-Irish Cunninghams practiced their Presbyterian faith as much as they could, given an irregular supply of pastors for their congregation. However, in the mid-1700s a Presbyterian minister established a school in nearby Moorefield which was attended by many of the children in the area, thus continuing the Scottish/Presbyterian tradition of literacy. That tradition followed the Cunningham/Jordan family to the communities they settled in further west—in Virginia, Michigan, Missouri, and Iowa. In Iowa the wife of Presbyterian minister Thompson Bird would start a school which James Jordan's daughter Emily would attend.

CHAPTER 10
The Second Great Awakening

When James Jordan was growing up, a religious phenomenon known as "The Second Great Awakening" dominated the lives of many in Virginia except the most traditional church-going Presbyterians, Lutherans, Catholics, and Episcopalians. This movement did not miss the Jordan clan, the majority of whom had cast aside their Presbyterian affiliation and plunged in to the emotion-packed worshipping opportunities the new churches of the day provided.

The Emergence of Methodism

Methodism gained popularity throughout America after the arrival in 1771 of an extraordinary Methodist preacher from England named Francis Asbury. One of his biographers, William Larkin, describes Asbury's inspired preaching: ". . . if when he lifted the trumpet to his lips the Almighty blew the blast." He spread Methodism in America as part of the

Francis Asbury. From *Appleton's Cyclopedia of American Biography*

Second Great Awakening. Traveling on horseback or by horse and carriage throughout the colonies, Larkin states Asbury "averaged 6,000 miles each year. For 45 years he preached daily and conducted meetings and conferences. Histories of the various counties in the Valley of Virginia document his visits there—always a heralded event."

In 1784, ten years after the Revolutionary War, the Methodist Episcopal Church of the United States was officially established due in large part to Francis Asbury. Methodism had actually experienced a *decline* during the war because, having originated in England, the denomination lost credibility to followers who despised "all things English." Every Methodist preacher who had come to America returned to England except two: Asbury and one other.

After the war, due in great part to Asbury's ongoing energy and enthusiasm, Methodism experienced a comeback. Possessing the foundation of an effective network, a workable evangelical approach, with a comprehensive missionary system and solid theological roots, Methodism not only recovered from its Revolutionary War slump, it survived, and in very little time it thrived.

For thirty-two years Asbury led all the Methodists in America. Under his direction, the church grew from 1,200 to 214,000 members and seven hundred ordained preachers, including Richard Allen, the first black minister in the United States. Francis Asbury died in 1816, the year James Jordan turned three years old.

The Significance of the Second Great Awakening Upon James Jordan's Life

The style of evangelicalism taking place during the Second Great Awakening was a vast and powerful religious movement, and by the l820s evangelicalism had become one of the most dynamic and important cultural forces in American life.

Many people, including James and his entire family, were brought into the charisma of the movement through participation in "camp meetings," where "revivals" took place. In the early nineteenth century when James was growing up, camp meetings were held all over western Virginia and North Carolina and on the Kentucky and Ohio frontier by Presbyterians, Methodists, and Baptists.

The revival, according to historian Donald Scott, "became a central instrument for provoking conversions: as much a human as a divine event, deliberately orchestrated and deploying a variety of spiritual practices which focused on the unconverted 'youth' (men and women between fifteen and thirty) in the community." James Jordan and many of his brothers and sisters and friends would have fallen into this category.

The Jordan family's commitment to Methodism was reinforced by their participation in these religious revivals, which were designed to connect the participants

Methodist Camp Meeting. Library of Congress

to their faith in wildly emotional ways. The mind-blowing experiences of his participation in revivals permanently burned a place in the heart and soul of James C. Jordan. Historian Edward Smith summarizes the impact revivals had on the souls living in western Virginia: "The influence of religion upon the pioneers often led to a combination of the wild and uncouth with the pure and noble. The great revivals of that day were calculated to instill the fear of God into the hearts of the people and to frighten them into the fold. Perhaps it was the only effectual means of accomplishing the end for which the frontier church existed. The influence of the church was always directed toward a higher plane of civilization. Many a community was 'cleaned up' by a vigorous revival meeting and sometimes the results were fairly permanent."

Donald Scott relates this story about a young man named James Finley who attended the famous twenty-thousand-person revival at Cane Ridge, Kentucky, in 1801, described as the "largest and most powerful revival in American history." Scott's description captures the spirit of this camp meeting and its effect on Finley: "The noise was like the roar of Niagara. The vast sea of human beings seemed to be agitated as if by a storm. I counted seven ministers, all preaching at one time, some on stumps, others on wagons. . . . Some of the people were singing, others praying, some crying for mercy. A peculiarly strange sensation came over me. My heart beat tumultuously, my knees trembled, my lips quivered, and I felt as though I must fall to the ground."

James Finley was so moved he went on to become a Methodist minister. James Jordan would name his fourth son after this man.

"Conversion" Leads to a New Way of Thinking

"The focal point of this movement," according to Donald Scott, ". . . was 'the conversion.' Religious gatherings featured public confessions and renunciations of sin and personal witness to the workings of the spirit, collective prayer, all punctuated with cries of religious agony and ecstasy, which promoted religious fervor and . . . conversions." Scott continues:

> People recognized the fact of conversion by the power and character of the emotions that accompanied it, that made it an emotional catharsis, a heartfelt rebirth. Most characteristically, conversion, often accompanied by tears, provoked a deep sense of humility and peace marked by an overwhelming sense of love toward God, a sense that one had entered a wholly new state of being—in which the paramount desire was to do God's will, a desire expressed almost immediately in active concern for the conversion of family, friends, and even strangers who remained unconverted.

> Once a person had gone through the experience of conversion and rebirth, he or she would join the ranks of visitors and exhorters, themselves becoming evangelists for the still unconverted around them.

Conversion brought participants into a new relationship with God; they were energized and redirected. They felt like they had acquired a powerful sense of control in their lives. As experienced by James Jordan and his peers, Scott explains that "it brought them collectively into a new and powerful institutional fabric that provided them with personal discipline, a sense of fellowship, and channeled their benevolent obligations in appropriate directions; accepting rules for behaving towards each other that were designed to counter the conflict of the outside world."

James Jordan learned that his self-esteem came from spiritual, not social, standing, and a person was "measured by intensity of feeling and dedication to evangelical disciplines." Disdaining the traditional goals of wealth and social status, he instead sought the respect of his brothers and sisters in the faith.

Church Becomes Central to James Jordan's Life

Influenced by the Second Great Awakening, Methodist gatherings James attended were organized around ideas of mutual concern, love, and obligation. Everyone participated together, singing many hymns and engaging in intense spiritual exercises. The congregation heard sermons from clergymen noted for their powerful "plain-speaking" preaching. Besides taking part in worship, members also immersed themselves in additional religious gatherings: prayer meetings, "class meetings," "love feasts," and membership in benevolent societies. This myriad of activities reinforced in them a deep and committed sense of fellowship with those with whom they worshipped and fostered a sense of responsibility and obligation to those they served.

James and his fellow converts were charged to tend to the needs of those less fortunate and offer aid to others who had suffered misfortune. James and many of his peers took this to the extreme, with them feeling the need to, according to Donald Scott, "enlist themselves in a broad set of campaigns to reform American society." Scott continues: ". . . this sense of participation in and responsibility for the vast outpouring of Saving Grace (caused them) to believe that it was given to them and their generation of evangelical Americans (the charge) to prepare the way for Christ's Second Coming . . . by working unrelentingly to bring about the thousand-year reign of righteousness that would precede his return to earth."

The converts were drawn into local evangelical Baptist, Methodist, or Universalist congregations, which became the foundation for an expansive "American religious denominational network" in which, according to Scott, "they could attend a familiar church in their faith wherever they moved, which many families did in the early to mid-1800s."

One of the first actions newcomers took when they entered a new town, Scott states, was to "seek the fellowship of their 'brothers and sisters' in a comforting church. Scores of young people embraced the movement and sought marriage partners from the ranks of their coreligionists." This would occur in the life of James Jordan and almost all of his brothers and sisters.

CHAPTER 11
A Visit to Cunningham Plantation

The South Branch Valley was one of the most fertile and prosperous valleys in the region, and in the early 1800s several large and gracious homes reflected that fact. The Van Meters in Old Fields improved theirs and eventually it became an iconic plantation "great house," which they called Fort Pleasant. The William Cunningham family, living about three miles away, did not have the ten thousand acres owned by the Van Meter family, but they did have over twenty-five hundred acres and possessed the same fertile soil as that on Van Meter's South Branch Farms.

At Cunningham Plantation, the entire family would gather for weddings, funerals, and other events. The children of John and Agnes Jordan and those of Agnes' many brothers and children—cousins that by now numbered around seventy-five—assembled at or near the old "Homestead" for several weeks of celebration and family reunion.

While visiting, James Cunningham Jordan got a taste of life in the area where his great-grandfather had settled and where his uncles had created an impressive home and agricultural business. Having been established about seventy-five years earlier, the area was on its way to becoming gentrified—a world apart from the rustic lifestyle in the wilds of back-country western Virginia where James was growing up.

Cunningham Plantation

The rustic farm James' grandfather, James Cunningham, had lived on as a child with his parents, "Lord" John and Mary, had become a smoothly functioning and successful enterprise. The living quarters, now inhabited by the descendants of James' great-uncle William "Irish Billy" Cunningham, reflected a significantly improved version of the dwellings lived in by previous generations. The rustic cabins and out buildings were replaced by fine houses made from milled lumber. If parts of the plantation house had previously been part of a log cabin, the logs were covered over with milled boards.

Windows were no longer the dangerous luxury they had been in the past. In the beginning there were few windows in the settlers' cabins, just slits carved between the logs in order to shoot at the Indians. The Indians were no more. They had been exiled to lands to the west. British rule was a thing of the past. The king's governors and armies had left, and it was a more peaceful time. Now it was possible to bring light into their more spacious homes, and windows were enlarged or added.

The homestead was heated with fireplaces (stoves would not be a fixture until the mid-1800s). There was adequate furniture in the house as well as metal eating and cooking utensils and china plates. Some cloth and clothing—hand woven, hand knit, and/or hand sewn—may still have been produced on the property, but fabric was also readily available in nearby towns for purchase. Gardens were established, orchards were in place, and crops were planted and harvested. The limestone soil in their fields was well suited to growing grass for grazing, corn, and tobacco. In the six or seven decades they had inhabited their land, the extensive Cunningham property had been transformed from a rustic cabin in the woodlands into a thriving and successful plantation.

Cunningham Plantation was conveniently located between Van Meter's Fort Pleasant/South Branch Farms (an area now called "Old Fields"), approximately three miles to the north, and the village of Moorefield, five miles to the south. Moorefield was in the area where the old Fort Buttermilk had stood during the French and Indian War. Many of the residents of Old Fields were displaced to Moorefield to make way for the successful farming and livestock enterprise that had been emerging on South Branch Farms owned by the Van Meter family.

Even though they had not moved, the members of the Cunningham family living on the plantation were now residents of Hardy County, with Moorefield as its county seat. Romney, twenty miles to the northeast, had been their county seat before Hampshire County was divided to create Hardy County. These boundary changes decreased the distance the Cunninghams had to travel to their county seat from twenty miles down to five.

Those living on Cunningham Plantation were also fortunate to be just a few miles from the road that linked the village of Moorefield with the next county seat town, Romney. The Cunninghams also had the advantage of traveling on yet another good road that took them further—out of Romney to the next county seat town of Winchester. As settlers continued to settle in Hampshire County (1,986 land entries were recorded in Hampshire County between 1788 and 1810), the Commonwealth of Virginia decided to build a forty-mile-long state road from Winchester, the county seat of Frederick County, east to Romney.

The road's construction was a boon to local economic development as several stage lines began operations, providing settlers ready access to eastern markets. With the stagecoach came the ability to deliver mail on a regular schedule, and in 1796 a post office opened in Romney. This gave the Cunninghams immediate access to the outside world, including postal service, on sixty miles of easily traversable roadway.

A Ride in South Branch Valley

James' Cunningham cousins and second cousins living on or near the plantation grew up in a comfortable and secure environment surrounded by family. The school they all attended, along with children living on neighboring plantations and farms, was in Old Fields, and the nearest village was Moorefield. Both could be reached by a short horseback or carriage ride and probably were visited by James and his cousins, brothers, and sisters when they went to South Branch Valley.

The community of Moorefield, which had been incorporated in 1777, became the county seat of Hardy County in 1785. When it was laid out, it was divided into half-acre lots. The stipulation to those buying property was they had to build a dwelling within two years, and the dwellings were to be at least eighteen feet square and have a brick or stone chimney. By 1825, when James was old enough to accompany his Cunningham cousins on horseback through town, he saw enlarged versions of the original small houses.

One of the most outstanding Moorefield buildings they would ride by was the Old Stone Tavern, a two-story building made of rough field stone with a "public house" or tavern on the first floor and a home for the tavern keeper and his family on the second floor. Moorefield settler Thomas Parsons, the brother-in-law and business partner of James' great-uncle Robert, had constructed this building in the late 1780s, combining the rugged stone with fine symmetrical details on the exterior. The interior featured large rooms, a wide stairwell, and a well-designed basement fireplace. James would note that the Old Stone Tavern was one of the finest buildings in town.

Another building James would see in Moorefield was a double log house with a brick chimney. Captain James Parsons, a Revolutionary War officer, also related to James' uncle Robert through marriage, had originally lived there with his family.

Riding on, James would see a log house built by Lieutenant Robert Higgins, who had served in the Revolutionary Army. Higgins built the 20 x 18 house as required by his deed and added the stone chimney. George Harness, another relative through marriage to the Cunningham clan, purchased the home in 1793 (not long before James' parents were married) and was raising his family there.

James and his fellow riders would also take note of the most significant building in Moorefield: the (second) Hardy County Courthouse, built in 1793, featuring graceful arches and entrances. There were other buildings in the town, all necessary for local sustenance: the gristmill, tannery, harnessmaker, shoemaker, wagonmaker, tailor, blacksmith, cabinetmaker, and merchants selling a myriad of items—food staples, fabric, and most likely candy for the children, etc.

Riding out into the valley to the north, James could see farmhouses and cabins tucked into the side of hilly acreages. A few miles to the north of the Cunningham property was the Van Meter family's "great house," called Fort Pleasant. This impressive residence was a massive double-chimney Federal-style building constructed of clay bricks which had been fabricated on the Fort Pleasant farm. Featuring colossal columns spanning two stories, it was by far the most magnificent residence in South Branch Valley.

About seven or eight miles to the north, at the end of the beautiful Trough of the South Fork Potomac, was the stone structure of old Fort Van Meter and a mile to the northeast of that was a stone Glebe House, a parsonage

The Van Meter plantation great house, Fort Pleasant. National Park Service, US Department of the Interior

and farm to support the Anglican church up the road in Romney. The Anglican minister and his wife lived on the glebe.

Returning to his Uncle William Cunningham's plantation house, James would note that even though the Cunningham property was not as sizable as Van Meter's South Branch Valley Farms, it was substantial and had most of the elements of the typical plantation estate—slave cabins, barns, stables, workshops, warehouses, and larger homes scattered here and there for the various families residing on the property.

James' visits to his great-uncle William's plantation were as good as attending school. James got a good look at some very successful large cattle and livestock operations. As an adult James would be known as "Uncle Jimmy" Jordan, a friendly and charming man. At Cunningham Plantation James observed and learned valuable social skills in a more civilized setting than where he was growing up.

He was given an opportunity to enjoy the many pleasures of living the fine plantation life but, conversely, saw firsthand a less impressive reality—slavery made this fine life happen. It was on one of these visits that James and the other men in the family were commissioned by the neighboring Van Meters to go, find, and capture escaped slaves who had run away from their plantation. Jordan biographer Johnson Brigham tells the story:

> James was a member of a party engaged in hunting up and returning to the owners a number of fugitive slaves who had escaped from the neighboring plantation. They were trying to elude pursuit by hiding in bushes and caves by day and by stealing out at night, enduring untold hardships to make a few miles toward the great free West, of which they had but a vague idea, from hearsay only.
>
> These people, men, women, and children, with hungry, pinched faces, sad longing eyes, bleeding feet, and scanty, ragged clothing were quietly caught while most of them were trying to pray for deliverance, and despite their pitiful pleadings and remonstrances, were marched back to their masters' homes and to their lowly life of servitude.

The memory of this slave-hunting expedition would haunt James Jordan for the rest of his life.

CHAPTER 12
Slavery in the Virginia Highlands

James Jordan's traumatic experiences hunting down runaway slaves in his youth would influence his abolitionist stance, his eventual membership in the antislavery Republican Party, and his active participation in the Underground Railroad.

Inspired by the Second Great Awakening, James Jordan, like many of his fellow Methodists, came to see freedom as a universal value. The Methodist church banned slaveholding among its members in 1837. They were not the only religious denomination to do so.

In the early years of the United States, when James Jordan was a child, farm machinery had not yet been invented. Manpower and utilizing beasts of burden was the only way to farm; it had been done this way since the beginning of time, and it was done this way by the settlers who first came into the western highlands of Virginia.

During the early decades of colonial settlement, the folks who could afford it contracted the five-to-seven-year assistance of (mostly European) indentured servants and German Redemptionists to lighten their labors. Seventy-five years later, when James Jordan was growing up, the situation had changed. The institution of slavery had arrived in the Valley of Virginia, and it had been inducted into the twenty-five-hundred-acre Cunningham Plantation. The Cunninghams owned slaves; many of them.

In 1756, forty black "tithables" (slaves) were listed on the tax rolls of Augusta County, the original county where Cunningham Plantation was located, indicating a slave population of not more than one-twentieth (5 percent) of the population of the county. By 1790, Cunningham Plantation was now located in the newly formed Hardy County, and the census for slave population in Hardy County (a much smaller area than Augusta County from which Hardy was carved) doubled to 10 percent, with 3,364 whites and 369 slaves. There were also 411 "free non-whites," a category not limited to black people and probably also including some Indians who had taken up permanent residence. A person with at least one-fourth Negro blood—and there was a large and increasing number of such—was counted as a mulatto. This ratio was low compared to some areas of Tidewater and Piedmont Virginia where, by 1860, 70 percent of that population was comprised of slaves.

The Impact of Slavery on the US Economy

Before 1776, when Virginia was a colony, slaves were real estate in the eye of the law. After the Revolutionary War they were regarded as personal property. Yale historian David W. Blight describes the impact the institution of slavery had on the American economy during the antebellum years: "In 1860 slaves were worth more than all of America's manufacturing, all of the railroads, all of the productive capacity of the United States put together. Slaves were the single largest, by far, financial asset of property in the entire American economy."

"Loans were taken out for their purchase to be repaid with interest," according to Ta-Nehisi Coates, journalist and author. "Insurance policies were drafted against the untimely death of a slave and the loss of potential profits. Slave sales were taxed and notarized." Coates continues, "Slaveholders had journals such as *DeBow's Review*, which recommended the best practices for wringing profits from slaves."

Slaves were often punished by whipping. Library of Congress

James Jordan: His Life and His Legacy 47

"The ten richest counties in the nation in 1860 were all in the South in fertile lands along the Mississippi River delta, the South Carolina coast, and the Alabama black belt, regions where thousands of slaves toiled on enormous plantations," states Bruce Gourley, an authority on nineteenth-century American history. "Thanks to the riches of slave-labor, most American millionaires were large-scale plantation owners."

Slavery in James Jordan's Life

James Jordan's relatives and close friends on the Cunningham side of his family had participated in the buying and selling of slaves. In his will, written in the 1790s, James Jordan's great-uncle Robert Cunningham left a total of nineteen slaves to his wife and children. The part of his will pertaining to the disposition of his slaves stated, "I give (the slave/s) to son/daughter and his/her heirs forever." Robert did not free any of his slaves. At the Van Meter family's ten-thousand-acre South Branch Valley Farms, in the shadow of which lay the Cunningham/Jordan holdings, Garrett Van Meter owned many slaves as would his son Isaac. In 1788, when Garrett made his will, he owned twelve slaves.

When he was growing up James Jordan heard countless stories about infractions and subsequent punishments of slaves:

- When settling an estate in 1828 in Pendleton County, near where James Jordan grew up, twelve slaves were sold at auction for $2,511.50.
- The Negro who stole a horse or a hog was hanged.
- In 1774 a slave by the name of Rockingham who killed a man was ordered hanged and his head set on a pole.
- In 1810 an escaped Negro was branded in the hand and returned to his master.
- In 1811 a Negro named Stevens was tried for plotting to kill but was discharged.
- In 1812 a Negro named Daniel was branded in the hand for stealing a calico habit and a piece of muslin.
- In 1813 a Negro named Lucy was sold for $11.25, the amount of jail fees, of which she was the occasion.
- In the same year a Negro named Ben stabbed John Davis. He was ordered burnt in the hand, given ten lashes on the bare back well laid on, and remanded to jail subject to the order of his master.
- In 1811 two men were tried for stealing a wench but were discharged. (In this case the slave was the occasion of lawbreaking on the part of the white man.)

Sometimes the freeing of a slave at a certain age was mentioned in a will. Western Virginia historian Oren Morton remembers, "A slave owner named Nicholas Harper provided that his slave Lydia be set free when she is sixty, if she behaves herself, and that her child Polly be free at the age of twenty-one."

Morton wrote in 1911, fifty years after the end of the Civil War, that the local white population of that pre-Civil War era generally felt the "laws relative to Negro lawbreakers were severe, yet not without reason." He further stated: "The slave had not the forethought, the initiative, nor the self-restraint which the white man had acquired through centuries of effort. He was a savage by instinct and heredity. Force, not suasion, was the one argument he could comprehend, and he expected it to be applied swiftly and vigorously. Leniency led only to a loss of respect toward those in authority over him."

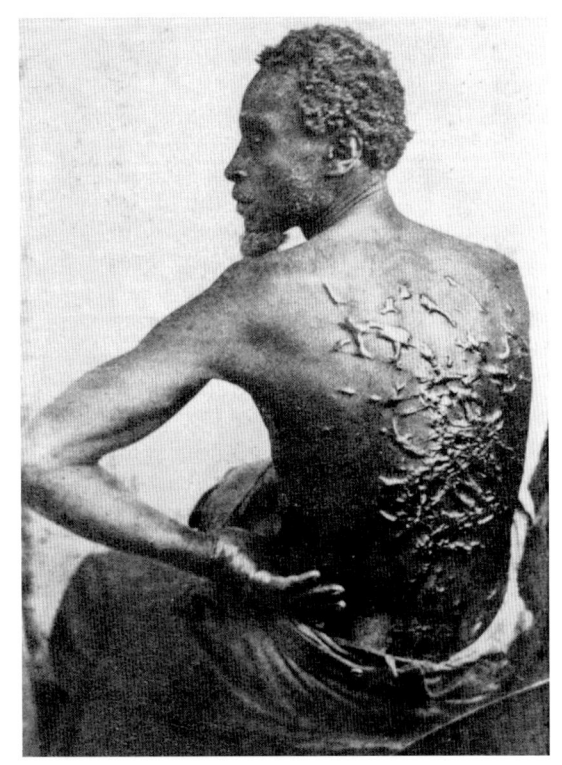

Photograph illustrating the brutality of slavery. National Portrait Gallery, Smithsonian Institution

Hill Farmers and Plantation Owners

In the back-country uplands of the northwestern Virginia mountains where James Jordan grew up, the area was breathtakingly beautiful, but the soil was not as rich and plentiful as that in the valleys below. The farmers raised crops and livestock, more for their own consumption than for a market. Land at higher elevations was less desirable; the "hill farms" were small and not as prosperous as the plantations occupying land in the valleys. These farms had few, if any, slaves. The farmers couldn't afford them and were typically against the concept of slavery. Furthermore, the hill farmers resented the slaves working down in the valleys—slaves robbed them of the opportunity to make extra income working for the prosperous large plantation owners.

The earlier generations of Jordan men were examples of this ongoing resentment. When James' great-grandfather, George Jordan, and his wife were first married and tending their own small "hill farm," George, by necessity, worked for landowners in the valley who owned larger parcels of land. At that time, slavery was just being introduced into the area, and any extra labor George Jordan could offer was gratefully welcomed.

George and later his son, George Jr., helped out doing seasonal work and providing assistance as the prosperous valley farmers transitioned their properties from rough land to productive fields and improved their cabins and outbuildings. The extra income George and his son earned was a welcome necessity. After slaves were brought to the area, George Jordan and other local farmers resented their presence because it lessened that opportunity.

James Jordan was probably familiar with these sentiments, which were passed down through the "hill farmer" Jordan side of the family from his grandfathers to his father, John Jordan. The feelings were further reinforced with recollections of the time when James' grandfather, George Jr., and James' father, John, had for a time lived in New Design, a community whose focal point was abolishing slavery.

In contrast to his Jordan ancestors, the Cunningham side of the family was rooted in the prosperous Cunningham Plantation; his uncle fully incorporating slave labor in order to operate the plantation. During his visits there, James became increasingly aware of the many negative aspects of this oppressive institution, and his perceptions were magnified when he was swept into the Second Great Awakening, experienced a conversion, and committed himself to practicing the abolitionist mandate of the (northern) Methodist church.

Escaping Slaves

Since the time Virginia was settled, it continuously held the largest number of slaves of any state in the United States. Virginia also had a large free black population. The advent of the cotton gin in 1790 forever changed how cotton was produced and that fueled the necessity for more and more slaves to work the now-burgeoning cotton industry. Eighteen years later, in 1808, the importation of slaves was outlawed in the United States. To compensate, multitudes of slaves from states in the upper South, such as Virginia, were sold to owners in the deep South, in the cotton-growing states where a slave's life would be much harsher and shorter.

As slave families were broken up, slaves became desperate and eager to run. In Virginia, the slaveholders were less likely than ever to free their slaves because they had become such valuable financial assets that could be leveraged, if needed.

Slaves living in Virginia who wanted their freedom faced limited choices: they could try to make their way up to the mountain highlands on Virginia's western frontier to one of the hidden, illegal communities of refugee Negroes; they could try to disappear into an

Slaves frequently tried to escape from their masters. *A Ride for Liberty—The Fugitive Slaves* by Eastman Johnson, ca. 1862. Brooklyn Museum

This portrayal of a poor fugitive was often used on handbills offering rewards for runaway slaves. From *The Underground Railroad from Slavery to Freedom* by Wilbur Henry Siebert and Albert Bushnell Hart, 2nd Ed., Macmillan, 1898

area located on the state line between southern Virginia and North Carolina known as the Great Dismal Swamp where thousands of escaped slaves (called "maroons") existed; or if they were light-skinned or trained as skilled craftsmen, they could try to settle in a community where they might pass as a free Negro. According to Virginia historian Oren Morton:

> The whereabouts and the doings of the slave were kept under scrutiny, and his liberty of movement was very much restricted. If a slave left his master's premises without a pass, any person might bring him before a justice, who at his option might order a whipping; or for every such offense he might be given ten lashes by the landowner upon whom he had trespassed. He might not carry a gun except by the permit of a justice. If he gave false testimony, each ear might by turn be nailed to the pillory and afterwards cut off, in addition to his receiving 39 lashes at the whipping post.

Virginia was a good place from which slaves could successfully escape. It bordered the free states of Pennsylvania and Ohio. Fugitives who journeyed through Virginia traveled high in the Appalachian Mountains, which offered safe refuge. From the state's northernmost point in western Virginia, across the Ohio River from Wellsville, Ohio, it was only ninety miles to Lake Erie, beyond which lay Canada. Sympathetic Pennsylvania Quakers offered safe refuge to escaping slaves as well. Fugitives fleeing from the Carolinas or Tidewater Virginia who made it to the western Virginia highlands were tantalizingly close to freedom.

This region in the back country uplands of northwestern Virginia was where James Jordan was raised. As he grew up he became very aware of slaves trying to escape and slave owners constantly searching the area to recover their "missing property." As a young man, he turned his back on all of it; he left Virginia to seek refuge from a way of life he had come to despise.

James Jordan was not alone; it was just a matter of time before the folks living in the western highlands of the Commonwealth of Virginia would angrily decide to split off and form a separate state. In 1861, the region known as western Virginia broke away from the Commonwealth of Virginia, became the State of West Virginia, and was admitted into the Union during the Civil War. The state motto said it all: *Montani Semper Liberi*, which is Latin for "Mountaineers Always Free."

State Seal of West Virginia designed by Joseph H. Diss Debar in 1863.

50   Pursuit of a Dream

CHAPTER 13
The Jordan Family Decides to Leave Western Virginia

The Jordan Sisters Get Married; One Elopes!

There were five daughters and three sons still living at home in 1821when little Agnes, named after her mother and grandmother, was born into the Jordan clan. Agnes may have been the flower girl when, five years later, her sister Anna was married in 1826 to William Smith in Nicholas County. After their marriage they lived close to Anna's parents on a farm near Blue Sulphur Springs in Greenbrier County. In 1828, the Jordan family celebrated James' sister Elizabeth's wedding to James Wood at the Jordan farm. The ink was hardly dry on her marriage certificate when Elizabeth died in childbirth less than a year after her marriage. She was twenty-six years old.

Most families are not without scandal, and the Jordan family was no exception. In 1831 James' sister Cynthia eloped with an exotic Hindu gentleman, Jordan Babar (or Baber). They were married on March 19, 1831, in nearby Kanawha County. Cynthia and Jordan had probably met at a camp meeting. Babar claimed he was a descendent of a great ruler of Afghanistan and his family came to Virginia by way of India, Spain, and Florida. According to him, he came from a wealthy family, but, alas, he had no money of his own. John and Agnes Jordan thought he was a fraud and disapproved of the match.

Agnes had barely finished dealing with the elopement of willful Cynthia when she was faced with another crisis. In early 1832 her husband, John Jordan, became gravely ill. He died at the age of fifty-seven on June 8, 1832. John's death was recorded in Lewis County, which had evolved from Harrison County—the place where John had been born, returned to, and become a bachelor farmer after living in New Design. He had taken his bride, Agnes, to live there after their wedding, and it was there they had started their family before moving south to Greenbrier County. Their daughter, Susan, and her husband, Abel Withrow, had been living there since their marriage in 1819. John Jordan died there and was probably buried on or near his old homestead.

The next year, in 1833, Agnes' oldest son, George, was married to Marie Taylor, the sister of their pastor. Marie's older brother, the Reverend John Wray Taylor, married them in a Methodist ceremony in Fayette County.

Agnes Jordan was now a fifty-one-year-old widow with five unmarried children: Phoebe, twenty-three; James, nineteen; Margaret, seventeen; John, fourteen; and Agnes, eleven. With her oldest son married and her husband deceased, it was time for Agnes to decide what to do with the Jordan property, which included land inherited from her parents. John and Agnes' property would eventually pass to George, as the oldest male son. Her other two sons would have little inheritance, and then there were the three unmarried daughters. Agnes wanted to be fair and her family to be happy, but in order to do so, difficult decisions needed to be made.

The Political Climate of Virginia in the 1830s

From colonial times Virginia was continually being carved up into more and more counties in response to the increasing population. There were always more than twice as many counties in the more populous eastern part of the state than over the mountains in the less developed west, thus creating an imbalance in state government. The western Virginians had fewer representatives in the Virginia legislature and were unable to successfully fund services and improvements like roads and schools in their area; most of the money stayed in the east. Western Virginians had felt ostracized and disenfranchised since the time of colonial Virginia's House of Burgesses before the Revolutionary War. By the 1830s, as legislators from western Virginia tried to bring their infrastructure up to nineteenth-century standards, the tension was at an all-time high.

As the white population grew in western Virginia, it declined in the eastern part of the state with a corresponding increase in the slave population. By 1860, in some counties in eastern Virginia, 70 percent of the overall population would be slaves.

The slave owners—mostly in eastern Virginia—were taxed 11 cents per $100 of valuation of their slaves, while the cattle in the western mountains were taxed 40 cents per $100 of valuation. Land was taxed at a lower rate than livestock, and slaves younger than twelve were not taxed at all.

In the 1828 presidential election between Andrew Jackson and John Quincy Adams, there was a relaxation of the voting restrictions, which meant nearly all white males could vote. Thus the "common man" was given a stronger voice in choosing his leader. This had a ricochet effect in western Virginia, and, starting in 1829, voices from western Virginia became louder, demanding better representation, changes in the state government, and more fair tax laws.

During the Nat Turner Rebellion in 1831, a slave living in the Tidewater area of eastern Virginia gathered fifty-six slaves together and slaughtered about the same number of white people. This greatly disturbed the residents in the western uplands, and they immediately demanded that the Virginia legislature consider abolishing slavery in the state. After debate, the more populous eastern plantation regions voted it down, which caused the citizens of western Virginia to move politically closer to the North.

In the 1832 presidential elections, young James Jordan "stood in" for his deceased father. James' older brother George was absent and, even though James was underage (nineteen), under the ruling of the election judges he was recognized as head of the family and invited to take his father's place at the polls.

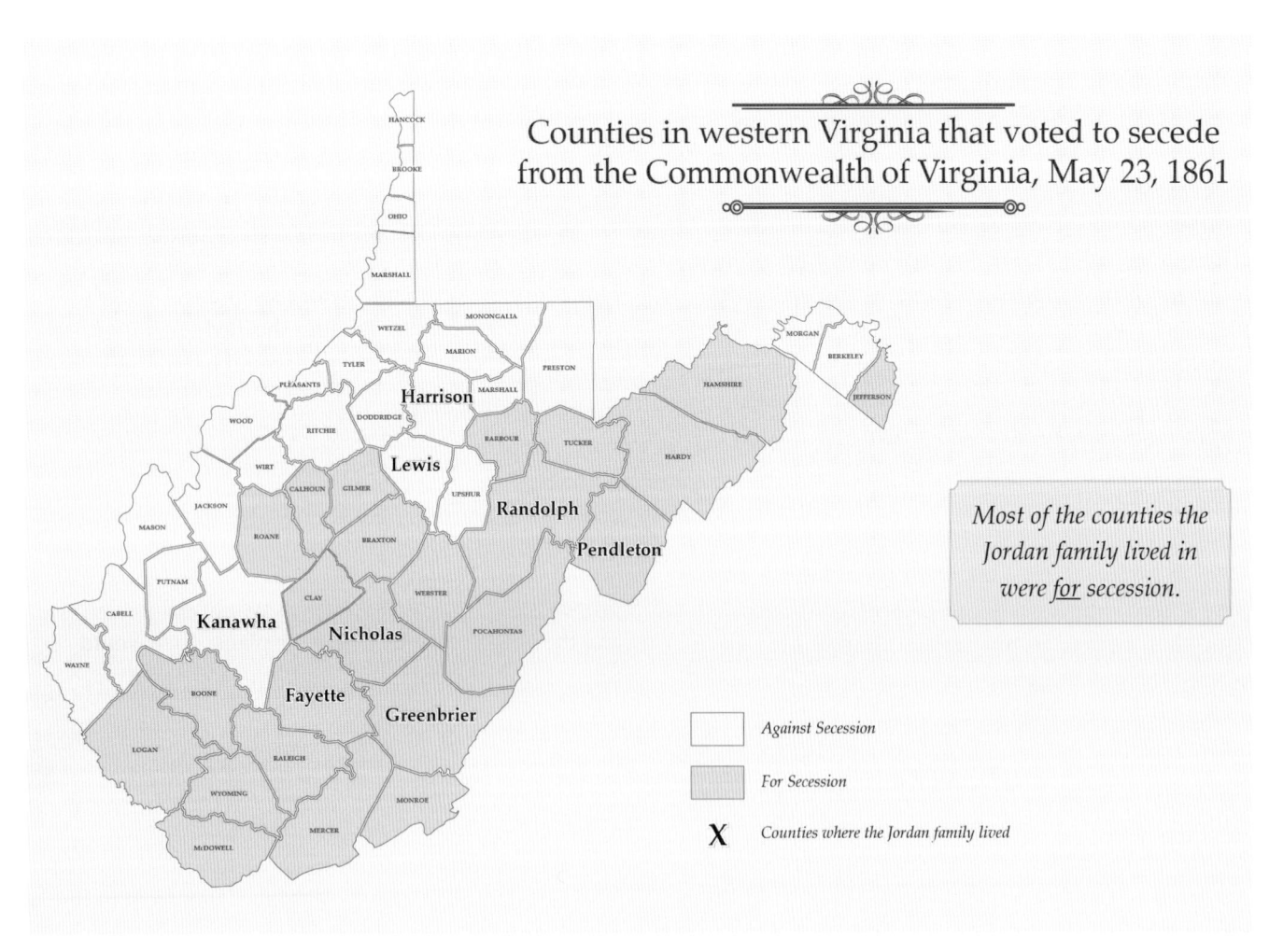

Counties in western Virginia that voted to secede from the Commonwealth of Virginia, May 23, 1861

Most of the counties the Jordan family lived in were for secession.

Prior to their departure from western Virginia, these are the counties where the Jordan family owned land.

52   Pursuit of a Dream

James proudly cast his first presidential vote—for Henry Clay. In doing so, young James was acting on the emerging principles and focus of his life:

- Clay was a member of the National Republican Party, which became the Whig party, the political party James Jordan would embrace.
- Clay was in favor of a National Bank; James Jordan would eventually help spearhead the State Bank of Iowa.
- Henry Clay had brokered the Missouri Compromise in 1820 which admitted one slave state and one free state into the union but also ensured that any states in the land acquired in the Louisiana Purchase would not be slave states. James would permanently settle in the "free" state of Iowa.
- Henry Clay championed his "American System" rather than the concept of "states' rights," which was fundamental to why the Civil War was fought. James fully supported Abraham Lincoln when the South seceded and the Civil War was fought to bring those states back into the Union.
- Even though Clay owned slaves, he freed them in his will. Jordan was an abolitionist.

Henry Clay lost the election to Andrew Jackson, but what was *not* lost was James Jordan's commitment to the ideals in which he believed. Voting in the 1832 presidential election was his first foray into politics, and with that the "hook had been set." James Jordan would be caught up in politics for the rest of his life.

The Decision to Move to Michigan

The contentious political situation in Virginia became the exit call for families living in western Virginia like the Jordans. The tax laws were unfair and the Nat Turner Rebellion had scared them; their local pastors repeatedly preached to them about the evils of slavery, and they realized they were allied more and more with the North than the South.

As soon as the Indians were cleared out of territories to the west, pioneers were pointing their covered wagons to those regions to start a fresh, new life, and hopefully one without political turmoil.

Furthermore, the First and Second Great Awakenings empowered these folks to think they could make a better life . . . and they wanted to pursue their dream in a new place.

In 1833, following the sad events of the previous year, the Jordan family learned more changes were imminent. The Reverend John Wray Taylor (brother-in-law of James' brother George) had heard about a pioneer settlement in Berrien County, Michigan, and was making plans to move there.

Located on the St. Joseph River near the town of Niles, the site was a former Pottawatami Indian mission settlement known as the Carey Baptist Mission. It had been established by the Reverend Isaac McCoy in 1822 with the assistance of Michigan Territorial Governor Lewis Cass, and while it was intended as a mission to the Indians, it had become a haven for pioneer settlers who were encroaching on the area. By 1831 the mission had been abandoned, and McCoy and the Indians had been forced to leave and resettle in the West through treaty agreements with the US government. Any remnants of the Indian tribes living east of the Mississippi River had been defeated in 1832 in the Black Hawk War in Illinois with the Indians being forced to cross into territory west of the Mississippi. Therefore, the Indian threat, which had been so pervasive in Virginia in earlier years, would not be a concern to folks settling in Michigan.

Disenchanted with the political situation in Virginia and relieved that the Indians were no longer a threat, Marie Jordan, Reverend Taylor's sister and George's wife, urged her husband to join the Taylors in their trek west. As the oldest son, George would have inherited the Jordan property in Virginia at the time of his father's death, but he instead was convinced a move to Michigan would offer a better future. George and Marie then encouraged George's widowed mother, Agnes, and her unmarried offspring to join them, and Agnes agreed. With the question of George's inheritance of the property resolved, the family was free to sell the farm, and they began formulating their plans. They would leave after the spring rains, traveling in covered wagons to a fresh start in southern Michigan.

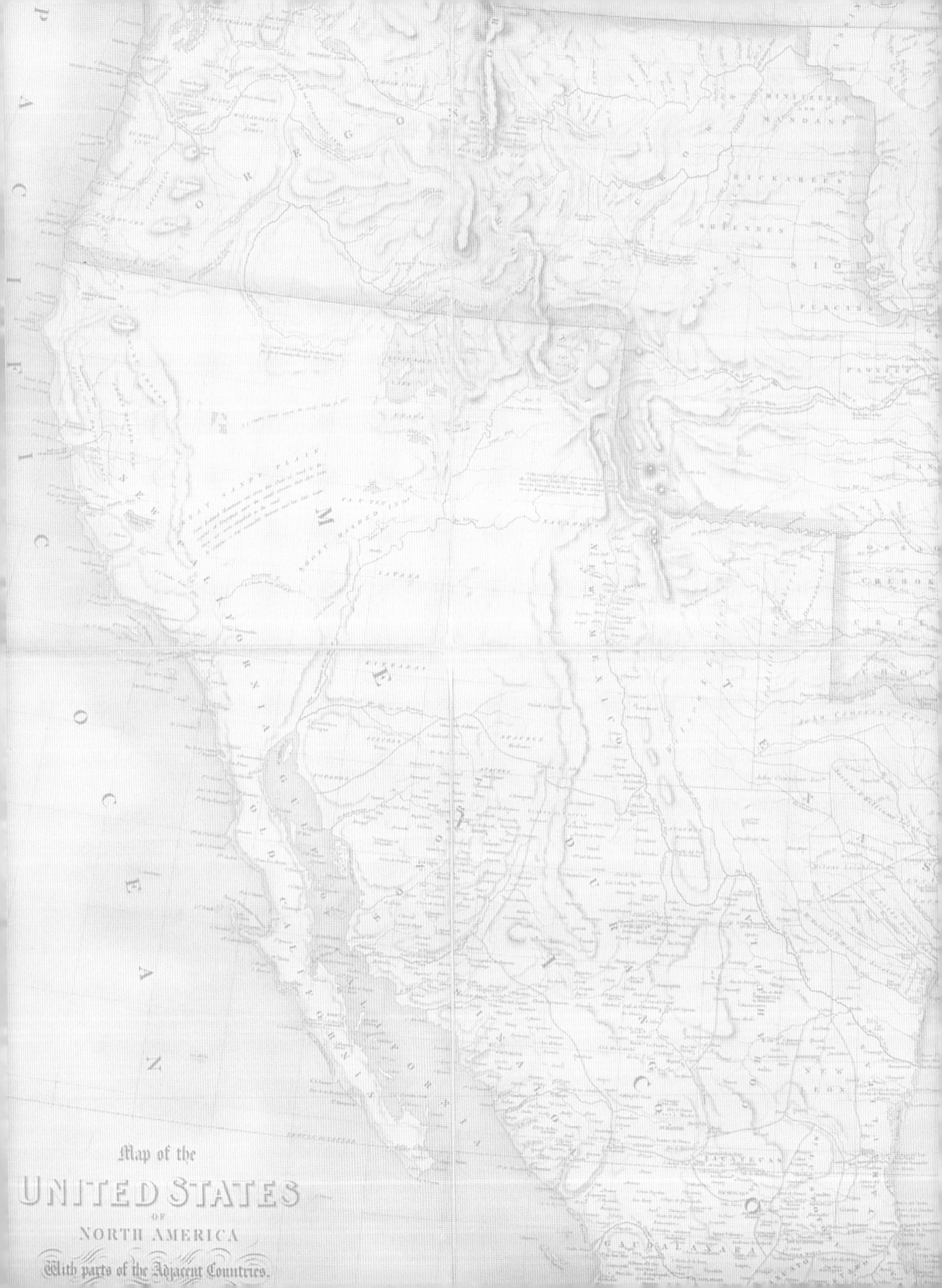

Map of the
UNITED STATES
OF
NORTH AMERICA
With parts of the Adjacent Countries.

Part Two

Pursuing a Destiny

"We wander, yes. There is uncertainty along the way. But we wander confidently, knowing that others have travelled this path before us, and filled with the assurance that God is with us. In response to a call that beckons us forward, and propelled by the promise that God is to be met along the way, there is something about the Christian life that keeps us on the move. And we discover who God is along the journey."
—Doug Workman, Presbyterian Pastor

"Press forward. Do not stop, do not linger in your journey, but strive for the mark set before you."
—George Whitefield

CHAPTER 14
A New Life in Michigan

Westward Ho!

Once the decision was made to travel to Michigan, the family prepared for the journey west, which would take place in the summer of 1834. According to Glenda Riley in the *Frontierswomen: The Iowa Experience:*

> After the basic wagon was selected, careful planning and long hours of labor were devoted to equipping the wagon box. The degree of thoughtfulness . . . in this task could spell disaster or success for the migrants. All of the family's needs had to be assembled and packed in that limited space. This meant that the usefulness of every item they owned or purchased had to be critically scrutinized.
>
> Equipment included all the clothing, food, cooking utensils, bedding, medicines, and tools that might be necessary to sustain family and animals along the trail as well as seed, farm implements, and furniture to carry them through the beginning phases of establishing a farmstead.
>
> The men were in charge of firearms, tools, and furniture, buckets of grease for the axles, barrels of

Map of the United States, 1839. Library of Congress

The Jordan family traveled by wagon train to their new home in Michigan. Library of Congress

water for the stock and spare parts for the wagon. Then they trained the team that was to pull the wagon as well as prepared the other stock for their long journey ahead.

Women made the cloth top for the wagon and prepared food and clothing and medicine. They dipped hundreds of candles, packed sacks with flour, cornmeal, dried fruit, and more; assembled dishes and cooking pots, and cooked enough food to last the first week. Canvas pockets were sewn on the inside of the wagon cover to hold miscellaneous items, such as cooking utensils, firearms, or toilet articles.

Decisions were made as to what to leave behind, and if it wasn't given to relatives, it was auctioned off.

In spite of the hard work, these were exciting times because the territory to the west was thought of as a "land of possibility" to the new pioneer settlers. Certainly the soil in Michigan would be far superior to the farmland in the western Virginia uplands. New opportunities could provide the optimistic pioneers with a fresh start.

Agnes Jordan sold the Jordan family farm, which provided adequate funds to start a new life in the West. They carefully chose which of their many possessions and supplies to pack in their wagons and sold the rest, providing them with more income to use to begin their new life. Sadly, they would leave four sisters behind; Mary, Susan, Anna, and Cynthia all chose to remain on their Virginia farms with their husbands and families.

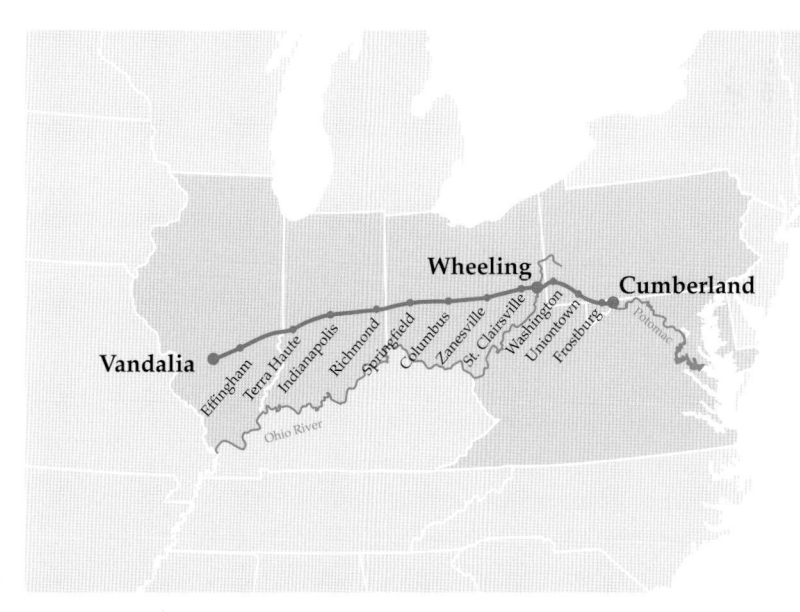

The National Road. Map by Citynoise at English Wikipedia.

James Jordan: His Life and His Legacy

Their plan was for the unmarried sons to farm the land Agnes would purchase with the proceeds from the sale of the Virginia farm. Her son George and his wife would also receive some of the proceeds to purchase their own homestead in Michigan. Agnes, James, and George and their unmarried sisters would all live together on the land Agnes would homestead.

The family also had made decisions about the dispersal of the Cunningham property in Lewis County that John Jordan had inherited from his father-in-law, James Cunningham. The two older daughters, Mary Jordan Cunningham and Susan Jordan Withrow, and their husbands both decided to move onto that land. They never left Lewis County, where they are buried.

Cynthia Jordan Babar, now reconciled with her family, had been living with her husband and children in Kanawha County, one county away from the Jordan farm. Just coming off of her third pregnancy, she and her husband chose not to travel with the rest of the family but joined them a few years later, in 1836.

Anna and her husband, William T. Smith, and their family stayed on at their farm near Blue Sulphur Springs in Greenbrier County the next four years, until 1837 when they sold their land and joined the Jordan clan in Michigan. Riley continues in the *Frontierswomen: The Iowa Experience*:

> A family's decision to leave (their) comfortable web was not only traumatic to those leaving, but also for the ones left behind. The announcement that a family was leaving initiated a transition period during which both the soon-to-be pioneers and those remaining at home attempted to adjust to the idea of separation. The rituals recognizing the impending departure included dinners, dances, family visits, and special church services, all designed to wrap the migrant family in a cloak of good wishes and friendship of the people they had known (and loved) for so many years.
>
> Defying their brave attempts to invest the coming break with a festive air, the actual departure usually presented a heart-rending scene. In the murky early morning light, people gathered around the migrants to help them load their wagons, to serve them breakfast, to grasp their hands one last time, and to wish them luck in the new country.

It was common practice for some friends to ride along with the migrants and their wagon for the first few miles for a sort of extended good-bye ceremony, but as the outskirts of town were reached, these rides gradually dropped back and returned home, leaving the travelers to begin the expedition on their own. Waving one last farewell to their friends and the life they had known, the would-be pioneers finally confronted the rigors of the trail which would lead them to a promising, unknown future.

The Road West

Members of the Jordan family participating in the caravan of covered wagons heading west were George Jordan and his new wife, Marie; Marie's brother and other siblings; George's mother, Agnes; his three unmarried sisters, Phoebe, Margaret, and little Agnes; and his two unmarried brothers, James and John.

During the summer of 1833, the caravan made its way, along with countless other covered wagons traveling westward. Fully loaded inside and out, most wagons had an assortment of farm animals tied to the back end and confined in crates that were leashed to the sides, so it was probably a noisy ride or walk.

Generally, there was little problem in providing adequate sleeping arrangements because there was space in the wagons. However, cooking and feeding the family was a chore. For the most part, however, travelers were excited to see the beautiful and ever-changing countryside through which they passed. One woman described the lands they traveled over as "one great flower garden."

The route they took west was over the National Road. The federal government had begun constructing the road twenty years earlier, in 1811, in Cumberland, Maryland. It ended 620 miles later in Vandalia, the territorial capital of Illinois. The first major improved highway in the United States, the National Road connected the Potomac and Ohio Rivers and was a main transport path to the West for thousands of settlers. When rebuilt in the 1830s, it became the second US macadam-surfaced road in the nation.

The covered wagons could travel ten to twenty miles per day. Many folks did not travel on Sundays, so they got a rest, but that added time to their trip. The journey to Michigan was approximately five hundred miles, which would take them about two and a half months. If things went well, they would arrive in late summer or early fall and have enough time to build a shelter before the snow fell.

The Jordan and Taylor families first journeyed north to Wheeling, Virginia (now West Virginia), on the Ohio River, and then west through Ohio to Indianapolis, Indiana. From Indianapolis they left the National Road and joined travelers heading north on the Michigan Road, stopping in South Bend, Indiana, and then in twenty more miles they reached their destination—Niles, in Berrien County, Michigan.

Berrien County, Michigan

Berrien County is located in the far southwestern corner of Michigan where the St. Joseph River enters Lake Michigan. As with Chicago for Illinois, in the early days the St. Joseph River was an important entry point from Lake Michigan into the southern part of the Michigan territory and northwestern Indiana. A crude harbor was built at the mouth of the St. Joseph River with initially small and then larger vessels landing there. Around 1825 the harbor was improved, with boating traffic increasing in the early 1830s, a few years prior to the arrival of an ever-increasing number of pioneer settlers, including the Jordan family.

The pioneers arrived on the heels of departing Indians who had been persuaded through treaties and some trickery to leave that area and settle in lands further west. Charles Cowles, a native of Vermont, arrived in Niles in 1932, and in June of 1833, he moved a few miles west to what became the village of Buchanan. He located a piece

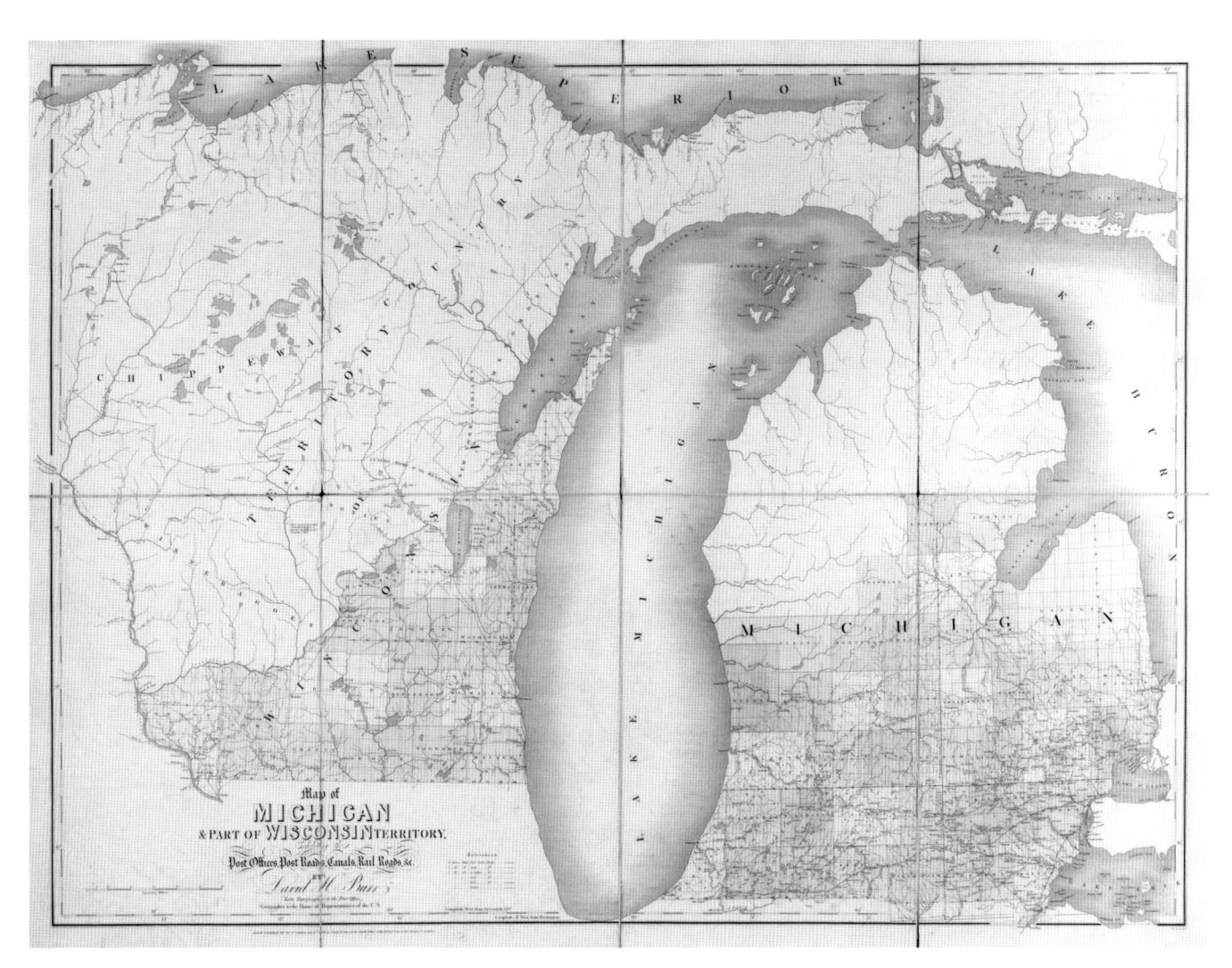

Map of Michigan, 1839. Library of Congress

of land near a creek, cleared it, built a cabin, and made his home. He was Buchanan's first white settler. The creek would eventually bear the name "McCoy Creek" after another Virginia native, Russell McCoy, who arrived a little later. Several pioneers built mills on the creek; the surrounding farmland was an excellent place to grow grain, and the village of Buchanan quickly became a bustling milling town. Many families from Virginia settled there—so many there would be a cemetery in Buchanan called "The Virginian's Burying Ground."

During their journey from Virginia to Michigan, the Jordans had followed Reverend Taylor, the leader of their group. Reverend Taylor had done a good job; all had arrived safely in Berrien County. Now it was time for them to break away from each other. The Jordans found land upon which to homestead a few miles west of Niles, near the confluence of McCoy Creek and the St. Joseph River in the vicinity of Buchanan Township. A. (Agnes) Jordan is listed as one of the original entries for land in Buchanan, in Section 36.

Berrien County historian Franklin Ellis describes the area where the Jordans settled as "a place that is not flat but undulating, with soil that was clay loam with a mixture of sand that was rich and productive, particularly for cereals." The highest point was Moccasin Bluff, located on a rise two miles north of town on the St. Joseph River that had been a sacred spot for the now departed Indians. According to Ellis: "The banks of the St. Joseph and the lands which extend thus southwesterly through the Bertrand and Buchanan Townships were (the Indians') favorite resorts and they had clung to these lands with great tenacity, for here were the homes and the graves of their fathers. The forests were abundantly supplied with game, the lakes and rivers were well stocked with fish, and much frequented by wild fowl. Moccasin Bluff, situated a short distance below the village of Buchanan, is well known as the site of one of the Indian villages, and numerous burial places along the river have been found."

Reverend Taylor and his family were joined by their relatives, Hiram Wray and his family, who settled there a year later, in 1834. Partnering with Russell McCoy, Wray built a sawmill on the creek that bore McCoy's name. Once settled in his new community, Reverend Taylor brought his dream to fruition by starting a Methodist church, which the Jordan family attended.

Making Farms in Michigan

The members of the Jordan family had found land to cultivate and upon which to establish their home. They may have chosen this area because it was not as difficult to make farm fields; unlike Virginia, the land was not covered with trees, and the soil was abundant and easy to till.

In order to supplement the farm income, George, James, and John may have helped out at the mills in Buchanan. No strangers to hard work, the Jordans were eager to make a successful new life for themselves. The problems facing the folks back in Virginia were now behind them.

As the farm became more established, the members of the Jordan family who were in their late teens and twenties were ready to begin new lives of their own, and several of them married, choosing the offspring of fellow settlers' families as mates. Margaret wed Jacob Eiler in 1834. Jacob's sister Barbara Ann Eiler had become the wife of Reverend Taylor and sister-in-law to Marie and George Jordan. The Eiler family had come from Montgomery County, Ohio.

Phoebe married Joseph Cannon on November 6, 1835. Joseph hailed from Shelby County, Ohio. Phoebe was twenty-seven years old and Joseph was twenty-five at the time of their marriage. During their years together, Joseph became a Methodist minister.

The passage of time and the weddings of their siblings may have prompted Cynthia and her husband, Jordan Babar, to finally leave Virginia in 1836 and make the journey with their three children to Michigan. They had sold their farm in the east and immediately upon their arrival in Berrien County found land on which to homestead in the vicinity of Agnes' farm.

William and Anna Jordan Smith arrived from Virginia in 1837, just in time to settle on their Berrien County homestead and attend the weddings of Anna's two brothers, James and John, who were celebrating nuptials with the two Pittman sisters, Drewsilla and Melinda. The Pittman sisters, who had both been born in Mount Vernon in Knox County, Ohio, were a year apart in age. They were from a Methodist family and had traveled with their parents, Benjamin and Jemima DeWitt Pittman, from Ohio to homestead in Michigan.

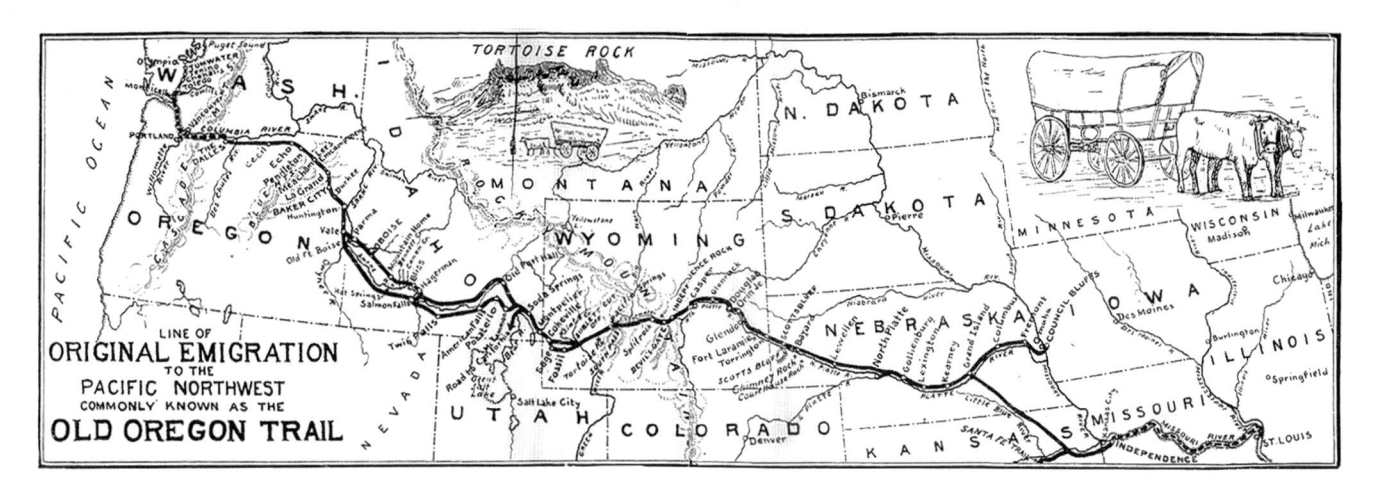

Map of the Oregon Trail. Courtesy of the University of Texas Libraries, The University of Texas at Austin

John married Drewsilla Pittman on August 24, and James married Melinda Dewitt Pittman a few months later on December 14. Young and free-spirited, both John and Drewsilla were nineteen years old when they married. Melinda, the more serious sister, was eighteen when she married twenty-four-year-old James.

The couples probably met each other at Reverend Wray's Methodist church. The two sisters were very close, as were the brothers, and in future years they would always remain near each other, even when points further west began to beckon. James and Melinda started their family shortly after their marriage; their first child, Benjamin Pittman Jordan, named after Melinda's father, was born in 1838.

The only unmarried Jordan remaining, besides their widowed mother, was little Agnes, who was sixteen years old.

Why Stop in Missouri?

The Jordans may not have known it when they left Virginia, but Michigan would only be their first stop in their journey west—a proving ground—a place where they learned and perfected their homesteading skills and prospered financially when they eventually sold their Michigan farms.

The entire Jordan family had been inspired by the stories of folks traveling to the western lands of California and Oregon. These stories had been circulating since the time of the Lewis and Clark Expedition just after the turn of the century. The stories often mentioned "the land of milk and honey"—Willamette Valley, Oregon—which had been a place of pioneer settlement since the 1820s. The inspiration for the Jordan family was Presbyterian missionary Henry H. Spaulding and his friend and colleague Dr. Marcus Whitman, who, along with their wives, had organized the first migrant wagon train in 1836 and successfully crossed the continent.

The Whitmans and Spauldings had left Independence, Missouri, in March of that year and traveled on a wagon trail that had been cleared as far as Fort Hall, Idaho. The trail, soon to be called the Oregon Trail, eventually reached all the way to the "promised land," the Willamette Valley in Oregon.

The Whitman/Spaulding wagon train carried people who were infused with the evangelical spirit of the Second Great Awakening and were traveling west to establish Christian missions. Upon arrival, the Whitmans established Whitman Mission near the Cayuse Indians by Fort Walla Walla, and the Spauldings established one near Lewiston, Idaho, near the Nez Pierce Indians. They were following the example of Methodist missionary Jason Lee, who had previously established a Methodist mission in Oregon.

The Spaulding's and Whitman's journey had originated in Missouri. It was the Jordan family's understanding that Missouri would be the place where their family members could acquire the necessary information on how to proceed to the western frontier.

Adventurous John was the perfect son to go, and he took his willing bride, Drewsilla, with him. The trip was to be a "scouting mission" to explore the possibility of the Jordan family traveling by wagon train over the Oregon Trail to the to the northwest and perhaps to the Willamette Valley.

John and Drewsilla waited until after James and Melinda's wedding in December to take off for Independence, Missouri. Upon arriving they settled in Andrew County, just north of Joseph Robidoux's trading post (which would become St. Joseph in 1843), just in time for Drewsilla to give birth to Charles Green Jordan on December 4, 1838. John, always the adventurer, was probably looking at the possibility of traveling on to the West Coast. The birth of his first child slowed him down.

Most likely John and Drewsilla's enthusiastic and encouraging letters to the folks back in Michigan prompted some members of the Jordan family to finalize their decision to venture further west . . . but how far west, they did not know.

Jacob and Margaret Jordan Eiler decided to leave Michigan immediately, which they did in early 1838. With them was their two-year-old daughter, Matilda. Later that year, after the Eilers arrived in Missouri, Matilda was joined by a sister, Eliza, who was born on October 17, just prior to the arrival of John's and Drewsilla's little Charles that December.

The plan was for their mother, Agnes, and her teenaged daughter Agnes to come with James and Melinda after that. The Smith and Babar families would remain for a time in Michigan.

Making a Profit on the Michigan Farms

Before she could move to Missouri, Agnes had to buy and then sell the Michigan farm on which James and Melinda and their son Benjamin, as well as James' little sister Agnes, were living.

In most states, pioneers had a four-year pre-emption deadline to purchase land they had chosen to cultivate. Once the land was being farmed, no other person could cultivate that land until four years had expired from the time land cultivation had begun, which, in the Jordan's case, was the spring of 1834.

Agnes needed to get her land officially purchased for two reasons: so she wouldn't miss the four-year "deadline" and lose her property to someone else wanting to buy the seemingly available acres from the land office, and so she could turn around and sell it herself in order to generate funds in preparation for the move to Missouri.

On September 15, 1837, Agnes officially registered the 140-acre parcel of land which had been cultivated by her sons and daughters for the past four years. A year later, on October 6, 1838, she moved forward to purchase that tract in the land office of Michigan at Kalamazoo, applying under the Pre-Exemption Act of 1838. She asked for 139 and 77/100 acres in Section 36 in Buchanan Township, Berrien County. In order to obtain the land at the lowest possible price, sixty-one-year-old Agnes said she was a widow who had children with her who depended on her for support. Her application was approved four days later. On October 10, 1838, Agnes Jordan bought her farm for $1.25 per acre, amounting to $174.70, which she paid in full.

Exactly two months later, on December 10, 1838, Agnes registered title and deed for her farm, whereupon she sold about one hundred acres of it to Benton Swift. At that time, re-sales usually netted the original owner (who had improved the land and built a home) a solid profit of at least three to five times the original price of the land. Very likely Agnes had at least tripled her money on the deal with Swift.

Four days later, on December 14, she sold the other forty acres to her son James and his wife, Melinda. One month passed, and on January 11, 1839, James sold his forty-acre parcel to the same Benton Swift who had previously purchased the one-hundred-acre tract from Agnes. James probably came away with a 300 to 500 percent gain in his monthlong real estate investment.

With the finalization of these transactions, this part of the Jordan family was ready to head west, setting their sights on Independence, Missouri.

CHAPTER 15
Platte County, Missouri

"Out-fitted and packed up, emigrant families headed out some time in the late winter or early spring for the Missouri River towns. Nearly three-fourths came in wagons rather than in steamboats, and for many this trip was a lark; roads were generally good, accommodations readily available at inns or friendly farmhouses. Often the route was set so the travelers could visit friends or relatives on the way. Before 1849 nearly everyone headed toward Independence . . . coming across the settled hills of central Missouri."

—John M. Faragher, Historian and Author

In 1838 Jacob and Margaret Jordan Eiler had arrived in Missouri and were settled on their farm. They had intended to homestead across the Missouri River in Kansas. However, in 1838 there were so many uprisings in the Kansas/Nebraska Territory over the question of slavery, they chose instead to homestead on the safer east side of the Missouri in Savannah Township, Platte County.

James and Melinda, their new baby Benjamin, and James' sister Agnes arrived in the early spring of 1839, their destination being the Eilers' Platte County

Sketch of a pioneer log cabin. Library of Congress

James Jordan: His Life and His Legacy   63

homestead. By late spring, James and Melinda Jordan and the Eilers were listed on the personal tax list as landowners in Platte County, Missouri. The Jordan homestead was described as follows: Platte County, Missouri. Deed Book C, page 212, Spring 1839. James C. Jordan and Melinda, his wife, and the County of Platte, west half of the northeast quarter of Section No. 13 in Township No. 53 of Range No. 34 containing eighty acres.

A Marriage in Missouri

The day she arrived in Platte County was a special one for James' youngest sister, Agnes, because it was the day she met the man who would become her husband. The Jordan family had stopped at a roadside spring to eat, water their animals, and determine the location of the Eilers' farm. A group of gentlemen arrived at the spring, and a tall, handsome, and personable 6'2"–6'4" man wearing a stovepipe hat introduced himself to James as Calvin Smith. Smith was on his way home after being the best man in a wedding in Westport (later renamed Kansas City). James asked him if he knew the whereabouts of his brother-in-law, Jacob Eiler. Smith said he was acquainted with Jacob, and the Eilers lived about twenty miles to the northwest, not far from the village of Smithville (a town Smith's father had founded in a fork of the Platte River).

About that time, Smith noticed a young woman (Agnes Jordan) gathering up the cooking utensils and other belongings as the family prepared to journey on to the Eilers' farm. Smith, age twenty-six, judged this woman to be about fourteen years old. He happily discovered later that Agnes was actually eighteen. He said, "I loved her from that first minute I saw her." After a yearlong courtship, the two were married on March 12, 1840.

Agnes' mother, Agnes Jordan, moved in with her daughter and new son-in-law, living with them in either Westport or Clay County for the next sixteen years. When she died she was buried in Clay County, Missouri.

This meeting at the roadside spring was significant not only for Agnes; it was the beginning of a steadfast and lifelong friendship between James Jordan and Calvin Smith, who were the same age. They became business partners in Missouri, and during the course of their lives each named one of their sons for the other.

Agnes and Calvin Smith made their home in Westport, a flourishing town primarily engaged in livestock trading. James and Calvin became partners in their own livestock venture, "running mules" back and forth from Westport, where Calvin and Agnes lived, to Independence, near James and Melinda's home. The business supplied the emigrants going west in the Oregon Trail wagon trains with hardy livestock to pull their wagons. Each made impressive profits from the business, which put both James and Calvin in strong financial positions.

This livestock enterprise was a pivotal factor in decisions James would make regarding his life's work. He understandably came to the conclusion that there was a lot of money to be made in the livestock business. Now he had the financial wherewithal as well as the practical experience to pursue the goal of becoming a livestock breeder and trader, just like his Virginia Cunningham/Van Meter cousins in South Branch Valley.

Smith's Fork and Smithville

Back in 1822, Calvin Smith's father, Humphrey "Yankee" Smith, settled his wife and family in Clay County at the confluence of a creek and the Platte River and named the area Smith's Fork. Two years later, in 1824, at that location, he built Smith's Mill, which was run by a flutter (water) wheel. At the time the only other gristmill in the county was a horse mill. For ten years these mills produced cornmeal and flour for Clay County.

"Humphrey Smith (had) Yankee enterprise and shrewdness when locating his mill, which earned the patronage of the government Indian agencies, and the business of settlers passing through to the Western frontier," states *A Pictorial History of Smithville, Missouri*.

Smith opened a store at his mill, and soon after other merchants arrived. A little village sprang up and, in 1827, Smith platted a small town he named Smithville. Frank Justus, a local historian, notes that when the town site was laid out in 1830, it was the westernmost settlement in the United States. The original town site was *officially* established in 1836, the year of the Platte Purchase, which extended Missouri's northwestern border.

The town consisted of eighty acres that was granted to Smith's twenty-three-year-old son, Calvin, by the US Land Office. All of the land was located on the south side of the river. At the time, the community was officially named "Smithville" by the US government.

The Smiths continued their milling enterprise, and when son Calvin was old enough he managed the mill store. After thirty years, in about 1854, the mill was sold, and shortly thereafter it washed away in a flood. By then Calvin and Agnes Jordan were married and living in Westport, engaged in their thriving livestock enterprise.

Clay County was proslavery and not at all sympathetic to abolitionists. In spite of living in a viper's nest of proslavery folks, Yankee Smith believed in human liberty for all, worked hard to make Missouri a free state, and kept up the struggle against the nefarious villains—whom he called "men stealers" and "negro-thieves"—who stole negro slaves away from their owners and resold them for a profit.

Missouri historian Howard Louis Conard provides a perfect description of how Smith was viewed as time went on: ". . . his uprightness, enterprise and public spirit (eventually) won the respect of his neighbors, and his non-resistance, maintained at all times under the greatest provocations, finally secured him exemption from personal violence. He was accustomed to tell the people about him that slavery would be abolished in the United States, little as they were inclined to believe it."

Family legend states that Smith's death in 1857 at age eighty-three was due to smallpox contracted from a contaminated abolitionist newspaper. He, in turn, spread the disease to visitors, causing a small epidemic. He was secretly buried in what is now known as Smith Cemetery in Ridgely, Missouri, just across the county line into Platte County. Fearing that "men stealers" would rob his grave, Smith's son, Calvin, wrote in his 1907 autobiography that his father left instructions: "Never let the [men-stealers] know where I am buried until my State is free; then write my epitaph: Here lies

Humphrey "Yankee" Smith and "Little Dixie"

Humphrey Smith, better known as "Yankee" Smith, was Calvin Smith's father. Humphrey's German ancestors arrived in New Jersey in 1714 where he was born on February 17, 1774. In 1803, Humphrey married Nancy Walker and they had four children. Their youngest son, Calvin, who would become James Jordan's beloved brother-in-law and close friend, was born on December 23, 1813, in Erie County, in the far western part of New York. Three years after Calvin's birth, Humphrey and Nancy emigrated to Missouri and settled near the Missouri River in Chariton County, in north central Missouri, where they farmed for the next several years.

Chariton County was one of several counties in the vicinity of the Missouri River that was settled mostly by Southerners, primarily from the states of Kentucky and Tennessee. The farmers brought slaves and slaveholding traditions with them and cultivated hemp and tobacco like they had done prior to settling in Missouri.

Given their culture and traditions, this area became known as "Little Dixie" and Chariton County was at its heart. Little Dixie was noted as a place embodying the very essence of the Old South and was described as "more Dixie than Dixie." On average, Missouri's slave population was only 10 percent, but in Little Dixie, county and township slave populations ranged from 20 to 50 percent by 1860. It was heavily pro-Confederate during the Civil War.

According to an article by Missouri historian Louis Conrad in the *Kansas City Star*:

> The Civil War was decades away, but passions already ran high in this Southern-leaning, pro-slavery region, where many families had slaves working the hemp and tobacco fields.

> Humphrey "Yankee" Smith was an outspoken abolitionist, and frequently provoked the resentment of the pro-slavery community in which he lived. . . .

> One night, he was mobbed by armed slave-holders; scourged, bruised and dragged at midnight from his house. His ever-faithful wife, coming to his assistance, received injuries at the hands of the mob which caused her years of affliction and the loss of one eye. He was compelled to leave. . . .

Smith's family fled from Howard County up the Missouri River to Carroll County where Smith joined them and they all scurried even further west to Clay County.

James Jordan: His Life and His Legacy

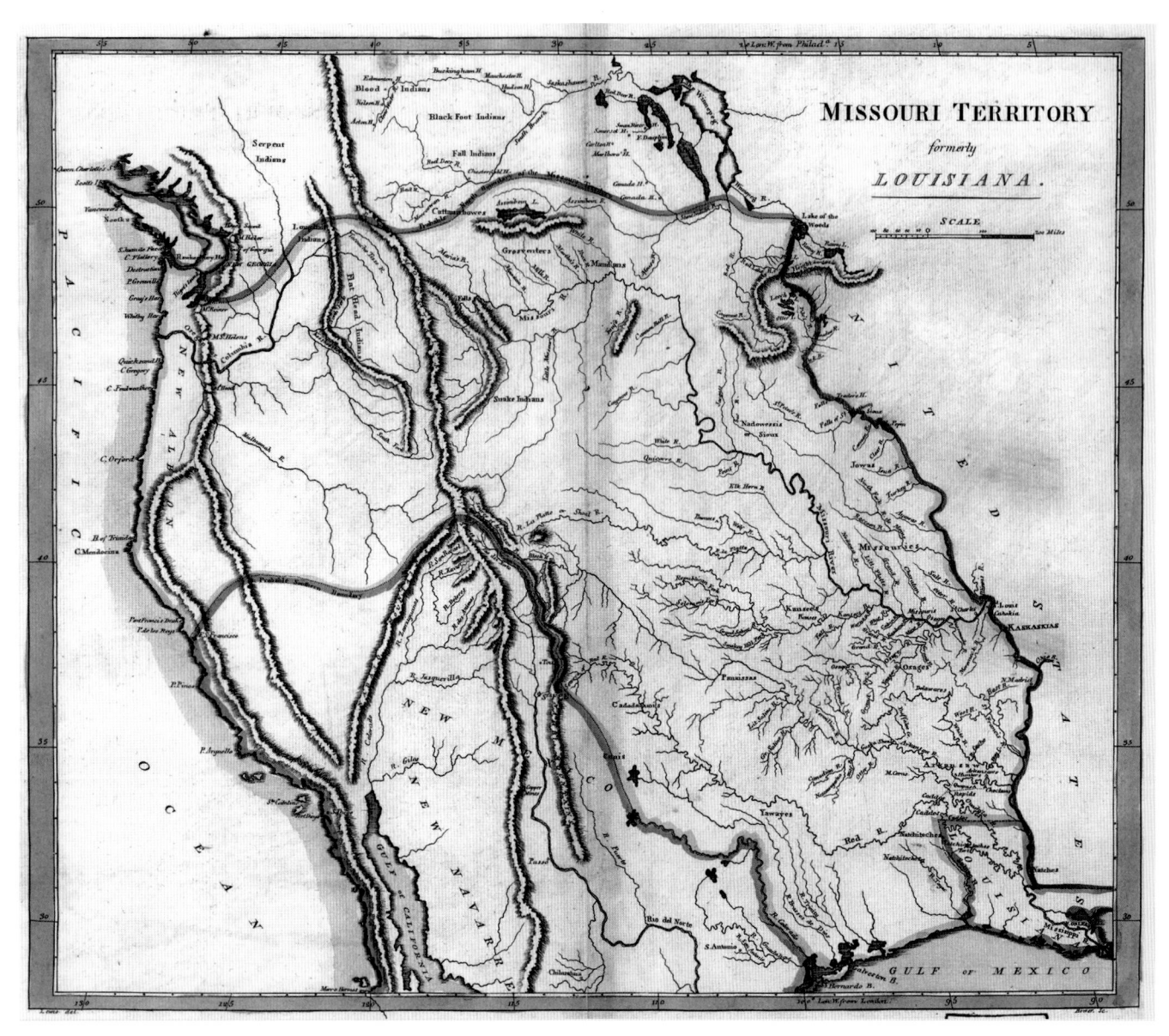

Early map of the Missouri Territory, 1814. Library of Congress

Humphrey Smith, who was in favor of human rights, universal liberty, equal and exact justice, no union with slave holders, free States, free people, union of States and one universal republic."

Poised to Go to "The Promised Land"

By journeying to the Independence area, the Jordans arrived at the perfect vantage point to consider all options for further migration. Since the 1830s, Independence and Westport were the starting points for the Oregon Trail to the west and the Santa Fe Trail to the southwest.

The Jordan family's timing was excellent. They preceded the "boom" which would take place in that region in the 1840s and 1850s as the territory between the Missouri River and the West Coast opened up for pioneer settlement. In fact, the Jordans' arrival in Missouri preceded the formation of the town of St. Joseph, Missouri. Trader Joseph Robidoux, owner of a trading post just upriver from Independence, observed Independence's burgeoning commercial activity. In 1843 he subdivided the land around his trading post and laid out a new town which he named St. Joseph, after himself. "Within two years, lots that initially sold for $100.00 were bringing $500.00," according to historian Bill Gilbert, "and there were 682 residents, nearly all of whom were in the emigration business."

James and Melinda chose to homestead between Independence and Joe Robidoux's trading post but closer to the bustling and commercial Independence. Bill Gilbert continues with a description of the chaotic activity occurring at the time in Independence and St. Joseph, Missouri:

> Noise and confusion reigned supreme; traders, trappers, and emigrants filled the streets. Mules and oxen strove for the right of way while the loud crackling of ox goads, squeaking of wheels and rattling of chains mingled with the oaths of teamsters produced a din indescribable.

> Independence, with its already established reputation and facilities for outfitting travelers, had a head start over the new town of St. Joe in attracting emigrants.

> In the 1840s and 1850s, fortunes were often and quickly made in western Missouri by the merchants, livestock dealers, blacksmiths, gun smiths and saloon keepers, con artists and travel agents who supplied and sometimes fleeced the emigrants. The latter made fairly easy marks.

After selling their property back East, they arrived at Independence or St. Joseph with considerable cash but little good information about how, and even where to proceed. Mostly they were from long-settled, well-watered and wooded regions, and were accustomed to eating regular meals, sleeping dry under roofs, crossing rivers on bridges or ferries. Rarely had they used firearms, cooked over buffalo dung fires, coped with hundreds of miles of treeless plains, deserts, September blizzards, grizzly bears, or Indian nations.

Consequently, when hard-sell Missouri entrepreneurs assured them that it was fool hardy to start without several items of food, ovens, odometers, canoes, feather comforters, snake oil or whatever else they had in stock, the green pioneers frequently believed and bought.

Many of the families who came to this area in Missouri had aspirations of traveling even further west—to California or Oregon. Emigration historian John Faragher states that "families drove out to Missouri in small groups, but few families thought of setting out for California or Oregon alone." Later on in the 1840s and 1850s, large wagon trains would move hundreds of thousands of people to the West Coast. Perhaps this was also the Jordan family dream . . . but not one that would happen immediately, and ultimately it would not be the dream for *every* member of the Jordan family.

CHAPTER 16
"Discovering" Iowa

The fortunate result of the Jordan clan's decision to move to Michigan from their established homes in western Virginia was that they were able to leave the chaotic political environment in Virginia and work themselves into secure financial positions through farming and profitable land sales during their time in Michigan. Their move to Missouri, however, was the result of subtle factors occurring in the lives of the various members of the family members.

In studies of families who made the westward trek, John Faragher suggests that "the life cycle of families was influential in the nature and timing of emigration and that family stages could be divided into four categories:
 Stage 1: Newly married couples, still childless
 Stage 2: Families with all children under fifteen years of age
 Stage 3: Families in which the oldest child has reached fifteen
 Stage 4: Couples whose children have grown and left to establish families of their own."

Fragher's research shows pioneer families moved once for each of the first three stages. In the first stage, "honeymoon emigrations, were a tradition." The Jordan family's move from Virginia to Michigan is a reflection of this first stage, when almost all of Agnes' children were newlyweds at that time. It could also have been true of Phoebe, Margaret, James, and John Jordan, who were "honeymoon emigrees" from Michigan to Missouri. The second stage is when couples with small children typically make a second move. "After eight or ten years of marriage, six to eight years of farming the same ground, perhaps setting aside a few savings, these families felt secure enough to try improving their situation" with a second move further west. This was true of George and Maria Jordan, Cynthia and Jordan Babar, and Anna and William Smith on their move from Michigan to Missouri and would be true of James and Melinda Jordan when they decided to move to Iowa. "Couples in the third stage," according to Faragher, "with older children near-grown and soon to set out on their own, a third move was perhaps the last chance to find the kind of home and farm suitable for their later years, perhaps in a region of abundant good land where their children would not be tempted so far afield in their own search for a place to settle." This third move for many emigrants, including some members of the Jordan clan, would be to the West Coast.

Iowa: "Land of Milk and Honey"

In Missouri, several of James' brothers and sisters arrived in Platte County with their young families at about the same time James and his brother John were scouting around Iowa. George, Anna, and Cynthia, with spouses and families, had all made their "second stage" journey to Missouri by 1845. Phoebe would come in 1847, at which time all the Jordans would have departed from Michigan, including the matriarch of the family, Agnes Cunningham Jordan.

By the mid-1840s, James and Melinda, also in the second stage of emigration, were ready to make a move. Their oldest child, Benjamin, was only seven years old. Their daughter, Agnes Emily (called Emily), had been born in 1842 and was a toddler, and Melinda had just given birth to their third child, Henry Clay, in 1844.

After seeing firsthand what was involved in traversing the Oregon Trail, James and Melinda probably realized the extraordinarily difficult move to the Northwest was out of the question. They were ready to settle down for good—James as a traditional landowner and businessman, Melinda as his helpmate—far away from the hustle and confusion of Platte County, Independence, Westport, and St. Joseph. Furthermore, "Little Dixie," with its growing population of slaves, was too close for comfort. Plans were made to go exploring, and James' brother John, the adventurer, was ready and willing to partner up with James on his journey to find just the right place.

They had both heard about the Iowa Territory, the eastern part of which had been open for legal pioneer settlement since 1824. Subsequent treaties with the Indians made land further west available in 1832, 1836, and 1837. By 1843, the Meskwaki Tribe agreed to release its land in central Iowa to the US government

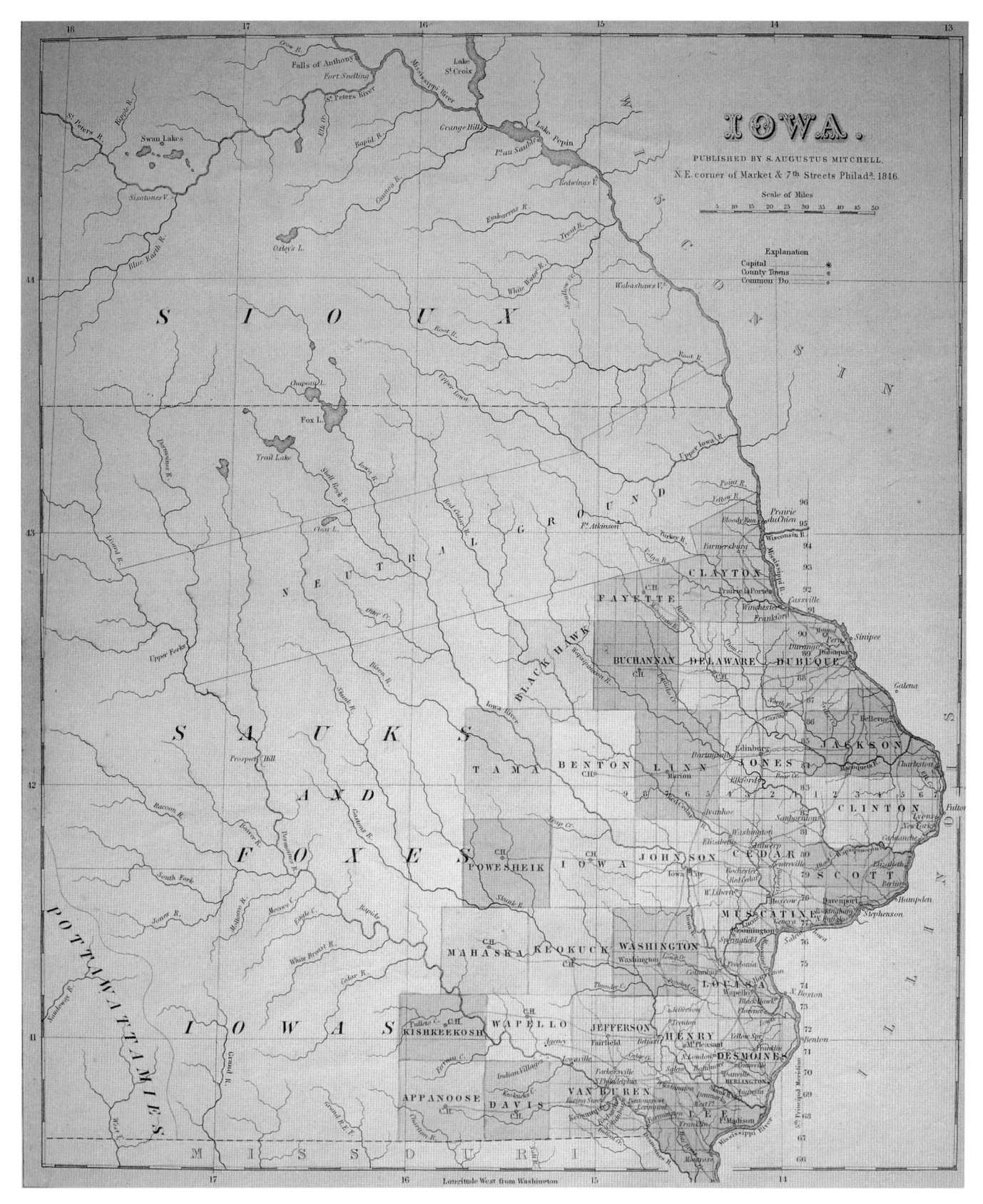

Map of Iowa Territory, 1846.

and promised to vacate the western region by 1845. A year later the Pottowatomie Tribe relinquished their lands in western Iowa, thus opening up all but the very northwestern part of the territory for pioneer settlement.

Since the 1830s, the Iowa Territory had been hailed by many as a "promised land," with its fertile soil, numerous rivers, plentiful woodlands, and endless prairies. J. B. Newhall, one of the better-known promoters, had published two widely circulated pamphlets—one in 1841 and another in 1846, one for Americans and one for the British. The pamphlets were entitled *Sketches of Iowa or the Emigrant's Guide*. In these pamphlets Newhall enthused in flowery prose every positive attribute of the Iowa Territory.

Newhall also traveled around the country and even went to England to give talks to local folks thinking about emigrating to Iowa. Excerpts from his pamphlets illustrate Newhall's contagious enthusiasm for the territory: "The rapid progress and present condition of this fertile region, stretching its verdant meadows and wooded banks along the majestic Mississippi, the variety and excellence of its agricultural productions, its richness of mineral wealth, its countless rivulets and streams which are destined to pour out its exhaustless treasures and carry back comfort and luxuries to its remotest boarders; its whole physical aspect, in short, combines as many requisites for human enterprise, as is developed in any tract of country of the same extent on the face of the globe."

Other excerpts:
- Physical Features: "The predominant features in the landscape of Iowa are prairie and timber; the face of the country is beautiful in the extreme. . . ."
- Soil: "The soil of the prairies of Iowa, and particularly the alluvial bottoms is extremely rich and fertile. It is a black vegetable mold, sometimes intermixed with a sandy loam, easily cultivated and stands a drought remarkably well. . . ."
- Crop Production: "All the grains, fruits, and plants of the temperate regions of the earth grow luxuriantly in Iowa. . . ."
- Timber: "The growth of the uplands consists of every variety of oak, sugar maple, hickory, hazel, cherry, white walnut, mulberry, hackberry, etc. . . ."
- Prairies: "They are, in fact, the gardens of nature. And who that has been an eye witness can ever forget the impressions made upon his feelings

What is a "Dragoon"?

The word dragoon comes from Europe and refers to a soldier who is part of the army infantry but who rode a horse. He would dismount, if needed, to fight. Captain James Allen was a member of the First Dragoons, whose headquarters were originally in St. Louis but, by the time he was assigned to lead the troops at Fort Des Moines, shifted to Fort Leavenworth in the Kansas Territory.

"Dragoons' principal missions," according to David Wiggins, "were to impress the Indians with the power of the United States, to protect settlements from attack and to discourage intertribal warfare. The soldiers were not expected to look only one way; they were supposed to crack down on white people encroaching on Indian lands and remove such undesirables as unlicensed traders and whiskey peddlers."

Dragoons. National Park Service

when, for the first time, he gazed with rapturous delight upon the boundless prairie? . . . The traveler now beholds these boundless plains, untouched by the hand of man, clothed with the deepest verdure, interspersed here and there with beautiful groves, which appear like islands in the ocean. . . . Many prairies . . . have been converted into highly cultivated farms. . . ."

In conclusion, Newhall stated: "It must be the settler's own fault if he does not enjoy in large abundance every substantial comfort and enjoyment of life, and rear around his frugal board all the choice blessings of a land flowing with 'milk and honey.'"

Fort Des Moines, Territory of Iowa

Despite the fact that western Iowa was still Indian Territory, several US government garrisons had been built in the 1820s and 1830s in southeastern Iowa Territory. Fort Atkinson was built in 1840 on the Turkey River on the Indian Neutral Ground in northeast Iowa. In May of 1843, another military outpost was established, this time in central Iowa at the confluence of the Des Moines and Raccoon Rivers, at a place known as "'Coon Point." It was called Fort Raccoon for a short time but then a more conventional name was chosen: Fort Des Moines No. 2. (Fort Des Moines No. 1 had been established many years earlier, in 1834, near the confluence of the Mississippi and Des Moines Rivers.) All of these forts needed to be supplied, and in the case of Fort Des Moines No. 2, provisions came up the Des Moines River by steamboat, which also brought the two US military companies—one infantry and one cavalry (Dragoons)—of soldiers who would build and occupy the fort.

Not far from 'Coon Point at the Raccoon Forks, about a mile *east* of the river, an Indian Agency House had already been built. According to Iowa historian Eugene Hastie:

> It was of log construction with two rooms downstairs and one above. Here was where Major Beach, the Indian Agent and his interpreter Josiah Smart lived and worked. Close by, south and east of where the capitol stands today, stood the Indian trading post of two brothers, George Washington Ewing and Washington George Ewing. They and the

Sketch of Fort Des Moines. From *Annals of Iowa*, October 1899

Indian Agency House near Fort Des Moines. From *Harper's Weekly: A Journal of Civilization*, 1861–2

fur trader, Phelps and Company, held licenses with the US government to do business with the Indians. Trading must have been brisk; the books kept by Phelps and Company showed the names of several hundred Indians that they had done business with during that time. There was also a gunsmith near the trading post and Indian Agency House charged with the mission of selling guns *only* to the Indians, not civilians or soldiers.

The military outpost called Fort Des Moines No. 2, constructed in 1843, was located on the *west* side of the Des Moines River and was home to about 120 soldiers. The little fort also sheltered a number of civilians who possessed special skills or had the ability to provide needed services to the fort. They were able to bring their families and live there at the invitation of the garrison commander, Captain James Allen. These included a "sutler" (a person who followed an army and sold provisions to the soldiers), a tailor, and a gunsmith. (This gunsmith did *not* sell guns directly to the Indians.) Even though they conducted

Thomas Mitchell. From *Hawkeye Insurance Company Atlas of 1875*

72   Pursuit of a Dream

business with the Indians at a location a mile away, the personnel at the Indian Agency House were considered members of the (non-Indian) community at the fort.

One family, J. B. Scott's, lived on the post and operated a farm. Other farmers lived nearby; two of them were Thomas Mitchell, who came in 1844, and John B. Saylor, in 1845. Each of them settled in areas where their name eventually identified their town: Mitchellville and Saylorville. In the next few years, other farmers were given permission to settle on Indian land and provide hay and food staples to the soldiers.

One man, John Parmalee, originally from Vermont, entered the area before the fort was even constructed. Considered the first white man to visit Polk County, he arrived in Wapello County, Iowa, in 1840 in the employ of a fur trading company. By 1843 he was relocated by his company to 'Coon Point at the fork of the Des Moines and Raccoon Rivers for a three-year assignment. He quit over lack of pay and decided to move southeast to the Middle River near where Carlisle now stands and build a mill.

When Captain James Allen arrived with his dragoons, Parmalee and his new wife were comfortably but also illegally established at their mill. Captain Allen made the decisions as to which non-native inhabitants could live in the Indian Territory that he was in charge of protecting from white pioneer encroachment. He allowed Parmalee to stay. After negotiating a lucrative and mutually beneficial business partnership with Parmalee, Captain Allen contracted Parmalee's mill to provide the lumber to build Fort Des Moines No. 2.

The Jordan Brothers' Iowa Adventure

In 1844, James and John Jordan decided to explore the Iowa Territory, traveling north out of St. Joseph. Independence and St. Joseph were on a national crossroads at that time, as was much of west central Missouri, and many roads and trails led in every direction in and out of this area, including several into Iowa. One such trail, known as the "Dragoon Trace," lead from nearby Fort Leavenworth on the Missouri River in the northeastern corner of the Kansas Territory to Fort Des Moines No. 2. The Dragoon Trace was, according to historian John Palmer, "originally made by the migration of animals, such as buffalo and deer, this trail was then used by the Native Americans who knew the animals had searched out the best place to cross the creeks and rivers, they, too traveled this narrow path. Later used by the pioneers, this was the road to change Iowa's civilization."

Following the Dragoon Trace, James and John made their way north, ending up at 'Coon Point, the location of Fort Des Moines No. 2. It is likely that along the way they found company because many people were doing the same thing as the Jordan brothers. In fact, the Fort Des Moines garrison had been established to keep the white settlers out. Too many of the interlopers were illegally "squatting" on Indian land, building cabins and starting to farm, even though the property still belonged to the Indians and would not be legally available for settlement until after the treaty commenced in October of 1845.

James, fondly known to his family as "Jimmy," had always had a reputation for sociability. His relaxed demeanor made it easy for him to make friends with the folks at the fort, even though the brothers were not supposed to be there. "Jimmy," along with his also-engaging brother John, probably stayed at or near Fort Des Moines for a while, camping out and exploring the region. Perhaps they were guided around the area by some of the local residents.

Since James had a plan in mind to start a livestock business, he probably paid particular attention to those geographical features which would be important for the kind of venture he had in mind. He needed a reliable and abundant water supply, easy access to transportation routes (rivers and trails), woods to provide protection for the animals, prairie for grazing, and a nearby town where he could market his stock.

One day, venturing out from the fort, he followed the Raccoon upriver. Traveling about five and a half miles in a westerly direction, he came to the place where he was to live for the rest of his life.

ROUTES TO THE PIKES PEA

Part Three

Settling in the "Land of Milk and Honey"

"It must be the settler's own fault if he does not enjoy in large abundance every substantial comfort and enjoyment of life, and rear around his frugal board all the choice blessings of a land flowing with 'milk and honey.'"

—J. B. Newhall, speaking about Iowa

CHAPTER 17
Staking a Claim in Iowa

"The (Iowa) settler had not to make his habitation on a battlefield or to live behind a stockade; every ounce of his effort was available for his assumed task. He went to his new home, not to wait for some servant to do his bidding, as had usually been the case in the oldest colonies, but willing and determined to do it himself . . . No dream of enslaving his fellow man, white or black, ever disturbed his hours either sleeping or waking . . . He no more questioned the wisdom and perfection of the ideas and institutions inherited from his ancestors or developed by himself during his tiresome journey through more than a thousand miles of wilderness, than he did the religion that he professed and tried to practice."

—George F. Parker, *Iowa Pioneer Foundations*

James Jordan, "Squatter"

In 1845, before the Indian Territory would be legally opened for pioneer settlement by the US government, the two brothers had already staked out their "claims." They had an abundance of company. Leland Sage, Iowa historian, states: "Long before the expiration of the Indian title, the settlers around the fort had organized in anticipation of this event, and had arranged with one another as to their so-called claims. Some had even gone so far as to measure and stake off their respective holdings—not that such course gave any validity to their claims, but to facilitate the official survey by preventing a possible duplication of claims."

The land, spoken for and "reserved" through a system of "gentlemen's agreements," would ultimately be occupied by "squatters," and before long, James and John joined their ranks. According to Sage, "Before the first land offices were open (in eastern Iowa) in 1838, thousands of settlers and speculators had put down claims to lands, all such claimants were trespassers . . . in the frontiersman's vocabulary these men were squatters."

"Jimmy" Jordan chose property in an area which would eventually be known as Walnut Township, five and a half miles west of the fort on the northern bank of the Raccoon River. Brother John's claim was in an area eventually called Hiner's Grove, only about four miles west of the fort and on the northern banks of what would be known as Walnut Creek.

One of James Jordan's biographers wrote, "James Jordan pitched his tent under burr oak trees that were later to shelter his log cabin." Most likely he was staying in a tent as he "stepped-off" his land: 750 paces each way from a given point would make a square that would mark his original 160 acres, "more or less." James drove stakes into the four corners and thus indicated his premature but eventually legal claim to the land.

James and John came into Iowa in 1844 quietly through the "back door," from St. Joe, Missouri, to the south. However, most settlers arrived in Iowa from points east. After crossing the Mississippi near Keokuk, they followed a trail heading northwest along the Des Moines River. The official borderline of the Indian Territory ran through Marion County and was designated by the "Red Rock Wall," a landmark well-known to the local Indians. A garrison in the settlement of Agency City (now Ottumwa) was supposedly guarding the entrance to the Indian Territory, and there the settlers stopped and waited for the US government to officially open the land for settlement.

The Indian Agency in Agency City had been established many years earlier in 1838 by General Joseph Street who was charged with the responsibility of keeping white settlers out of Indian Territory. By the early 1840s and until the territory was opened to settlement, Street spent much of his time protecting the Indians from the traders and other white entrepreneurs who continually took advantage of the Indian braves by selling them useless trinkets which the Indian men sold back to the traders to get money to buy whiskey.

In 1844, at the same time the Jordan brothers were looking at property and choosing their claims on Indian land upriver near Fort Des Moines, there was chaos downriver at Agency City near the borderline "Red Rock Wall." Iowa historian Ilda M. Hammer described the bedlam as follows:

> While the traders at the fort were growing rich and the soldiers were watching over the Indians,

settlers anxious to secure choice pieces of land were waiting for the opportunity to enter the forbidden territory. Poor people had come from the East and South with the hope of buying the good land cheaply. They knew it had been bought from the Indians for about 75 cents an acre and that it would be sold for very little more.

Many came into the eastern part of the state and settled there temporarily, waiting for the opening of the reservation. Some of them arrived a year or two before this was to take place.

While they waited, they explored the reservation, selecting the favorable spots on which to locate when the time came. Every month more and more settlers came in and camped along the border, eagerly awaiting the appointed time.

A group of land speculators was also waiting to enter the reservation. They wished to buy land at the cheap government price and then dispose of it at a neat profit. Men like this were always present when newly opened Indian Territory was to be sold.

Iowa historian Jacob Van der Zee presented a description of the frenzy prior to the land exchange: "As the time for removal drew closer, hundreds of vagabond settlers squatted along the border ready to pounce on the Indians' land. A number of white men crossed over the border onto Indian land, plied the braves with liquor and staked out land claims. When forcibly removed by a detachment of troops, the angry whites retaliated by killing a number of Sac and Fox Indians."

Upriver, Fort Des Moines No. 2 was not exempt from the hysteria taking place. The local Indian agent, Major John Beach, was there to observe it all and penned his disgust in his 1845 report to the commissioner of Indian Affairs in Washington, DC, regarding the loathsome treatment of the Indians: "It is not a subject of astonishment that the education, the civilization, and especially the glorious religion of the white man, are held by them (the Indians) in so little estimation. Our education appears to consist in knowing how most effectively to cheat them; our civilization in knowing how to pander to the worst propensities of nature, and then beholding the criminal and results with a cold indifference—a heathen apathy; while our religion is readily summed up in the consideration of dollars and cents."

The Great Iowa Land Rush of 1845

At last the day came that everyone had been waiting for—October 11, 1845. The Indians had been herded by the Dragoons to the Kansas Territory. Iowa silently awaited its fate.

Jimmy Jordan and brother John had probably quietly returned to Fort Des Moines for the big event. In Agency City and at Fort Des Moines, the firing of a musket from each locale at midnight would be the signal to begin the land rush. An account, written by H. B Turrill in 1857, described what took place at Fort Des Moines:

> Precisely at 12 o'clock the loud report of a musket fell upon hundreds of eager ears. Answering reports rang out upon the night air in quick succession from every hill top and in every valley, 'til the signal was conveyed for miles around. . . . The moon was slowly sinking in the west and its beams afforded a feeble and uncertain light for the measurement of claims in which so many were engaged.
>
> Ere long the landscape was shrouded in darkness, save the wild and fitful glaring of the torches carried by the claim makers. Before the night had entirely worn away the rough surveys were finished and the Indian lands had found new tenants. Throughout the country thousands of acres were laid off in claims before dawn. Settlers rushed in by hundreds, and the region so lately tranquil and silent felt the impulse of its change and became vocal with the sounds of industry and enterprise.

Abstract of the James C. Jordan Claim:
NE 1/4 of the SE 1/4 lying East (except the East 4 1/2 acres of the North half of the NE 1/4 of the SE 1/4) all in Section 16, Township 78, North Range 25 West of the 5th P.M. Polk County, Iowa. North half of the SE 1/4 and SW 1/4 of NE 1/4 and SE 1/4 of the NW 1/4 of Section 16, Township 78, North Range 25, West of 5th P.M. Contains 160 acres.

James Jordan's claim, dated March 1, 1852, was not legally and officially filed until May 12, 1887. The property claimed was recorded in 1848 at the Claims Club in Des Moines, which was as official as the pioneer infrastructure could be in the Iowa wilderness.

It would be the first permanent claim in the area that would be designated, in 1860, as Walnut Township, Polk County, Iowa.

Meanwhile, back in Platte County, Missouri, James' and John's wives, Melinda and Drewsilla, and the rest of the Jordan clan continued to go about their daily lives. By then, all of the Michigan Jordans had relocated to Missouri. Brother George and his family and sister Cynthia and her family had arrived around 1845. When Cynthia and Jordan Babar came, they purchased the land adjacent to James' and Melinda's Missouri farm.

In early 1846 Melinda gave birth to another son, John Quincy Jordan. His name reflected James' admiration for the nation's sixth president. John Quincy Adams sided with another politician James revered; Henry Clay and his American System called for high tariffs, federally funded internal improvements, and a National Bank. When John Quincy Adams was elected US president in 1830, he appointed Henry Clay Secretary of State. After his presidential term, Adams spent seventeen years in the United States House of Representatives. Paul Nagel, John Quincy Adams historian, wrote: "A longtime opponent of slavery, Adams used his new role in Congress to fight it, and he became the most prominent national leader opposing slavery. His opposition to slavery made him, along with Henry Clay, one of the leading opponents of Texas annexation and the Mexican–American War. He correctly predicted that both would contribute to civil war."

James was back from Iowa and at the Platte County homestead in time for the birth of John Quincy. The family then included four children: eight-year-old Benjamin, four-year-old Emily, two-year-old Henry, and the new baby, John.

During the spring and summer of 1845 the family began to prepare for their move to Iowa. Winter passed, and in the spring of 1846 James planted their last crops in Missouri. They made arrangements for James' sister Cynthia and her husband, who had farmland adjacent to James' and Melinda's Missouri property, to continue to farm their land, as the property was not sold prior to their leaving Missouri. In fact, James had placed a mortgage on his Platte County land which wasn't paid off until March 3, 1890.

After the fall harvest, they collected their livestock and, along with John and Drewsilla, departed Missouri and made their way up the Dragoon Trace to Iowa. In late September 1846, the two Jordan families arrived at their new homesteads west of Fort Des Moines.

Fording the river. Author's personal collection.

78   Pursuit of a Dream

What Happened to the Indians in Iowa?

The primary Indian tribes in Iowa have been referred to as the "Meskwaki," the "Sac" (also called "Sauk"), and the "Fox." Historically, the Fox are the Meskwaki. The tribe has had two names: the one they always had—Meskwaki, and the one the French gave them—Fox. Although both the Meskwaki and the Sac tribes have the same Algonquin language base, the Sac were a completely different tribe from the Meskwaki. Neither tribe was indigenous to Iowa.

There were also three other Indian tribes. Forced into Iowa from their tribal lands to the east were the Winnebago and the Pottawatomie. The Sioux, originally woodland Indians from the upper Mississippi in Minnesota, Iowa, and Wisconsin, were forced west by the French and their Chippewa allies.

The Early Years of the Meskwaki Tribe

From prehistoric times, both the Meskwaki and the Sac Tribes lived in the Great Lakes Region along the St. Lawrence River northeast of Lake Ontario. The Meskwakis remained there with their tribe growing to over ten thousand members. The Sac left when early Indian tribes drove them out, and they moved into the Great Lakes Region, settling in present-day eastern Michigan by Saginaw Bay. The Sacs took their tribal name from that area; the Ossaakiiwaki, which mean "yellow-earth," due to the yellow-clay soils found around Saginaw Bay.

The Meskwaki name of origin is *Meshkwahkihaki*, which means "the Red-Earths," related to their creation story in which their culture hero, Wisaka, created the first humans out of red clay. When French fur trappers came to the St. Lawrence River area in 1698, they mistakenly applied what was a clan name, "Fox," to the entire Meskwaki Tribe calling them *les Renards*—the French word for "fox." Later the English and Americans adopted that name, also calling the Meskwaki the "Fox," and the name has remained since then.

Moving to Wisconsin

Disease brought by the trappers and battles for their territory drove the Meskwaki out of their homeland in the very early 1700s. They resettled initially between Saginaw and Detroit, near the Sac, but then moved to the southern side of the Great Lakes and eventually into the Fox River Valley, in what became the state of Wisconsin. There the Meskwaki engaged in fur trading with the French.

It was just a matter of time before the French wanted rights to the Fox River system, where the "Fox" (Meskwaki) Indians had settled, to gain better access to the Mississippi River from the Great Lakes. The Meskwaki fought against the French in the "Fox Wars" from 1701 to 1742 to preserve their adopted homelands. By 1712 the number of Meskwaki had declined to thirty-five hundred; however, the Meskwaki resistance to French encroachment was so persistent and successful that the frustrated and angry king of France signed a decree commanding the complete extermination of the Meskwaki, the only edict of its kind in French history. According to historian Louise Kellogg: "The Mesquakie were the most fierce and most interesting of the Wisconsin tribes. They managed to maintain their primitive independence longer than any other Wisconsin tribe because of their great courage and determination to live as their forefathers did."

After the Second Fox War of 1728, the US government estimated the Meskwaki were reduced to some fifteen hundred people. After further fighting with the French, two years later, in 1730, there were only nine hundred Meskwaki remaining: three hundred warriors and the remainder mostly women and children.

In order to advance their agenda, the French gathered up Indian allies who were willing to fight with them against the Meskwaki. In a huge battle which took place on September 9, 1730, between the French and their Indian allies against the Meskwaki, most of the three hundred Meskwaki warriors were killed. Many of the women and children were either killed or taken captive.

Moving to the Mississippi Valley

In 1735, the Meskwaki allied with the stronger Sac tribe, which had about fifty-five hundred members. Both tribes had been friends and together relocated southward from Wisconsin along the Mississippi River and into Iowa, Illinois, and Missouri, where they lived cordially, but separately, for almost a century. The Sac settled in Saukenuk at the confluence of the Mississippi and Rock Rivers in Illinois, and the Meskwaki settled by the Mississippi River, near Rock Island, Illinois. Starting about 1804, Meskwaki braves began to penetrate further and further into Iowa because they needed more hunting land. Both the Sac and the Meskwaki continued to engage in the lucrative business of fur trading, that turned out to be detrimental to the Meskwaki traditional way of life, as explained by Helen Blair:

> Although the habits of the Mesquakie had changed little during the years since 1804, the emphasis they placed on the occupations of agriculture and hunting had changed dramatically. In the years after 1804, the Sac

and Fox became increasingly dependent upon hunting as the principal means by which they could purchase the merchandise offered by the traders. In 1805, the Sac and Fox brought approximately 1,000 deer, bear, raccoon, otter, and beaver pelts to the traders. By 1819, the number of pelts brought to the traders had increased to 60,082. On the other hand, the number of acres cultivated by the Sac and Fox decreased from 800 acres in 1804 to only 300 acres in 1819."

Donald Ewing provides further clarification: "As the Indians turned more and more to hunting as their prime activity, they required more, not less land on which to hunt. Only by maintaining their thousands of acres of land could they provide themselves with the necessary meat, furs, guns, gunpowder, traps, yard goods, blankets, and colored glass beads they desired."

Even before white settlers were allowed to live in Iowa, the Indians were ceding land to the US government:

- Starting in 1804 and ending in 1824, a series of controversial treaties were negotiated in St. Louis between Territorial Governor William Henry Harrison and other US government officials and the Sac and Meskwaki. In the 1804 treaty, the Indians supposedly sold a swath of land on the east side of the Mississippi River, fifty miles or more wide, stretching from St. Louis five hundred miles north into Wisconsin. For this enormous amount of territory, the United States paid $2,200 in goods and annual payments of $1,000 in goods. The Indians felt they had been tricked but the treaty was enforced by the US government who said the Indians could use the land until it was surveyed for white settlement, which happened around 1828.
- In 1824 the Sac and Meskwaki gave up a triangular shaped region in what is now Lee County, Iowa, for the half-breeds. But white traders soon gained control of this land.
- The Sioux, Sac, Fox, and other tribes who were at odds with each other's claims to hunting grounds in northeastern Iowa agreed to appropriate a strip of Indian land twenty miles wide in that area designated as a "Neutral Ground" to enforce separation of the tribes. The Indians turned this strip over to the US government in 1830.

Black Hawk War

The US government estimated that by 1829 there were fifteen hundred Meskwaki and about fifty-five hundred Sac. Continued pioneer expansion began to again pressure the Indians to move off their lands. The signing of the Indian Removal Act of 1830, authorized by the US Congress and signed into law by President Andrew Jackson, mandated the permanent removal of Indians to territory west of the Mississippi River.

The Black Hawk War (May–August 1832) started over Sac Tribal Chief Black Hawk's allegation that the United States was not providing adequate supplies, per treaty agreements, to his tribe. Chief Black Hawk had allied with other Indian tribes, including some Meskwaki braves and members of the British military from Canada—a group called the "British Band." The conflict started slowly but escalated into a "throwback" to the War of 1812 (through the "British Band") when Britain had tried to gain or regain US territory they had lost during the Revolutionary War. It was also an attempt by Chief Black Hawk to regain the land of his birth on the eastern side of the Mississippi River between the Mississippi and the Rock Rivers that had been lost in the 1804 Treaty of St. Louis.

Meskwaki historian Richard Frank Brown cites reasons why the Meskwaki tried to stay out of the conflict and why the Sac engaged in the war: ". . . rumors of the eminent war between the British and the Americans reached the Sac and Fox. The Mesquakie had determined to live in peace with the white man and wished only to remain neutral should conflict occur. The Sauk, however, favored the British. The British agent, Colonel Dixon, held talks with the Sauk leaders and gave presents to the different bands."

In his autobiography, the Sac (aka "Sauk") Tribal Chief Black Hawk recalled the events of this time and wrote: "I had not made up my mind whether to join the British or remain neutral. I had not discovered one good trait in the character of the Americans that had come to the country. They made fair promises, but never fulfilled them! Whilst the British made but few—but we could always rely upon their word."

"Sac and Fox Confederacy"

The Indians and British, far outnumbered and out maneuvered by the US troops, were not successful. During the signing of the treaties after the Black Hawk War, the United States officially combined the Meskwaki and Sac Tribes into a single group known as the Sac and Fox Confederacy. Thus, to the US government, the Meskwaki ("Fox") and the Sac became one tribe. From then on all treaties, agreements, or actions negotiated with the US government were determined by the leaders of this tribal combination.

The US government's 1832 treaty with the Indians also included the relinquishment of six million acres of Indian Territory. The transaction was first called Scott's Purchase and later called the Black Hawk Purchase. Charles Aldrich, Iowa historian, described the terms: "The United States paid the Sac and Fox $655,000, which included a $40,000 cash payment to the traders to pay for the accumulated debts of the Indians, and an annuity of $20,000 for a period of thirty years to the relatives of the warriors killed in the war. The price came to about 14 cents per acre."

Sac Chief Keokuk was granted a reservation, called Keokuk's Reserve, within the cession and was recognized as the primary chief of the Sac and the Meskwaki because he had not sided with Black Hawk.

Moving into Iowa

Manifest Destiny was being realized. White settlers were on a rampage for the beautiful and fertile Iowa land the Indians occupied. As the settlers approached, the Sac and Fox were compelled to leave hunting lands and villages they had occupied and move further west, this time into Iowa.

When negotiating treaties and agreements for land, the Indians usually were given (or requested) amenities from the US government: money for guns and whiskey and goods such as blankets, cloth, salt, tobacco, and gun powder. Oftentimes the government promised to lay out farms, establish a school, build a blacksmith shop, and provide one or two blacksmiths and gunsmiths. All of this made them increasingly dependent on the white man and contributed to the eradication of their traditional Indian way of life.

As time went on, more and more lands were ceded by the Indians, until the United States had gobbled up almost the entire area of what is now known as the state of Iowa.

- At the close of the Black Hawk War, in 1832, the Sac and Fox gave up a strip of land along the west side of the Mississippi River. This was about fifty miles wide and extended from the Neutral Ground on the north to Missouri on the south. The land secured from the Indians was first called Scott's Purchase and later the Black Hawk Purchase.

- In 1836, the four hundred square miles on the Iowa River, known as Keokuk's Reserve, was sold by the Sac and Fox to the US government. This was the tract given to Sac Chief Keokuk and his band because they did not join Sac Chief Black Hawk in his war against the whites.

In 1837 an agreement referred to as the Second Black Hawk Purchase was executed between the United States and the Sac and Fox, involving 1,256,000 acres of land. In exchange for the land, the United States agreed to pay $377,000 divided up as follows: $30,000 to the Indians in cash; a payment of $48,458.87 to traders for Indian debts; two hundred horses valued at $9,341; and $4,500 in presents to the Sac and Fox. The treaty called for $200,000 of this money to be put in trust for the Indians with the promise of a $10,000 annuity for ten years.

- In 1837 the government made another purchase from the Sac and Fox. This tract lay west of the Black Hawk Purchase. The new purchase was about twenty-five miles wide in the middle and tapered off at either end and it made the boundary between the land of the government and the Indian land to the west almost straight.

- In 1841, the US government offered a $1 million deal to the Sac and Meskwaki for the remainder of their Iowa land. The United States promised the Indians they would be able to settle in Minnesota. The offer was rejected by Meskwaki Chief Wapello, who did not want his tribe to be so close to their adversaries, the Sioux in Minnesota. One of the comments in the speech he gave to the US officials when he rejected the offer follows: "I remember when Wisconsin was ours; and now it has your name; we sold it to you. Dubuque was once ours: we sold it to you. . . . And they are occupied by white men who live happily. Rock Island was the only place where we lived happily; and we sold that to you. . . . This land is all we have; it is our only fortune."

Guns Were the Problem

Richard Frank Brown, in his thorough study of Meskwaki history, presented his opinion about the demise of the Meskwaki:

> In the years after the Black Hawk War, the Sac and Fox became increasingly dependent upon the traders for their food. In 1804, the two bands of Sac and Fox living at Rock Island had cultivated over 800 acres of land. By 1837, the entire tribe of Sac and Fox cultivated only 450 acres of land. What had happened to the once proud Sac and Fox Indians? What had reduced them to dependence upon the traders and the government in such a short span of time?
>
> The Indians' reduced reliance upon agriculture as their major supply of food, came about primarily because a white man's invention—the gun. The gun promised

the Indians an easier life but its use proved to be a "Pandora's Box." The use of a gun made hunting much easier for Sac and Fox braves because they could easily kill more than enough game to meet the needs of their people. But a gun required ammunition and needed fixing or replacing. Thus the Indian braves sold their surplus and pelts to the traders in exchange for guns and ammunition. Before long, the Indians had destroyed all the game in their immediate vicinity and it was necessary to travel many miles away to good hunting grounds. The Sac and Fox reached this stage by 1824.

The Sac and Fox braves no longer considered hunting easy when they had to travel 200 to 400 miles to find game but they had no choice. The increased emphasis on hunting had decreased their reliance on agriculture, and by 1819, they barely harvested enough for their needs. By 1824, the Sac and Fox had reached the point of no return. They could not go back to their old ways. The Sac and Fox were primarily meat eaters, and the game had departed long before.

Indian Agent Thomas Forsythe supports Brown's opinions with a observation he made in 1820, saying that "many of the old Indians told (him) that they were happier before they began to use firearms, because then they had to kill only what they needed for food. Since that time, however, they had to destroy all the game in order to purchase merchandise from the traders."

The Meskwaki and Sac Agree to Leave Iowa

In February of 1842, the United States induced the Sac and Fox to sell one-half of their holdings with the qualification that, instead of having to move north to Minnesota, they would instead eventually be removed to a location south of the Missouri River. A date for the treaty to be signed was set for October. Leland T. Mitchell, who witnessed the negotiations, provides this description:

> On the opposite side sat Poweshiek, the head chief of the Foxes, backed in semicircles by the prominent chiefs of his tribe. His appearance is not so striking as Keokuk's but there is something in his countenance which denotes a warm heart. One expression of his we well remember. Speaking to the Agent of having to leave the land they had sold to the United States, he said he "knew it was right that they should leave, but, says he, there will be crying in the bottoms." How natural the expression of the old chief. Here was the land where their fathers had lived for ages and here rested the bones of some of their greatest chiefs and most renowned warriors for whom it was fit that there should be crying in the bottoms. Several chiefs spoke upon the subject of their leaving and others connected with their tribe, but Poweshiek's regret still hung upon our memory.

At the Indian Council of 1842, held at Agency City, a treaty was signed on October 11 by the Sac and Fox Confederacy whereby the Indians agreed to sell all their land east of the Missouri River for $1,058,566, or about 10 cents per acre. The government paid $258,566 of this amount to the traders to whom the Indians owed money and placed the $800,000 in trust at 5 percent interest, which the United States agreed to pay to the Sac and Fox in allotments, as an annual annuity.

The Sac and Fox agreed to evacuate as far west as a line north and south through the Red Rocks in Marion County in about six months, by May 1, 1843, and after that live in the western half of Iowa. They agreed to then vacate that in three years, in October 1845. The United States promised to remove the Indians at that time to a tract of land on the Missouri River or one of its tributaries in the Territory of Kansas, which was, as yet, not a part of the United States.

Meskwaki Indians. Minnesota Historical Society

Chief Keokuk. From *High Points of Iowa History* by Eugene N. Hastie, 1971

Chief Poweshiek featured in the *Iowa History Journal*.

In response to this development, squatters immediately came in and settled on the land that was to be (eventually) vacated by the Indians. When Indian Agent Beach responded by forcibly evicting the squatters, they burned the mills the government had built for the Indians.

Moving to Kansas

For the next three years, two groups of Sac and one group of Fox lived separately but harmoniously not far from Fort Des Moines. After receiving their annuity payment from the US government in the fall of 1845, they kept their promise and mournfully made ready to leave their beloved Iowa.

Each of the three groups of Sac and Fox Indians left Fort Des Moines in separate groups. A witness is quoted by Ambrose Fulton who watched the Indians leave: "A solemn silence pervaded the Indian camp; the faces of their stoutest men were bathed in tears and when their cavalcade was put in motion, toward the setting sun, there was a spontaneous outburst of frantic grief."

A large group of Sac were led out of Fort Des Moines by Chief Keokuk in a single file on September 10, 1845. A small band of Sac led by Chief Hardfish had kept to themselves after the treaty was negotiated during the Indian Council of 1842. They were the remnants of Black Hawk's tribe, bitter from having lost so many loved ones during the Black Hawk War. They were one of the three groups of Indians at Fort Des Moines, and they followed Keokuk's footsteps a few days later.

Meskwaki Chief Powieshiek tried to delay the move of his group; his people were in poor health and too weak to travel, having suffered through a bad winter. US authorities allowed only about one hundred of the sick to remain, and on October 8, 1845, Poweshiek reluctantly led the Meskwaki out of Fort Des Moines.

All of the Indians—braves, women, and children, half wrapped in blankets, some riding ponies, with some ponies only carrying bundles of belongings—were walking silently, single file with sadly bowed heads. They traveled over two hundred miles on the Dragoon Trace; first going to what is now known as the town of Ellston, then over to and along the Grand River as it enters Missouri, then following a southwest diagonal line leading to the Missouri River crossing at Fort Leavenworth and into Kansas where their reservation was located.

Most reached Fort Leavenworth in late October 1845; however, Poweshiek's group did not. According to Dragoon Trace historian, John Palmer:

> When he reached the Missouri border around October 11, Poweshiek met a white settler, perhaps Charles Schooler, whom he knew would not have been allowed to inhabit the Iowa Territory under the treaty agreement. Thinking he had reached the state of Missouri and had gone far enough, Poweshiek turned west to camp where the Grand River met the Missouri border. This was the territory of the Pottawattomies, friends of the Mesquakie, and they invited them to stay.

> Poweshiek established his village of about forty lodges on the Grand River, not far from the white settlement. Culturally different and fearful, the settlers reported the Native Americans to Fort Des Moines. Rather than sending soldiers which could have inflamed bloodshed, three civilians acquainted with Poweshiek went to talk to the old chief: Dr. Campbell, J. B. Scott (hauler of supplies), and Hamilton Thrift (a tailor). Within the year, the Mesquakies removed to the reservation in Kansas.

The following spring, on March 10, 1846, Dragoons from Fort Des Moines marched the three hundred remaining Meskwakis out of the fort and down the Dragoon Trace to join the other members of their tribe who were now living on a reservation in northeastern Kansas, not far from Fort Leavenworth.

The Meskwaki and Sac Return to Iowa

When the Meskwaki and the Sac were deported to Kansas, a few Meskwaki secretly remained in Iowa. Many who moved to Kansas were unhappy with the poor water, lack of wooded streams, and bad soil. While the hunting was adequate at first, game soon became scarce. Around 1850, smallpox broke out and then the flu. Many Indians were consuming too much alcohol.

While some Indians (mostly Sac) adapted to the new way of living and started farms in Kansas, another group (mostly Meskwaki) decided to return to Iowa in 1852, settling on some of their old land on the Iowa River. "The chiefs and the old people became fearful lest their children and grandchildren adopt the new ways and forget how to be good Indians," according to Richard Brown. "The Mesquakie knew they were dying and longed to return to the home of their ancestors in Iowa. They remembered only the good times they had spent in Iowa before 1845. They remembered the numerous streams, the well-timbered lands, the good hunting, and the wonderful feasts."

Richard Brown continues:

> The Mesquakie realized, however, that in order to settle permanently in Iowa, they would somehow have to circumvent the treaty. Consequently, they began an all-out negotiation with the State of Iowa to permit the legal return of all Meskwaki to their beloved homeland. Many sympathetic settlers came to the aid of the Indians and circulated a number of petitions requesting that the entire tribe be allowed to return to Iowa. One petition carried the signatures of the Secretary of State of Iowa, George McCleary, and his deputy, John M. Davis. In spite of the large support the settlers gave the Mesquakie, the United States government refused to allot any land in Iowa for use by Indians who belonged in Kansas.
>
> Somehow (probably from sympathetic white settlers) they learned that they could buy land in Iowa and acquire title to it. Then the land would be theirs and no one could take it from them until they decided to sell it. Accordingly, one band in Kansas collected $735 for the purpose of buying land. The chief of the band, Ma me nwa ne ke, held council and sent his brother, Pa ta co to, and four other councilmen to Iowa to make the purchase.
>
> Jubilant and anxious, the delegation of Indians left for Iowa without any real plan of action, without any idea of the process required in buying land. What is more, not one of the Indians could speak English. Consequently, upon arriving in Iowa, the delegates were unable for a time to carry out their objective. however, the Mesquakie met a Chippewa-Ottawa Indian, Qua ti bi ta la, who could speak English and who agreed to act as an interpreter. Through this interpreter, the Mesquakie councilmen told some white settlers of Chief Ma me nwa ne ke's plan. These white men in turn contacted three farmers, Phillip, David, and Isaac Butler who agreed to sell the Indians eighty acres of land. The farmers, however, wanted $1,000 for the land.
>
> The determined Mesquakie delegation set out to find the other Mesquakie Indians who had remained in Iowa. Again and again they reiterated their chief's plan and the urgency of their need for money. The Iowa Mesquakie could raise only $15 in cash but they offered to give up some of their ponies to make up the $250 difference.
>
> In the meantime, the sympathizing white settlers continued to use their influence on the Iowa legislators. On July 15, 1856, the Iowa Assembly passed an act permitting the tribe to reside in Iowa. There was one legal snag, however. The Mesquakie were not citizens of the United States; therefore, they could not own land. Knowing this, those settlers favorable to the Mesquakie's cause once again prevailed on the Governor of Iowa, James W. Grimes, to hold the newly purchased land in trust for the Indians. After much deliberation, the governor agreed to the trust, and on July 13, 1857, he signed the deed in the names of the five Mesquakie from Kansas. Thus, for $1,000 the Mesquakie Nation acquired possession of eighty acres of land west of the present towns of Tama-Toledo, in Tama County, Iowa. The Mesquakie Nation thus became the first Indian tribe in United States' history to actually purchase their land.

When the Meskwaki returned to live in Iowa, the federal government withdrew financial support promised in earlier treaties. Years of hardship followed as the tribe worked to make a living on an area of land too small to support so many people. Finally, state officials convinced the US government to resume the annual payments. The tribe used the money to purchase more land. According to Fred Gearing:

> Actually the Mesquakie did not really care to use the land for farming, but preferred to leave it in its natural state. They had always lived in harmony with nature and felt safe among the trees, the river, and the hills. When the Mesquakie returned to Iowa, the land became a symbol of safety. It became a place of refuge from the white man. The symbol of land signified to the Mesquakie all that was good in their lives. Thus the close relationship of the land to the Mesquakie concept of security created in them an almost fanatic desire to increase the size of their holdings.

Today, the Meskwaki continue to purchase land as opportunities for economic diversification arise. They currently own more than eighty-one hundred acres in Tama, Marshall, and Palo Alto Counties. Since their return to Iowa over 150 years ago, the Meskwaki have worked diligently to adhere to the values and spirituality of the indigenous native, support themselves, and to recover their traditional way of life.

CHAPTER 18
A Cabin in the Woods

James and Melinda chose to bring their family to Iowa in the fall of 1846 after completing their final harvest in Platte County, the yield of which was brought to Iowa to sustain them that first winter. By arriving in the fall they were able to posture themselves for an Iowa spring of planting, calving, etc., and they also avoided traveling through the spring floods.

When Melinda Jordan arrived in Iowa and James took her to their Jordan claim west of Fort Des Moines, she was probably quite pleased. To mark his 160 acres, James had driven stakes into the ground of the lush grassy areas of their extensive holdings and blazed trees in the timbered sections. Upon the land, she observed quiet acres of oak, walnut, and hickory trees; rolling hills; the Raccoon River with its many sandbars; and, flowing into the Raccoon near an area James had previously cleared for a cabin, a little winding creek. There were some open spaces, but much of the land was covered with brush and towering trees—brush which was perfect for sheltering their livestock and trees which would provide lumber for building barns and a cabin.

Unseen were the many animals in the woods—wild turkeys and pheasants and other fowl, raccoons and other fur-covered animals, even some bear and buffalo. These animals could be hunted to provide food for the family. Berry bushes, wild fruit trees, and other vegetation offered sustenance, as well.

After the 1845 Iowa land rush and prior to bringing his family to Iowa in 1846, James had probably taken time off from his Missouri farm and livestock enterprise to come north and get the Iowa homestead started. To preserve his Iowa claim, James had to make some improvements on the land. According to Hubert and Hugh Moeller, Iowa historians, "If a settler broke 5 acres of ground, it was generally considered sufficient proof of ownership for at least 6 months. Then if the settler built himself a cabin eight logs high with a roof, that was adequate to hold a claim for another 6 months. If a settler did these two things, his neighbors considered he had a full and recognized title to the land he claimed and they would gladly join him in defending his rights . . . if another settler tried to come in and take over the claim."

Cattle Grazing in the Lowland, artist unknown. Author's personal collection

The site James had chosen for their cabin was on a rise about a quarter mile north of the Raccoon River, next to the little stream they would later name Jordan Creek. Camping out in a tent, James had probably previously cleared some land and prepared and stacked up logs which would be used to build the cabin he and his family would construct after they arrived. He also may have dug a cellar, which would be the foundation of the cabin. A giant oak tree behind the cabin became a popular place later on for the family to stay cool on hot summer days.

There is a question as to exactly when the Jordan cabin was built. A Jordan biography states that, after living in a tent under the burr oaks, "a log cabin was soon erected." Most likely, a small but cozy cabin was built immediately after the family arrived in 1846 and enlarged over the next two years. The actual presence of a cabin was not listed in any official record until 1848 when James was able to (semi-officially) record his claim with the Fort Des Moines "Claims Club."

James' brother John, who had come with him earlier in the spring, helped James with his building project just as James helped his brother. John's claim and cabin were about one mile to the east in an area which came to be referred to as Hiner's Grove and later called the Walnut Creek Settlement. It was located near where the present-day Fifty-sixth Street and Welker Avenue run along Walnut Creek in Des Moines.

Besides wanting to get their farms going and cabins built, there was another good reason for the early settlers to improve and live on their land. They wanted to protect it from claim jumpers, as the area was beginning to attract more folks, some of whom were already claiming land nearby.

James was not the first pioneer settler to live in what would become Walnut Township. Preceding him during the spring of 1846 were a number of folks from Missouri: Hinton Lyons, Towne Hall, B. F. Jesse, and Samuel Shaw. They and their families all moved up from Clay County, Missouri, which was adjacent to Platte County where the Jordans had lived. Besides James and John Jordan and their families, Hinton Lyons' brother Jacob also arrived that fall. Of this entire group, only James Jordan and his family stayed in the area and became permanent residents. All the others farmed for a few years and then moved on to California or Oregon.

Now settled in Iowa, both Jordan families planned to use the long winter days to get organized in their new lives and get ready for planting in the spring. They also looked forward to winter as a good time for James and Melinda and John and Drewsilla to become acquainted with their neighbors. One way to meet them would be through church services and gatherings, held in settlers' cabins and very possibly conducted by John, as he later became a Methodist exhorter.

Affable Jimmy Jordan was probably quite interested in making friends in the little community that had sprung up around Fort Des Moines. These initial friendships would be the basis of many future business associations. However, the winter they hoped for was not to be.

The Winter of '46

No matter how organized James and Melinda were when building and settling in their new cabin that fall, they could not have been prepared for the terrible winter of 1846, the winter of "the big snow," unprecedented in the history of the country. Polk County historian L. F. Andrews writes: "The snow began to fall early in November and continued at intervals until December 21, when over 22-1/2 inches fell, and during the entire month the depth was over 3 feet. Frequent violent winds, low temperatures and deep snow made travel outside impossible and if a person did venture out the winds closed up his tracks as fast as made so that he could not retrace them."

James and Melinda were particularly concerned with their livestock, which lacked proper protection in the cold and were vulnerable to exposure and attacks from timber wolves. Legend states that friendly Indians who were still living in the area helped James and Melinda survive that first winter by bringing them food. James would not forget this. Later, as a state senator, he would take advantage of the opportunity to repay the life-saving assistance the Indians provided his family by voting favorably for them to buy back some of their Iowa land.

Jimmy's Cabin

The Jordan cabin, when finally completed in 1848, was very fine indeed. Additional cellar space had been created by further excavation under the enlarged cabin. The milled lumber for the building had been purchased from Parmalee's Mill in Carlisle and hauled to the Jordan claim. The cabin featured windows and "battened" doors, which were unusual for the time.

Doors were typically made of a slab of wood, hung on wooden hinges, and fastened with a wooden latch operated by leather thongs through a hole in the door. If the pioneer family were exceptionally poor, the "door" would simply be heavy cloth quilts, hung to cover the opening. However, the Jordans' cabin door, an object of much admiration, was more like doors in the homes back east—far more secure and able to keep the cabin much warmer.

Most likely, this cabin also had wooden floors rather than dirt. The fact James used milled lumber, had windows, and a modern door in his large cabin shows he arrived in Iowa with enough money to construct a first-rate shelter for his wife and family. Although there is no further description of the Jordan cabin, others of that time have been described. The following is a description by Edward and Rebecca Burlend of a cabin that may have been similar to the Jordans' home:

> There were two rooms, both on the ground floor, separated from each other with (a board wall). The rooms were nearly square, and might contain from 30 to 40 square feet each; beneath one of the rooms was a cellar, the floor and sides of which were mud and clay, as left when first dug out; the walls of the house consisted of layers of strong blocks of timber, roughly squared and notched to each other at the corners; the joints filled up with clay.
>
> The house had two doors, one of which was always closed in winter, and open in summer to cause a drought. There was a fire on the floor at the end of the building where a chimney had been constructed of stones gathered out on the land, and walled together. It was necessarily of great width, to prevent fire from communicating with the building.
>
> The house was covered with oak shingles; that is to say, thin riven boards railed upon each other, so as just to over-reach. The floors of the house were covered with the same material, except for a large place near the fire, which was paved with small stones, also gathered from the land.
>
> It was quite common to see at least one bed in the same room where the fire is kept. There was a sort of loft, constructed rather with a view to make the house warmer, than to afford additional room. One corner of the house was occupied with agricultural implements, consisting of large hoes, axes, flails, and wooden forks. Various herbs were suspended from the roof with a view of being medicinally serviceable, also two guns, one of them a rifle. There were also several hams and sides of bacon, smoked until they were almost black; two or three pieces of beef, etc. Under one of the beds were 3 or 4 pots of honey. The furniture in the other room consisted of two beds and a hand loom, with which the family wove fabric for the greater part of their own clothes. In the cellar . . . were 2 or 3 large tubs of lard and a lump of tobacco.

Furniture in pioneer cabins was traditionally crude, handmade, and very utilitarian. However, Melinda's was probably somewhat more refined, as she did not have to bring it far, and, while in Missouri, she had several years to accumulate cast-off pieces from emigrants getting ready to embark on the Oregon Trail. St. Joseph by then enjoyed steamboat service from the Mississippi River and on up the Missouri River, which could bring fine things from New Orleans and the east. Home furnishings imported from the eastern states could be purchased in St. Joe, Independence, and Westport (Kansas City). Since James and Melinda were not poor, they had bought what they needed and then figured out a way to haul it north to Iowa. Besides furniture, Melinda brought along a stove to cook on rather than preparing meals over a fire in the fireplace. The fireplace was probably used mainly for heat and light.

Dresser belonging to Melinda Jordan. Courtesy of West Des Moines Historical Society

James Jordan: His Life and His Legacy

CHAPTER 19
Making the Farm

Creating a farm was hard work, but Jimmy and Melinda, now thirty-three and twenty-seven years old, were used to it. During the years the Jordan family lived in Michigan and later in Missouri, they gained the knowledge and experience they would need to build both their Iowa farm and also a successful livestock business. By the time they arrived in Iowa they were well trained, but it was still a strenuous and challenging endeavor.

The first year of establishing a farm was the hardest. The crop was small; only a few acres of timbered land were cleared for planting the first season. Corn was their first regular crop. The roots of the cornstalk, it was believed, loosened the soil better than the roots of any other plant.

The soil was the big challenge. Upon the virgin prairie soil, grasses and weeds, flowers, and brush grew in profusion—plants whose network of tangled roots went almost a foot deep into the soil. Breaking into this earth was not the task of a solitary man. It usually took a group of neighbors and eight to ten yoke of oxen to do the job. The oxen would be borrowed from all the neighbors in order to make a large team. Three to four men were needed to drive the animals; the oxen being guided by twenty-foot-long whips.

The swath cut into the earth was only two feet wide, but once they all got started, the job went quickly and quite a bit of sod could be broken. If the team couldn't cut through a particular patch, the men would use axes to hack up the earth. Sod was broken during May and June. If not done by then, the prairie grass would be too tall for the plow to get into the earth. Once the sod was broken and the fields planted, crops appeared in abundance.

James first cleared his timbered bottomland along Jordan Creek and the Raccoon River, saving the large logs to build a barn. His earliest crops were planted on the bottomland, as it was easier to plow than the virgin prairie soil.

His livestock was left to forage on this bottomland near the creek and river, so building fences was especially important. James probably used the "worm"

Breaking sod on the prairie. Library of Congress

Building a "worm fence." From *The Palimpsest: Iowa's Popular History Magazine*, Vol. 70. No. 2 (Summer 1989)

fence which was about ten feet high and consisted of sections of ten-foot rails stacked on top of each other in a zig-zag fashion. By the time it was completed it was impervious to livestock or other animals. That was the object of fences—to keep animals out. No farmer wanted livestock, deer, or other wild animals in his cornfield.

Starting the Livestock Business

In the early days, James' large livestock herds were turned out to graze upon unsold Iowa land. As there was much unusable river bottomland in the immediate vicinity of the Jordan farm, James showed wisdom in choosing a farm site—he always had local pastureland available for his livestock. His herds were guaranteed virtually unlimited free pasturage in a fairly protected, well-watered location. George F. Parker, Iowa historian, states: "The farmer who had the training and persistence to pursue cattle raising soon found himself independent if not wealthy. Often the first year would provide him with the modest capital necessary to go on to improve his stock and equipment and keep him out of any considerable debt. In another few years he would be able increase his holdings of land, to erect better buildings and finally, when markets (or the railroad) came nearer, to enjoy the fruits of his labor."

Not many cattlemen succeeded, however. As pioneers moved into Iowa, more and more prairie was bought and farmed, which left fewer acres for grazing herds. But James, an astute businessman, succeeded where others failed. When the land immediately around his farm became more and more settled he sought out new pastureland further west for his herds. James Jordan eventually grazed cattle as far west as Atlantic, Iowa, in much the same fashion as cattle was grazed in Texas or Oklahoma.

After being out on the range in western Iowa, the herds were driven into market in Des Moines. The next markets were to the south and east. From Des Moines the animals were shipped downriver, probably first on flatboats and later on small barges to the town of Keokuk on the Mississippi and from there on larger barges south to St. Louis. After the Civil War, trains took the livestock east to Chicago.

Four or five years after the Jordans settled in Iowa and their sons got a little older, they worked with the hired farm hands who were entrusted with the job of going out on the western Iowa range and supervising these grazing animals; two hundred to three hundred head of cattle was not an unusual responsibility for a trustworthy worker. James' oldest son, Benjamin, worked for at least two decades as a cowboy on the western range of Iowa. In the 1850s James' sister Anna and her husband, William Smith, moved with their family from Missouri to Winterset, Iowa, where they were locally positioned to assist James with his herds in the summer and fall.

The first Jordan herds were comprised of cattle indigenous to the United States. Originating from the British Durham breeds brought over in the 1600s by the nation's first settlers, the herds owned by the pioneers

Shorthorn cow. Author's personal collection

evolved into small but hardy cattle that were almost impervious to disease. After the Civil War, midwestern stockbreeders quit breeding the indigenous cattle and shifted to specialized breeds.

James' eventual choice was the Shorthorn, a dual-purpose breed known for its meat as well as milk production. Shorthorns originated in England, but the Scots refined them into excellent meat producers and introduced them to the United States in the late 1700s. They were brought to Iowa by breeders—including James Jordan—in the late 1860s.

As time went on, James would become very prosperous and acquire more and more land. His modest claim of 160 acres would grow to local holdings of over 1,800 acres. It would not be long before he was noted on the tax rolls as paying $1,000 per year in taxes on the income from his livestock business.

His livestock was not limited to cattle; he also raised hogs, and they were probably more useful to him in the early years than the cattle. At a time in Iowa's history when there was no authorized currency, the resourceful pioneers used livestock, especially hogs. Parker continues:

> In addition to furnishing wholesome food in ample quantities at a nominal cost for labor, the universal demand for hogs soon made it a producer of ready money. This was increased as wild game declined as the settler plunged further into the wilderness. Once in the business it was as easy to raise two hogs as one or 20 as 10, and as there were many families who needed food, there was an assured demand for surplus hogs for a decent price. In the

scarcity of money, a married hired man could be paid in part with a ham, a shoulder, a side of bacon or some lard, which he could carry home to his family. Or these meat articles could either be traded for something else or traded to the general store in payment for necessary products from the outside world.

Farmers often relied on hogs as a source of "cash" to pay their debts, taxes, or doctor bills or to purchase land, farm equipment, etc. Hogs were often the only meat-producing animals that were moved bodily as population shifted from place to place. It is interesting to note, prior to the Civil War, livestock was rarely weighed when bought or sold. There were few, if any, scales. The buyer and seller simply came to a mutual agreement on the weight of the animal and agreed on a price they both thought fair.

Besides growing corn for his stock, James also harvested wild hay which the animals needed for the long, hard winters. The hay was cut by hand with a scythe and raked over to dry. When it was ready to store away it was piled high in a stack beside the barn. Corn was stored in dried cobs in the barn and later threshed. Corn for domestic use was dried and either ground at Parmalee's Mill or by hand to be made into cornmeal, which was the staple starch in a pioneer household. In the early days, flour from wheat was scarce. Housewives waited for the steamboats to bring it up the Des Moines River and knew it would be costly once it arrived.

In addition to yielding crops and pasturing livestock, the land also offered any number of berries, nuts, herbs, roots, and other useful vegetation. Bees that were common in the woods provided honey, which was often used in the early days instead of sugar. Eventually the Jordan family had their own beehives from which to procure honey. Hunting provided all kinds of game meat—turkeys, ducks, pheasants, and quail, as well as deer, elk, bear, and raccoon. The rivers were full of fish. The largest fish caught in Des Moines in those early days was a thirty-pound walleye which sold for forty cents.

While James was tending to the fields and herds, Melinda was planting her garden. Historian John M. Faragher wrote she, "began by setting out onions and potatoes in early April, following up later that month by planting lettuce, beets, parsnips, turnips, and carrots in the garden, tomatoes and cabbages in window boxes

Hogs were a valuable commodity on pioneer farms. Title of painting and painter unknown. Library of Congress

indoors. When danger of late frosts had passed, the seedlings were moved outside and set out with May plantings of cucumbers, melons, pumpkins, and beans. (She may also have) laid down a patch of buckwheat and a garden of kitchen and medicinal herbs—sage, peppers, thyme, mint, mustard, horseradish, tansy, and others."

To supplement her garden Melinda would constantly search for wild berry bushes such as gooseberry and currant that she might replant in her yard. She also searched for wild flowers she could transplant by her doorstep or wild fruit-bearing trees she could use to create an orchard.

Jimmy also grew tobacco for himself, as most farmers did. It was sown in beds like onions in the spring of the year and grew into a rhubarb-looking plant. The leaves were cut, dried, and bunched together to "sweat" and then stored in the cellar. Jimmy would bring up his homegrown tobacco when his friends came to visit, and they would all have a good chew.

Separately, James and Melinda went about the jobs traditionally defined as men's work and women's work. But the really big jobs of harvesting or slaughtering had to be done together. Since the Jordan children at the time were still young, their parents had to work together to plant, harvest, and bring in their crops and to butcher and preserve the meat from the cows, hogs, and wild animals. With both of them working very hard, James and Melinda thus began their Iowa adventure by creating their farm which, along with the livestock operation, would become one of the most well-run and successful enterprises of the region.

CHAPTER 20
Making Friends in Town

Jimmy and the 'Coon

This story by Polk County historian L. F Andrews about James Jordan was told when he was an old man:

> The winter of 1847 was very severe and wolves were a source of much trouble to settlers on bottom lands along the streams. "Uncle Jimmy" walked to the Fort nearly every day to help build a rail fence around Hoxie's big cornfield, which lay along what is now Grand Avenue and West 12th Street.
>
> The cornfield belonged to Melville Hoxie, a carpenter, who, with his wife and four children in 1846 had taken up residence in one of the deserted officer's cabins at Fort Des Moines 1/2 mile away from the cornfield. He died in 1847 leaving his young wife, Ruth, a widow.

The beginning of this story illustrates how pioneers helped each other and is especially poignant because Jimmy Jordan and a friend were helping out the widow of a man he knew through the local Fort Des Moines Methodist worshipping community he and Melinda had joined. Melville and Ruth Hoxie were related to B. T. Hoxie who was one of the founders of the First Methodist Church in the village of Fort Des Moines.

The story continues:

> As James and his friend were splitting the rails for the fence, a light snow fell, and the two men decided to suspend the fence-making as the weather conditions were perfect for going on a "coon hunt." James and his friend found 'coon tracks and followed their game to a large tree. When they got to the tree the question of how to capture the 'coons without a dog or a gun became the challenge.
>
> They agreed that the best way to get the 'coon was to cut down the tree and kill the 'coon with clubs. Down came the tree but no 'coon came out. Then they cut a hole in the tree and discovered that the tree was home to a whole 'coon family! They decided that James would pull out the 'coons one by one while his friend would kill them.
>
> All went well until James reached in for the fifth raccoon and discovered that he was pulling the wrong end of the animal. Instead of Jimmy having the 'coon, the 'coon had Jimmy by his thumbs. The result was that Honorable J. G. Jordan did not catch any more 'coons nor split any more rails for some time thereafter.

"Claims Jumpers" vs. the "Squatters"

During the winter of 1847 "Jimmy" spent a great amount of time in Fort Des Moines becoming acquainted with the people in the town he now considered his home. At that time there were around 150

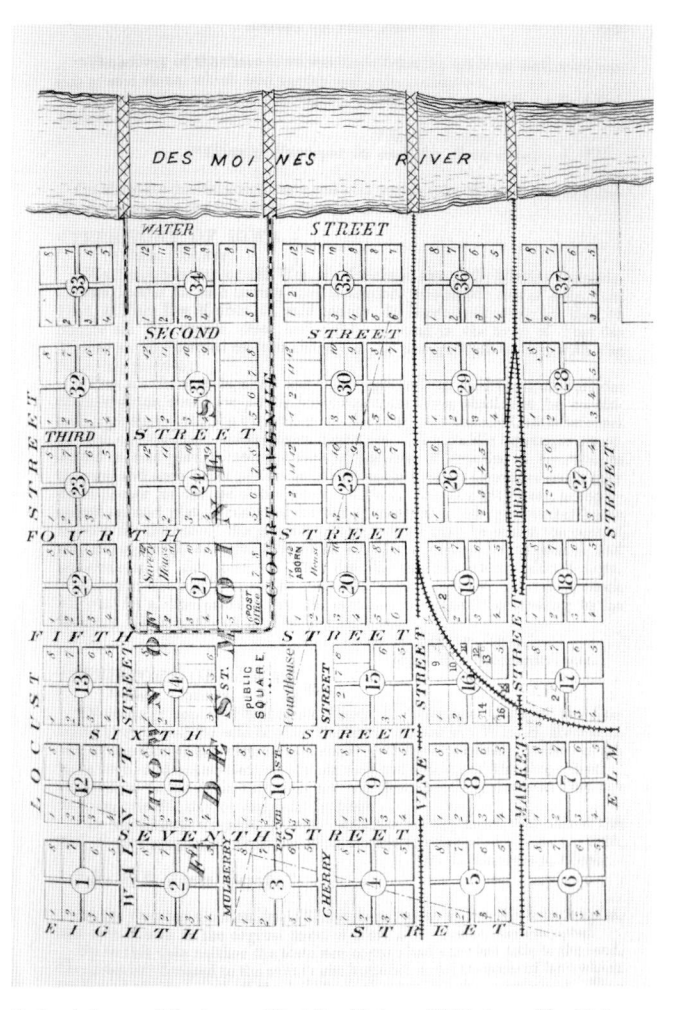

Early plat map of the town of Fort Des Moines, 1846. From *The History of Polk County, Iowa*

James Jordan: His Life and His Legacy

First Des Moines Post Office. Library of Congress

residents, including twenty-four families, living in and around the village, which was beginning to turn into a small town. The garrison had closed down in March of 1846, when the Indians were relocated to Kansas so the residents of Fort Des Moines were no longer restricted to living in or immediately around the fort.

They expanded their village to the area bounded by the Des Moines River to the east, the Raccoon River to the south, Eighth Street to the west, and Locust Street to the north. The area laid out contained the ever-important post office, the business district near the commercial wharf on the Des Moines River, the houses of the residents as well as their small farm fields to grow food, and outbuildings to shelter their horses, pigs, cows, and chickens.

In 1846 Fort Des Moines had been named the county seat of Polk County. The first businesses to serve the town would be some general stores, groceries (which were licensed to sell liquor), blacksmith shops, drug stores, and a hardware store. In a short time, a fashionable tailor would open a shop; there would be a clothing store, a furniture store, and several lawyers' and doctors' offices.

As time went on, Fort Des Moines evolved into a small city and boasted a hotel, several mills, and a Methodist church. Although closed in winter, there was a wharf on the Des Moines River where steamboats arrived when the river was high enough. A pontoon bridge spanned the Des Moines River at Grand Avenue, and another bridge crossed the river in Carlisle, about ten miles southeast of Des Moines. Iowa historian Eugene Hastie describes the early town: "The (Fort Des Moines) barracks had been laid out at right angles with the river and not according to the cardinal points of the compass. All the west side streets followed this policy. Proceeding northward the streets were Elm, Market, and Vine before coming to Court Avenue. Prior to 1855 most of the stores were on Second Street but south of Court Avenue. Present-day Grand Avenue was called Sycamore Street west of the river and Keokuk Street east of the river."

Jimmy Jordan could count as his friends most of Fort Des Moines' early settlers, many of whom had been attached to the garrison in either a military or civilian capacity. In the ensuing years he would be elected as a trustee of the first town council of Fort Des Moines, even though he lived almost six miles outside of town.

The big topic amongst the settlers that winter was the possibility of losing their claims. The US government had not yet fully surveyed the Indian Territory upon which the residents of Fort Des Moines had settled. Even though the government allowed pioneers to settle the area in October of 1845, they did not complete official land surveys until November of 1847 and were not allowing claims to be officially filed until late 1848. When that time came, Fort Des Moines residents would be directed to file their claims at the nearest land office, which was in Iowa City. (The other land offices in the Iowa Territory were in Burlington, Dubuque, Fairfield, and Marion.)

So, even though the settlers (also called "squatters") of Fort Des Moines had started to build homes, businesses, and farms and make improvements on "their" land, the land still legally belonged to the government and would not be officially available for a registered sale until the fall of 1848. The hard fact was the settlers had no legal right to the land upon which they were living and they had no assurance they could buy it when it was put up for sale.

In 1848 when the surveyed land *was* officially for sale, it would be sold to the highest bidder. James and the others, therefore, risked losing the hard work of two or three years of sod breaking, construction, and other improvements they had made on their land. If two people claimed the same tract of land, as sometimes happened, there was sure to be trouble.

And then there were the land speculators—the "shady" dealmakers who would arrive at the land office and file claims on land already being homesteaded by pioneer families, offering the government more than the going rate of $1.25 per acre. These nefarious men, known as "claim jumpers," were in it only for the quick profit. Most settlers, who were trying to make a homestead for their families, hated the claim jumpers and wanted to be rid of them.

In other parts of the Iowa Territory, earlier disputes over claims had been numerous and often had become so contentious that there was mob violence. By the spring of 1848 Fort Des Moines citizens were nervous and upset, distrusting any stranger in their midst. They decided it was necessary to develop some method of local control, whereby the settlers' claims could be protected. On April 8, 1848, a "Claims Club" was formed to do just that.

According to Iowa historian Ilda Hammer, the purpose of the Claims Club was "to get security and protection for the citizens of Polk County in their claims against speculators and all persons who may be disposed wrongfully to deprive settlers of their claims by preemption or otherwise." The Claims Club asked that all pioneer settlers put their claim on a list. James Jordan and forty-four others, all of whom were Fort Des Moines' earliest squatters, did so. Hammer continues, "If there was a problem with a claim, it would be resolved with a Claims Club adjustment committee that consisted of five Fort Des Moines residents."

Claims Club meetings were held right up until the fall of 1848, when the former Indian land officially went up for sale in Iowa City. At the last meeting of the club, the settlers appointed Robert L. Tidrick, a trustworthy local lawyer, to act as their agent and sent him to Iowa City accompanied by an armed corps to ensure no one interfered with the registration of their claims. After he left for Iowa City the squatters were on pins and needles.

The happy outcome was that Mr. Tidrick was successful in registering all of the claims at the minimum price of $1.25 per acre. Under the Iowa Pre-Exemption Act of 1841, Jordan had four years in which to pay for the land and receive title to it, which he did in 1852 when a land office was conveniently opened in Fort Des Moines.

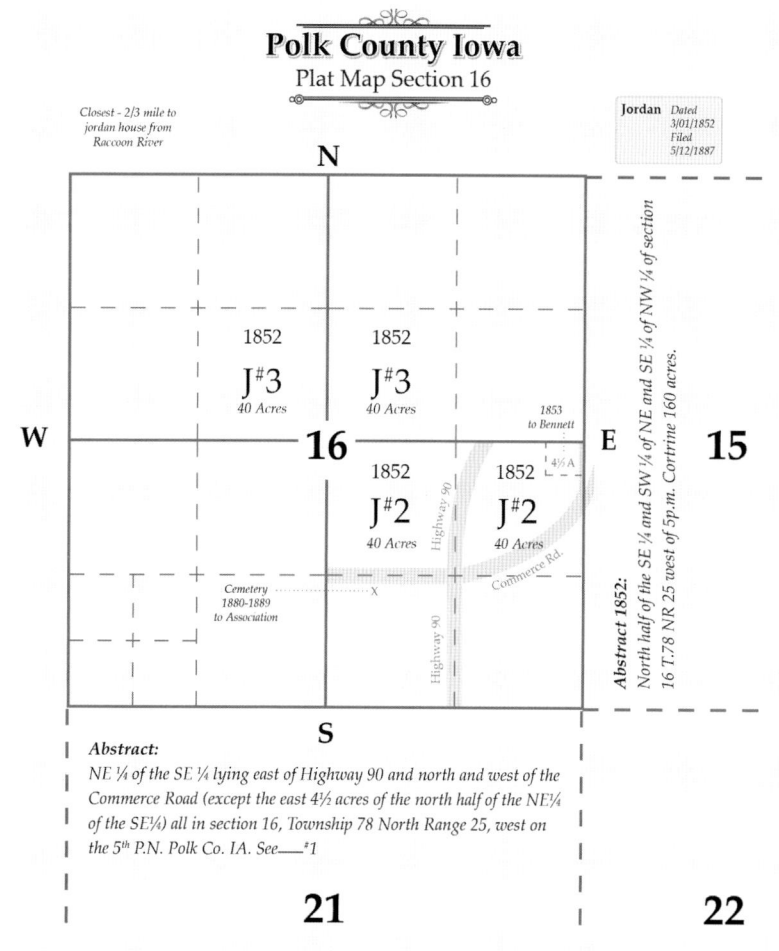

Polk County Iowa
Plat Map Section 16

Closest - 2/3 mile to jordan house from Raccoon River

Jordan Dated 3/01/1852 Filed 5/12/1887

1852 J#3 40 Acres
1852 J#3 40 Acres
1853 to Bennett
16
1852 J#2 40 Acres
1852 J#2 40 Acres
4½ A
Highway 90
Commerce Rd
Cemetery 1880-1889 to Association
X
Highway 90
15
Abstract 1852: North half of the SE ¼ and SW ¼ of NE and SE ¼ of NW ¼ of section 16 T.78 NR 25 west of 5p.m. Cortrine 160 acres.

Abstract:
NE ¼ of the SE ¼ lying east of Highway 90 and north and west of the Commerce Road (except the east 4½ acres of the north half of the NE¼ of the SE¼) all in section 16, Township 78 North Range 25, west on the 5th P.N. Polk Co. IA. See___#1

21
22

"The road to the south of the Jordan Property coming from the east was called "Wagon Trail Road". It was changed to "Commerce Road". Later, the names of both changed. The part of Commerce Road south of the Jordan property going towards Commerce is now known as Grand Avenue. East of that road was called "Valley Drive" and then became "Fuller Road", which was a continuation of the old "Wagon Trail Road" heading west.

James Jordan: His Life and His Legacy

CHAPTER 21
Building a Community

The Birth of the First Pioneer Child

By the time the citizens of Polk County had settled the question of securing their claims in the fall of 1848, a second crop had been harvested at the Jordan farm and the place was beginning to run more smoothly. Melinda had recently given birth to a little boy, the very first pioneer baby to be born in their emerging community that would eventually be known as Walnut Township.

Most of the settlers who had arrived before James and Melinda had left the area. They probably had never intended to stay and put down roots like James and Melinda were doing. The birth of their son caused the young couple to understand that in order for their community to survive and thrive they had to lead the effort.

James and Melinda named their son James Finley Jordan, again after an individual for whom James had great regard: Reverend James B. Finley, a Methodist circuit rider. Finley and other circuit riders he inspired helped bring about a virulent spread of the Methodist religion. He was also notable for other important reasons: Finley himself became involved in prison reform, temperance, rights for Native Americans, women's causes, and slavery. His father freed the slaves he had when Finley was a teenager. When Finley spoke on the subject at a contentious Methodist conference, he said: "How any man can say it is right for him to hold his fellow being in bondage, and buy and sell him at pleasure, put him under an overseer, and drive, whip, and half starve him, and that this is connived by the Methodist Church, I cannot comprehend." When the conference ended, the denomination divided between north and south.

James Jordan, Road Builder

In the early years of pioneer settlement, folks were exploring central Iowa, traveling on the crude wagon paths and "roads" of the time. As a property owner, James had the responsibility to maintain the roads on or adjacent to his farm.

Proceeding right through his property in far western Polk County was a busy wagon trail that ran west out of Fort Des Moines right past the Jordan farmhouse. On the northeast side of his property, the trail crossed Jordan Creek, which was difficult to get over without a bridge, especially during the spring and early summer rains. James was responsible for maintaining the wagon trail roadway and constructing and maintaining the bridge across the creek. No doubt he did an excellent job because he traveled often into Fort Des Moines, and many visitors came out to visit him and Melinda at their home.

Personal convenience was not the only reason James needed to keep his roadway and bridge maintained. In the late 1840s and early 1850s the Mormons were going west, and, even though the "official" Mormon Trail passed south of Des Moines through Osceola, family legend recalls members of the Jordan clan seeing covered wagons belonging to Mormons pass by the house.

Folks were also heading west to the California Gold Rush. Iowa historian Eugene Hastie relates that "during the '40s the state established a state road from Davenport to Council Bluffs. This ran through Fort Des Moines and was the route of the 49er's on their way to the California gold fields. Hastie continues with an excerpt from an article from the *Des Moines Gazette* published on April 26, 1850: "The number of teams that have crossed the Des Moines (River) at this place, for the past week amounts to 199—with 540 men, making the total up to this time of 690 teams and 1,797 persons."

Hastie provides another description of gold rush frenzy:

Many departed for "the land of promise" in the fall of 1849, and an enormous number were planning on leaving the first thing in the spring. The spring of 1850 was a never-to-be-forgotten one. Such a scene was never seen before or since. The mad rush westward gained momentum the further it went, for every section through which it went added some to the swollen numbers. Haste and greed characterized the gold seekers. The old proverb, "The early bird catches the worm" had a real meaning to them, and to get there first was the all-important thing. Delay might cost them a fortune, so they reasoned.

Pursuit of a Dream

Those who joined the gold rush westward were fortunate they departed in the spring of 1850. In 1851 a great flood occurred in the river bottomlands around Fort Des Moines. Flood waters submerged the town and the surrounding area—an event that was remembered for decades.

"Readin', Writin', an' 'Rithmetic"

By 1848, families were beginning to settle in the area around the Jordan farmstead and it was time to get a school started for the children. A young couple, Reverend and Mrs. Ockerman, arrived in Fort Des Moines and Mrs. Ockerman was hired as the teacher in the tiny community beginning to form in western Polk County. In the tradition of the early schoolteachers, she and her husband would "board around," which meant they would live with different families every month during the school year. She was paid $12.00 per month.

The parents of the children provided Mrs. Ockerman with a little log cabin in which to teach their children. It was probably a relief to James and Melinda to now have a schoolhouse in their community. Even though school was being taught in Fort Des Moines in one of the recently abandoned soldier's cabins in Raccoon Row, it was too far away for the young Jordan children to conveniently attend every day. So, in addition to all their other tasks, Melinda and James also had been teaching little Benjamin and Emily at home since their arrival in Iowa two years earlier.

James and Melinda sent Benjamin, nine, and Emily, six, to the local school, but Henry, four, and John, two, were too young. Henry stayed home and helped Melinda with brother John and the new baby. Benjamin and Emily's cousins, Charles, nine, and Jemima, six, the son and daughter of John and Drewsilla Jordan, also attended the school, as well as many others from the many families who by then had settled nearby.

The community was growing and the cabin in which Mrs. Ockerman was teaching was not large enough to hold all the children who wanted to attend school. In 1849 James Jordan, whose farm and stock venture were already beginning to become profitable, commissioned Samuel Hiner, probably a neighbor of his brother John who lived in "Hiner's Grove," to plan and build a real schoolhouse for the children.

The log building Hiner constructed had one log cut out lengthwise the entire length of the building, about four feet from the floor. This opening was for a window which would provide light to the students inside. The cost of construction was $69.00.

Jimmy became the school superintendent and cashier. As superintendent, one of his main responsibilities was to either personally supply firewood to the school or to see that the parents of the schoolchildren took their turn to supply it so the building would be kept warm in winter when school was in session.

James determined the school schedule (students usually got a day off on Christmas and New Year's Day) and was in charge of hiring and firing the teachers. He also found them a place to reside and purchased whatever school equipment the community could afford, such as a blackboard, maps, or a globe.

As cashier, James' job was to pay the teacher; at that time there were no taxes supporting the schools. He did this by collecting money from the parents based on the number of children they had attending the school. Very likely James subsidized the budget, as his biographies all state he was a strong supporter of local education.

The actual location of the Hiner-built schoolhouse

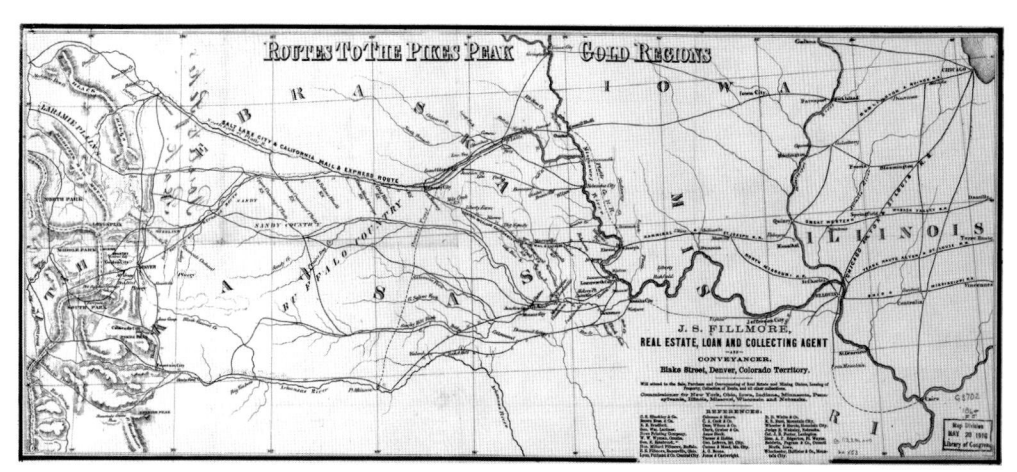

Wagon trails heading west. Library of Congress

has been a puzzle. An account written around the turn of the century states the school was located near the banks of the Raccoon River in the vicinity of what would become Valley Junction but further south and west of there. This was entirely possible, as the school predates mandatory state requirements whereby Section 16 of every township was granted to the state for construction of a school. It would have been equidistant from James Jordan's and John Jordan's cabins.

Early on, James and the other parents in the pioneer community were able to select their own site, convenient to the settlers who were living there at the time. Later, James would build a second log schoolhouse, this one on a hill just east of his house (which was on Section 16) and close to the banks of Jordan Creek. This log schoolhouse was torn down in the 1880s to make room for a new, "modern" building named "Jordan School" build on its footprint. Eventually Jordan School was moved down Fuller Road and became a storage building.

School was usually held only six months of the year during two terms, one in the summer and one in the winter (to coincide with times children were not needed on the farm for planting and harvesting). Thus the building was available for more than educational purposes. Until church congregations constructed buildings, the schoolhouse was often used for Sunday services and perhaps religious revival gatherings in the summer.

The school building was also the community's "advertisement" to attract new settlers to the area. Each schoolhouse competed with the next one. Pioneers like James and Melinda wanted people to settle in their community. The more people living in their area, the greater the chance of establishing a real town. They knew settlers traveling through might be attracted to a well-maintained, warm schoolhouse with a competent teacher and decide to permanently settle in their area.

Pupils often had to travel several miles to attend the school. In the early years, they had come into a sparsely furnished room with almost no equipment. These early schoolhouses were not unlike the one James Jordan had attended thirty years earlier; the seats would be long benches made of planks or split logs, usually along three sides of the room with a few at the front by the teacher. Desks were a slanting shelf fastened to the wall. The blackboard, if there was one, would be a plank or two painted black and fastened to the wall. Erasers were a rag or made of sheepskin wool.

The earliest pupils had no regular textbooks but brought whatever books their parents had carried with them in their covered wagons—maybe a few classics and always the family Bible—standard reading material in most schools. Some students brought almanacs. The few books which the teacher personally owned made up the school's "library." In later years, the schools acquired books for the students: primers for reading, arithmetic books, spelling lists, and so on.

There could be fifteen to thirty children, maybe more, of all ages in a one-room school with only one teacher. The most desirable teacher was a man because he could exert greater discipline. Discipline was harsh—children were often spanked or whipped if they didn't behave. Single female schoolteachers were less desirable because they usually got married upon coming to a new community and quit their teaching job to keep house and raise their families. They might not even finish out the six-month school term. Teachers were hired by the term, so in one year students could have two or three different teachers.

Pioneers traveling by covered wagon. From *A New and Popular Pictorial History of the United States* by Robert Sears, 1848

Just like James Jordan's school back in Virginia, the "Three Rs" (readin', writin', an' 'rithmetic) were taught along with spelling, geography, and history. Probably due to scarcity of books and materials, there was very little emphasis on the classics. Spelling was considered very important. As in James' boyhood school in western Virginia, to be able to "spell down the room" in a spelling bee was a real honor.

In writing, the boys and girls used small slates or copy books, if available, and pens made from goose quills. Mothers made the ink at home from maple bark and copperas. The pupils would practice their writing by copying a sentence the teacher had written.

The level of instruction was completely individualized based on the student's competency in the books he or she presented to the teacher on the first day of school, as well as on the teacher's own preparation. The teachers had very little education and schools were not graded, but students usually started at the front of their book at the beginning of every term and went as far as they could, then started all over again at the beginning of the next term.

The school day always opened with the reading of a chapter from the Bible by one of the students. Often they could read better than the itinerant preachers who spoke on Sundays. Most instruction revolved around small groups of students called up to the benches in the front of the room to recite for the teacher. Because of this there was perpetual noise in the classroom.

The day was not all work and no play. During lunchtime students would play outside at games such as Pussy Wants a Corner, Pull Away, I Am On Dickie's Land, Ring Around the Rosie, Needle Eye, Drop the Handkerchief, Poison, Annie Annie Over, and other games. In the winter they slid on frozen ponds, sledded down hills, and had snowball fights.

To spend a little time away from the schoolhouse, a student could volunteer to carry the water bucket and go after water from a spring or farm. Sometimes these were as much as a quarter mile away. Upon returning to the room, the student would offer water first to the teacher and then to the pupils, all drinking out of the same long-handled dipper.

In later years, the schools, school supplies, and quality of teaching improved; however, many things did not change. Children were a necessity as helpers on the family farms, but if they stayed in school, they might progress by age sixteen or eighteen to long division in arithmetic. These proficient students could then qualify to become teachers themselves. Many young men who became teachers lasted one or two years until they were either exhausted, had saved up enough money to purchase some land and become a farmer, or finance the pursuit of further educational or professional goals. Becoming a teacher was generally the means to an end, not a career goal.

Several of the Jordan children progressed to high school and into college. Henry attended Forest Home Seminary (later the Baptist College) and after the Civil War, at the age of nineteen, won an appointment to West Point. James studied to be a teacher at Simpson College in Indianola.

Emily attended Mrs. Thompson (Anna) Bird's Female Seminary, which was located in Fort Des Moines near Second and Walnut Streets. Mrs. Bird was the wife of the Presbyterian minister who was also Fort Des Moines' first mayor. In keeping with the Presbyterian tradition of literacy, Mrs. Bird established a school where children of the settlers would learn to read—and study other subjects as well. Starting in an abandoned cabin at the former fort, Anna Bird's school soon moved into a newly constructed building in 1851. Emily attended there before continuing her education at Northwestern University in Chicago. Many years later, the Des Moines Public Schools would remember Anna P. Bird when they built a schoolhouse at Twenty-first and Woodland and named it "Bird School."

Reverend Thompson Bird, Fort Des Moines' first civil leader. From Beginnings: Reminiscences of Early Des Moines by Tacitus Hussey

CHAPTER 22
James Jordan, Methodist

For over half a century, being a Methodist had been the Jordan family tradition. When individuals married into the family they became Methodists if they weren't so already. And, of course, all the new babies born into the Jordan clan were baptized as Methodists. James Jordan biographies never fail to mention what a zealous Methodist he was throughout his life.

Local Church Services

Pioneers like James Jordan were puritans. They were devoted to working their land, tending their livestock, raising their families, and adhering to their religious beliefs. While the few newspapers and almanacs available were read, there was a noted absence of books in most pioneer homes. A major reason was difficulty in transporting them. Books were not necessities like food and tools. However, the main reason there were few books in pioneer cabins at the time was because only one book was important to these settlers, and that was the Bible.

Pioneers followed the Bible literally. It was the one great and universal guide. Pioneers focused on the life hereafter. They did their best to live their lives as free from sin as possible so they could hope to go to heaven. They did not want to burn in hell, which they fully believed was a possible fate.

Pioneers put a great burden on themselves to lead perfect lives, and for some this could lead to a narrow life, possibly one laced with bigotry. However, it enforced a code of behavior and provided valuable structure to citizens who were trying to forge a lifestyle out of the wilderness where it was every man for himself, with no one to enforce rules and laws.

The calendar the early pioneers followed was secular, and religious holidays such as Christmas and Easter were minimally celebrated. Fourth of July was the "Big Day" of the year. In the early years, musical instruments were banned from homes of the higher-class settlers, and in the more conservative Methodist families, such as the Jordans, dancing was not allowed. Whiskey was consumed only for medicinal purposes.

On Sunday, worship services were held all day. In the early years, hymns might have been sung in church but without a piano or organ. At that time many Methodist services were led by untrained preachers who were not scholarly people; however, they had "heard the calling" and had been ordained, which authorized them to preach.

People spent most of their week working, establishing their homesteads, building and maintaining their cabins and outbuildings, tending to children and livestock, and farming their land. Sunday church meetings gave them all a welcome break in a monotonous routine of hard work.

Church was an important way for folks to socialize. Opportunities for socializing generally occurred before and after worship and during the noon-time break, when neighbors could relax and enjoy each other's company.

The only "entertainment," aside from the summer camp revival meetings, might be an occasional traveling circus. In the evenings, the families in pioneer homes spent the close of the day reading a chapter or two from the Bible. While sending their children to school was important to pioneer parents, with school held only six months out of the year, children learned much more from the role-modeling and training provided to them by their parents, neighbors, and relatives—all based upon the puritan pioneer lifestyle on the prairie.

Circuit Riders and Itinerant Preachers

In the early settlement days of Fort Des Moines and Walnut Township, "Uncle Jimmy" opened his cabin to the itinerant Methodist preachers who "rode circuit" in the area. There was no church in Fort Des Moines until 1848 when the Methodists built the first one at Fifth Avenue and Walnut Street. When possible, the Jordan family would attend services there, but often the Sabbath was honored in the Jordan home or at the community school, with either John Jordan, a neighbor, or an itinerant preacher leading the services.

One circuit rider by the name of Reverend Raynor preached in the Jordan cabin in 1849. When another itinerant preacher came to the Jordan home the story was told that Uncle Jimmy mistakenly handed him a bound version of the *Congressional Globe* instead of the family Bible from which to read. The Jordan cabin was described, according to L. F. Andrew, as "the mecca of circuit riders and preachers. They liked his yellow-legged chickens and sumptuous table spread, for he was a good provider."

A religion particularly suited to "Westward Expansion," Methodism's system of circuit riders was key in carrying the church's message to the widely scattered people of the frontier. Perhaps of greater importance was the denomination's willingness to use local preachers and lay ministers of limited educational backgrounds during the first generation or two of frontier life. In the early years of Methodism, ministers were drawn from the neighborhood. No special training was needed, just a deep belief and commitment. In this way, new congregations could begin immediately if there were enough families to form one. This facilitated the rapid growth of the Methodist church all over the United States and specifically in the early years in the state of Iowa.

Prayer Meetings and Camp Meetings

In Iowa pioneer communities like the one in which James and Melinda lived, the absence of church buildings at times necessitated holding prayer meetings in people's homes. James and Melinda always made their home available. These meetings in the Jordan parlor may have been emotional and animated.

A meeting similar to those at the Jordan's house is described by Rebecca and Edward Burland:

> The company being assembled and seated, the one acting as leader rose from his seat which was the signal for the others to do the same. A sort of circle was then immediately formed by the whole assembly taking hands and capering about the house surprisingly. Their gesture could not be called dancing and yet no term describes it better. This done, worship commenced with extempore prayer, not in language or style the best selected. All the persons being again seated, an individual started from his seat, exclaiming in a loud and frantic shriek, "I feel it!," meaning what is commonly termed the power of God. His motions, which appeared half convulsive, were observed with animated joy by the rest, till he fell apparently still upon the floor where he lay unmolested a short time and then resumed his seat. Others were affected in a similar manner, only in some instances the power of speech was not suspended and the person lying on the floor continued to shout.

As back in western Virginia and points west, the early churches in Iowa collaborated interdenominationally and sponsored religious gatherings called "camp meetings." These were held annually during the warm months at some gathering spot, with everyone camping out in the open air. Camp meetings were advertised as two-day meetings, but generally took up the greater part of the week. According to W. J. Petersen, Iowa historian:

> While the hysteria for religious expression which had swept through the nation a little earlier had somewhat died away by the time Iowa was settled, revival services were popular and there were many camp meetings in Iowa during the early days. Whole families for many miles around came to these meetings and sometimes stayed for several days. Exhortations and threats and joyful singing, accompanied by tears, moans, and abasement, followed in swift succession. The repressions stored up in the lonely lives of toiling men and women found an opportunity for release in these religious experiences.

Women were particularly fond of the camp meeting, which was the one public event they claimed as their own. When it was camp-meeting time, work was put aside and a family might camp out for a few days of vacation. The simple cold meals freed women from most of their cooking chores, and it was one of the only times of the year when wives were free from housework. Women responded by getting into the thick of the meeting; it was often women who were the most prone to emotionalism, who would "get the jerks."

Men were freed from work, too, and many used camp meetings as occasions for general rowdiness and recreation. Only about three-fourths of the men actually came into the meetings; the rest stayed on the fringes and got into mischief, which included drinking, wrestling, playing, swearing, and yelling. According to John M. Faragher, "There was more harm done to the morals of the youth in this fringe area than there was religious good effected on the campground." This may have been one of the many reasons why James was such an advocate of prohibition.

James Jordan's biographer L. F. Andrew said: "Jordan was a firm believer in the school and church as promoters of civilization and good government, and his labor and purse were given freely to each." James would eventually build two Methodist churches on or near his property. He would die while attending services on the far west side of Des Moines in a church that was named after him—Jordan Methodist Church.

Methodism and the Abolitionists

Scores of Iowans who were abolitionists embraced the Methodist religion. Back East during the Methodist annual general conferences in the late 1830s and early 1840s, the slavery question was debated back and forth. The antislavery folks were led by Reverend James B. Finley (for whom James Jordan named his son James Finley Jordan). These disagreements lasted until 1845 when, during a meeting in Louisville, Kentucky, proslavery Methodists separated and formed their own church, the Methodist Episcopal Church, South. The split with the southern Methodists resulted in a renewed abolitionist commitment and stronger resolve by northern antislavery Methodists, especially those in New England and New York.

Methodists from southern states who did not want to be a part of a slave-enmeshed society were attracted to Iowa, which was a "free" territory. It is interesting to note that, in 1844 and 1845 when the Methodist split took place, James and Melinda and John and Drewsilla Jordan moved out of Missouri, a slave state, and up to Iowa, a free state. They did not want to deal with slavery in "their own back yard," as they had been forced to do in Virginia.

Family Transitions

The strong faith of the Jordan family members held them in good stead during some sad times. On the Fourth of July 1849, Melinda's sister, Drewsilla, died while giving birth to her fourth baby. She had lost a previous pregnancy a few years earlier, and this one had been difficult as well. The baby, named Mary Melinda Dewitt Jordan, survived and was cared for by Melinda. However, little Mary died of congestion a few months later on October 2. How devastating it must have been for Melinda to lose her beloved sister, whom she had been separated from only a few short times in her life, and then to suffer a second loss—her namesake, the little baby, Mary Melinda.

Drewsilla's husband, John, was also devastated. Always emotional and ebullient, he threw himself into his religion, becoming officially sanctioned in 1850 by the Methodist church to be an "exhorter," a title he held for the next twenty years. Bereft and miserable, John decided to get away for a while. Always the adventurer, he decided to go off to the Gold Rush and joined the stream of wagons winding their way through Iowa in 1849 bound for California.

John left his two children, Charles and Jemima, in the loving hands of Aunt Melinda and Uncle Jimmy. They would remain with them until Melinda's death six years later.

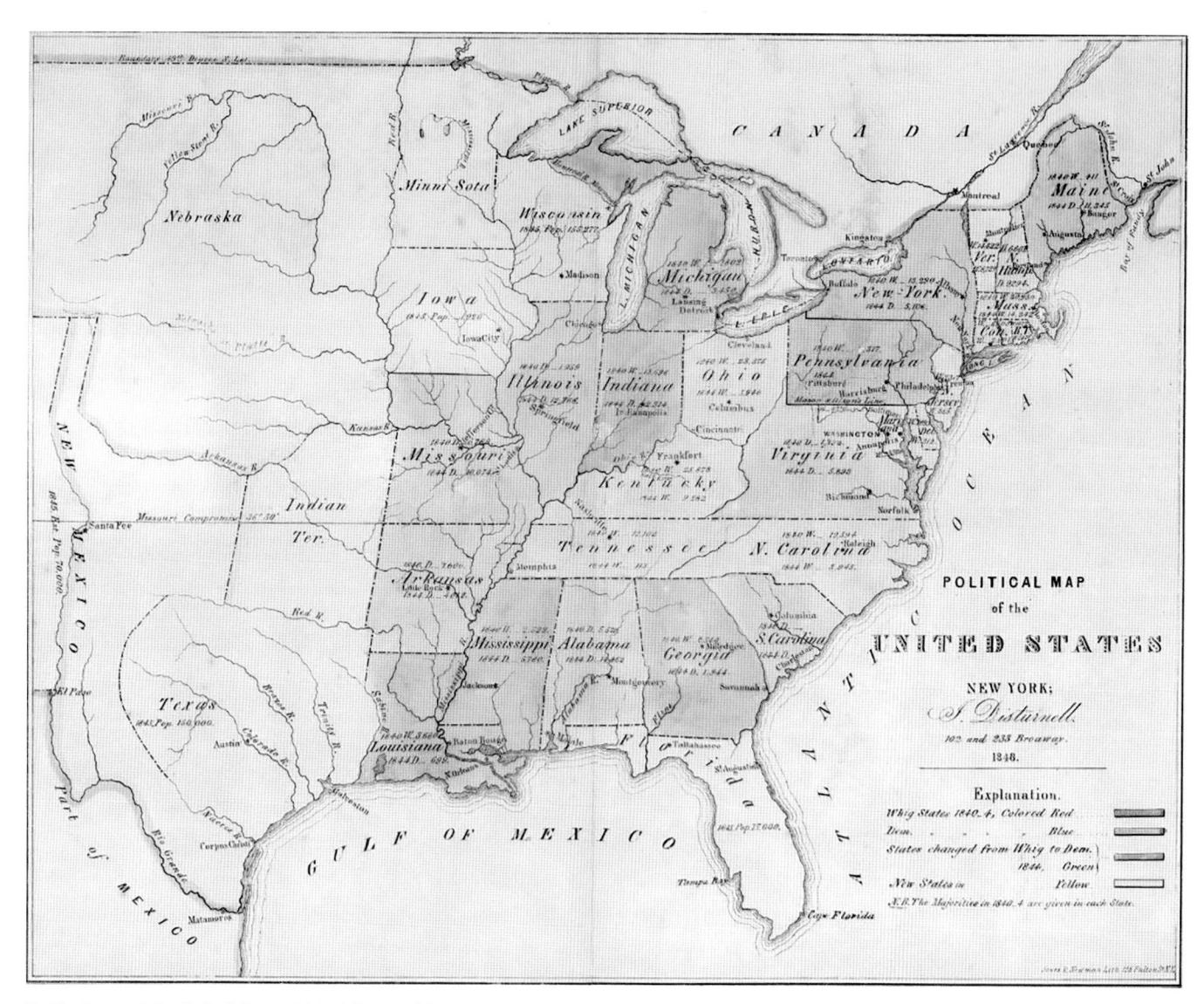

Political map of the United States, 1848. Library of Congress

CHAPTER 23
Uncle Jimmy's New House

The seven children of James and Melinda Jordan and their siblings John and Drewsilla were growing up. Charles and Ben were both twelve, Jemima was eleven, and Emily nine. Henry was seven, John was five, and there was the toddler, James. In 1851, baby George Benton Jordan was born, bringing the number of children in James and Melinda's household up to eight.

George Benton Jordan was named for several Georges: George Jordan, James' German great-great-grandfather; James' beloved older brother George; and also George Washington, the first president of the United States. His middle name was from Thomas Hart Benton, a five-term senator from the state of Missouri. Benton was the author of the first Homestead Acts and pushed hard for public support of the transcontinental railway. Though he owned slaves, Benton came to oppose the institution of slavery and demonstrated this by opposing the Compromise of 1850 as too favorable to proslavery interests.

Building a "Real House"

As James and Melinda had hoped would happen in the five years since their arrival in Polk County, Iowa, their livestock business had become quite successful. It was time for them to provide their family with a "real house" instead of a log cabin. Since the arrival of nephew Charles and niece Jemima, and with new baby George, James and Melinda needed more room.

There was another reason the Jordans wanted a bigger place in which to live. James' sister Anna and her family had moved from Missouri to Madison County, Iowa, and settled near Winterset. James' brother George and his family were planning to move north to Iowa, as well. Being a close-knit group, the relatives were sure to visit James and Melinda often.

Melinda and James had already built a kitchen house about twenty-five to thirty feet west of the cabin. This building was comprised of two rooms: a kitchen and an office on either side of a massive double fireplace. On the kitchen side the fireplace offered a large interior space in which to place Melinda's cook stove. In future years, the front of the fireplace would be cemented shut and a very large wood-burning stove would be placed in front of the fireplace, with the chimney in use to vent the smoke from the stove.

On the other side of the fireplace was James Jordan's warm and cozy office. It was divided into a small sitting area with a separate closet-like room just off of it. The sitting room, which contained a small fireplace, was a place for his clients and friends to come and visit. The adjacent closet was where he kept his desk and safe. It was a secure space with a door he kept locked when he was not in the office.

A covered breezeway had also been constructed between the back of the cabin and the kitchen/office building. Porch-like, it was a place where the family gathered for meals on the warm summer days, as well as a protected passageway to go back and forth from the cabin to the kitchen and office. To the south of the breezeway was a giant old oak tree that offered shade during mealtime on hot summer days.

James retained the breezeway but had the cabin taken down and the logs hauled away. He had the cellar under the cabin re-excavated, enlarging the space. The new cellar walls were then lined with limestone blocks. After the house was finished, a stairway was built where a trapdoor had been that led down into the basement. The stairway divided the cellar into two rooms, one on the north side and one the south side. An exterior stairway on the north side of the foundation was also dug that led down to a door opening into the basement for easier access from outside.

The cellar had a packed dirt floor and a brick chimney, in front of which stood the iron stove that had been salvaged from the old cabin. This stove would provide heat to the bedroom above.

The two-story house faced east, and upon entering the front door one was impressed by a great staircase leading to a wide upstairs hallway. Opposite the front door at the end of the first floor hallway was the back door to the breezeway.

On the first floor, there were two rooms directly above and larger than the basement rooms. These two rooms were used as living quarters—the one on the south was a parlor with its entry immediately to the left of the front door and the room on the north, a bedroom for James and Melinda. The bedroom was entered through a door behind the stairway. This room contained a closet, which was unusual for the times. The bedroom was located above the room in the basement that had the stove, which kept the room above it warm and cozy in the winter. Because of that, this room was where the family spent a lot of time together during the colder months.

Proceeding up the stairway to the second floor was a hallway parallel to the stairway, on either side of which was a bedroom. The larger one on the south side of the stairs was for the five boys. The smaller one on the north side of the stairway was for the two girls. The girls' bedroom may have been warm in the winter, as it was above the parents' bedroom. The boys' bedroom was heated by a small stove in the room. The baby slept in a cradle near James and Melinda in their cozy first-floor bedroom.

To finish the project, the house, breezeway, and kitchen/office in the rear was sided with milled boards, probably from Parmalee's Mill in Carlisle. They were probably left unpainted.

The logs from the dismantled Jordan cabin were taken across Jordan Creek and rebuilt into a schoolhouse. It was appropriate to do this, as schoolhouses were supposed to be built on Section 16 of a township and that section was on the Jordan farm.

Except for the schoolhouse, the new Jordan parlor was the largest room in their local community. In addition to being used for social gatherings, it was also put into use for other functions. For many years it served as the community meeting place and also as a gathering place for religious meetings when itinerant preachers passed through. It also provided a large space needed for funerals. Bodies were "laid out" in the northeast corner of the room. When James became involved in politics, the leaders of the state of Iowa and beyond assembled in this room to discuss the issues of the day.

On April 5, 1852, James was elected as a township trustee of Fort Des Moines. The Jordans had become respected leaders in their local community. Melinda Jordan was recognized as an exemplary wife and mother, and James' reputation was that of an affable, generous, and hospitable host. His door was always open to travelers, circuit riders, friends, relatives, and anyone in need. As he matured, James' nickname changed from "Jimmy" to "Uncle Jimmy." It was *more* than a reflection of his Virginia roots; it was an old-fashioned way of showing respect to a man well-liked and highly regarded, locally and beyond.

The new home was symbolic of all the hard work they had accomplished together. One could not have done it without the other. True partners, they worked together toward common goals, and their success was a result of their combined diligence and faith, that with hard work they would create a good life for themselves, their family, and their community.

Jordan farmhouse sketch by Bill Wagner.

James Jordan: His Life and His Legacy

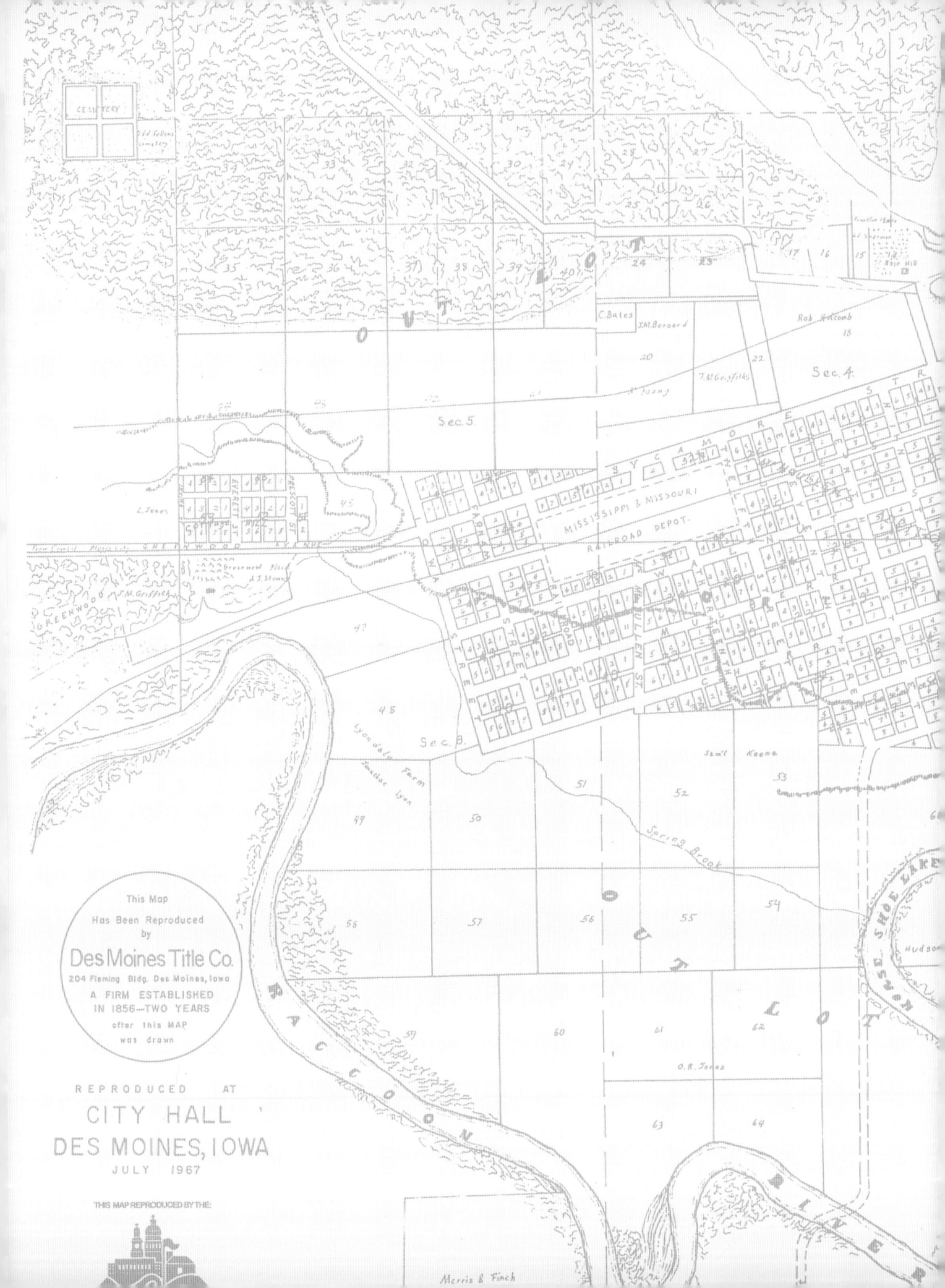

This Map
Has Been Reproduced
by
Des Moines Title Co.
204 Fleming Bldg. Des Moines, Iowa
A FIRM ESTABLISHED
IN 1856—TWO YEARS
after this MAP
was drawn

REPRODUCED AT
CITY HALL
DES MOINES, IOWA
JULY 1967

THIS MAP REPRODUCED BY THE:

Part Four

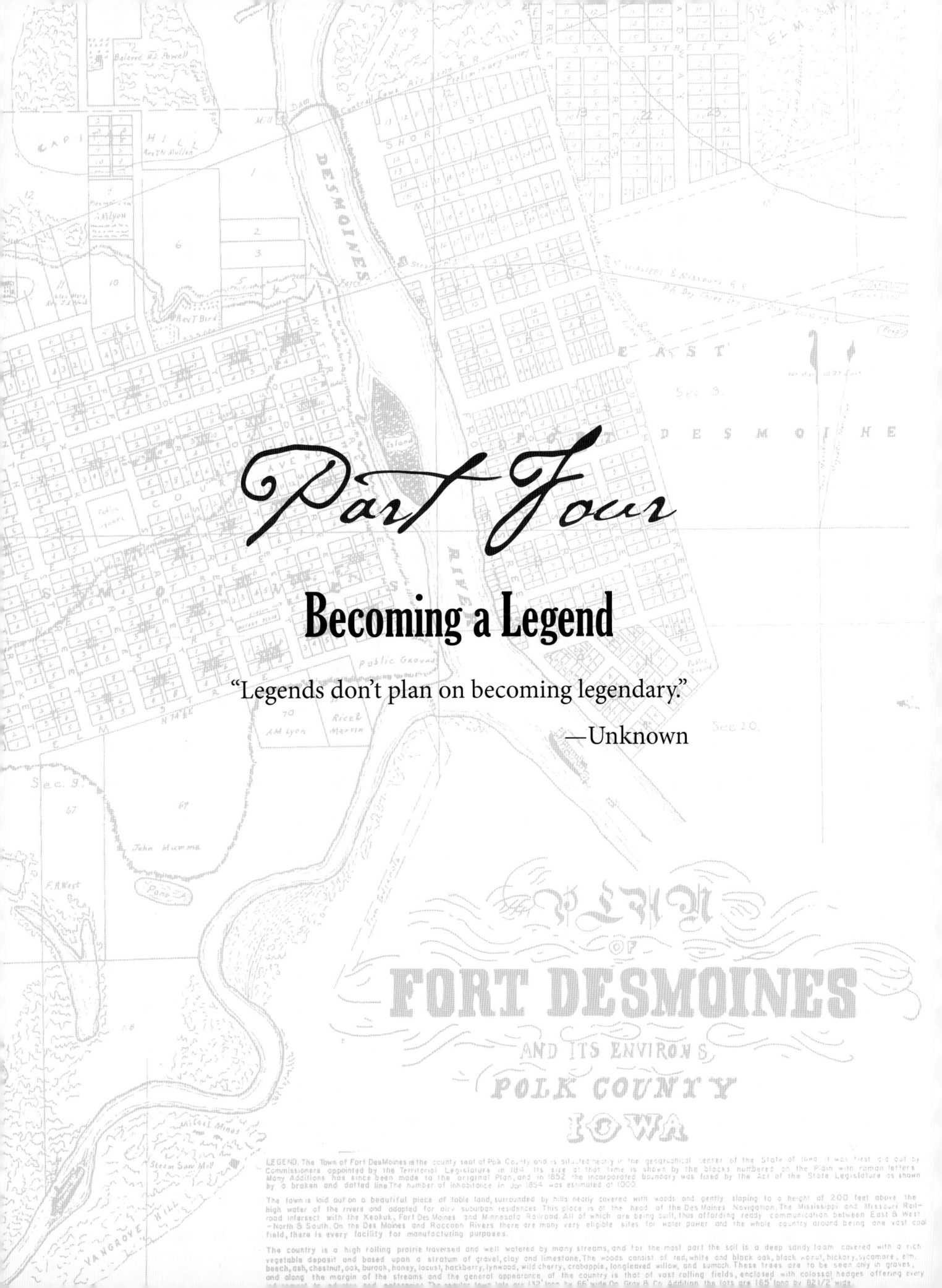

Becoming a Legend

"Legends don't plan on becoming legendary."

—Unknown

CHAPTER 24
"Honorable" James C. Jordan

To receive the title of "honorable," one has to be elected to an honorable political position. James Jordan, Fort Des Moines Township trustee, livestock dealer, and successful farmer, decided—with some persuasion— to enter the world of state politics. The title was not important to him but getting the job done was.

Fort Des Moines, 1854

Probably because he was a township trustee, it had become Uncle Jimmy's habit to make regular trips into the city of Fort Des Moines. Only five and a half miles away, Fort Des Moines was a quick ride on a horse-drawn sleigh in the winter or with a horse and buggy in the summer and fall. During the spring, travel was a little more difficult, as the roadways became muddy and could be temporarily impassable.

During the months school was in session, he probably took his daughter Emily to Mrs. Bird's Female Seminary at Second and Walnut Streets. From there it was a short trip to the post office, located near the wharf, where mail would arrive once a week from downriver in Keokuk, past various stops on the Des Moines River.

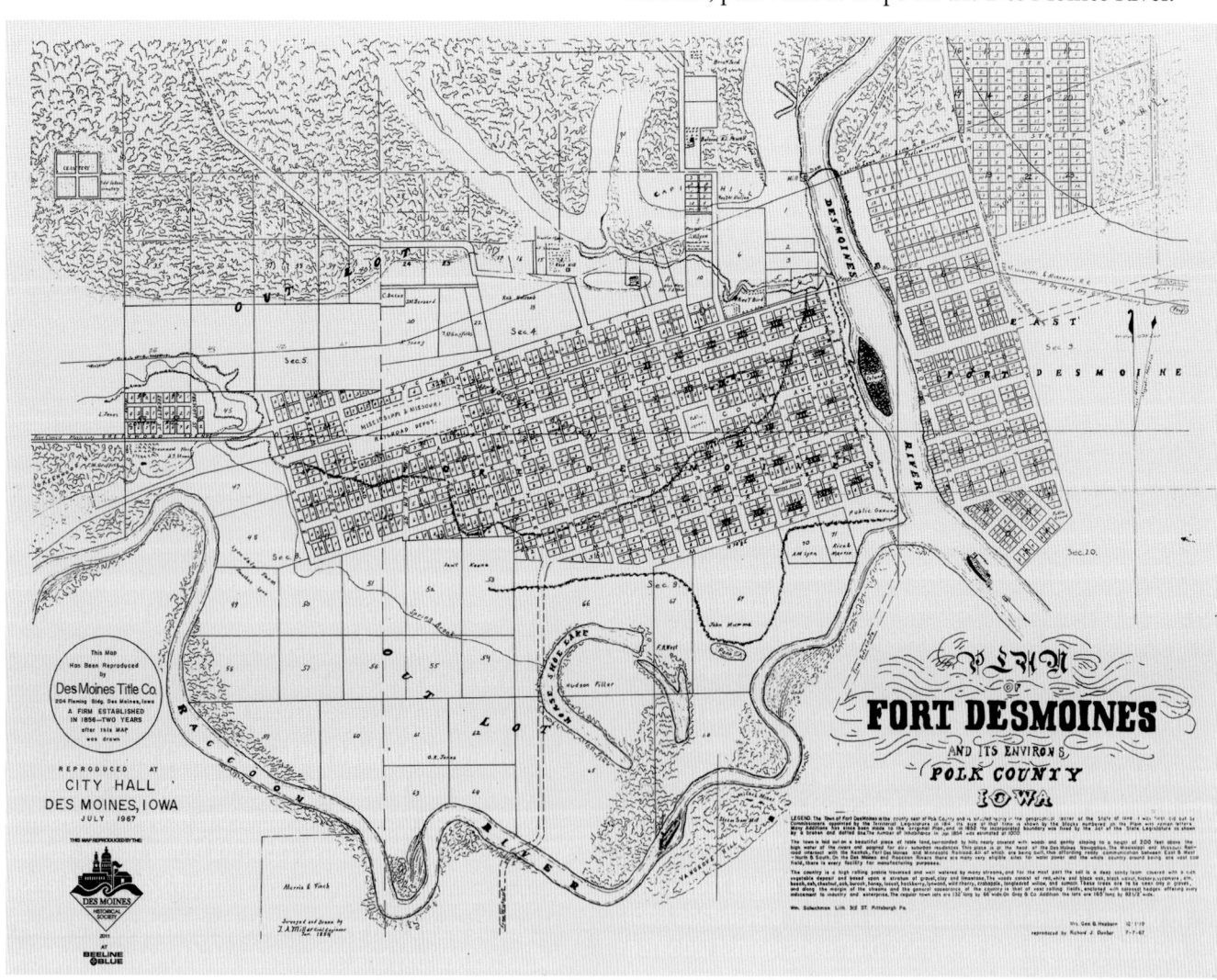

Map of Fort Des Moines, 1854. Courtesy of Des Moines Historical Society

106 *Pursuit of a Dream*

Once James got into the town of Fort Des Moines, travel wasn't much better than in the springtime months, as the city streets resembled cow paths. They were narrow, without curbs, dark at night, and ankle deep in dust or mud, depending on the precipitation. People complained of mud holes, piles of wood, and other debris in the streets. Horses, hogs, chickens, dogs, and cows wandered freely around the town. An early schoolteacher, Arizona Perkins, described her less-than-favorable impressions of the town in a letter she wrote to the folks back home in 1851:

> This is one of the strangest looking "cities" I ever saw. . . . This town is at the juncture of the Des Moines and Raccoon Rivers. It is mostly a level prairie with a few swells or hills around it. We have a court house of "brick," and one church, a plain, framed building belonging to the Methodists. There are two taverns here, one of which has a most important little bell that rings together some fifty boarders. I cannot tell you how many dwellings there are, for I have not counted them; some are of logs, some of brick, some framed, and some are the remains of the old dragoon houses. . . . The people support two papers and there are several dry goods shops. I have been into but four of them. . . . Society is as varied as the buildings are. There are people from nearly every state, and Dutch, Swedes, etc.

In the early days the residents held horse races on the main streets of Fort Des Moines. That was how the Methodist church got its bell. One of the parishioners jokingly said he would pay for a church bell if the Sexton dared to use it to start a horse race. The Sexton, dearly wanting the bell, complied, but the bell was used by the conservative Methodists only once, for the reason that it was won on a bet. Gambling was not an acceptable activity in the Methodist church.

In spite of its backwoods location and provincial lifestyle, after the early 1850s Fort Des Moines was starting to take off. The town had competed with Oskaloosa for the lucrative appointment as the next site in Iowa for a land office. Because of the intense lobbying efforts of Des Moines lawyer Phineas Casady, Fort Des Moines was chosen.

Starting about 1853, land agents were numerous in Fort Des Moines, and hotels were crowded with hopeful homesteaders and scheming speculators. Livery men did a big business renting trams and carriages to prospective buyers who drove outside of town for miles to find land in good locations. The volume of business in land sales was extraordinary. Sometimes the land office would take in as much as $25,000 in gold for one day's business, and that was at a rate of $1.25 per acre for government land.

Uncle Jimmy and all of his cronies were in the thick of this extremely profitable sport. He and his friends bought and sold land, constantly making profits each time they closed a sale. At the time of James' death he had holdings all over Des Moines and central Iowa. During his lifetime he gave entire farms to most of his children—because he owned thousands and thousands of acres.

The 1854 Election

Some of the visitors James and Melinda entertained in the parlor of their new house were politically inclined friends who, early in 1854, attempted to persuade James, now known as "one of the leading farmers of interior Iowa," to run for the state senate seat being vacated by Dr. Andrew Hull. Iowa historian Johnson Brigham wrote of Dr. Hull:

> An interesting product of frontier conditions was Andrew Y. Hull, of Polk County, who took his seat in the Senate of the Fourth General Assembly representing twenty-four counties in the then sparsely settled interior of northern and northwestern Iowa.
>
> Hull was the pioneer physician of Polk County but opportunities for public and private service were so numerous that we find him rounding out a mixed career as land speculator, town promoter, editor, politician, and legislator.
>
> He was equally "at home on his feet" as pleader for the relocation of the state capital or as lecturer before the pioneer medical society of Central Iowa on "The Wants of the Medical Profession." He was the father of John A. T. Hull, a longtime representative of the Des Moines District in Congress.

Fort Des Moines had been successful in 1846, when on May 25 of that year the village had been officially named the county seat. Another town to the east, called Brooklyn, two miles back from the river near the present state fairgrounds, was in hot contention for the honor. A commission, which had been called by the state legislature, was appointed and Fort Des Moines was named the county seat of Polk County.

A few years later, in the early 1850s, the burning issue amongst the movers and shakers in Fort Des Moines was how to get the state legislature to approve moving the capital from Iowa City to their town. At that time, only those with vision could imagine that the town of Fort Des Moines would have the potential to be grand enough to be the capital city of Iowa. It was so far away from the more-settled eastern part of the state. Traveling to Fort Des Moines could be challenging; in the winter it was a long, cold ride by stagecoach, wagon, or horseback and impossible to get to by steamboat on the frozen rivers. During some of the warm months, when the spring floods were over, it *might* be approachable by steamboat if the water was high enough in the river, but there was no guarantee of consistent steamboat transportation to Fort Des Moines from points downstream. The railroad, which would make travel to western Iowa much easier, did not yet reach the city, and it would be a long time coming.

However, there was a contingent of local Fort Des Moines advocates, including Senator Hull, who had the mindset that it could be done. According to Des Moines historian H. B. Turrill, "... scarcely had the Raccoon Fork (another way of referring to Fort Des Moines) emerged from the wilderness before the builders of Fort Des Moines began to think of their little town as the future capital of Iowa."

Senator Hull had been campaigning for years to move Iowa's capital to Fort Des Moines, and during the fourth legislative session in Iowa City (1852–53) he formally introduced a bill to the Iowa Senate to move the Iowa capital to Fort Des Moines.

This issue was of great interest to James Jordan, but other political issues of the time deeply interested him as well. One was the establishment of a state bank. Another concern was the myriad of slavery issues being argued in the political arena at that time. Plus, there was an opportunity to enact prohibition, a cause dear to James Jordan's Methodist heart.

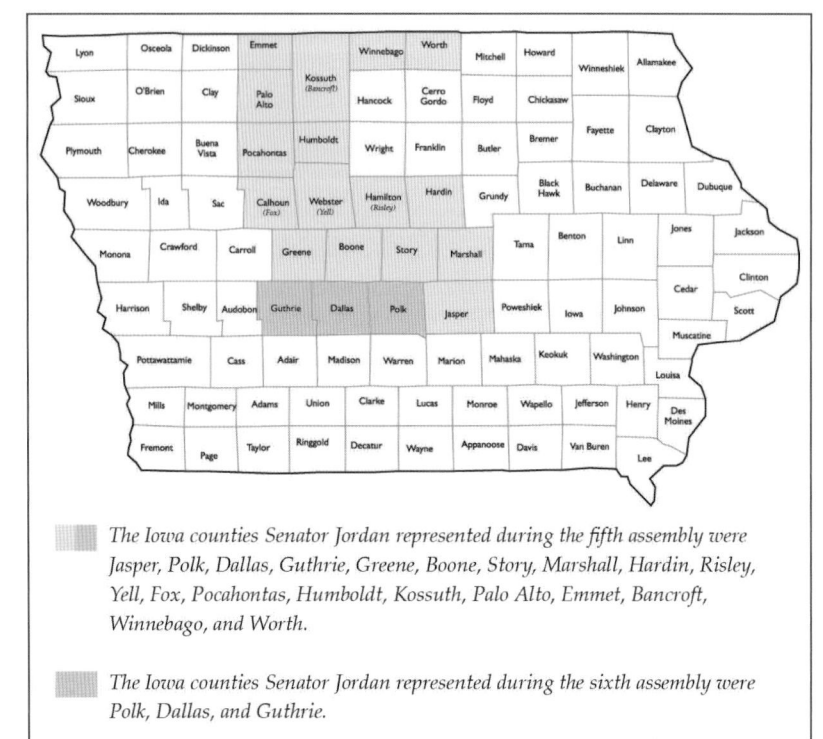

The Iowa counties Senator Jordan represented during the fifth assembly were Jasper, Polk, Dallas, Guthrie, Greene, Boone, Story, Marshall, Hardin, Risley, Yell, Fox, Pocahontas, Humboldt, Kossuth, Palo Alto, Emmet, Bancroft, Winnebago, and Worth.

The Iowa counties Senator Jordan represented during the sixth assembly were Polk, Dallas, and Guthrie.

Initially reluctant, James accepted the challenge and entered the state senatorial race to replace Hull. The slavery issue ended up being the most prominent in the election of 1854, which James was very comfortable embracing. Moving the capital would have to take a back seat.

The Democrats had dominated US Senate representation since Iowa had begun sending senators to Washington. However, a new wind was blowing. Too many federal laws, supreme court decisions, and other resolutions made in Washington had compromised the focus on antislavery and state's rights of many Iowans. They knew the only way for the nation to change its pattern was to vote for antislavery candidates at the grass roots level.

Among those addressing that mandate in the 1854 Iowa elections were:
- James W. Grimes, a fervent abolitionist characterized as a "radical Whig," who was running for the office of governor.
- James Harlan of Mount Pleasant, who was running for the US Senate position as an antislavery candidate. He was the president of Iowa Wesleyan College. Opposing Harlan was the Democrat and proslavery incumbent Augustus C. Dodge.

108   **Pursuit of a Dream**

James W. Grimes. Library of Congress

James Harlan. From *High Points of Iowa History* by Eugene N. Hastie, 1971

- James Jordan, an antislavery candidate from Polk County's Whig Party, running against proslavery candidate Theophilus Bryan, a Guthrie County Democrat. This contest would decide who would become the state senator representing a twenty-county area in north central Iowa.

The US Senatorial election at the time was a sort of domino-effect process. After the citizens cast their votes for either Jordan or Bryan to become a member of Iowa's general assembly, the winning candidate would proceed to the Iowa legislature where another election would be held. There the state senators would vote for one of the two candidates running for the US Senate seat to represent Iowa in Washington, DC. The two contestants in the US Senate race were James Harlan (antislavery) and Augustus Dodge (proslavery).

It would turn out to be a race where each step in the election process was hotly contested because the stakes were high; nationwide, the proslavery and antislavery forces each wanted control of the US Senate as a result of the 1854 election. It was up to each state senate to decide whether their state would be represented by a proslavery or antislavery US Senator.

"Aliens" are Discovered!

Initial election returns were not favorable for Jordan; his opponent Theophilus Bryan had gotten a majority of the votes, thus winning the election. Bryan received the commission, accepted his seat, and voted for Dodge for US Senator, who was officially appointed by the Iowa legislature as the US Senator from Iowa.

Senator Dodge would not be in office for long. It was discovered that in Jasper County, just prior to the election, a large number of "aliens" (people not eligible to vote) had been recruited on the streets and roads, and their names were recorded in the poll books as having voted for James' opponent, Theophilus Bryan. The Whigs contested the election count and the votes were recounted, removing the "aliens'" votes. This time, Bryan was eighty-five votes short. Bryan was ousted, and James Jordan was seated.

James Jordan: His Life and His Legacy

A reelection then took place for US Senator. With James' vote, proslavery incumbent Senator Dodge was dismissed and antislavery Harlan was elected to the US Senate. With the election of James Grimes for Iowa governor, James Harlan for US Senate, and James Jordan for state senator, the antislavery candidates had won in Iowa.

A New Location for Iowa's Capital

Having won on the issue of abolishing slavery, Senator Jordan was now free to promote the cause of his predecessor, Dr. Hull, the leader of the movement to change the Iowa capital from Iowa City to Des Moines.

In 1846, when Iowa had become a state, and then again in 1848, bills had been introduced to the state legislature to move the capital to a more central location in Iowa. There was reluctance initially because the majority of Iowa's population at that time was in eastern Iowa. Legislative discussions in 1847 concluded, *if moved*, the capital should be in the exact geographical center of the state. This location, according to their calculations, turned out to be in Jasper County between the Skunk and Des Moines Rivers about two miles southeast of Prairie City.

A tract two miles north and south by two and one-half miles east and west was laid out and named "Monroe City." A group was charged with the responsibility of preparing the site. They all happened to be Quakers. The Quakers selected the site and platted out the land on an open prairie, punctured with gopher holes and inhabited with prairie dogs, six miles from the Des Moines River and so uninhabitable it was several miles from any settler's cabin. After platting the land of the imaginary community that would be located there, they bought up all the choice lots. Speculators joined the Quakers and invested in lots the Quakers had not purchased, in nonexistent "Monroe City."

When they heard about the isolated location of "Monroe City" and the shenanigans happening there, the Iowa legislature decided the site was inadequate, and in 1848 the Iowa General Assembly voted to vacate the land, refund the investors' money, and look elsewhere.

The positive result of this aborted attempt to relocate the capital was that Iowans were introduced to and accepted the concept that ultimately the capital *would* be moved, and it would be moved to a site *further* west.

The principal of "manifest destiny" had become a reality; central and western Iowa were filling up with people.

The question was again: Where? The cities of Marshalltown, Newton, Oskaloosa, Pella, Red Rock, and Fort Des Moines were all favored spots, with Oskaloosa and Fort Des Moines being the most frequently discussed.

The race was on, and citizens of the two towns worked diligently to persuade the legislature that their town was the best place. They gathered names on petitions, offered free land for the site of the capitol building, and promised money to build it.

In 1852, Senator Hull formally introduced to the Iowa Senate the bill which he had been championing for years: to move the capital specifically to Fort Des Moines. Discussion and arguments followed, including a suggestion that a university be established in Iowa City to replace the soon-to-be-vacated seat of state government. Even though Fort Des Moines agreed to bear the entire expense to move and build a new capitol in Des Moines, the bill failed by one vote. The discussion then shifted to striking a specific location but favoring a move. Pella then made an attractive offer as did other cities. Ultimately, the bill was referred to committee, debated, referred, etc., for the next two years.

Newly elected State Senator James Jordan reintroduced the bill in December immediately after the 1854 election. L. F. Andrews, Polk County historian, wrote: "Jordan's bill was specific, it designated Fort Des Moines as the objective point. Immediately it was loaded with amendments and dilatory motions.... Jordan, with his genial, conservative ways, and the aid of his colleagues in the lower House, and active lobbies from The Fort, carried the bill through. The seat of government was to be located within two miles of the junction of the Des Moines and Raccoon Rivers. Iowa City, robbed of her considerable prestige as the seat of government, was placated. She was given the Statehouse, then uncompleted, for a State University."

The Iowa Senate officially passed the bill to move the Iowa state capital from Iowa City to Des Moines on January 11, 1855. A week later it passed in the House. It would be two and a half years before the actual move would take place.

CHAPTER 25
"... and her loss was keenly felt."

During the early months of 1855, while James was in Iowa City finalizing details around his successful effort to bring the Iowa capital to Fort Des Moines, Melinda remained at home managing the farm and tending to their family. The life of a pioneer woman was challenging—full of constant and never-ending hard work. If a job description were written for Melinda, it would have been worded similar to an account by Glenda Riley, pioneer life historian: "Economic producer who manufactured all manner of domestic goods, gave birth to and trained future laborers, helped with 'men's work' and generated small amounts of cash income."

The Pioneer Housewife

It was Melinda's responsibility to supervise the children. Together they tended the henhouse and gathered the eggs. She was in charge of the dairy, and Melinda either milked the cows herself or enlisted the children to do it. Milking was done twice a day, in the morning and again in the evening. Besides milking, Melinda made butter, cottage cheese, and farmer's cheese. She baked bread daily, hauled water from the creek or, eventually, the well, and tried to keep her home neat, clean, and free from small rodents that tried to sneak in.

Responsible for producing three heavy meals every day, Melinda probably would spend her entire morning cooking. The meals she cooked were typical midwestern farm fare. "Over the course of the day," according to Riley, "there would be two kinds of meat, eggs, cheese, butter, cream (especially in gravies), corn in one or more forms, two kinds of bread, three or four different vegetables from the garden or from storage, several kinds of jellies, preserves and relishes, cake or pie, and milk, coffee, and tea."

Melinda's afternoons were probably devoted to her other jobs tending her enormous garden, making jellies and preserves, canning vegetables, smoking meat, making soap, making candles, washing and ironing clothes, and perhaps spinning yarn to knit socks and mittens.

Other chores she performed, according to Riley, "included food preservation, such as covering tomatoes in red wax and placing them in cans, salting down cucumbers and placing them in large crocks and converting cabbage into sauerkraut in huge wooden barrels." She also would have "wrapped apples in paper or hay, cut them up for drying, or cooked them into apple butter. In the late summer, she would gather root vegetables such as potatoes, rutabagas, and turnips to store in the cellar." Melinda "cleaned hogs' heads and feet for souse, salted pork, dressed down chickens, and dried or preserved wild meat" the men brought home from hunting and stored in their cellar.

Throughout the day she was responsible for the care of her young children, the health of her family, their general well-being, and their cleanliness and grooming. Baths were rare, and in the winter Jordan Creek could not be used. Nor were there any toothbrushes. Probably in very cold weather Melinda was content if her boys washed their face and hands before eating. She probably cut James' and the boys' hair and tried to keep her hair and the girls' hair combed and tangle-free. At night she tended to the mending and the knitting, read the evening Bible passage with the family, and put the younger children to bed.

If friends came by or travelers were passing through, as they always were, Melinda would extend the now-renowned warm Jordan hospitality. Inns and hotels were nonexistent at that time in or around the western part of Polk County, and the Jordan House was located next to a busy wagon trail. Travelers often needed a place to spend the night, maybe up to a week. When someone stopped, Melinda would see to it the group was fed, no matter what time of day or night. If they were sick she helped nurse them back to health.

Melinda sewed all the clothing for her husband, herself, and the eight children living in the house. This included all the undergarments and outerwear as well as everyday work clothes, Sunday suits, and gowns.

Typical dress Melinda would have worn. From Godey's Lady's Book and Magazine

Melinda's Sunday gown was her one good black silk dress which lasted most of her lifetime and which she remade every four or five years to reflect the current fashion. Per historian Riley, "It seems strange but even in such rude and self-sustained times, the women insisted upon being fashionable. These were the days of hoop skirts. They would have been both dangerous and a nuisance when working before the blazing kitchen hearth or going out to milk the cows and were discarded except on special occasions."

Melinda also sewed all of the sheets, blankets, curtains, and table linens. She made pillows and featherbed mattresses from feathers she plucked from ducks and geese and annually cleaned the pillow feathers and restuffed the featherbed mattresses.

Melinda, as a pioneer housewife, was also the druggist and the family doctor. According to Riley, " . . . it was her responsibility to have on hand herbs and other medicinal plants which she either grew in her garden or collected in the wild. She would then dry them and make them into medicinal teas, tonics, bitters, or poultices to cure whoever was sick or hurt." These remedies had been passed down to Melinda from her mother, but she also referred to her recipe book which had recipes for both food and medicine. In addition to home remedies, Melinda also used "store-bought medicines such as quinine, morphine, and whiskey." When her son John's right arm was severely burned after falling into a bonfire as a young child, Melinda undoubtedly knew what salves to apply to his tender skin.

Childbearing had been a focal point of Melinda's life. The typical emigrant family produced an average of five or six children—Melinda had six. Most pioneer wives bore their children between the ages of twenty to thirty-five, and most gave birth every two and a half years.

When James married Melinda, there is no doubt he loved her, but he was also interested in her domestic abilities, good health, and religious fervor. He was looking for a life partner with whom to build a successful life, and when they married it was the beginning of not only a congenial and affectionate journey together, it also became a shared business venture. Their mutual desire to work together and succeed is evident. By 1855 they were more financially successful than they had ever imagined. However, James would have probably given up all this success to avert the tragedy which was about to occur.

James Loses Melinda

Since December of 1854, James had experienced remarkable success as a state senator in Iowa City. He had accomplished the extraordinary task of getting a positive vote from the state legislature to move Iowa's capital from Iowa City to Des Moines. Furthermore, he was a distinguished member of the strong antislavery "team" now ensconced in the Iowa government.

The Iowa legislature met on even years during the winter months from early December to late January, a quiet time for the many Iowa farmers who had been elected to serve in Iowa City. James had been living there most of the months of December and January while Melinda was back in Des Moines in charge of the farm. After returning from the legislative season around January 26, James went back to Iowa City in late February to wrap up some legislative business.

While in Iowa City, James got word that his wife had become very ill. Greatly disturbed, he made immediate plans to return to the farm. A fierce snowstorm slowed his travel, but he fought his way through it. James arrived too late. Melinda had passed away a few hours before he got to his house. On March 1, 1855, Melinda died at the age of thirty-five. James and Melinda had been married eighteen years.

Although they are uncertain about the cause of Melinda's death, family legend recalls three possibilities. The first was Melinda was working outside in the cold during early calving season, gathering baby calves during a blizzard, and had gotten pneumonia. The second was she had an attack of appendicitis. The third was she was pregnant, either miscarried late or had given birth early and died from childbirth, in much the same way as her sister had a few years earlier.

Melinda Dewitt Pittman Jordan was eulogized by Johnson Brigham, Des Moines historian, as follows: "She inherited the industry and thrift of her parents and while many privations incident to Iowa pioneer life were her daily portion, yet her modest and well-kept home, her well cared for family and her husband's well-preserved pocket book were constant witnesses to the indomitable energy, the continued watchfulness and devotion to the better life of this admirable woman. She was a lovely Christian wife and mother whose life faded far too soon for the world's good. She was but 35 years of age at the time of her demise and her loss was keenly felt."

Widower James buried his beloved wife in a secluded burial plot northeast of their home on a hill beneath the shelter of towering walnut, hickory, and oak trees. There, she joined her sister Drewsilla and her little namesake niece, Mary Melinda.

Melinda Dewitt Pittman Jordan, James Jordan's first wife. Jordan Family Collection

CHAPTER 26
Uncle Jimmy Meets a Yankee

After Melinda's death James went to the post office in Des Moines and sent a letter, which would be carried by Pony Express to his brother John, asking him to return from California as soon as was possible. There were too many children for James to care for alone. John Jordan rushed back to Iowa, crossing the continent and returning several months later that year. When he reached James' house he moved in.

Chaos and Confusion

Fortunately for John and James, their sister Anna and her husband, William Smith, had moved their family from Missouri to Madison County near Winterset. Only a short distance away, Anna was able to come up to the Jordan farm and help out until John Jordan's return and then for some time afterward. She was assisted by her two nieces, thirteen-year-old Emily and eleven-year-old Jemima. Family life in the Jordan House was probably chaotic. At the head of the household were two widowers, John and James, caring for their combined family of eight children: Benjamin and Charles, both seventeen; Emily, thirteen; eleven-year-olds Jemima and Henry; John, nine; James, eight; and George, four.

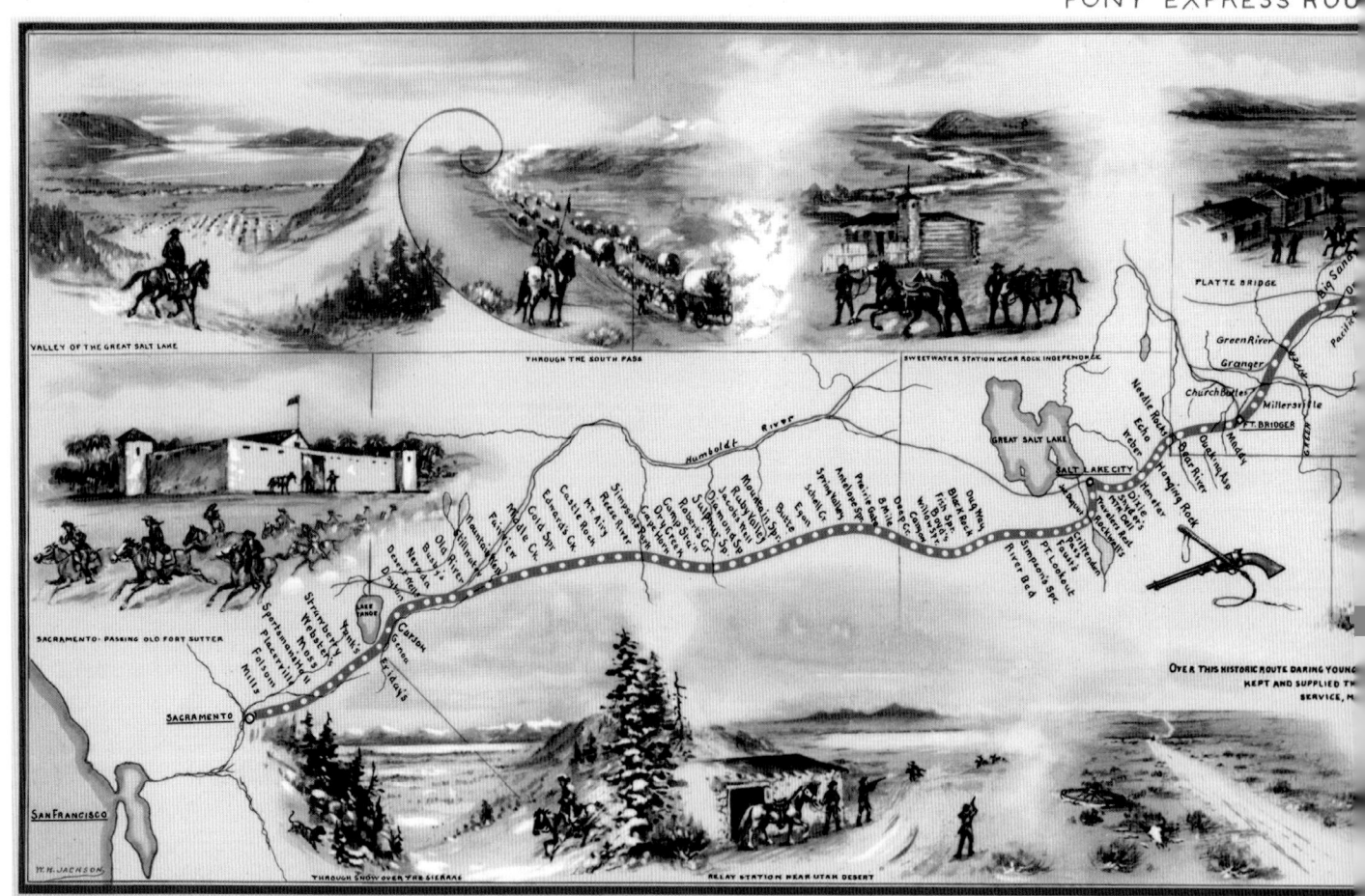

Map of the Pony Express Route. Library of Congress

114   Pursuit of a Dream

To add to the confusion, James was finishing up a term as a senator in Iowa City in the Iowa state legislature. The out-of-town political responsibilities, combined with an already busy life of running his local business affairs and supervising his household, clearly mandated additional help. The two Jordan widowers could not continue as they were.

It was about this time that George Jordan and his wife, Marie, and their family also left Missouri and settled near Winterset. They also were probably enlisted to help the two widowed men. No doubt their sister Anna, as well as their brother George and his wife, were on the lookout for brides for the brothers!

Before long, thirty-seven-year-old John met Mary Magdalene Worley, a young woman aged seventeen who was living with her family in St. Charles, Madison County. By then, John had become a licensed Methodist exhorter and may have spent time in Madison County preaching to rural congregations. He could have met Mary on one of those occasions or was introduced to her by his brother or sister. Not long after they met, John and Mary Magdalene were married on November 17, 1855. John moved Mary to Polk County, possibly into his old cabin in Hiner's Grove or to the Jordan farm. Their first child, David Simpson Jordan, was born on July 18, 1857.

John's heart, however, was back in California. In 1858 he left Iowa and took his family west—by wagon train—back to Gold Rush country in Shasta County, California. There they lived for another ten years, and five more children were born.

In the early 1870s John finally fulfilled his longtime intention of living in what he had always dreamed to

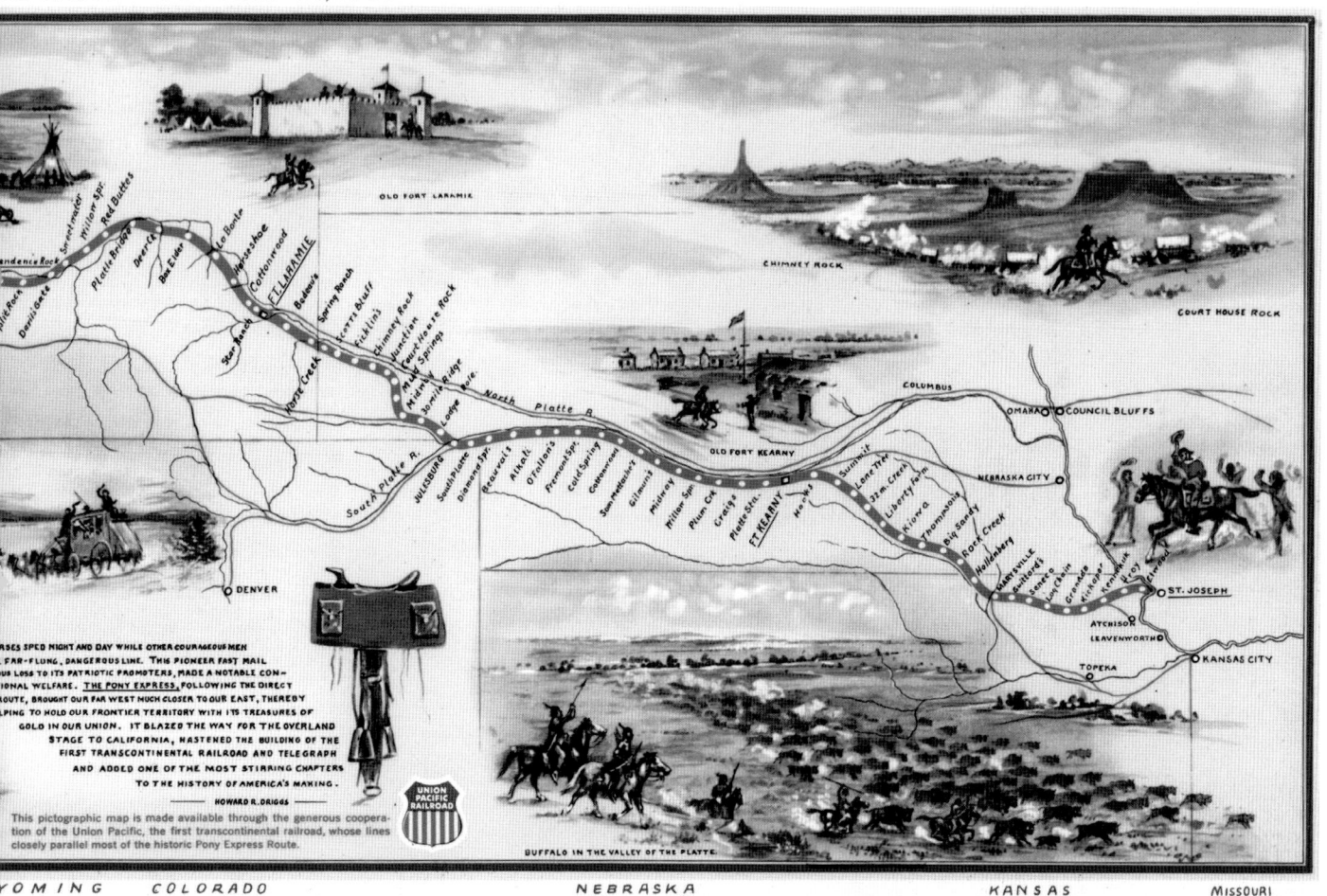

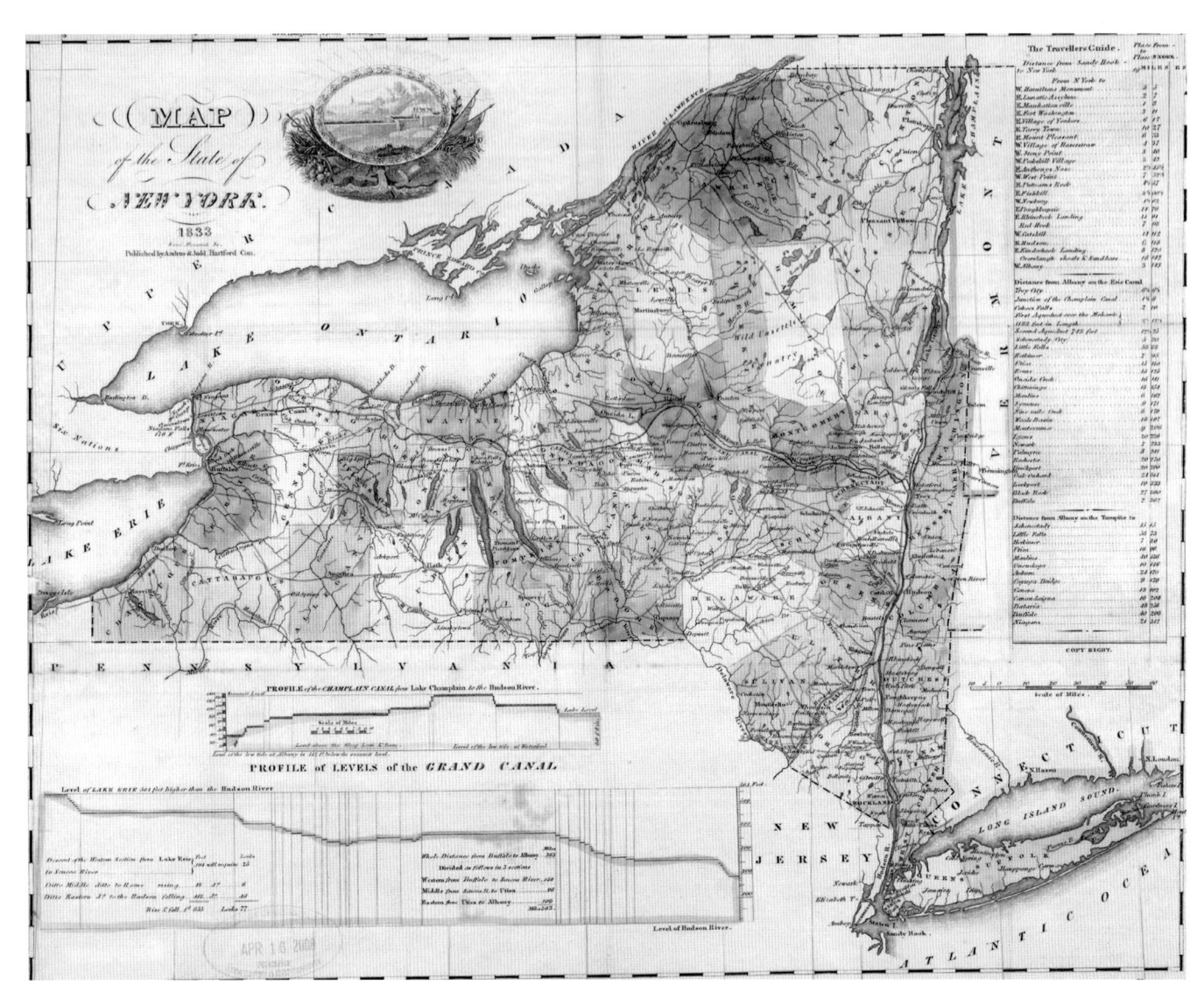

Map of Cynthia Jordan's home state of New York, 1833. Library of Congress

be *his* "Land of Milk and Honey"—Willamette Valley, Wendling, Lane County, Oregon. He had first heard about it as a young man living in Michigan. After finally settling in Oregon, four more children were born to John and Mary Magdalene, making John ultimately the father of twelve children.

The New Teacher

Autumn was approaching, and James—in addition to doing all his other jobs—needed to turn his attention to the fall term of their local school, as he was its superintendent. The log cabin schoolhouse on the other side of the creek needed a new teacher for the 1855–56 term.

By then there were over thirty children on the school rolls. With so many students, including James' five and John's son and daughter, a strict young man would have been the ideal candidate to interview, but time was running out and the school term needed to begin shortly. At about this time James heard from his sister Anna about a young Madison County widow who was living with her father and looking for a place to teach school. James interviewed her as soon as he could and was impressed.

During his interview with the twenty-four-year-old schoolmarm, James had been informed she was born in Canandaigua, Yates County, New York, and had grown up in nearby Middlesex where her father was one of the leaders in the Methodist church. She had traveled to Winterset with her husband, Mr. Sheppard, who had died. She had summoned her father who had arrived in Iowa to help her make decisions about her future, which

116   Pursuit of a Dream

had become cloudy. With no means of support, this widow needed to find a way to carry on. It was natural for her to consider becoming a schoolteacher. James decided she was perfect for the job and hired her for the fall and spring terms. The new teacher's name was Cynthia Disre' Adams Sheppard.

As James became better acquainted with her, he learned Canandaigua was located near the Canadian border in an area that was a hot bed for abolitionism and she shared the abolitionist sentiments. She was pleased to learn James was an abolitionist, as well.

The young woman told fascinating stories to James about slaves who came to her home town from the South and how they were hidden in homes in and around Canandaigua. When the coast was clear the fugitive slaves were spirited to freedom over the border into Canada. Harriet Tubman personally led over three hundred slaves to freedom through that part of New York.

Cynthia's father, Cyrus Adams, had everything in common with James insofar as religion was concerned; they were both ardent Methodists and sincere in their desire to end the institution of slavery. A family legend suggests that Cynthia may have had relatives in the family of former presidents John Adams and his son John Quincy Adams; however, that has not been proven.

As the schoolyear went from fall into winter, James decided Cynthia was a person he might want to have permanently in his life—but so did his son, seventeen-year-old Benjamin. According to stories passed down by the Jordan family, after Cynthia started teaching in the school Benjamin asked his father if he could "pay Cynthia court." James replied, "No, you're far too young, and I'm going to marry her." After the winter term was over and the spring crops were planted, forty-three-year-old James became the bridegroom of twenty-five-year-old Cynthia Sheppard on May 21, 1856. The wedding celebrants included James' children, the spouse and children of James' older brother George, and his matchmaking sister Anna and her family.

George had just moved to Madison County from Missouri to operate a sawmill owned by his brother James on the Middle River. George and his family ran the mill for two years, and then James sold it to Cornelius Haight in August of 1858.

Cynthia Disre' Adams Sheppard Jordan, James Jordan's second wife. Courtesy of West Des Moines Historical Society

A New Family

Cynthia married into a ready-made family. She may have been especially fond of James' ten-year-old son, John, with whom she shared her maiden name—John Quincy Adams Jordan. Less than a year later in March 1857 she would add her own child to the clan, baby Ella. Over the years Ella would be joined by four others: twins Eva and Eda and sons Calvin and Edward.

With Cynthia's arrival, James no longer needed his sister Anna to fill in as a housekeeper, but she and her husband decided to assist James in another way. They moved to the little community of Greenfield in western Iowa, where they established a farm and helped manage the Jordan cattle herds which were sent there to graze. Most likely, George and his family left the mill they were running for James and took over Anna and her husband's Winterset farm.

Following in the Jordan family tradition, Cynthia joined the local Methodist church, which happened two months after their wedding. In July 1856 both James *and* Cynthia were listed as members of the First Methodist Church of Des Moines.

CHAPTER 27
The Capital Comes to Des Moines

Even though he was a newlywed, James could not divert his attention from his long list of responsibilities, a major one being his job as a state senator. Having been reelected to a second term, James needed to again focus on Iowa politics: in December 1856 he would be returning to Iowa City to the sixth session (1856–57) of the Iowa state legislature.

By now Senator Jordan was fast friends with many notable leaders in state and federal government—powerful men who were influential in shaping the future course and direction of Iowa and, in some cases, the nation. Among them were colleague and friend James Harlan, now representing Iowa as its US Senator. James Grimes of Burlington was Iowa's governor, and Samuel Kirkwood, a resident of Iowa City, was James' colleague in the Iowa Senate.

The Meskwaki Tribe Buys Land in Iowa

One of the measures passed during the sixth legislative session had to do with the Meskwaki Indians, who had been previously exiled to a reservation in northeastern Kansas and who wanted to return to Iowa and purchase land. In addition, some remnants of the tribe who had not left the state and were in hiding wanted to continue to live in their Iowa homeland. The way to accomplish this was to purchase back some of the land they had relinquished in the treaties, and they assembled the funds to do just that. All they needed was get permission from the State of Iowa.

This was difficult because the Indians were not even thought of as human beings. It would follow that they were also not considered to be citizens of the United States. There were no laws in Iowa for people who were not citizens, much less non-human, to purchase property. However, following the lead of Governor Grimes and his staff, the majority of the Iowa legislature was persuaded to vote affirmatively to allow members of the Meskwaki Indian Tribe to purchase and own land in Iowa. James Jordan helped this legislation pass, and in doing so showed his gratitude to the Indians who had helped his family survive their first very hard winter in Iowa.

The Meskwakis found and purchased eighty acres along the Iowa River near Tama and Toledo. The Meskwaki Nation of Iowa was unique in being the first Indian tribe in the United States to purchase their land.

The Constitutional Convention of 1857

The legislators' main focus was on the new year, when Iowa's constitutional convention would take place—in February and March of 1857. This would be the last constitutional convention for Iowa. (Earlier ones had occurred in 1844 and 1846 as the state was forming.) Major items to be dealt with included establishing a safe and sound state banking system, prohibition, addressing the slavery question, and finalizing the move of the capital from Iowa City to Fort Des Moines.

Even though the Iowa legislature had voted to relocate the capital in 1855, since then there had been much foot-dragging with regard to the actual move. Several legislators and many citizens wanted to rescind the decision. An affirmation of the new Fort Des Moines location was included as part of the revised constitution which would hopefully be approved during the 1857 constitutional convention. However, there was concern that when this new Iowa Constitution was put to a public

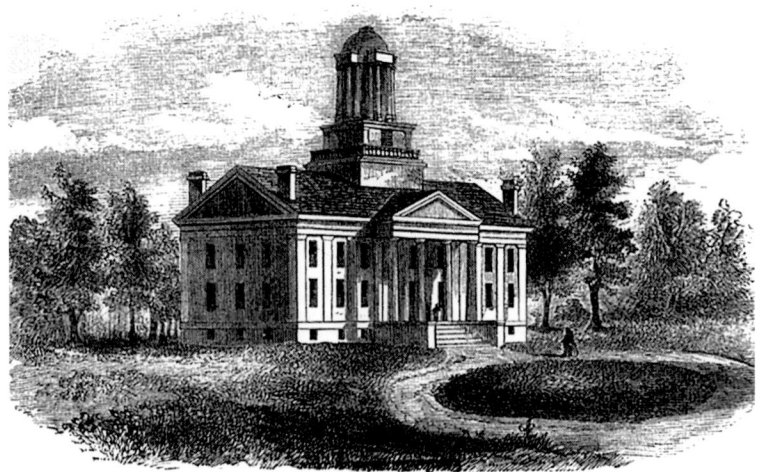

Old capitol building in Iowa City, 1855. Public domain

118   Pursuit of a Dream

vote, many counties would vote against it, therefore once again putting the capital relocation in jeopardy.

It was no surprise that eastern Iowans continued to lobby against moving this important focal point of the state to the west. Eastern Iowans would be inconvenienced, but more importantly, they would lose an economic asset. These were, of course, the exact reasons why people in Fort Des Moines and central and western Iowa wanted the capital further west in their part of the state.

Fort Des Moines fortunately had a contingent of "allies"—the counties stretching south and east from Fort Des Moines down to Keokuk along the Des Moines River basin. They figured it would be important for citizens and business enterprises to have good access to the state's capital city and if Fort Des Moines were the capital, the Des Moines River would be the easiest and best way to get there. Goods would need to be transported by steamboat to Fort Des Moines, which would stop at points along the river. Business would improve in those river towns. The counties along the Des Moines River were excited at the prospect of increased business opportunities up and down the river. For all of that to be possible, however, the river would have to be engineered to be more navigable, which would further increase the significance and value of the Des Moines River basin in Iowa and their towns and counties, in particular. According to L. F. Andrews, Polk County historian:

> Residents of Keokuk, Keosauqua, and Ottumwa, imagined that the Des Moines River would be made navigable, at least as far as the Fork. ("The Fork" was an early reference to Fort Des Moines.)
>
> In their imagination they saw all obstacles to navigation removed by the government, the state co-operating, the steamers coming and going, carrying from the cities rich cargoes to be exchanged for the corn and hogs and the products of the orchards, vineyards, and mines of the interior. The development of the little garrison town at the Fork into a populous city would mean a rich central market for their wares and a depot of farm and field supplies. They had little to expect from Iowa City, with its nearness to the Mississippi towns above Keokuk and everything to gain from Fort Des Moines.

With the hard work of Jordan and his colleagues, the Iowa legislature approved the 1857 constitution. In the fall it would be presented to Iowa citizens to accept or vote down. Work needed to be done to secure a positive popular vote. Polk County businessmen together devised a plan to focus their efforts on counties along the Des Moines River basin, particularly down in Lee County, home of Keokuk. However, instead of pushing for steamboat transportation, they decided to take advantage of nineteenth-century technology opportunities and focus on railroad development, promising $100,000 to be pledged toward the development of the Des Moines Valley Railroad linking Keokuk to Fort Des Moines.

Voters in the southeast Iowa counties along the Des Moines River, especially those in the city of Keokuk in Lee County, had the perfect incentive to turn out and vote in favor of the new constitution, which they did. The vote passed by a slim but successful margin of 1,630 votes. The new constitution became the "law of Iowa" in September of 1857. On October 19, Governor James W. Grimes issued a proclamation declaring "the capital of the State of Iowa to be established, under the (new) Constitution and laws of the state, at Des Moines in Polk County." This constitution also changed the future capital city's name. "Fort" was eliminated and the name was shortened to "Des Moines."

A New Capital for Iowa

Governor Grimes directed that the seat of Iowa government be moved to Des Moines to a three-story brick building that business leaders there had already constructed for this purpose. It was located at the top of a hill just east of the fork of the Des Moines and Raccoon Rivers, where the Iowa Soldiers and Sailors Monument now stands.

Even though the commercial area of Fort Des Moines had been built primarily on the *west* side of the river, close to where the old fort had been, the capitol building was erected on the *east* side. Bill Wagner, Iowa historical architect, explained that the contentious statewide dispute to locate the capital in Des Moines was nothing compared to the battle waged in Des Moines as to which side of the Des Moines River the capitol building would be located.

> A commission was appointed to select a site for the new capitol which was to be located within a radius of two miles of the junction of the Raccoon and Des Moines Rivers. It is doubtful if any other commission serving in connection with

First capitol building in Des Moines. From *History of Iowa from the Earliest Times to the Beginning of the Twentieth Century*, Vol. 1, by Benjamin F. Gue, 1903

a public building project has ever been so criticized and accused of under-the-table dealings as was the one locating the building for Iowa's capitol in Des Moines. Nothing came out of any of the investigations to prove bribery and corruption, probably because it is doubtful if bribes had anything to do with the selection.

Governor James Grimes liked our present capitol hill. He was a Republican and at the time, the East side was Republican and the West side Democrat. Maybe he had a better feeling for his political allies. Also entering the picture was a man, Wilson Alexander Scott. He and two other East siders gave fifteen acres to the State in 1856 for a new capitol and even provided the financing with which to build the new building by borrowing up to thirty-five thousand dollars.

The businessmen who built the capitol building intended to donate it to the state; however, there was an economic recession in 1857 and they were unable to do so. Retaining ownership and the debt, they instead rented the building to the state for one dollar per year and paid back the debt to the state school fund, from which they had borrowed the money. Later on, the state released them from their indebtedness to the school fund in exchange for title to the land. This capitol building was used as the seat of Iowa government for the next thirty years.

Moving the Capital

Getting the capital moved in late 1857 was a major endeavor and was later described by Iowa historian Johnson Brigham as follows:

In these days of ample transportation facilities, it is not easy to realize the difficulties under which Dr. Jesse Bowen labored in removing the four safes of the four departments of state from Iowa City to Des Moines. There were no railroads in the state. The roads were mere wagon tracks on the open prairie. Most of the streams had no bridges.

Men and teams were sent from Des Moines, for no one in Iowa City would contract to do the job. Many days were consumed before the removal was complete. The state treasurer's safe was left for several days and nights on the open prairie, near Four-Mile Creek, until a storm abated and the ground was sufficiently frozen to enable ten yoke of oxen to haul it to town on a bob-sleigh. Its arrival was a great relief to the treasurer, and to the employees of the state as well, for it contained the coin with which the month's salaries were to be paid.

The state officers were brought to Des Moines through the courtesy of Colonel Hooker of the Western Stage Company, the stage drawn by four horses. The deputies chartered a hack and on Friday they started out. The weather was delightful. The second day out closed with a wind and snow-storm. Sunday morning the snow was more than a foot deep—and Des Moines twenty-five miles away. The driver refused to go farther.

A farmer with a lumber wagon offered to take them. Using their trunks as seats they started out and late that afternoon they were safely landed at the Shaw House, near the Capitol. On the following Monday the departments were in running order in the new state house.

After the capital was established in their city, the big changes folks in Des Moines had been dreaming of did *not* occur. A major reason for this was the financial crash of 1857. There was little money for "extras," such as improved transportation to the new capital city. An account, also by Johnson Brigham, follows:

It is hard to realize the isolation of the new capital city in the late '50s. It was without a railroad connection. Steamboat navigation on the Des Moines was suspended much of the time in winter

120   Pursuit of a Dream

Early legislators traveled by stagecoach to Des Moines. *From The History of Polk County, Iowa*

by ice, in spring and fall by floods, and in summer by low water. The roads leading to the capital were made nearly impassable by rains, and creeks and rivers were made unfordable by floods. Members of the General Assembly were frequently compelled to face fierce winds and below-zero weather.

Senator Pusey long afterwards related the story of his hard ride from Council Bluffs in January 1858, 150 miles in a stagecoach with the mercury more than twenty degrees below zero. On inauguration day the weather turned abnormally warm. Ice in the streams had melted, making the streams well-nigh impassable. But a cordial welcome awaited those who "pulled through."

Two years later the situation was not improved. In 1894 Julius H. Powers, of New Hampton, told the pioneer lawmakers the story of his wedding journey in January 1860. The story well illustrates the inaccessibility of the new capital in midwinter. Having been elected senator and having married a young wife, and unwilling to leave his bride, he employed a man to drive him and his wife in a democrat wagon to Des Moines.

Starting December 31, 1859, with the mercury twenty-six degrees below zero, on the 3rd of January they joined several other legislators at Cedar Falls and started across Grundy County in a snowstorm. The temperature lowered toward night and the young wife became numb with cold, and before reaching their destination she barely escaped freezing.

The two stopped over for the night at Steamboat Rock, and the rest of the party went on. The food supply in the hotel was low, their bedroom was icy cold, and the wife discovered that the upper sheet in the bed was a linen tablecloth! They took an early start the next morning, intending to breakfast at Eldora. But, going through the tavern kitchen, they lost appetite entirely.

Another weary day brought them to Nevada, where they passed their first comfortable night since leaving home. The next day they took the wrong road, and when night came found themselves still eleven miles from Des Moines and the party (for they had rejoined their legislative friends at Nevada) were informed by the man of the house that they must move on.

At this Uncle Zimri Streeter jumped out and told the rest of the party to unload, for he knew there was plenty of room for man and beast. Another party came on and they, too, were commanded by "Old Black Hawk" to stay overnight. The invaders took down the beds to make more room on the floor. They turned the cattle out and put their horses into the straw barn. The bride and groom slept in a shed, and were made comfortable with robes and blankets. Next day at 11 a.m. they put up at the Grout House at the foot of Capitol Hill.

James Jordan: His Life and His Legacy

CHAPTER 28
Further Changes in the Iowa Constitution

Three important issues were addressed by Iowa State Senator James Jordan and his legislative colleagues during the Iowa Constitutional Convention of 1857; the question of enfranchising the blacks, the problems with banking, and one especially dear to James Jordan's Methodist heart, the question of temperance.

A Temperance Law is Passed

Problems with drinking and drunkenness had followed the pioneers from the eastern states into the Midwest, and the new state of Iowa was not exempt. "There is no question that the early explorers, trappers and soldiers, away from their family life and Christian influence, led rather wild lives," stated Iowa historian Eugene Hastie. "Whiskey by the barrel was a common thing on the frontier." The pioneers who were present during the Iowa land rush in the mid-1840s also saw what a travesty liquor was to the Meskwaki Indian tribes. Rumor has it that in 1845, while the Indians were staying in Fort Des Moines prior to their exile to Kansas, Captain James Allen sold them liquor from barrels he had hidden in the woods.

The various religious denominations strongly addressed drinking and drunkenness, and there were several, like the Methodists, which forbade it. "Not until permanent settlers came did things improve," Hastie continues. "Some of these people were drinking people too, but the majority of them were strongly opposed to drinking and adhered to Christian standards."

James Jordan was a sincere and vocal advocate of the Methodist mandate on temperance. He and other like-minded legislators worked hard for temperance reform and were ultimately successful. In Section 26 of Article 1 of the Constitution of 1857 it states: "No person shall manufacture for sale, or sell, or have for sale as a beverage any intoxicating liquors whatever, including ale, wine and beer." Iowa was one of only a few states in the nation to enact a temperance law, which was in effect for the next thirty-seven years and not modified until 1894.

The Rights of Blacks

The antislavery Republican Party was on the rise in a legislature filled with men who were entrenched in the national status quo. According to Steven Cross: "There were lengthy debates as to whether blacks could vote, join the militia, testify in court, and so on. In 1857, those who favored restricting most rights of blacks won, although the issue of whether blacks could vote was submitted to the people as a referendum. In the referendum, the extension of the franchise to blacks

---

The Methodist Church's Position on Temperance

James Jordan was a strict prohibitionist. His views, fostered and mandated by his Methodist religion, insisted on abstinence of all alcoholic beverages, including liquor, wine, and lager beer. Only unfermented wine was allowed during Communion in Methodist churches.

The Upper Iowa Conference of the Methodist Church expressed their position on temperance at their annual conference in 1856 and again in 1859. As a state senator, James Jordan would introduce legislation to accomplish the goals set by his church.

"From the beginning, the Conference has taken strong position in favor of total abstinence and prohibition of the liquor traffic. Thus in 1856 it declared intemperance to be a great and serious evil, destructive alike of social happiness and religious prosperity, and dangerous to our civil institution; and that the Conference would labor to secure a prohibitory law that would accomplish the entire overthrow of the liquor traffic."

In 1859 they extended support of additionally prohibiting lager beer. "We will use our influence and our votes to secure the election of members of the Legislature, who have appetites that will favor and backbone that will enable them to enact a prohibitory law that will include lager beer."

The Upper Iowa Conference stated in 1884 that "voluntary total abstinence from all intoxicants as the true ground of personal temperance; and complete and legal prohibition of the traffic in intoxicating liquors as the duty of civil government."

was defeated. After the Civil War, Iowa voters approved a constitutional amendment giving the ballot to black males in 1868."

Banking Challenges in the New State

When the Iowa Territory was released by the Meskwaki Indians and the land became available for purchase by settlers and speculators, there were extraordinary opportunities for money to be made—in real estate and in other business ventures. At that time there were two kinds of banks operating in Iowa: "Banks of Issue" and "Banks of Deposit."

When Iowa became a state in 1846, the state legislature had reversed the territorial laws on banking. In the actions of the 1844 and 1846 Iowa legislatures, "both of them prohibited banks in Iowa," historian Steven Cross explains. However, "the 'banks' which were prohibited were the then frequently existing '*banks of issue*.' These banks printed and issued notes which were similar in appearance and use to our paper currency today. These banks were numerous in the early 1800s and were often wildcat operations. When one of these banks closed, those who held notes issued by that bank suffered a significant financial loss."

Stephen Hempstead, Iowa's second governor, elected in 1850, declared, "If the whole concern—banks, officers and all—could be sent to the penitentiary, I would be glad of it."

"Another kind of bank, a '*bank of deposit*,' was *not* prohibited," Cross continues, "and folks could continue to deposit money in these 'banks of deposit,' as they had done when Iowa was a Territory."

By shutting down banks of issue, the printing of currency became prohibited in Iowa, and the only legal currency options available in Iowa for the next twelve years were paper money printed out of state (unreliable) or solid gold and silver coins (very reliable). Most businessmen and bankers alike kept large accounts in eastern cities—usually New York—and drew drafts against them when they needed to complete a financial transaction. Local banks were used to store gold and silver until it could be transported to banks in the east.

B. F. Allen. From *Hawkeye Insurance Company Atlas of 1875*

It was not desirable to carry around unwieldy bags of gold and silver, and so, there was a demand for the convenience of paper money. This demand was addressed in Iowa by enterprising financiers like Des Moines banker B. F. Allen, who circumvented Iowa law by opening a bank in Nebraska (where it was legal for banks to print money) and issuing currency which local residents knew was backed up with gold Allen had in his vault.

A poster inspiring the temperance movement. Library of Congress

James Jordan: His Life and His Legacy 123

At that time, Allen was reliable, but many others, both in Iowa and outside the state, were not. They circulated worthless bills, hoping these would be acceptable currency to the unsuspecting person. In order to avoid problems, lists were distributed regularly that told people which bills were acceptable and which were worthless. Tacitus Hussey, early Des Moines historian, paints a picture of the precarious state of the financial situation in Des Moines:

> The paper money in circulation was usually either counterfeit or had no gold to back it up—thus it was usually worthless. . . . We had very little, if any, paper money in circulation in Des Moines that New York bankers would accept. Western currency (Des Moines was considered to be a part of the West) would not do, and that was about all the paper money we had, so gold and silver was the only kind a Western banker could trust to keep his credit good and to draw drafts against in the Eastern cities.
>
> Merchants and businessmen would meet daily and prepare a list of banks deemed good for the day, at par, at discount and worthless. The list would be revised on the arrival of each mail.
>
> All bankers, tradesmen, merchants, etc. studied the "Bank Note Reporter" and "Counterfeit Detector," a copy of which was hung by every prudent businessmen's desk with the utmost diligence and in receiving money a merchant would have to satisfy himself by consulting the "reporter" that it would be accepted by the bank "if he ran all the way" to deposit it as soon as received. Otherwise he would lose it in case he couldn't find "the man who passed it off on him," and compel him to take it back. So if the receiver's bump of caution was well developed and the amount considerable, it took about as much time to receive the money as to sell the goods.

S. Goettsch and S. Weinberg, Terrace Hill historians, told a story about a Des Moines merchant who went to St. Louis to buy goods: "He carefully selected the best notes he could to take with him to pay for the merchandise, but when he got there he could not get a dollar for the whole of them."

Commerce was brisk in Des Moines during that time and money was flowing:

- During this decade the land office took in an average of $25,000 a day in gold.
- In addition to pioneers purchasing homesteads, people in the East sent money to people in the West to invest in land for speculation purposes.
- In 1849 a merchant went to Ohio to purchase over $100,000 of items for his store in Des Moines which, upon his return, he sold "in no time."
- Des Moines businessmen were easily able to raise $100,000 in 1856 for the dual purpose of securing the state capital and bringing the railroad to town.
- Frank Mills, who operated a Des Moines printing business, at one time was depositing $1,000 a day and had loans of over $150,000 spread around five different banks in the city.

In 1855 there were seven private banks in Des Moines and thirty-eight banks in seventeen other Iowa towns. Their legitimate purpose was to lend money, but their most important function was to store gold and silver in their locked vaults. In order to pay bills, patrons would authorize gold or silver to be transferred through Iowa's central clearing house in Iowa City. From Iowa City, gold and silver would be transported to banks within the state or region or to the banks back East.

Tacitus Hussey illustrates how these transfers of gold took place in the early years of Fort Des Moines: "The express company in those days sent out only one shipment a week to Iowa City in an express stagecoach in the charge of George Butts. As this express stage had no regular time to depart, the express agent usually went around to his customers and notified them privately of the time of intended departure so that shipments might be ready in time, and they would accordingly prepare the shipment and carry it to the express office after night, thereby avoiding a display of the treasure on the streets in daytime."

Reforms in Iowa Banking

When James Grimes became Iowa's third governor in 1854, Iowans had a leader who was an adept businessman. He was a banker, a real estate speculator, and a lawyer and, like most of his fellow Whigs, was committed to making revisions in the Iowa Constitution to permit banks and banking in Iowa.

During the constitutional convention of 1857 the bank problem was addressed by a committee of thirty-six Iowans who spent the majority of their time writing laws to provide for a workable banking system in the state. The system, according to Iowa historian Leland Sage, "basically authorized the creation of a 'free' (private) banking system and a state bank, which was not a state-owned bank at all but a private bank, with branches to be set up in towns and cities wherever a chartering group could meet the requirements. It should be noted that the Constitution did not create such banks; it merely authorized their creation." When the Iowa General Assembly, of which Senator James Jordan was a member, and later the Iowa citizens approved the new constitution, wherein these new banking principles were included, they were pleased to vote for a constitution which brought safe and convenient banking to Iowa.

The new laws authorized the issuance of local paper currency backed up with gold and silver. This had not been the case for over a decade.

Rather than one umbrella bank with branches out in the state, state banks of Iowa were instead a network of independent banks who had each qualified for the charter as a state bank. Approximately fifteen were quickly chartered around the state, all of them with different owners and boards.

In October 1858 several affluent businessmen joined together to create a state bank in Des Moines, which was one of the first. They were able to meet all the chartering requirements set forth in the new Iowa Constitution. The largest shareholder, B. F. Allen, was elected bank president. One of the original investors and directors of the bank was James C. Jordan.

James' involvement with this bank underscores his financial stability and affluence, as well as his entwinement with the Des Moines business community. "James Jordan was largely interested in and identified with town affairs," stated Polk County historian L. F. Andrews. "In fact he was always considered a part of the city."

As a director of a state bank in Des Moines, he was subject to bank inspections. After one inspection he was quoted as saying, "The financial cost is clear—no tempest to catch me and destroy."

"Saving the Bank"

The state banks in Iowa enjoyed a fair degree of success and played a large part in financing the state's activities during the Civil War. During that war, James Jordan was called upon in 1862 to save their state bank in Des Moines. The story by L. F. Andrews follows:

> In 1862 during the Civil War, a rumor came that a band of Missouri bushwhackers led by "Missouri Bill" were on their way to loot Des Moines and there was great apprehension as the city was virtually defenseless. Many residents were alarmed but particularly the merchants and bankers.
>
> The banks at once sought refuge for their funds. Those of the State Bank were removed to "Uncle Jimmy's" place where he cached them beyond the probability of seizure.
>
> The marauders, however, ran up against some of Uncle Sam's blue coats and didn't get to Des Moines. The blue coats were local citizens Captain Henry Griffith and Colonel James A. Williamson who were in Des Moines on furlough. They organized a company to man a battery of two guns, which were stationed on the State House grounds ready for any emergency.
>
> It was learned, however, that "Missouri Bill'" was going the other way, and the battery was disbanded, much to the regret of Harry, whose dander was up.

In 1863 the National Banking Act, which was amended in 1865, directed that the Iowa State Bank and all its branches convert to national banks. James had championed the concept of a national bank since he had heard Henry Clay speak about it as a part of his "American System" in the 1830s. After the changes in the banking system created by the new 1857 Iowa Constitution, James kept bank accounts locally, but in years hence he would have his most significant deposits and accounts in banks in Chicago where he would trade his livestock.

James Jordan: His Life and His Legacy 125

CHAPTER 29
James Jordan, Republican

Many settlers were drawn to Iowa simply because of the fertile soil and cheap land. Others chose Iowa more specifically; in the growing national dispute over slavery, they wanted to live in a "free state." This issue was the most important factor that led to the birth of the Republican Party.

National Politics

Over the years, the US government tried to address the problem of slavery, first in 1820 with the Missouri Compromise and later on with other legislation. All of these measures were designed to keep the Union together and the American people tranquil over slavery issues.

The Missouri Compromise addressed the challenge of how to keep the Union 50 percent slave states and 50 percent free states. Prior to 1820, there were eleven of each. The Territory of Missouri asked to join the Union in 1818 and wanted to come in as a slave state. Allowing this would have given slave states the advantage in the US Congress, so Missouri was denied. The problem was solved when Maine was admitted in 1821 as a free state, thereby allowing Missouri to enter the Union as a slave state, bringing the number to twelve of each.

Continuing debate and discussion determined that from then on any states formed from the Louisiana Purchase north of the southern boundary of Missouri, but not including Missouri, would enter statehood only as free states. Despite this measure, to assure many new western states would have free-state status, the federal government continued to admit older southeastern territories as slave states, thus maintaining the balance between slave and free as new states came into the Union. Hence, when Iowa became a state in 1846, it was offset by Florida, which was admitted as a slave state at about the same time.

The Compromise of 1850 addressed non-Louisiana Purchase territories and illustrated the growing debate of the pro- and antislavery factions. It admitted California as a free state and let New Mexico and Utah Territories decide the slavery question when they became states. It abolished slave trade in Washington, DC, and enforced the constitutional provision for the return of fugitive slaves.

The Kansas-Nebraska Act of 1854 provided for the organization of a territorial government in the then unorganized country west of Missouri and Iowa. The act provided that the people of the two areas of Kansas and Nebraska (which were much larger than they are today as states) could decide for themselves whether to be slave or free. It also repealed the Missouri Compromise.

With the passage of the Kansas-Nebraska Act, antislavery factions were outraged. Intended to be a means of lessening friction between the slave and free proponents, it only increased opposition. US politics as it had been up to that time would never be the same again.

Iowa Politics

In Iowa there was intense interest about which way the Kansas Territory would go. Antislavery and proslavery factions from all over the United States gathered to influence the decision. The Kansas problem drew activist John Brown to the Midwest. An ardent abolitionist, he traveled from the East with his sons, intent on making Kansas a free state.

Towns along the Missouri River's southwest border of Iowa were often used as a staging ground for bloody encounters in Kansas between pro- and antislavery groups. It was said the town of Tabor in southwest Iowa at times looked like an armed camp.

Kansas became known as "Bleeding Kansas" because of all the bloody skirmishes around the issue of slavery. This had been the reason James' sister Anna and her husband, who originally had intended to settle their family in Kansas, had decided instead to live in Missouri. When the

James W. Grimes. From *Portrait and Biographical Album of Polk County, Iowa*, 1890

slavery issue got to be too much in Missouri, they moved to Iowa.

In Iowa, Governor James Grimes was inaugurated in December 1854. He won on an antislavery platform, severely condemning the Kansas-Nebraska Act. There is no doubt he and James and their other abolitionist colleagues engaged in long discussions about this issue.

Contributing to their concern, just over the southern border of Iowa, in north central Missouri, there was a collection of seventeen counties along the Missouri River that referred to themselves as "Little Dixie." The area was populated with tobacco and hemp plantation owners and scores of slaves. It was described as "more 'Dixie' than Dixie." By 1860 the population of half of the counties in Little Dixie was 25 percent slaves. Little Dixie was the area John Brown would rampage through as he and other like-minded folks endeavored to liberate slaves

The Methodist Church's Official Position on Slavery Prior to the Civil War

The Methodist church in Iowa would eventually be divided into four areas of governance. The "Upper Iowa Conference" of the Methodist church was organized in 1856 when it geographically subdivided from the "Iowa Conference" which had been established in 1844 in the southeastern quarter of the state. The "Des Moines Conference," originally called the "Western Conference," included the southwestern part of the state and was not established until 1860. Eventually the Northwest Conference was formed in 1872.

James Jordan and his family, who lived in the area of the state where the to-be-organized "Des Moines Conference" would be located, embraced the resolutions against slavery as declared by the Upper Iowa Conference of the Methodist Church. The strongly worded resolutions, written in 1856, 1857, and 1858 during their Annual Conference, follow:

Slavery

The Upper Iowa Conference has from the beginning maintained an advanced position on all questions of moral reform. When burning issues were pending, and the public mind was unsettled, the Conference has not hesitated to express its convictions without fear. The Conference was initiated in the midst of the great antislavery movement. Political parties were being reorganized, the north and the south were being arrayed against each other and mutterings of war were already heard.

At its first session in 1856 the Upper Iowa Conference adopted the following:

Resolved 1st, That slavery is opposed to the spirit of Christianity and the promulgation of the Gospel, as well as an aggravating sin against God.

Resolved 2nd, That as the ministers of Christ we will make every reasonable and consistent effort to maintain a healthy antislavery sentiment in our several congregations, in order to prevent the extension of slavery in our country, and to effect the extirpation of this great evil.

During the year 1856, the United States Supreme Court, through Chief Justice Taney, rendered a decision of the famous Dred Scott case, in which the court declared that, 'They (the Africans) had for more than a century before been regarded as beings of an inferior order, and altogether unfit to associate with the white race, either in social or political relations, and so far inferior that they had no rights which the white man is bound to respect.'

At the next session, in 1857, the Upper Iowa Conference adopted the following:

Resolved, That while as an ecclesiastical body we claim no authority over the courts of our land, and, that while we inculcate respect for our judicial authorities, yet we deeply deplore the recent decision made by a majority of the United States Supreme Court in the Dred Scott case, as being contrary to the historical truth, subversive of the most common principles of justice, destructive of natural rights, as was clearly shown by Justices McClean and Curtis, and is therefore calculated to destroy public confidence in that high tribunal.

Resolved, That we look with mingled sorrow and abhorrence on all attempts, by whomsoever made, to pervert Scripture to the sanction of American slavery."

In 1858 the Conference adopted the following:

Resolved, While we see with surprise and sorrow the efforts made by selfish and unprincipled men to revive the slave trade, we do believe that God in His providence, is so directing events as to secure at no very distant day the overthrow of this deplorable evil.

THE GREAT REPUBLICAN REFORM PARTY,
Calling on their Candidate.

Political cartoon, 1856. Library of Congress

and guide them to freedom by way of the Underground Railroad through Iowa.

Grimes and Jordan were both Whigs, one of several political parties active in Iowa at the time, including the antislavery Seward Whigs or Free Soilers. Proslavery political parties were the Democrats and the Hunkers. The Silver Grey Whigs did not like slavery but did not oppose it, and the American Party (aka the "Know-Nothing Party") was a semi-secret group which wasn't telling which side they were on.

When Grimes ran for governor, he worked hard as a Seward Whig to ally the Free Soil Democrats and the Silver Grey Whigs, which he successfully accomplished. This coalition was uniformly antislavery but the movement, at that time, was not fully developed. According to Iowa historian W. J. Peterson, Grimes assisted in its development by putting words to a cause: "As he campaigned the state, his speeches actually molded antislavery sentiment, for he gave expression to what most citizens had only vaguely believed."

In 1856 Iowa's Governor Grimes issued a statement with national implications: "(Slavery) is a local institution, and to States that maintain it, brings its responsibilities and its perils.... It is both the interest and the duty of the free States to prevent the increase and extension of the slave power, by every constitutional means.... Congress can pass no law establishing or protecting it in the territories. If Congress can pass no such law, much less can it delegate such authority to the territorial legislatures, over those whose act it has ever exercised supervisory and restraining power."

Nationally, Grimes' statement became the doctrine which later helped unite opponents of slavery into a new political party—the Republican Party. Republicans, formed as a coalition of citizens, were not only opposed to slavery but also opposed to a Congress dictating the decisions the states felt they could make for themselves.

James C. Jordan. From *The History of Polk County, Iowa*

After serving a two-year term in the Iowa Senate, James Jordan was reelected in 1856 as a Free Soiler Whig. Southwest Iowa was a hotbed of abolitionism which was being watched closely nationwide. Tabor, Iowa, had become the center of antislavery activity. It was no secret that easterners were sending money and arms to Tabor to help equip those who were willing to risk their lives in their effort to make Kansas a free state. Hubert and Hugh Moeller, Iowa historians, explained, "Tabor at times looked like an armed camp. As many as 200 men, heavily armed, were seen drilling in the Town's square. Many wounded were brought to Tabor from Kansas and the place became both a storehouse for arms and a hospital for free-state sufferers of Kansas."

It was not much better in Des Moines. According to Johnson Brigham, there were several Underground Railroad stations in Polk County. "The tricks and devices practiced to escape the vigilance of slave-hunters, close on their track, were numerous and often ludicrous, for there was a strong proslavery sentiment in the county. *The Statesman* (a local newspaper) frequently gave voice to it in vigorous editorials, denouncing the opposition to the Fugitive Slave Law, with special anathemas against the Methodists." In fact, slavery *existed* in Polk County at one time. Joseph Smart, the Indian interpreter at the trading post, went to Missouri, bought two Negro women, brought them to Des Moines, and kept them for some time as servants. When he got through with them, he took them south and sold them.

The Republican Party Begins

The first *private* meeting of what would become the National Republican Party took place when a group of Whig Party defectors called together by Samuel Kirkwood and other abolitionists met in Crawfordsville, a part of Iowa City, in February of 1854. The meeting was to lay the groundwork for the creation of a new political party—the Republican Party. Its first *public* meeting would be held in Ripon, Wisconsin, one month later.

In January of 1856, Iowa newspapers announced a call for the organization of the Iowa Republican Party. The meeting took place in Iowa City on February 22. It is suspected but never confirmed that Governor Grimes instigated this meeting. After the group met, the Iowa Republican Party was officially launched. Folks were also working hard to get the party established in Illinois, which happened on May 29, 1856.

By 1858 Republican State Chairman John Kasson had successfully organized the election of Republican Governor Grimes to the US Senate. Grimes joined fellow Republican Senator James Harlan, who had been representing Iowa in Washington since 1855.

In 1859 homespun Republican Samuel Kirkwood battled against polished Democrat Ambassador Augustus Dodge for the office of governor. The race was likened to the Lincoln-Douglas contest; Kirkwood won by three thousand popular votes.

All of these Iowa leaders—Governor Kirkwood, Senators Grimes and Harlan, and Republican State Chairman John Kasson—were close personal friends of Senator James Jordan. He had served with them in state government. He entertained all of them in his home, and they spent a tremendous amount of time together discussing the complicated politics of the day. They probably were aquainted with Abraham Lincoln, whose political views were by then well-known.

Samuel Kirkwood. From *Portrait and Biographical Album of Polk County, Iowa*, 1890

James Jordan: His Life and His Legacy

Kasson, who became a prominent politician in Iowa's early years of statehood and then nationally through the turn of the century, was an especially frequent guest of the Jordans. So much so that James' son Henry named his first son "Kasson."

Kasson had been a newcomer to Iowa in 1857 but quickly understood Iowa politics and knew how to get Republicans elected. Probably James was of assistance to Kasson in the beginning, providing friendship and a welcome introduction into the Iowa Republican enclave. This would ultimately facilitate Kasson's appointment as Republican state chairman in 1858.

Senator Jordan was also a close friend of Samuel Kirkwood, who was secretly active in the Underground Railroad in Iowa City. James and Kirkwood had a lot in common. According to Iowan historian Leland Sage, "Born and reared in the border state of Maryland as a Democrat, Kirkwood was shocked and disillusioned by what he saw as a youth of the slave trade in Washington, D.C., and was completely won over to antislavery views during his residence in Ohio before coming to Iowa in 1855, so he could not in good conscience remain a Democrat."

"If you are a Republican you are probably also a Methodist. . . ."

By 1859, the dreams of these dedicated political leaders had come true as the lines between Free Soil Whigs and all the other antislavery groups blurred and then coalesced under the Republican banner.

The Republican movement came together in Iowa for many reasons, not strictly political ones. Credit must also be given to shared religious views often reflective of the antislavery movement. When contemplating this religious perspective, the powerful influence of the Methodist church must be considered.

In Iowa, the growth and maturation of Republican politics strongly paralleled the growth and maturation of the Methodist church. The church's organizational structure was perfectly attuned to the Iowa pioneer and his developing lifestyle. Everyone was welcomed into the church and urged to play an active role, and many Iowans became members of Methodist congregations sprouting up in every Iowa community.

Abraham Lincoln, 1857. Library of Congress

"At every step in the scheme Methodists found a place for the humblest of youngest layman, the woman and child, on through the Sunday School, the class leader, the exhorter, the local preacher, the circuit rider, up to the Senior Bishop. The way was clear and open to all. . . ," stated George Parker, Iowa historian.

The structure and operational style of the church groomed its members for leadership, if they so desired. Thus it was natural for some of these members to become leaders in politics.

Because Iowa Methodists were abolitionists (the slave-owning Southern Methodists had seceded from the church decades earlier), they aligned with antislavery political groups: first the Whigs and later the Republicans. If a person was a Democrat, it was unthinkable for that person to consider becoming a Methodist preacher. Several Iowa historians have noted that the Methodists were a one-political-party church. Horace Greeley said

130 Pursuit of a Dream

that "all Republicans were not Methodists, but Methodists were distinctively Republican."

Abolitionist James Harlan, both a Methodist and a Republican, was the president of Mount Pleasant's Iowa Wesleyan College, a Methodist school. He was elected US Senator from Iowa, a seat he held for eighteen years. Harlan's daughter would eventually marry Abraham Lincoln's son.

Beginning in 1854, the newly forming Republican Party was dominated by Methodists. Republicans dominated Iowa politics exclusively until 1873 after Harlan lost his seat in the US Senate. According to Parker, during those years it was a known fact in politics at all levels that "where worthwhile patronage was to be distributed or influence exerted, the Methodist church, both in its clergy of every rank and in its membership, could be counted upon almost to a man as a Republican

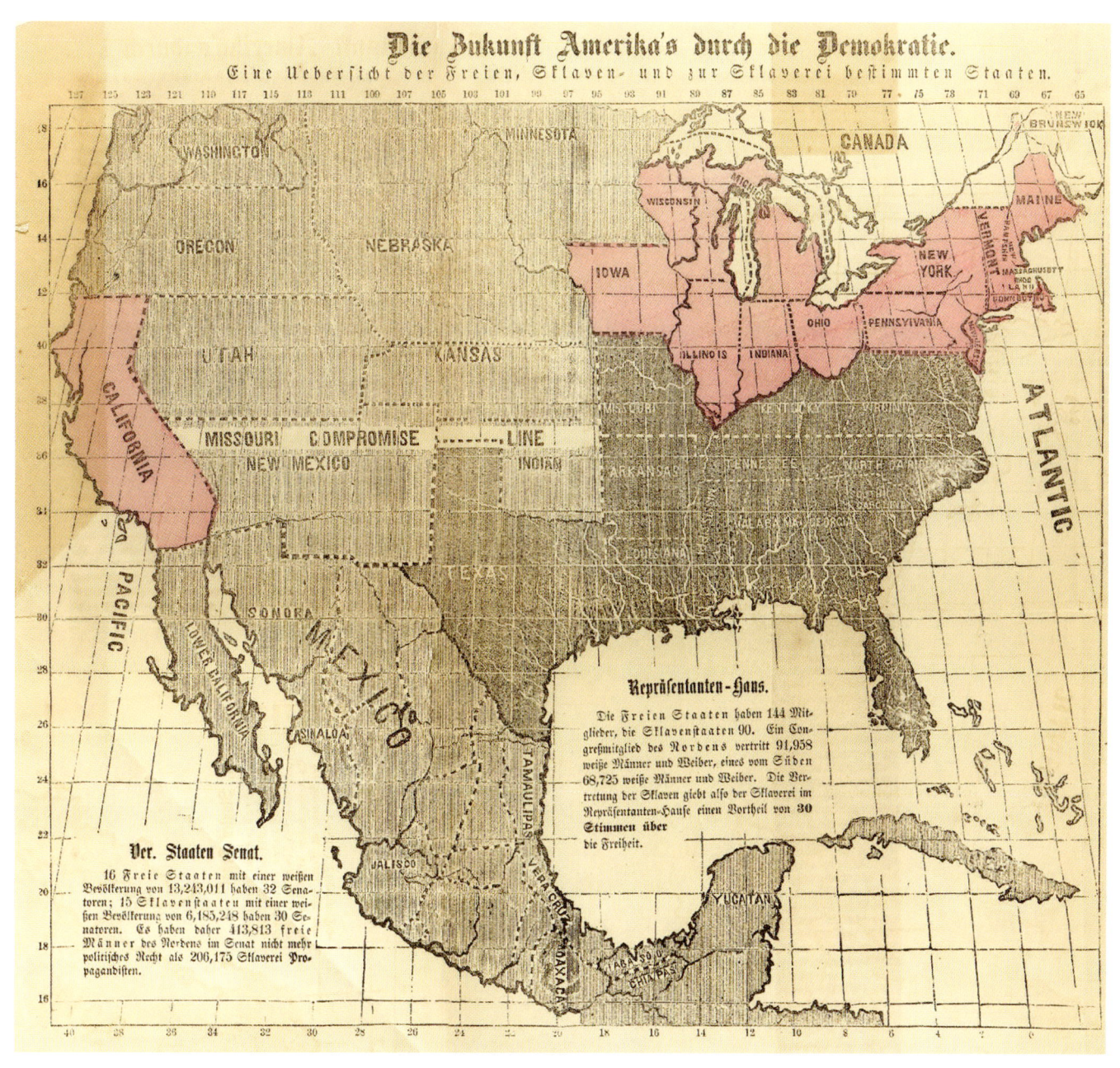

Antislavery map, in German, from the 1856 presidential campaign. Cornell University—The P. J. Mode Collection

Party force." Parker continues: "When it could not elect a Methodist Republican, it would make terms with and support only the most-friendly or eligible of the remaining Republican candidates presenting themselves. "This powerful unity of Methodist Republicans continued for decades and had a vital influence on the religious and political life of Iowa. Almost a revolution was required to break its hold."

In seventy-four years, from 1848 to 1932, Iowans elected only *one* Democratic US Senator and only *one* Democratic governor. The revolution which broke the Republican domination of Iowa politics was the Great Depression of the 1930s. Since the Depression, with a few exceptions, Republican governors have been an Iowa norm into the twenty-first century.

It should be noted that Governor (later Senator) James Grimes, so influential in early Iowa politics, was *not* a Methodist. He belonged to the Congregational church. He had been influenced by the "Iowa Band" of Congregationalists, a group which included Josiah Grinnell, also an abolitionist. Grinnell's friend and fellow "Iowa Band" member William Salter was the pastor of the Congregational church Grimes and his family attended when he lived in Burlington. Another Congregationalist active in the abolitionist movement was Reverend John Todd, who with others came to the southwestern Iowa town of Tabor to found a school they named Tabor College. Like James Jordan, John Todd was a friend of John Brown and active in the Underground Railroad.

Besides being a Republican abolitionist, Grimes was also a strong temperance man, as was James Jordan. When he was elected governor in 1854, Grimes, James, and other prohibitionists had tried to introduce permanent prohibition in Iowa. The effort was unsuccessful, as prohibition lasted only one year, 1855. However, when it was reintroduced in the Iowa Constitutional Convention of 1857, it passed and continued until the end of the century.

From State Senator to County Supervisor

Senator Jordan accomplished all he had set out to do in the Iowa state legislature. He brought the capital to Des Moines, helped get a banking system started in Iowa, and was part of the Republican movement to assert Iowa's stance against slavery. He had helped to successfully pass temperance laws, a cause very dear to his heart. He did not continue in the Iowa Senate after 1858 but instead directed his attention to Polk County government. In 1858 he was elected to the county board of supervisors and was reelected for three subsequent terms.

During his tenure he served as president of the board and in 1865 helped acquire the Polk County Poor Farm. James and two others, Dr. Brooks and D. C. Marks, were charged with the responsibility of purchasing land to care for the poor and incurably insane residents of the county.

In prior years, indigents and paupers had been served by caretakers who charged the county for the expense of caring for them. This proved to be too costly, and the taxpayers demanded a more economical system. James and his committee found a 120-acre parcel of land about five miles north of Des Moines. The county took $4,000 from the Polk County Swamp Land Fund and purchased the land for the Polk County Poor Farm. An additional 160 acres was subsequently purchased, thus enlarging the farm to 280 acres.

James eventually retired from Polk County politics and ended his political career, except for one brief two-year term as a representative in the Iowa legislature in 1878. Attesting to his local popularity, he was elected by a vote larger than his party ticket—both Republicans and Democrats voted for "Uncle Jimmy" Jordan.

CHAPTER 30
The Underground Railroad

The Underground Railroad (URR) was a secret route that runaway slaves followed as they escaped their southern owners and traveled north to freedom. Its name was influenced by the new phenomenon of railroad transportation in the United States. The idea behind the establishment of the URR was that it would mirror the new speedy and efficient railroad transportation system. The difference between the two was that the destination of folks traveling on the URR was either a "free" (nonslave) state or, even better, Canada, where slavery was not allowed.

Because the Underground Railroad was an illegal enterprise, secrecy was of utmost importance. Families sheltering slaves dared not breathe a word to anyone about what they were doing. Despite these dangerous and isolating circumstances, families like the Jordans, who offered their home as one of the "stations," sheltered the fugitives, provided whatever care or supplies they needed, and then sent them on or gave them escort to the next "station." The fact that Jordan House was located outside of Des Moines on a large wooded acreage west of the city ensured secrecy.

Cynthia and James Jordan joined this secret network shortly after their marriage in the mid-1850s. They were so caught up in the endeavor to help the escaping slaves that James *led* the effort in his area, becoming the "chief conductor" of the URR in Polk County.

The Antislavery Supporters

The First Great Awakening, which occurred in the mid-1700s, was a precursor of the antislavery movement. The Second Great Awakening of the 1820s and 1830s inspired reform. For some that included the immediate abolition of slavery; most considered it sinful to hold slaves or to tolerate slavery.

In 1830 William Lloyd Garrison, publisher of the abolitionist newspaper *The Liberator* and one of the founders of the American Anti-Slavery Society, demanded "immediate emancipation, gradually achieved;" slave owners should repent immediately and set up a system of emancipation.

Frederick Douglass was an escaped slave who became a national leader of the abolitionist movement.

William Lloyd Garrison. Digital Collection of New York Public Library

Frederick Douglass. National Archives and Records

He was known for his dazzling oratory and incisive antislavery writings. The most influential abolitionist literature, however, was a book entitled *Uncle Tom's Cabin*, written in 1852 by Harriet Beecher Stowe. The book emphasized the horrors abolitionists had long claimed about the institution of slavery. Read by many members of the white establishment, the book raised people's consciousness of the atrocity of slavery.

Women played a crucial role as leaders in the antislavery movement by helping to fund the printing and dissemination of antislavery literature throughout the country. They also pursued typically feminine endeavors such as the sewing and selling of quilts that provided money for the abolitionist cause. Women sponsored petitions, campaigned to Congress, and wrote articles and editorials for abolitionist newspapers and magazines.

The politicians of the Whig Party were abolitionists, the most famous of which was Henry Clay. Clay and the Whig Party (which transitioned into the Republican Party) wanted to achieve the gradual extinction of slavery by market forces because its members believed free labor was superior to slave labor.

Nationally, several Christian faith traditions participated in the antislavery movement; the most noted were the Quakers and Congregationalists.

"Northern" Presbyterians, Baptists, and Methodists, who would eventually sever their traditional ties with their denomination over the issue of slavery, also supported the abolitionist movement.

In Iowa the Quaker communities of Earlham, Salem, Low Moor, and Springdale are probably remembered the most for their abolitionist stance, but the Congregational church in Iowa was also very active. The abolitionist towns of Tabor and Grinnell were both Congregationalist strongholds. Although the Methodists in Iowa may not have been as vocal as the Congregationalists or the Quakers, the denomination may have been the most collaboratively supportive entity of the abolitionist movement, due to its many Republican members.

The Underground Railroad in Iowa

Slaves started to escape through the Iowa Territory before it became a state. According to Tacitus Hussey, early Des Moines historian, the Indians had reported they had seen "men who looked like bears" traveling through the woods of southern Iowa. These were probably escaping slaves. The Indians had never seen black people; they thought they were some kind of bear.

The Underground Railroad began operating in Iowa to assist runaway slaves sometime after statehood occurred, probably in the early 1850s. Iowa was a natural thoroughfare for slaves escaping from the slave state to its south, Missouri, where the "Little Dixie" counties along the Missouri River were heavily involved in slavery.

Intersected by navigable rivers, streams, and wooded, hilly terrain, Iowa provided camouflaged avenues for escaped slaves to find their way, usually on foot or hidden in wagon beds. Once the fugitives made their way through the state, they typically traveled to Chicago, and from there to Canada. There is no way to know actual figures, but it is estimated that during the decade of the 1850s, hundreds of slaves found their way through Iowa to freedom by way of the Underground Railroad.

In Iowa, the main route started at Tabor in southwest Iowa and continued in a northeasterly direction, passing through Lewis, Atlantic, Fontanelle, Winterset or Earlham, Jordan House, East Des Moines, Mitchellville, Lynnville, Grinnell, Iowa City, Tipton or Springdale, Clinton, and on to Canada. Along the way were homes, churches, and commercial buildings that provided shelter to the fugitives.

There is a good possibility that, between East Des Moines and Lynnville, the home of Ishmael and Marion Lee was also a refuge for the escaping slaves. The Lees had been active in the URR in Cass County, Michigan, and later, the Quaker community in Warren County, Iowa, before finally moving to Franklin Township near Mitchellville in Polk County. They most likely continued their URR activity there. Another option was the hotel constructed by Thomas Mitchell, a supporter of the URR in Mitchellville.

Refletions on the Treatment of Slaves

"Think of being compelled to live all your life with the man who is stealing the babies from your cradle and you dare not say one word; think of being compelled to associate with the despised and hated Southerner who is constantly robbing you; think of the being compelled to separate from your dear brother, loving sister, only father and mother, never to see them again. The agonizing groans of mothers when separated from their crying children were heart piercing. See the slave scarred veterans who are before me today and have witness to their once cruel and inhuman treatment. For 243 years the slave pen, the auction block, and the whipping post were all perpetuated within the sunny south; for 243 years the blood hound was raised to trace women through tangled swamps and craggy mountains. . . . Four million souls in fetters, 4,000,000 bodies in chains; all the sacred relations of wife, fathers, and mothers trampled beneath the brutal feet of avarice and might, and yet, fellow citizens, all of this was done under our beautiful and so-called flag of the free."

From an Emancipation Day speech in 1898 by John L. Thompson, editor of the *Iowa State Bystander*, Iowa's most prominent black newspaper, who reflected on the treatment of slaves prior to their emancipation.

Some "Known" Members of the Polk County URR

When the Underground Railroad network worked its way into his central Iowa area in the early-to-mid-1850s, James Jordan volunteered to become its chief conductor in Polk County. He was joined by four other "known" volunteers: Isaac Brandt, John Teesdale, Reverend Demas Robinson, and Jeremiah G. Anderson.

Isaac Brandt

In his youth while living in Ohio, Isaac Brandt apprenticed to be a shoemaker. Later as a young man living in Indiana, he expanded his trade into a very profitable boot and shoe manufacturing business. After traveling to Iowa, he decided to move there, and in 1858 he brought his wife and three young children to Des Moines, where he established another very successful boot and shoe manufacturing enterprise in Fort Des Moines. That same year he began welcoming fugitive slaves to his home, located at "Cherry Place" on the east side of Des Moines, near is what now known to be East Twelfth and Grand Avenue. At that time, it was merely a roadway through the timber leading southeast out of town. It follows that Brandt was a Republican; he lived on the east side of the river.

Isaac Brandt. From *Portrait and Biographical Album of Polk County, Iowa*, 1890

Brandt and URR Chief Conductor James Jordan probably "connected" because they were both Republicans but also because of the fire-hot issue of temperance. In the *History of Polk County, Iowa*, published in 1880, it says Brandt "has always been an active advocate of temperance and can say what can be said by few, that he never tasted a drop of alcoholic drinks, wine or beer, and this is an experience of fifty-three years." It further states that Brandt's "oldest child is thirty years of age, and none of his children have ever taken a cup of tea or coffee; neither have they tasted any alcoholic drink."

Isaac Brandt served in various leadership positions in local and national temperance organizations, and he "devotes his entire moral powers to the cause of temperance, which costs him $100 to $300 a year, without counting his time."

After the Civil War, Isaac Brandt served the State of Iowa as an elected official and was a member of many important legislative committees. In 1877 he was elected to the Des Moines City Council and then elected mayor of the city in 1880.

John Teesdale

John Teesdale was a newspaper editor and printer and was, for a short time, the owner of the Des Moines newspaper called *The Star*. The newspaper offices were located in one of the barrack buildings near "Coon Point" and because it was on the *west* side of the river, it was Democratic in politics. When he bought it in 1856, Teesdale, an abolitionist Republican, shifted the paper's viewpoint to Republican. In order to expedite the printing of the news, he invested in the first steam-powered printer to come to Des Moines. Shortly before he sold it in 1860, he changed his newspaper's name to *Iowa State Register*. It was the early predecessor of the *Des Moines Register*. After the Civil War, Teesdale invested in Wesley Redhead's Des Moines Coal Company, the first organized coal mining enterprise in the city.

Reverend Demas Robinson

Reverend Demas Robinson was a well-known pioneer Baptist preacher who was an early settler in the area that would be known as Four Mile Township.

Jeremiah Anderson

Jeremiah Anderson assisted slaves through Polk County until the summer of 1856, when he joined a group of armed young men who were marching from Iowa City to fight in the Kansas War against a pro-slavery group known as the "Border Ruffians." Anderson served under abolitionist John Brown, who had fought and won the Battle of Black Jack, the first battle in the Kansas War.

Slaves escaping in winter. Library of Congress

James Jordan, Abolitionist

Abolishing slavery became an ongoing objective in James' life from the time he was a young man until he reached adulthood and was able to take a leadership role in the antislavery movement:

- When he was nineteen he voted in the US presidential election of 1832 for Henry Clay, who was against slavery.
- During his life he became active in the (Northern) Methodist church, which was antislavery.
- His sister married a man whose father, "Yankee" Smith, was a well-known antislavery activist in his area of north central Missouri.
- He became a member of the Whig and then the Republican Political Parties which were antislavery.
- He and his family settled in the "free state" of Iowa where slavery was not allowed.
- Documentation exists that he was a friend of and co-conspirator with John Brown, a notorious abolitionist who operated out of Tabor, leading attacks into Kansas and Missouri and helping slaves escape through Iowa.
- Every one of his political cronies were abolitionists. Three of them were associated with the Underground Railroad: Governor Grimes and Samuel Kirkwood, both residing at the time in Iowa City, and J. B. Grinnell of Grinnell.

James' marriages to Melinda, a devout Methodist who was profoundly influenced by the antislavery message of the Second Great Awakening, and later to Cynthia, raised in an area of New York state where the Underground Railroad flourished, further influenced and reinforced his abolitionist commitment and activity. It was said that Cynthia and Melinda were as strong in their advocacy and support of abolition and the antislavery movement as James.

Traveling on the URR in Iowa

Slaves usually traveled in small groups, the largest normally being no more than seven to ten people. Generally escaped slaves traveled at night, but sometimes they could disguise themselves and travel during the day. Sometimes when it wasn't safe to travel a certain route, they would have to try a different one. One Jordan biographer, Johnson Brigham, stated that to elude bounty hunters "the Negroes would have to be returned to stations past, and routed another way."

When the fugitives arrived at a safe house, as the Jordan House was, they would first look around the yard for clues to see whether or not it was safe for them to approach the door. At night a lighted lantern might be placed on a post or during the day a particular quilt might be hung on the clothesline to signal a welcome to the fugitives. If it appeared safe, they would approach the house and would be provided a much-needed shelter in which to hide and rest before continuing on their journey to freedom. Jordan family legend tells of a time in the 1850s when the Jordan children remember seeing the faces of slave youngsters peering over their picket fence into their front yard.

The escape route often began in Nebraska City, in the Nebraska Territory. Considered to be outside the United States, Nebraska City was a safer place than Iowa, and it was strategically located on the Missouri River with access to a ferry (although many runaways were rowed across the river in rowboats). In Nebraska City, Allen B. Mayhew and his wife would shelter the escapees. Their cabin is considered to be the oldest building still standing in the state of Nebraska.

When the number of escaped slaves grew to greater numbers, Mayhew's brother-in-law dug a cellar under the cabin from which he further excavated a tunnel leading to a nearby ravine. Iowa historian Eugene Hastie describes the tunnel: "The ceiling of the tunnel was several feet beneath the surface, and at frequent intervals was supported by strong timbers. To the sides of the tunnel were three secret rooms, each capable of holding

Iowa Underground Railroad display at the Jordan House. Courtesy of West Des Moines Historical Society

about a dozen people. All of this was for hiding the slaves and eluding their pursuing owners."

Many were secreted in the caves in the Mayhew cabin tunnel. Others were hidden elsewhere, such as the thirteen slaves who were concealed in a wagon train crossing the Missouri River on the ferry.

Another cave, known as the "Black Din," also hid slaves. In 1928 Calvin Chapman, a local resident of that era, reminisced about when, as a sixteen-year-old in 1859, he drove his brother's wagon from the "Black Din" fifteen miles west to Lickskillet, which is now known as Knox, Iowa.

Hastie tells a riveting story which illustrates the tremendous danger to those helping folks make their way on the URR:

In November 1858 two female slaves were enticed away from their owners. A reward of $200 was offered for their capture and return to Nebraska City. The "Nebraska City News," among other things, said, "They will doubtless be found in some abolition hole." Fifteen armed men set out to capture them. The first place they went to was Civil Bend (Percival), Iowa, where a Mr. Williams was known to be a strong abolitionist. Williams refused to let them search his house, which resulted in him being struck and temporarily put out of commission. The posse continued on until the whole group was arrested at Tabor.

The Williams incident was taken into court, where a Fremont County jury awarded Williams a

James Jordan: His Life and His Legacy 137

Sketch of Hitchcock House by Bill Wagner.

considerable sum of money for damages. He invested this money in a large barn and opened a hotel for the use of people going to and from Nebraska City. One night two strangers sojourned with Mr. Williams. That evening the barn was found to be on fire. The ropes to the well had been cut and the strangers had vanished.

The next station after Nebraska City was Tabor, Iowa. Reverend John Todd, leader of Tabor's Congregational church, was in charge of the URR activity there and also may have been involved in the comings and goings of the militia John Brown was forming that eventually ended up at Harper's Ferry, Virginia.

After Tabor, fugitives were either led or directed to a two-story house southwest of Lewis, Iowa, on a hill overlooking the western bank of the East Nishnabotna River. Built in 1856 by Congregationalist minister George B. Hitchcock, it is now known as Hitchcock House. In this dwelling, there was a basement chamber where slaves could be hidden when necessary. The access to this chamber was concealed by a false cabinet. The other basement room was fitted with a cooking fireplace and was accessible via an exterior entrance and by stairs from above, very much like at the Jordan House.

From Lewis the fugitives hurried through western Iowa to sympathetic folks in the Quaker community of Earlham and then on to a safe haven offered either in Indianola or at the Jordan House. While slaves were sheltered at the Jordan House, they probably were hidden in the barn, in the creek bed, in the cornfields, or under hay in wagon beds that were taking them to freedom. If brought inside the house, they may have been concealed in the attic, in the cellar, or in a secret space under the front hall staircase.

There was a legend that two tunnels were constructed for hiding slaves on the Jordan property—one from the basement running east to Jordan Creek and another running west from the fireplace area of the kitchen house to Jordan's barn. No evidence, however, has been found to support the existence of these tunnels.

Traces of a hole in the basement floor were actually the remains of a recessed place where the family stored potatoes, and Jordan family members recall playing in it. More likely, the slaves passing through the Jordan House were hidden in the brush and ravines adjacent to the sometimes ten- to fifteen-foot deep creek bed, which people may have mistakenly assumed was a "tunnel" that led to the basement. "Evidence" of a purported tunnel leading from the kitchen house to the barn was actually from a large drafty crack in the fireplace foundation.

If they had been led to Indianola instead of the Jordan House, the escaped slaves probably made their way from there to the home of Reverend Demas Robinson at Four Mile Creek in southeast Des Moines. There were other safe houses in and around the nearby community of Rising Sun, where Robinson hid slaves as well. From both the Robinson's and the Jordan House, the slaves were assisted by Jeremiah Anderson as they continued through Des Moines, sheltering, if necessary, with either John Teesdale or Isaac Brandt. From there they may have stopped at the Lee's house near Mitchellville, or at Thomas Mitchell's hotel, before moving on to Lynnville and then Grinnell, into the welcoming sanctuary offered by Congregational minister Josiah Grinnell. Grinnell then sent the fugitives east to Iowa City

Josiah B. Grinnell. Library of Congress

John "Osawatomie" Brown. Library of Congress   John Brown's home in New York. Library of Congress

and the URR network led by Samuel Kirkwood. Next they traveled to the Quaker communities of West Branch and Springdale. From those towns it was over to the Mississippi River and on to Chicago, where the slaves would be able to travel to Canada on trains or ships traversing the Great Lakes.

Bounty Hunters

Participation in the Underground Railroad was serious business. By sheltering fugitive slaves, James and first Melinda and then Cynthia Jordan put their family and their livelihood at risk. In addition to the possibility of being killed by bounty hunters or having their house and outbuildings burned down, James and Cynthia risked being taken to court and fined heavily or imprisoned for breaking the law by sheltering or assisting fugitive slaves.

Bounty hunters and slave catchers were exercising their legal rights to recover escaped "property," which was what slaves were considered to be. Slaves were considered less than 100 percent human; they were white men's possessions—beasts of burden—particularly those engaged in hard, physical labor in the fields. Generous rewards were offered to those who caught and brought back runaway slaves. It was a lucrative business, and at any given time there were many people searching Iowa for slaves missing from their Missouri masters.

James, Melinda, and Cynthia were law-abiding citizens who were morally opposed to slavery. Following their moral and religious principals, they made the decision to risk the safety and well-being of their family to assist the fugitives in their quest for freedom. They must have strongly stressed to their children what a secret affair it was. Only one documented comment affirming the family's involvement in the Underground Railroad appeared from the Jordan children, made in a biography about son James Finley Jordan, published several decades after the Civil War.

John "Osawatomie" Brown

It was said in the late 1850s that the only person who knew the entire route system of the Underground Railroad was John Brown. During that decade deviations off the main Underground Railroad route were introduced to maintain secrecy, and these new routes were also known only to him.

Brown was born in Connecticut in 1800. As a youth he wanted to be a Congregationalist minister but instead he apprenticed with his father and became a tanner. He plied his trade in Ohio, Pennsylvania, and Massachusetts, where he also farmed and raised livestock—cattle and sheep.

He moved to Springfield, Massachusetts, where he worked with wool growers, and while living there

James Jordan: His Life and His Legacy   139

he joined St. John's Congregational Church, one of the most prominent platforms in the United States for abolitionist speeches. From 1846 until he left Springfield in 1850, Brown witnessed abolitionist lectures by the likes of Frederick Douglass and Sojourner Truth. "During Brown's time in Springfield, he became deeply involved in transforming the city into a major center of abolitionism, and one of the safest and most significant stops on the Underground Rail Road," claimed St. John's Congregational Church in Springfield, Massachusetts.

Business failures forced him to homestead for two years in Upstate New York. In 1855 he left and joined his six abolitionist sons who were all homesteading in the Kansas Territory. At that time there was an intense struggle over the future status of Kansas eventually coming into the Union as a "free" or "slave" state. Carrying his passionate abolitionist zeal with him to "Bleeding Kansas," John Brown first sought to mitigate the introduction of slavery in Kansas by trying to persuade people that the practice of owning, buying, or selling slaves was evil.

Brown was as successful in Kansas as his contemporary, "Yankee" Smith—James Jordan's brother-in-law and Calvin Smith's father—had been a few years earlier in "Little Dixie," Missouri. Yankee Smith, along with his wife, had been beaten up, terrorized, and run out of town by the slave-owning residents there when he voiced his abolitionist views. The same thing would happen to John Brown in Kansas.

Tired of Brown's rhetoric, 150 pro-slavery Kansas border ruffians attacked and burned his camp in 1856 in Osawatomie, Kansas. Four of his six sons were either killed or maimed and at that point Brown decided it was time to retaliate. According to Iowa historian Benjamin Gue, as Brown watched the flames he exclaimed: "God sees it. I have only a short time to live—only one death to die, and I will die fighting for this cause. There will be no more peace in this land until slavery is done for. I will give them something else to do than to extend slave territory. I will carry the war into Africa."

His new nickname—"Osawatomie"—became a battle cry and from then on Brown shifted from verbiage to violence. "Osawatomie Brown" was obsessed with the abolitionist cause. He was described as a "splendid fanatic," and many people thought he was just plain crazy. Brown was continually and proudly responsible for many heroic but brutal actions as he routinely led raids into "Bleeding Kansas" and "Little Dixie" in Missouri.

John Brown and the URR in Iowa

Osawatomie Brown eventually made his headquarters in Tabor, Iowa, and became a leader of the Underground Railroad in the state. There are several documented accounts of John Brown stopping along the Iowa Underground Railroad network. One of these visits was to the Isaac Brandt home on the east side of the Des Moines River. "Very early one morning in April, 1859," Iowa historian Ilda Hammer relates, John Brown "came in a wagon filled with corn fodder, under which lay four hidden runaway slaves. The slaves were cared for, and John Brown and Isaac Brandt had breakfast together. They told each other goodbye, shaking hands across a little white picket gate in the front yard." The group had probably spent the previous night at the Jordan House.

Another book, *Portrait and Biographical Album of Polk County, Iowa*, documents a visit by John Brown to the Jordan House: "After coming to Iowa, Jordan's home

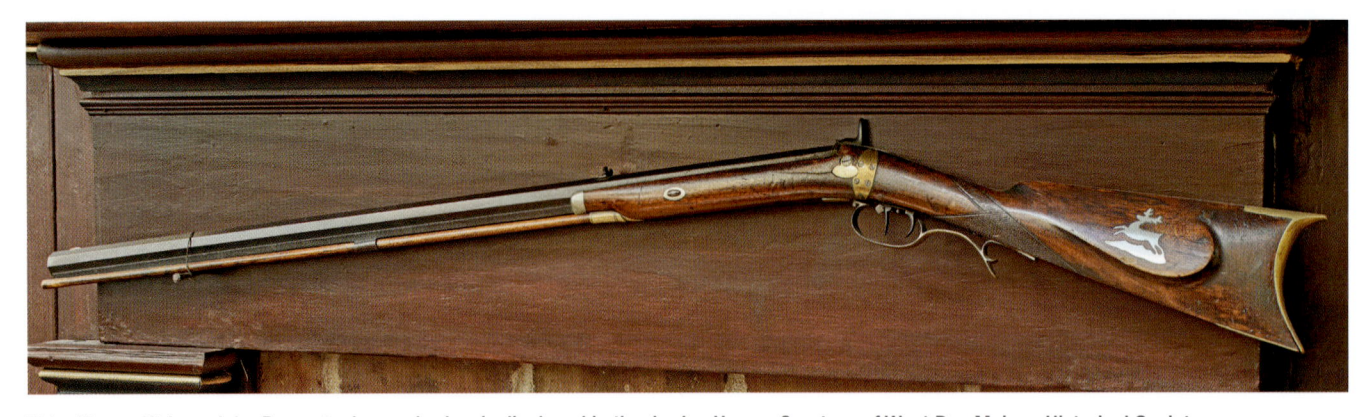

This rifle, a gift from John Brown to James Jordan, is displayed in the Jordan House. Courtesy of West Des Moines Historical Society

140   Pursuit of a Dream

in Walnut Township was often a haven for fugitive slaves while escaping to Canada. John Brown, with a small party of colored people whom he was leading to freedom, was once his welcome guest. He was on his way to Virginia accompanied by the principal ones of that band that met defeat shortly after Harper's Ferry. Twenty-four colored people accompanied him at that time."

An account of this incident in *Pioneers of Polk County, Iowa* also mentions John Brown "being quartered" at the Jordan House and saying that "once all 24 Negroes were there, it took good engineering to get them disposed of, for the stations were at many angles."

The book *Iowa, Its History and Its Foremost Citizens* states, "John Brown, the noted abolitionist, was a guest at (Jordan's) home and more than once received assistance in different ways from Mr. Jordan."

In the book *History of Des Moines and Polk County*, under the biography of his son, James F. Jordan, it states James F. Jordan "distinctly recalls seeing John Brown on one of his expeditions, that gentlemen having stopped at his father's home . . . a station on the Underground Railroad prior to the Civil War."

Family legend recalls a tale about one of Brown's visits to the Jordan House. The Jordan children saw men with guns who they later realized were slave catchers chasing John Brown. Fearing that Brown would be outspoken and belligerent with the authorities, James "knocked John out" and hid him away until the slave catchers finally left, so as to not risk being "found out."

Grandchildren of Benjamin Jordan tell another story that was passed on by his son Charles. While Benjamin was overseeing the Jordan cattle north of the Jordan farm in an area near where Dallas Center now stands, he remembered John Brown coming through in the middle of the night, lost. He asked Benjamin where the Jordan farm was, and Benjamin escorted him there.

Legend also tells us that John Brown never slept inside Jordan's house. Constantly worried about being found by slave catchers, he wanted to be able to move on at a moment's notice, so he always slept out in the bed of his wagon.

James Jordan and John Brown were co-conspirators who became good friends. Besides offering friendship, Brown gave James the gift of a rifle that hangs on the mantle at the Jordan House.

"Brown's Band"

In spite of the secrecy of the Underground Railroad, one particular story from 1859–60 is recounted in bits and pieces in a number of history books. It concerns one of the last journeys John Brown made through Iowa, and it occurred on the eve of the Civil War. Perhaps that is why this story, unlike most of the others, was actually told and not kept secret.

It involved a group of men Brown recruited to help liberate and transport a number of fugitive slaves. They were Albert Hazlett, Aaron D. Stevens, John Henri Kagi, C. P. Todd, George B. Gill, and Jeremiah G. Anderson. Anderson was the same person who had been active in the Polk County Underground Railroad.

F. B. Sanborn, John Brown historian, recounts a letter written by John Brown in January 1859 from Trading Post, Kansas, that begins the story:

On Sunday, December 19, a Negro man called Jim, came over the river to the Osage (Kansas) settlement, from Missouri, and stated that he, together with his wife, two children, and another Negro man, was to be sold within a day or two and begged for help to get away.

On Monday (the following night), two small companies were made up to go to Missouri and forcibly liberate the five slaves, together with other slaves: One of these companies I assumed to direct.

We proceeded to the place, surrounded the building, liberated the slaves, and also took certain property supposed to belong to the estate. We, however, learned before leaving that a portion of the articles we had taken belonged to a man living at the plantation as a tenant, and who was supposed to have no interest in the estate. We promptly returned to him all that we had taken.

We went to another plantation, where we found five other slaves, took some property and two white men. We moved all slowly away into the Territory (Kansas) for some distance, and then sent the white men back, telling them to follow us as soon as they chose to do so.

The other company freed one female slave, took some property and as I am informed, killed one white man (the master), who fought against the liberation.

When the time was right, Brown led his men in the capture of the arsenal in Harper's Ferry on October 16, 1859. He entered the town with eighteen men (including five blacks), murdered four men, and took hostages. One of the captives was Colonel Lewis W. Washington, a great-grandnephew of George Washington. The raid failed because Robert Elise, under the command of Robert E. Lee, intercepted Brown and his followers and captured many of them. Brown was wounded and ten men were killed, including two of Brown's sons. Brown was arrested and stood trial.

During his trial, per Brigham, John Brown was quoted as saying: "If it is deemed necessary that I should forfeit my life for the furthering of the ends of justice and mingle my blood further with the blood of my children and with the blood of millions in this slave country whose rights are disregarded by wicked, cruel, and unjust enactments, I say let it be done."

John Brown was hanged along with others, including Iowan Edwin Coppoc. According to Iowa historian Benjamin Gue, Iowans reacted to the news of the raid and the executions with "surprise, shock, and passion. The execution of John Brown aroused magnificent indignation. . . . For the first time, responsible men began to believe that the issue between North and South could be settled only by armed conflict."

Delivering a lecture on "Courage" at Boston on November 28, 1859, Ralph Waldo Emerson referred to John Brown as "that new saint." The November 2 edition of the *Richmond Enquirer* stated, "The Harper's Ferry invasion has advanced the cause of disunion more than any other event that has happened since the formation of the government."

Barclay Coppoc escaped from Virginia after the raid, and his story according to Iowa historian William Peterson, follows:

(The Commonwealth of) Virginia requested the apprehension and delivery of the youthful Barclay Coppoc of Springdale, Iowa, who had assisted in the raid upon Harper's Ferry. He had escaped to Iowa and Virginia demanded his arrest and return for trial.

(Iowa's) Governor Kirkwood discovered legal and technical flaws in the Virginian extradition warrant and declined to surrender Coppoc. Three weeks passed before Virginia could return another requisition for the youth and by that time, Coppoc had been safely transferred out of American jurisdiction to Canada. Iowans had contributed funds for his escape and formed an armed guard about Springdale to prevent his arrest before his flight. That is how Iowa felt about slavery!

By 1860, abolitionist James Jordan and his family were finally in good company in Iowa. For the preceding five years they had quietly assisted escaping slaves—doing so as secretly as possible. However, by 1860 public sentiment in Iowa supported James' position by voicing its collective indignation at the execution of John Brown. Very likely James and Cynthia and their family mourned the loss of a man so dedicated to a movement in which they all believed. Certainly Brown's memory was fresh in their minds, as only a few months before his execution he had been welcomed as a guest in their home.

James Jordan, A Friend to John Brown

"Mr. Jordan, though raised on slave territory, has been a life-long enemy to slavery; his devotion to political life as a staunch and stalwart Republican is the outgrowth of a deep-seated conviction; it is among the pleasant things to remember that under his protecting roof John Brown and his associates, with more than a score of recently liberated slaves, have offered their prayers and sung their first jubilee hymns on their way to Canada, in the old slave days; said Brown, when forecasting the next day's journey, with a view of safe quarters the next night, 'we can stay with our enemies but prefer to stay with our friends.'"

—*History of Polk County, Iowa*

in Walnut Township was often a haven for fugitive slaves while escaping to Canada. John Brown, with a small party of colored people whom he was leading to freedom, was once his welcome guest. He was on his way to Virginia accompanied by the principal ones of that band that met defeat shortly after Harper's Ferry. Twenty-four colored people accompanied him at that time."

An account of this incident in *Pioneers of Polk County, Iowa* also mentions John Brown "being quartered" at the Jordan House and saying that "once all 24 Negroes were there, it took good engineering to get them disposed of, for the stations were at many angles."

The book *Iowa, Its History and Its Foremost Citizens* states, "John Brown, the noted abolitionist, was a guest at (Jordan's) home and more than once received assistance in different ways from Mr. Jordan."

In the book *History of Des Moines and Polk County*, under the biography of his son, James F. Jordan, it states James F. Jordan "distinctly recalls seeing John Brown on one of his expeditions, that gentlemen having stopped at his father's home . . . a station on the Underground Railroad prior to the Civil War."

Family legend recalls a tale about one of Brown's visits to the Jordan House. The Jordan children saw men with guns who they later realized were slave catchers chasing John Brown. Fearing that Brown would be outspoken and belligerent with the authorities, James "knocked John out" and hid him away until the slave catchers finally left, so as to not risk being "found out."

Grandchildren of Benjamin Jordan tell another story that was passed on by his son Charles. While Benjamin was overseeing the Jordan cattle north of the Jordan farm in an area near where Dallas Center now stands, he remembered John Brown coming through in the middle of the night, lost. He asked Benjamin where the Jordan farm was, and Benjamin escorted him there.

Legend also tells us that John Brown never slept inside Jordan's house. Constantly worried about being found by slave catchers, he wanted to be able to move on at a moment's notice, so he always slept out in the bed of his wagon.

James Jordan and John Brown were co-conspirators who became good friends. Besides offering friendship, Brown gave James the gift of a rifle that hangs on the mantle at the Jordan House.

"Brown's Band"

In spite of the secrecy of the Underground Railroad, one particular story from 1859–60 is recounted in bits and pieces in a number of history books. It concerns one of the last journeys John Brown made through Iowa, and it occurred on the eve of the Civil War. Perhaps that is why this story, unlike most of the others, was actually told and not kept secret.

It involved a group of men Brown recruited to help liberate and transport a number of fugitive slaves. They were Albert Hazlett, Aaron D. Stevens, John Henri Kagi, C. P. Todd, George B. Gill, and Jeremiah G. Anderson. Anderson was the same person who had been active in the Polk County Underground Railroad.

F. B. Sanborn, John Brown historian, recounts a letter written by John Brown in January 1859 from Trading Post, Kansas, that begins the story:

On Sunday, December 19, a Negro man called Jim, came over the river to the Osage (Kansas) settlement, from Missouri, and stated that he, together with his wife, two children, and another Negro man, was to be sold within a day or two and begged for help to get away.

On Monday (the following night), two small companies were made up to go to Missouri and forcibly liberate the five slaves, together with other slaves: One of these companies I assumed to direct.

We proceeded to the place, surrounded the building, liberated the slaves, and also took certain property supposed to belong to the estate. We, however, learned before leaving that a portion of the articles we had taken belonged to a man living at the plantation as a tenant, and who was supposed to have no interest in the estate. We promptly returned to him all that we had taken.

We went to another plantation, where we found five other slaves, took some property and two white men. We moved all slowly away into the Territory (Kansas) for some distance, and then sent the white men back, telling them to follow us as soon as they chose to do so.

The other company freed one female slave, took some property and as I am informed, killed one white man (the master), who fought against the liberation.

Staging area for John Brown's raid on the arsenal at Harper's Ferry. Library of Congress

Other accounts "credit" John Brown with the raids on both farms and report several horses, wagons, cattle, and other property were taken because, Brown claimed, "the slaves were entitled to it after all their years of unpaid labor." The number of slaves rescued varies from nine to twelve in these accounts. Brown's letter suggests ten were rescued. Soon after the raid the furious governor of Missouri offered a large reward for the arrest of John Brown and the members of "Brown's Band."

With the dozen or so slaves in their charge, the band left Kansas and hid out in Nebraska for almost a month. When it seemed like things had quieted down, they traveled to Tabor, Iowa, arriving there on February 5. There was a problem in Tabor, however. Because Brown and his men were in such trouble in Missouri, the citizens of Tabor, fearing armed retaliation by Missourians, were nervous about keeping the Brown party in their town. Brown's group left Tabor on February 11.

Traveling through southwestern Iowa, they stayed with Lewis Mills on February 13 and with the Murray family on February 15. On February 17 they spent the night at the Jordan House. The next day John Teesdale paid for their ferry ride across the Des Moines River. The party continued on to Grinnell where on February 20 they were welcomed by J. B. Grinnell and citizens at a town meeting. Five days later the group arrived in Springdale by way of Iowa City. There the fugitives were quartered by Quaker friends.

After leaving Tabor there had been no threat of slave hunters coming after them, but when they passed through Iowa City on February 25, two men from there tried to put together a slave-hunting posse. Their intent was to capture the slaves in Springdale, collect the slave bounty, apprehend John Brown and his men, and collect the reward money.

Pursuit of a Dream

Over the years, Brown and his men had brought an arsenal of guns and ammunition to Springdale. Even though it was supposedly a nonviolent Quaker settlement, the Quakers must have turned their heads; Springdale had turned into an armed camp similar to Tabor.

The two men in the "slave-hunting posse" were unsuccessful in their plan to capture the slaves in Springdale because nobody would join them. No one wanted to risk a fight with the well-armed and tenacious John Brown and his sharpshooting friends in Springdale.

It was now almost March. The fugitives had been traveling since late December and problems had arisen in getting the slaves out of Iowa. The exciting story that follows by Benjamin Gue, Iowa historian, tells how this was accomplished:

> After resting at Springdale some days, arrangements were made by Wm. Penn Clark and others at Iowa City, to procure a boxcar on the Rock Island Railroad to convey the fugitives and their escort to Chicago. Laurel Summers, United States Marshal at Davenport, was quietly organizing a posse to arrest them when the train reached that city. But Clark had outwitted the officers by arranging for a boxcar to be side-tracked at West Liberty.
>
> Brown and Kagi slept at Dr. Bowen's at Iowa City on the night fixed for departure. Workman's spies were watching for Brown, intending to arrest the leader while his party was absent and then seize the slaves. But the slave rescuers were hunting men who were on the alert and not easily trapped.
>
> At four o'clock, long before daylight, Brown and Kagi, mounted on fast horses, and piloted by Colonel Trowbridge, eluded the spies of watch and were on their way to West Liberty, where the slaves had been secreted in a mill, guarded by Stevens and others. A boxcar stood on the side track waiting for its human freight. As soon as Brown arrived the slaves were quickly transferred to the car, while Stevens and Kagi, leaning on their Sharp's rifles, their belts filled with revolvers, kept guard.
>
> Soon the train arrived from the West. It was a thrilling moment, as the guards with rifle in hand, anxiously watched the passengers alighting, to discover indication of officers coming to arrest them. The train backed down the side track, the car with locked doors was attached, the guards stepped into one of the passenger coaches, the train started and John Brown and his companions were leaving Iowa for the last time.
>
> At Davenport the marshal and aides walked through the passenger cars in search of the twelve slaves, but no Negroes were found, and no suspicion was aroused by the freight car in the rear. At Chicago, Allen Pinkerton, the famous Detective, conducted the slaves to a waiting car, which took them safely to Canada.

John Brown and Harper's Ferry

The most famous story involving John Brown was his raid on a government arsenal in Harper's Ferry, Virginia, located at the confluence of the Shenandoah and Potomac Rivers, not far from where James Jordan had grown up. This incident became a major provocation for the Civil War and further coalesced Iowans in a unified position against slavery.

Brown's plan was to capture the federal arsenal and steal its guns and ammunition. His intention was to give all these arms to slaves so they could form an army and start a revolution to free the slaves. Brown could not do this alone so he gathered an "army" of equally fanatic men around him, including two Quaker brothers, Edwin and Barclay Coppoc of Springdale, Iowa. The story by Johnson Brigham, Iowa historian, continues:

> Ossowatamie (John Brown's nickname) Brown had already made Iowa his rallying point. He had ridden across the state to Tabor, where the Reverend John Todd had long kept in storage for him arms for the relief of "bleeding Kansas." Thence, after furbishing the arms, learning their use, and recruiting a band of faithful followers, Brown rode on to Springdale, accompanied by his faithful allies, arriving there near the close of 1857. He had intended to go to Ashtabula, but the panic of 1857 compelled him to remain among his Quaker friends. Here his men were drilled for service, and were instructed in parliamentary usages, in anticipation of future public duties. Brown went on east to raise money for his purpose. Late in April he returned. His party at once proceeded to Chatham, Canada, from which point they separated to reassemble at Harper's Ferry. Lack of funds deferred the raid until 1859.

When the time was right, Brown led his men in the capture of the arsenal in Harper's Ferry on October 16, 1859. He entered the town with eighteen men (including five blacks), murdered four men, and took hostages. One of the captives was Colonel Lewis W. Washington, a great-grandnephew of George Washington. The raid failed because Robert Elise, under the command of Robert E. Lee, intercepted Brown and his followers and captured many of them. Brown was wounded and ten men were killed, including two of Brown's sons. Brown was arrested and stood trial.

During his trial, per Brigham, John Brown was quoted as saying: "If it is deemed necessary that I should forfeit my life for the furthering of the ends of justice and mingle my blood further with the blood of my children and with the blood of millions in this slave country whose rights are disregarded by wicked, cruel, and unjust enactments, I say let it be done."

John Brown was hanged along with others, including Iowan Edwin Coppoc. According to Iowa historian Benjamin Gue, Iowans reacted to the news of the raid and the executions with "surprise, shock, and passion. The execution of John Brown aroused magnificent indignation. . . . For the first time, responsible men began to believe that the issue between North and South could be settled only by armed conflict."

Delivering a lecture on "Courage" at Boston on November 28, 1859, Ralph Waldo Emerson referred to John Brown as "that new saint." The November 2 edition of the *Richmond Enquirer* stated, "The Harper's Ferry invasion has advanced the cause of disunion more than any other event that has happened since the formation of the government."

Barclay Coppoc escaped from Virginia after the raid, and his story according to Iowa historian William Peterson, follows:

(The Commonwealth of) Virginia requested the apprehension and delivery of the youthful Barclay Coppoc of Springdale, Iowa, who had assisted in the raid upon Harper's Ferry. He had escaped to Iowa and Virginia demanded his arrest and return for trial.

(Iowa's) Governor Kirkwood discovered legal and technical flaws in the Virginian extradition warrant and declined to surrender Coppoc. Three weeks passed before Virginia could return another requisition for the youth and by that time, Coppoc had been safely transferred out of American jurisdiction to Canada. Iowans had contributed funds for his escape and formed an armed guard about Springdale to prevent his arrest before his flight. That is how Iowa felt about slavery!

By 1860, abolitionist James Jordan and his family were finally in good company in Iowa. For the preceding five years they had quietly assisted escaping slaves—doing so as secretly as possible. However, by 1860 public sentiment in Iowa supported James' position by voicing its collective indignation at the execution of John Brown. Very likely James and Cynthia and their family mourned the loss of a man so dedicated to a movement in which they all believed. Certainly Brown's memory was fresh in their minds, as only a few months before his execution he had been welcomed as a guest in their home.

James Jordan, A Friend to John Brown

"Mr. Jordan, though raised on slave territory, has been a life-long enemy to slavery; his devotion to political life as a staunch and stalwart Republican is the outgrowth of a deep-seated conviction; it is among the pleasant things to remember that under his protecting roof John Brown and his associates, with more than a score of recently liberated slaves, have offered their prayers and sung their first jubilee hymns on their way to Canada, in the old slave days; said Brown, when forecasting the next day's journey, with a view of safe quarters the next night, 'we can stay with our enemies but prefer to stay with our friends.'"

—*History of Polk County, Iowa*

CHAPTER 31
The Civil War Years

Despite the distractions of politics during the past six years, the devastating flood of 1851, the financial panic of 1857, and a disastrous farming season in 1858, by 1860 life was finally again running smoothly at the Jordan farm.

James, having given up his state senatorial post, was involved locally in county government, on the Polk County Board of Supervisors. He was also concentrating his efforts on enlarging and developing his cattle herds and raising hogs for market. Hogs were raised locally, near his farm. The cattle, by now numbering in the thousands, were pastured all over southwestern Iowa. Many were "ranged" as far away as Atlantic, sixty miles to the west. When it was time for the cattle to be brought to market, the Jordan sons, nephews (sons of his sister Anna Smith), and other hired hands served as cowboys to drive the herds to Des Moines. The cattle and hogs were herded into the stockyards along the river. The livestock then was shipped on flatboats or steamboats downstream on the Des Moines River to Keokuk and from there on Mississippi barges to the markets in St. Louis.

The Jordan children were healthy and numerous. James' and Cynthia's first daughter, Ella, had been born in March 1857 and would soon celebrate her third birthday. Cynthia had just given birth in February to twin girls who were named Eva and Eda. James now was the father of nine children:

- Benjamin (aged twenty-one), who along with the other hired hands worked for his father as a cowboy, was in charge of the cattle herds grazing in western Iowa. When Benjamin's brothers became old enough, they were put to work as cowboys along with Benjamin and the hired hands.
- Emily (eighteen) was attending Mrs. Thompson Bird's Female Seminary at Second and Walnut Streets near old Fort Des Moines on Coon Point. She would in years hence complete her education at Northwestern University in Evanston, Illinois.
- Henry (sixteen) attended the Forest Home Seminary (later called the Baptist College) of Des Moines.
- John (fourteen), James (twelve), and George (ten) went to the nearby one-room schoolhouse and helped out on the farm.
- Ella (three) and the new twin babies, Eda and Eva, along with household responsibilities, probably kept Cynthia very busy, although by now hired help assisted her in some domestic responsibilities.

Until 1860, the area of southwestern Polk County where the Jordans lived was considered by many of their friends as part of far western Des Moines, but by March of that year the population had grown sufficiently for it to be organized into its own separate community, Walnut Township. The area included the land north of the Raccoon River, extending from the west boundary of the county to within about a mile of the city of Des Moines. Two branches of Walnut Creek—Little Walnut and Walnut Creek proper—formed the township's north boundary. It also included what would become Webster Township in 1878.

Abraham Lincoln assumed the office of president on March 4, 1861, and one month later the Civil War began. Despite concerns about the political state of affairs nationally, life at the Jordan farm carried on pretty much as usual. Eventually, however, the Jordan family would experience direct repercussions of the war.

In the meantime, the family celebrated two joyous occasions. Cynthia gave birth to a son, Calvin, and their oldest son Benjamin got married. Benjamin and his bride, Mary Elizabeth Haines, made their home at the Jordan House after their wedding. When Benjamin was needed out on the range, he left Mary at home with his parents and siblings. Eventually Benjamin and Mary would have a farm of their own when James allocated land southeast of his homestead to them. This began James' tradition of gifting a farm to each of his married children.

Baby Calvin had been named after James' favorite brother-in-law, former business partner, and good friend, Calvin Smith. Smith was the husband of James' youngest sister, Agnes, and they had a large and prosperous farm and stock business in Westport (now known as Kansas City), Missouri. As transportation and roads improved, the James Jordans and the Calvin Smiths spent time together on a regular basis. James still owned a farm in Missouri, and he and Smith continued to collaborate on livestock business deals.

The Civil War

About a year after the start of the Civil War, the war's impact was felt with full force at the Jordan farm. In July of 1862 Governor Kirkwood called for five new regiments of infantry volunteers from Iowa—at least one from the western part of the state. Des Moines businessmen, seeking government contracts, said Des Moines should be designated the rendezvous location for the recruits.

After some debate, a camp to train the recruits was placed on the city limits east of the capitol building, located at the present area of Dean Avenue and East Eighteenth Street. It was named Camp Burnside.

Two Iowa regiments were assembled and trained there during the summer and fall of 1862: the Twenty-third Regiment Iowa Volunteer Infantry from Des Moines was mustered into service on September 19, 1862, and the Thirty-ninth Regiment Iowa Volunteer Infantry from Des Moines and Davenport was mustered on November 24, 1862.

Recruits who came to train at Camp Burnside saw an impressive business district when they arrived in the bustling city of Des Moines. An article in the *Des Moines Register* states the area "spread west from 2nd Avenue along Court Avenue and Walnut Street with lots in the western part of town selling for about $400.00. A large Catholic Church and about 100 other buildings were under construction." Des Moines had grown to a population of 5,451. Most remarkable was the presence of shade trees in the city where a decade earlier no such trees had existed.

Civil War Soldier

Eighteen-year-old Henry Jordan heard the governor's call to duty. After the spring term ended, he joined Company A of the Twenty-third Iowa Infantry. The Iowa Twenty-third was also served by another Walnut Township citizen, thirty-four-year-old Abraham Ashworth, who joined Company E.

The Twenty-third Iowa Infantry included recruits from counties in central, south central, and southwest Iowa: Polk, Dallas, Story, Wayne, Page, Montgomery, Jasper, Madison, Cass, Marshall, and Pottawattamie Counties. In all, 960 men made up the regiment, which was recruited in July and August and mustered into service in September. They were ordered into combat in Missouri. On the way there, Henry wrote a letter to his parents, family and friends:

Keokuk September 26, 1862
Dear Friends,
I arrived here yesterday noon and will start tomorrow on the road for St. Louis. I am well and hearty at present and I hope that you are all well. There is but a few in the camp that is sick. I was down in town this morning and saw (words missing) in my life. Some with their arms off and others with their legs off walking on wooden legs. The Colonel thinks that we will be in a battle within 10 days in Rolla, Mo. We are all ready. There is a part of our boys staying in a large schoolhouse which was used for a hospital and the rest of us are in camp close by, and enjoy ourselves very well better than we did at the barracks. We have hired a cook for our company. He was a soldier under General Mulagen. I can't think of anything to write as there is so much noise but I will write soon again. If I can get out today I will have my picture taken and send it. Write soon and let me know how you all are getting along and I remain your son.
Henry Jordan
Direct to the 23 Iowa Company A and it will follow.

Vicksburg, Mississippi

At first Henry saw service in Missouri, but by November the regiment was marching down to Vicksburg, Mississippi, where they were assigned to join General Grant's army as part of the United States First Brigade under General Carr. A second letter from Henry arrived in Walnut Township, this time for his sister Emily:

Patterson, Mo. Nov. 6th, 1862
Dear Sister,
Received a letter form you yesterday or day before that I forgot when. I received one from Pa the 27th date. I am well and hearty and hope this will find you the same. I will write to father tomorrow or next day we have had one man to die since I wrote you. He was from Story Co. Caused by the measles. I sent my picture a few day ago. I did not know that I could have

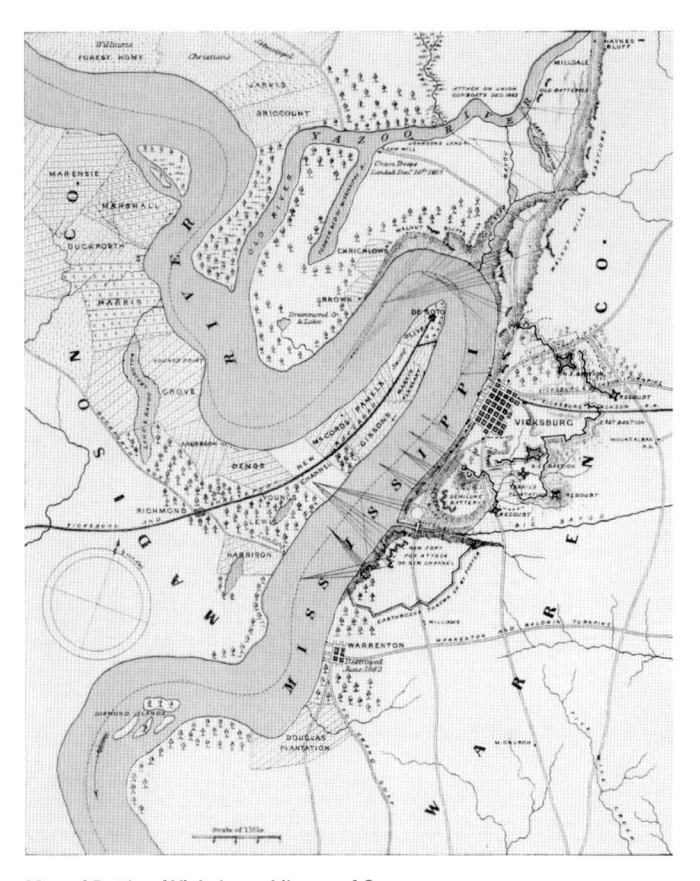

Map of Battle of Vicksburg. Library of Congress

Civil War soldiers in battle. "The War for the Union, 1862—A Bayonet Charge." This *Harper's Weekly* illustration is by Winslow Homer.

it taken here. The boys is generally healthy. Joe Fagen is Company Commissary Sergeant. Will Saylor is quarter master Sergeant Assistant. There is any amount of wild deer, turkeys here. There was one Company got back today. While the boys was gone they got 20 prisoners and one Sesesh* Captain. He talks as sassy as you please. There is some of them that say that they give themselves up on purpose. They are a dirty lousy Scout without overcoats. There is troops in every direction here. We have got more troops in Missouri now than were before this. If we have not enough to whip them now we never will have. There nobody that likes our brigadier commander there is too much Sesish about him he shafts the Iowa boys. His name is Boyd. I got a letter from John Preston. They are at Davenport. They have got neither arms nor uniforms. I must close. I will write again soon. Take good care of your selves. I hope to see you again. I remain your brother.
Henry Good-bye

*A shortened version of the word "seccessionist."

Henry Jordan and his regiment were sent south of Vicksburg to Port Gibson to fight. During their victorious engagement at the Battle of Port Gibson, the Iowa Twenty-third lost thirty-three men. One outcome of the battle was that Union troops forced the retreating Confederates to make a last stand on the banks of the Black River. It was here the Iowa Twenty-third helped defeat Confederate troops in the Battle of Black River Bridge.

Despite a substantial depletion of their numbers, the Iowa Twenty-third was assigned to fight in the siege and eventual capture of Vicksburg, Mississippi, a Confederate stronghold on the Mississippi River. The siege lasted for forty-two days and nights, during which time there was continuous fighting. The Union Army, utilizing thousands of troops, was finally victorious on July 4, 1863, when they captured Vicksburg. Leland Sage, Iowa historian, recounts, "The power of the Southern Confederacy was broken and the capture of Vicksburg ensured the North's total control of the Mississippi River in the Confederacy's western plank."

The War Comes to an End

At the close of the Vicksburg Campaign Henry Jordan and the Twenty-third saw further action near Jackson, Mississippi, where they fought under General Sherman. A month later, in August, the Twenty-third Regiment was transferred to the Department of the Gulf of Mexico and for the next year they served in Texas and the islands along the Texas coast.

By the spring of 1864 they were ordered back to New Orleans, and from there they were sent to Fort De Russey in Arkansas' Red River country. Together with the Iowa Twentieth, a regiment from Wisconsin, and another from Illinois, the Iowa Twenty-third spent the rest of 1864 in Arkansas but never saw the enemy.

There is a family story about Henry which has been handed down through the generations. Apparently soldiers were issued woolen long underwear to wear under their uniforms. While stationed in Arkansas, Henry and his companions were so uncomfortable in the woolen underwear that, to stop itching, they threw handfuls of Arkansas dust down their long johns as a soothing antidote to the scratchy wool.

The Peacemakers by George P. A. Healy, 1868, depicts the March 28, 1865, strategic session by the Union high command on the steamer *River Queen*. Left to right are Major General William T. Sherman, Lieutenant General Ulysses S. Grant, President Abraham Lincoln, and Rear Admiral David D. Porter. The White House Historical Association

Mustering Out

In early 1865 Henry and his regiment were ordered back to New Orleans where they were fitted out for the last campaign of the war against Mobile, Alabama. Their numbers were stronger now, as many of those who had been ill or injured had recovered and were able to fight. The Iowa Twenty-third stormed Mobile's Spanish Fort. Twenty-five men were wounded and only one killed. The regiment remained in the vicinity of Mobile for two months and then was ordered to Columbus, Texas.

Soon thereafter, on July 26, 1865, the regiment was mustered out of the service at Harrisburg, Texas. Traveling up the Mississippi River they reached Davenport on August 8 and disembarked. Of the original 960 troops from Iowa, 417 survivors remained.

Henry Jordan returned home a local hero. Instead of continuing his studies at the Forest Home Seminary in Des Moines, he received an appointment to West Point Military Academy in New York as a reward for his meritorious conduct while serving the Union. No doubt this appointment was won upon strong recommendations from his father's close friends: US Secretary of the Interior James Harlan, US Senator James Grimes, and Iowa Governor Samuel Kirkwood. Henry attended West Point for six months and then returned to Iowa.

Crest of West Point Military Academy. US Army Institute of Heraldry

148   Pursuit of a Dream

CHAPTER 32
Supporting the War Effort

Most Iowans were fervently supportive of their state's involvement in the Civil War, and most who were able to serve joined the Union Army. Iowans wanted to save the Union. The abolition of slavery was an important incentive, but it was incidental to what they perceived as the war's central focus, which, in their opinion, was to keep the Union together.

For the Iowa pioneer, "Union (of the country and the government) was a necessity," George Parker, Iowa historian states, "the pioneers had never known anything else. They had no experience or knowledge of monarchy and knew nothing of the strong jealousies that had torn the Thirteen Colonies, so as children of the Union, dependent upon it for protection to life and property . . . they came to know it as a fostering mother and were attached to it accordingly."

Iowans supported the credo, "Our Federal Union: it must be preserved." They also agreed with President Abraham Lincoln who had declared, "My paramount object in this struggle is to save the Union." Thus, Iowa pioneers preserved their traditional political ideas, held onto their concept of duty to the whole country, and supported the goal of preserving the Union as they fought in or helped support the troops fighting in the Civil War.

The Jordan Family Helps Out

During this time, James Jordan's close friend and confidante Governor Samuel Kirkwood offered him many administrative military positions, but he declined, saying at age forty-five he was too old and he could best serve the Union cause by *producing* the dollars needed by the government to finance the war. Because funding the war effort was of critical importance to the state and the nation, James' decision was very wise. Most likely his oldest son, Benjamin, stayed back to assist his father in their giant family livestock and farming enterprise. According to the *Iowa State Register* on December 20, 1862, "J. C. Jordan of this county is feeding this winter 700 head of cattle. They are disbursed around Polk, Dallas, Madison, and Jasper Counties."

Funds from the many state banks in Iowa—which James Jordan played a significant role in creating—also played a role in helping provide funds for the war effort and helping folks remain financially stable during hard times.

While the men were off fighting, the citizens of Des Moines sent food, clothing, money, and medicines to the front for their use. At the same time, soldiers' families at home had to be cared for. Concerts and entertainment

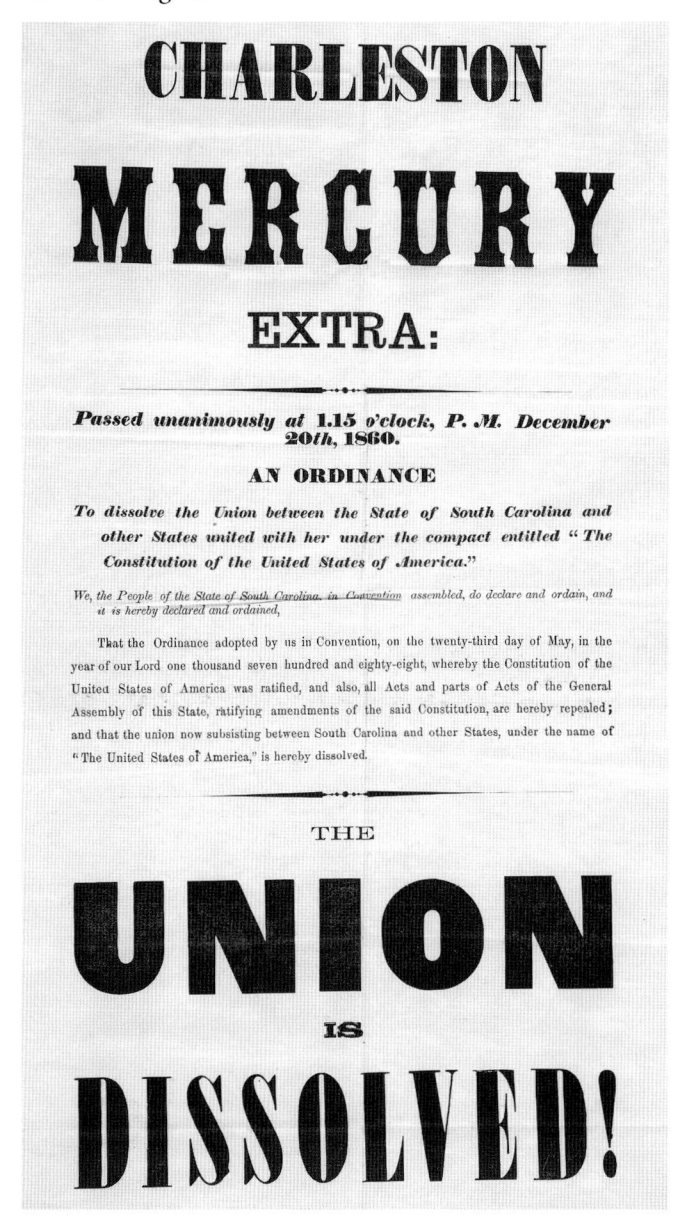

Public domain

for the benefit of soldiers' families raised large amounts of money. Many private individuals and club groups helped in this way. A permanent relief society was organized to raise and supervise the use of relief funds.

In Walnut Township James and Cynthia and their family were in a secure financial position, which enabled them to offer assistance to wives and families of soldiers gone to war. They provided them with food, clothing, and assistance on their farms, as it was common during the war that those left behind tended to the farms of men who were away fighting.

Four of James' sons were at home—Benjamin in his twenties and John, James, and George, all in their teens. Benjamin was in charge of the outlying herds, and the other boys were undoubtedly kept busy helping to plow, plant, and harvest their neighbors' fields and tend to their livestock as well as help with their own.

It is probable that daughter Emily, also in her twenties, as well as Cynthia Jordan, assisted in the war effort by aiding families, putting together medical supplies for wounded soldiers, and helping to raise money for the war effort.

In spite of the many acts of charity and kindness the Jordan family offered to those in need, sometimes the "good" was overshadowed by the "bad." During the later years of the war, in 1864 and 1865, the *Iowa State Register* reported consistent and repeated incidents where, much to his consternation, Uncle Jimmy's horses were stolen. In one article, "Rebs" stole his horses. Another one reported the "Monarch of Horse Thieves" stole the horses. Other accounts related how the thieves would be captured and jailed, and then they would escape, and the cycle of thievery would continue.

Emancipation!

The year following the beginning of the Civil War marked the end of the Underground Railroad. In September 1862 Abraham Lincoln's Emancipation Proclamation officially freed all of the slaves. The following story by early Des Moines historian Tacitus Hussey, describes the arrival of the first company of freed slaves in Des Moines in 1862:

> They traveled all night to reach the borders of Iowa and then felt safe. There were 13 in all; they traveled with two-horse teams, "borrowed" for the occasion and one of them, Jeff Logan, rode his master's horse "for this occasion only."

General William Duane Wilson, uncle of Woodrow Wilson, who was always on the lookout to do good, organized them into a Sunday School at Central Presbyterian Church and with the aid of others, taught them to read and laid the foundation for an education, with other teachers and scholars of the school assisting.

Previous to coming to Iowa, the slaves had never seen any white bread and could hardly believe their eyes when it was placed before them.

In a story told by Ella Jordan to her children and grandchildren, she remembered when she was about four years old (1862) climbing the big white fence at the Jordan House. When she got to the top she saw a black man who was a freed slave.

Uncle Jimmy Builds a Church

During that time of war and strife, Uncle Jimmy decided to build a local Methodist church, Jordan Chapel, for his family's use as well as for the other

Free at last! Public domain

families living in Walnut Township. He chose land about a half-mile west of his house, down the wagon trail (now Fuller Road) which led through the farm. He had a parsonage built next to the Jordan Chapel and later, in 1880, a cemetery would be added.

In spite of James' and Cynthia's pleasure at having a Methodist church so close to home, they were brokenhearted when it was used in 1863 for the funeral of their little three-year-old daughter Eda. She had tried to slide down the long banister in the front hall staircase of the Jordan home. Descending rapidly, upon reaching the bottom she flew off the railing, landed on the back of her head and broke her neck. After funeral services in the Jordan Chapel, her sorrowful parents buried her small body in the burial plot adjacent to the house. It is possible that an old gravestone, now broken, belonged to her grave. This stone reads: "What to us is life (broken piece) and despe (broken piece) When with signs residlo (broken piece) This lamb proclaims that thou art gone."

A year later Jordan Chapel was the sight of a joyful celebration on the occasion of the baptism of the first Jordan grandchild. Benjamin and his wife, Mary, chose the Jordan Chapel as the place to have their son, John Cunningham Jordan, christened. Sadly, two years later Baby John died at age two in 1866 and was buried close to little Eda in the Jordan family burial plot near their home.

Jordan Chapel was part of this Walnut Township neighborhood for about fifteen years, but the succession of eleven ministers who were appointed to live at the parsonage were known to protest the desolate aspect of the location. The chapel was abandoned in the early 1880s and the land upon which it stood became Jordan Cemetery which still exists. The Jordan Chapel building was moved to 1950 Southeast Fourth Street in Des Moines where it was renamed the "Jordan United Methodist Church." It was later torn down.

This document freed the slaves. Library of Congress

James Jordan: His Life and His Legacy 151

CITY OF DES MOINES AND ENVIRONS.

Part Five

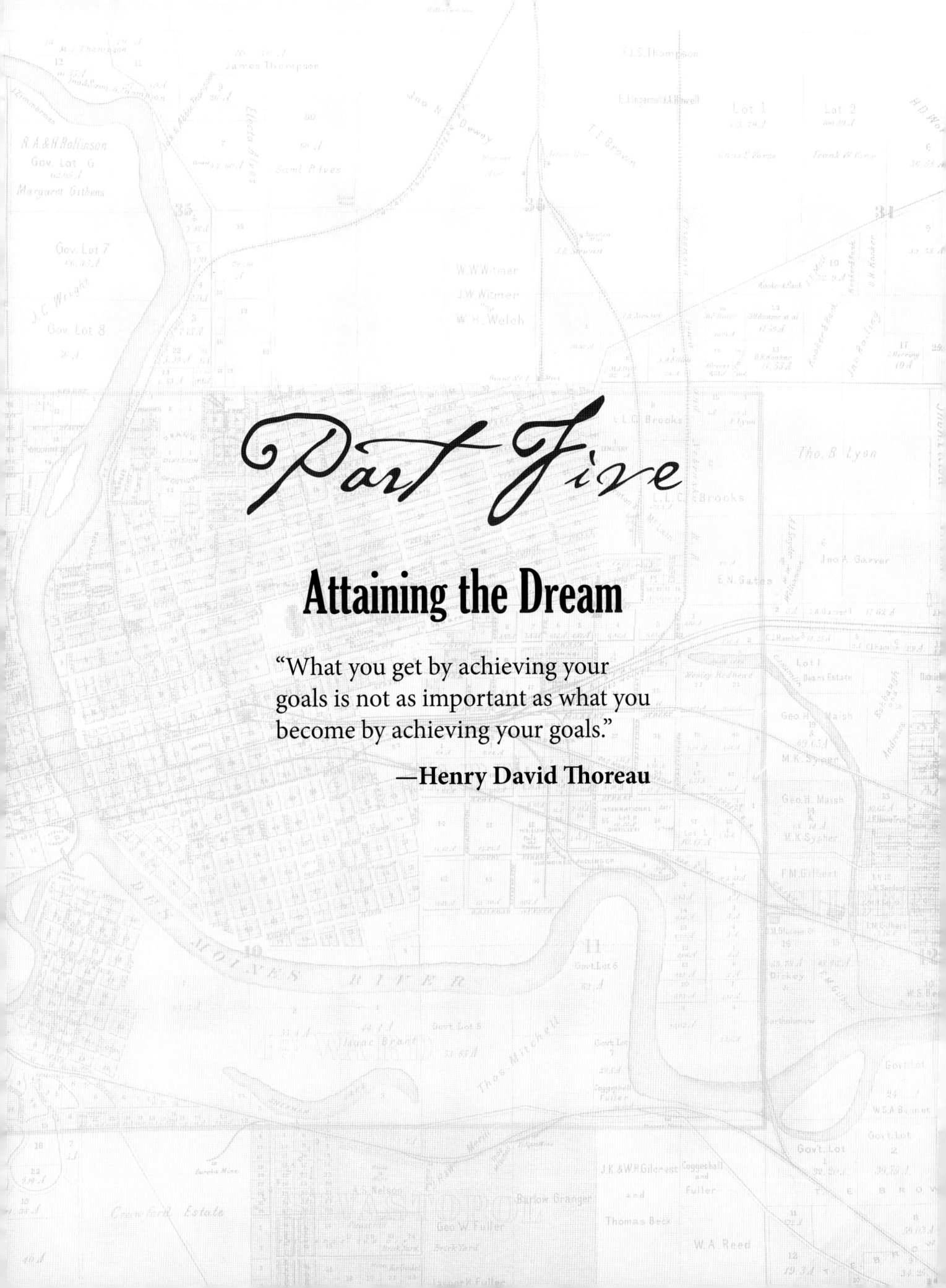

Attaining the Dream

"What you get by achieving your goals is not as important as what you become by achieving your goals."

—Henry David Thoreau

CHAPTER 33
The Coming of the Railroad

A few years into the Civil War, business in Des Moines, as elsewhere, slowed down and times became more difficult, but as the war continued the slump began to reverse. More money came into circulation, prices rose, demand for labor increased, and wages were high. New settlers came to Des Moines and the farming region around the city. New businesses were organized, and new buildings were planned and constructed. The war ultimately created a time of prosperity and growth in the city.

By 1866 the population of Des Moines had risen to about ten thousand, and the city had been the state capital for nine years. Many new roads leading into the city had been built, and the area enjoyed excellent stagecoach and fairly reliable steamboat service. When navigable, the rivers were busy with dozens of steamboats transporting goods. Stagecoaches regularly carried folks to and from the city when roadways were traversable. Several bridges had been built across the Des Moines and Raccoon Rivers. In twenty years, the pioneers had converted the area from a wilderness to a small but prospering metropolis.

However, traveling on rivers was dependent on the rise and fall of water levels, and when journeying over stagecoach trails or plank roads during inclement weather, travelers had to contend with ravaged road beds. The solution to these problems was the railroad.

The Railroads Come to Iowa

When Iowa became a state, the federal government, acting in response to the concept of Westward Expansion, directed four tiers of railroad tracks were to cross Iowa, east to west with spaces in between from north to south. They would be like four evenly spaced horizontal stripes flowing across the state of Iowa.

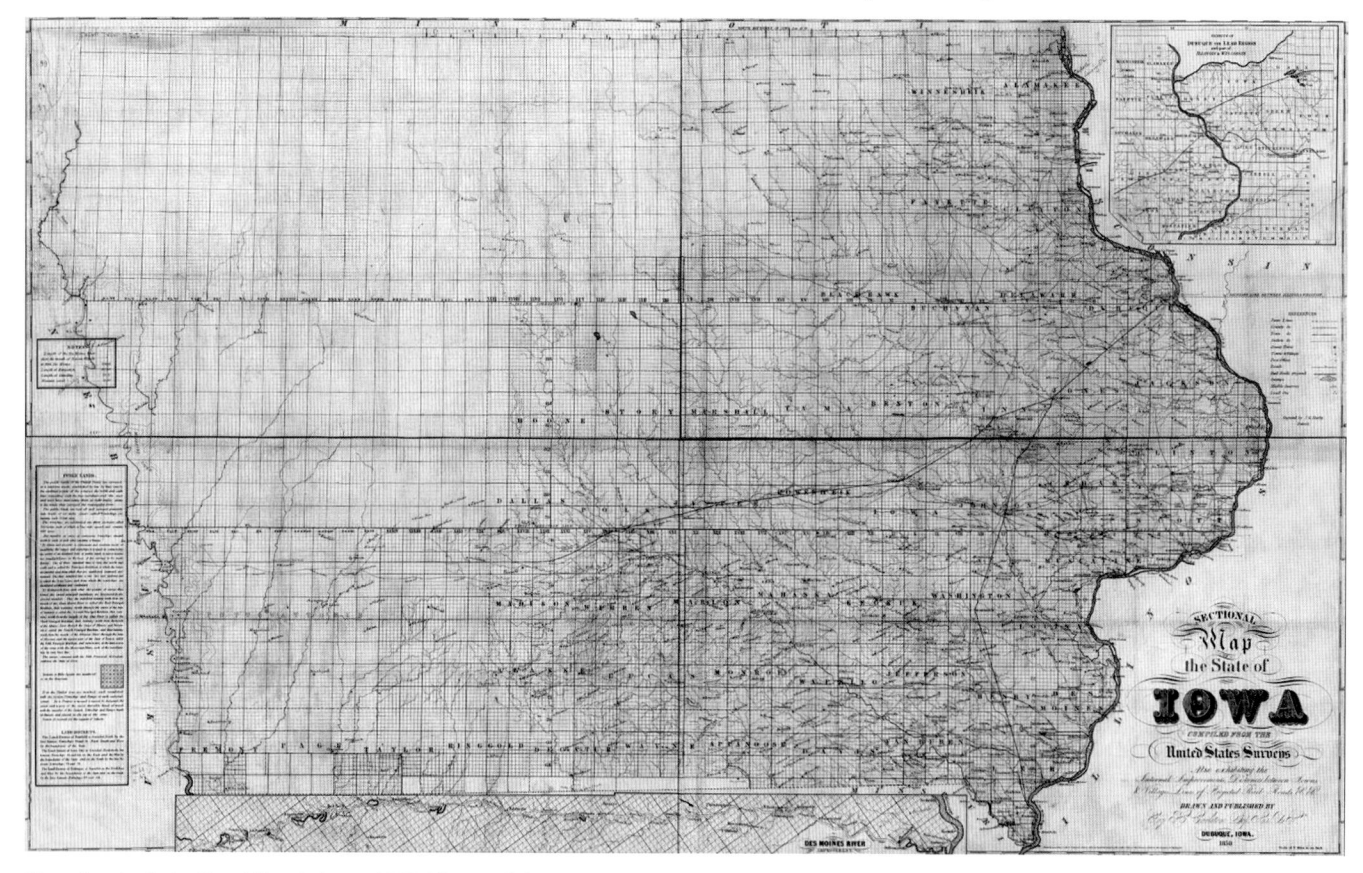

Map of projected railroad tiers in Iowa, 1850. Library of Congress

154   Pursuit of a Dream

Companies to build the tracks and railroads to run them would be selected by Congress to manage each of these four lines of tracks. Because most of the population in Iowa was in its southeast corner, and because the area around Rock Island, Illinois, offered a suitable site for a bridge across the Mississippi River to Iowa, work on building railroads across Iowa began in the southernmost tier. By the mid-1850s, the Chicago and Rock Island Railroad had completed the difficult and challenging job of building a bridge and tracks across the Mississippi. This accomplishment resulted in linking eastern Iowa cities to all points east in the United States.

In 1856 the US Congress, anxious to see cross-country railroad lines completed across the *entire* continent, helped facilitate those in the Iowa corridors by increasing the three-mile-wide swath of land on either side of the four proposed rail lines to six miles of freeland right of way on either side of the tracks. Because Congress had planned for four major lines to pass east to west through Iowa, the amount of land Congress granted on either side of those four lines added up to about four million acres. The freeland right of way was to be used to "bait" railroad builders to get the lines built as soon as possible.

In addition to granting freeland right of way, the US government also subsidized railroad construction at the national, state, county, and local levels, and, as government officials hopefully envisioned, there was a huge rush to build tracks. The enormous amount of money that could be made encouraged under-the-table deals, illegal maneuvering, bribes, and generally poor (but profitable) business practices. It was every man (or town) for themselves, and Des Moines would be no exception.

Building the Railroad to Des Moines

Several factors led to the assumption that Des Moines would eventually secure railroad service: Des Moines was the state capital; Des Moines citizens desperately wanted the railroad; and on the national scene, Iowa had been designated by the US Congress as an ideal site for multiple rail lines. Its location—west of Chicago, east of Omaha, and close to the western frontier—made it a "natural."

However, actually building a railroad to Des Moines was another matter and, although the desire of the Des Moines citizenry was there, execution of a plan— choosing the location for the tracks, surveying the land

Crossing the Mississippi River

- A subsidiary of the Rock Island Railroad, the Railroad Bridge Company, built the first bridge across the Mississippi River, at Rock Island, Illinois, in April 1856. It was the *first* bridge to be built across the river, from St. Paul, Minnesota, to the Gulf of Mexico. Besides being an engineering challenge, the construction of the bridge was opposed by the steamboat companies who had been running their boats up and down the Mississippi for decades. They did not want anything to endanger their vessels or obstruct steamboat traffic on the river

- Less than a year after it was built, a steamboat, the *Effie Afton*, crashed into the new bridge, destroying the boat and damaging the bridge. The steamboat company sued, and "fledgling" lawyer Abraham Lincoln represented the Railroad Bridge Company in US Circuit Court in Illinois. Neither side won the case, but a committee was appointed by the US House of Representatives to study the matter

- In 1859 a steamboat company from St. Louis filed a bill in US Circuit Court in southeastern Iowa to remove the bridge across the Mississippi River and won. The judge, calling the bridge "a common and public nuisance," ordered the Iowa side of the bridge be removed within three years

- The Railroad Bridge Company took the case to the US Supreme Court, and in 1862 the ruling in the lower court was reversed and the bridge was allowed to remain. The argument that won the case was one which had been introduced earlier by Abraham Lincoln when he argued before the Circuit Court in Illinois in 1857.

Frank P. Donovan, railroad historian, quotes Lincoln as follows: ". . . there is a travel from east to west whose demands are not less important than that of a river. . . . This current of travel has its rights, as well as that north and south . . . the statement of its business during a little less than a year shows this importance. It is in evidence that from September 8, 1856, to August 8, 1857, 12,586 freight cars and 74,179 passengers passed over this bridge. . . . This shows that this bridge must be treated with respect in this court and is not to be kicked about with contempt."

THE RAIL CANDIDATE.

Poster showing the railroad's support for Lincoln as a presidential candidate. Library of Congress

and building the line—was fraught with problems. These problems were generally due to money mismanagement, corruption, fraud, and broken promises by the builders. Additionally, the financial panic of 1857 and the Civil War had cut off and diverted funding for any and all railroad construction in central Iowa for almost eight years.

As it turned out, from beginning to end, building a railroad from the Mississippi River into Des Moines would take fifteen long, tedious years. However, toward the end of those years, it became an exciting contest among three railroads as to which would get to Iowa's capital city first.

The First Contestant: The Mississippi and Missouri Railroad

The company managing the first line of tracks to cross Iowa—and the one with which Des Moines initially assumed it would be involved—was the Mississippi and Missouri Railroad (M&MRR), an Iowa subsidiary of the Chicago and Rock Island Railroad. The M&MRR was organized as an *Iowa* company in 1852 as a means for the *Illinois* company of the Chicago and Rock Island Railroad to continue their route across Iowa once they completed the Illinois portion—from Chicago to the Mississippi River at Rock Island, Illinois. During 1853 Iowa land was selected and surveyed and some was actually graded in preparation for laying the rails. Not long afterwards, however, work slowed as the M&MRR became preoccupied with bringing service from Burlington, Iowa, to eastern Iowa towns such as Iowa City. The population was much larger in that area of Iowa, and building railroad lines there would garner the railroad more profits, so the decision was made to set aside work on the Des Moines link.

156   *Pursuit of a Dream*

Next: The Keokuk, Fort Des Moines and Minnesota Railroad Company

The following year, a promising candidate entered the race for rail service to Des Moines. The Keokuk, Fort Des Moines and Minnesota Railroad Company presented itself in 1854.

When Iowa became a state in 1846, $70,000 had been earmarked by the Iowa state legislature for a Des Moines River Improvement Land Grant to straighten and deepen the river for easier steamboat travel. A New York company bid for and won the job. In eight years, however, all that had been done was the surveying of the corridor of land designated for the project.

Des Moines, with its location in the Des Moines River Valley, had enjoyed a decades-long relationship downriver with Keokuk. This relationship was fostered by steamboat traffic traveling on the Des Moines River between the two towns and was cemented later when Keokuk produced enough votes to assure Des Moines would win the election as the new state capital.

During this time, transportation modes were changing, with the railroad replacing the steamboat. In response, the Iowa state legislature reallocated the $70,000 intended originally to enhance Des Moines River steamboat travel and reassigned it for railroad development along the Des Moines River.

Following the money, the New York company that had won the river development project earlier refiled as a railroad franchise and called themselves the Keokuk, Fort Des Moines and Minnesota Railroad Company. Their plan was to lay tracks up the Des Moines River Valley from Keokuk to Des Moines, north to Fort

Aerial view of Des Moines, 1868. Library of Congress

James Jordan: His Life and His Legacy

Trains arrive in Des Moines, 1866. From *The History of Polk County, Iowa*

Dodge, and on up to Minnesota. Work began on the line in the mid-1850s with steady progress being made.

The Competition Continues

In the meantime, the M&MRR was able to process $300,000 in bonds to begin building a rail link across Iowa from Davenport to Council Bluffs. Just when the dream of having rail service in and out of Des Moines seemed a bit more possible, and it appeared the company providing the service would (again) be the M&MRR line rather than the Keokuk, Fort Des Moines and Minnesota Railroad, the Panic of 1857 and the Civil War slowed what little progress the M&MRR had made since 1856, and the $300,000 in bonds was rescinded.

In 1856 and 1857 the Keokuk, Fort Des Moines and Minnesota Railroad took over where the M&MRR left off; the contract had been re-awarded to them. The railroad was steadily progressing up the Des Moines River, first to Buena Vista in 1856, then to Farmington and Bonaparte in 1857, Bentonsport in 1858, Agency City in 1859, and Ottumwa in 1861. Finally, that same year the railroad reached Eddyville, only sixty-eight miles southeast of Des Moines, and then ran out of money.

The arrival of the railroad in Eddyville did make rail service somewhat available to the citizenry of Des Moines. Soon plans were in the works to continue this line up the river, and folks in Des Moines hoped it was only a matter of time before their city, too, would be joined to this great network.

The Des Moines Valley Railroad Enters the Race

In 1862, a newcomer, the Des Moines Valley Railroad, took over the project, and the Iowa legislature granted them the rest of the land they needed to complete the tracks into Des Moines. However, with the Civil War raging, there were no available funds, manpower, or raw materials to work on any of the railroads. Completion of rail service to Des Moines would take four more years.

A Railroad (Finally) Arrives in Des Moines

With the close of the Civil War in April 1865, the stage was finally set to complete the rail line from Eddyville to Des Moines. There remained one last but significant problem: the Des Moines Valley Railroad needed $70,000 to finance the completion of the line.

The city of Oskaloosa knew about these money problems and decided to make a last-ditch effort to try to divert the line away from Des Moines, offering bonuses to the Des Moines Valley Railroad to build in their direction instead. However, Calvin Leighton, who was involved in the railroad and friendly to Des Moines' effort to secure rail service, quietly told Des Moines Judge Phineas M. Casady, Senator Jordan, and other prominent Des Moines businessmen that a fund of $70,000 would secure completion of the line into Des Moines.

Leighton knew that James Jordan in particular would be proactive in helping to get the money raised and the line built. As a big-time stock breeder and owner of over eighteen hundred acres of Des Moines-area land, James wanted the most reliable and practical transportation to carry his sizable herds to market. At this point his livestock grazing in central and western Iowa were still being driven by cowboys to stockyards in Des Moines and then floated down the Des Moines River to markets in St. Louis. It had gone on too long.

James had known for years he wasn't alone in his intense desire to see the railroad completed from their city to Des Moines, and it would not be difficult to solicit others to the cause. Upon hearing the news from Leighton, he immediately offered $1,000 of his own money, challenging his colleagues to do the same. Proclaiming, "I'll be one of two hundred who will give a thousand dollars each," a scheme was devised to come up with the $70,000, whereby Des Moines businessmen would voluntarily tax themselves according to their last assessment. Hundreds of men came forward with their quotas. B. F. Allen gave $10,000. In all, approximately two hundred rallied around the cause and donated a total of $100,000.

158 Pursuit of a Dream

The city of Keokuk was so pleased the railroad could finally be completed from their city to Des Moines they invited all of the financial contributors, including James Jordan, to a riverboat excursion down the Des Moines River to the Mississippi and a triumphant celebration in Keokuk.

The first passenger train entered Des Moines on August 29, 1866. It stopped on the east side of Des Moines because there was no railroad bridge built over the Des Moines River or tracks past it. It had taken seven and a half hours to travel from Keokuk to Des Moines.

The train was met by almost all of the residents of Des Moines. According to a newspaper report by historian Hussey: "When the train came in sight as far down the track as could be seen was a wilderness of waving handkerchiefs, hats, and hands. The citizens were jubilant. Some in the greeting crowd had never seen an 'iron horse' on rails and others were grateful that the horseback and stagecoach days were now gone."

In 1866 the bankrupt Mississippi and Missouri Railroad was sold to the Chicago, Rock Island and Pacific Railroad. A year later, in 1867, the Rock Island Railroad finally completed their lines into Des Moines. Des Moines now had rail service from two lines: the Rock Island, which entered Iowa at Davenport, and the Des Moines Valley Railroad coming from Keokuk.

The Des Moines Valley Railroad was eventually absorbed into the Chicago and Rock Island Railroad, but not before each line had built a bridge across the Des Moines River in Des Moines. The Rock Island built theirs in 1868, and the Des Moines Valley Railroad bridge was built in 1869, the same year the Rock Island completed their tracks across Iowa to Council Bluffs. In 1871 the Rock Island Railroad constructed a bridge across the Raccoon River at Seventh Street with a wagon track on it. Iowa historian Leland Sage stated: "No other facet of the westward movement is more important than the story of the railroads. No agency contributed more to the buildup of Iowa."

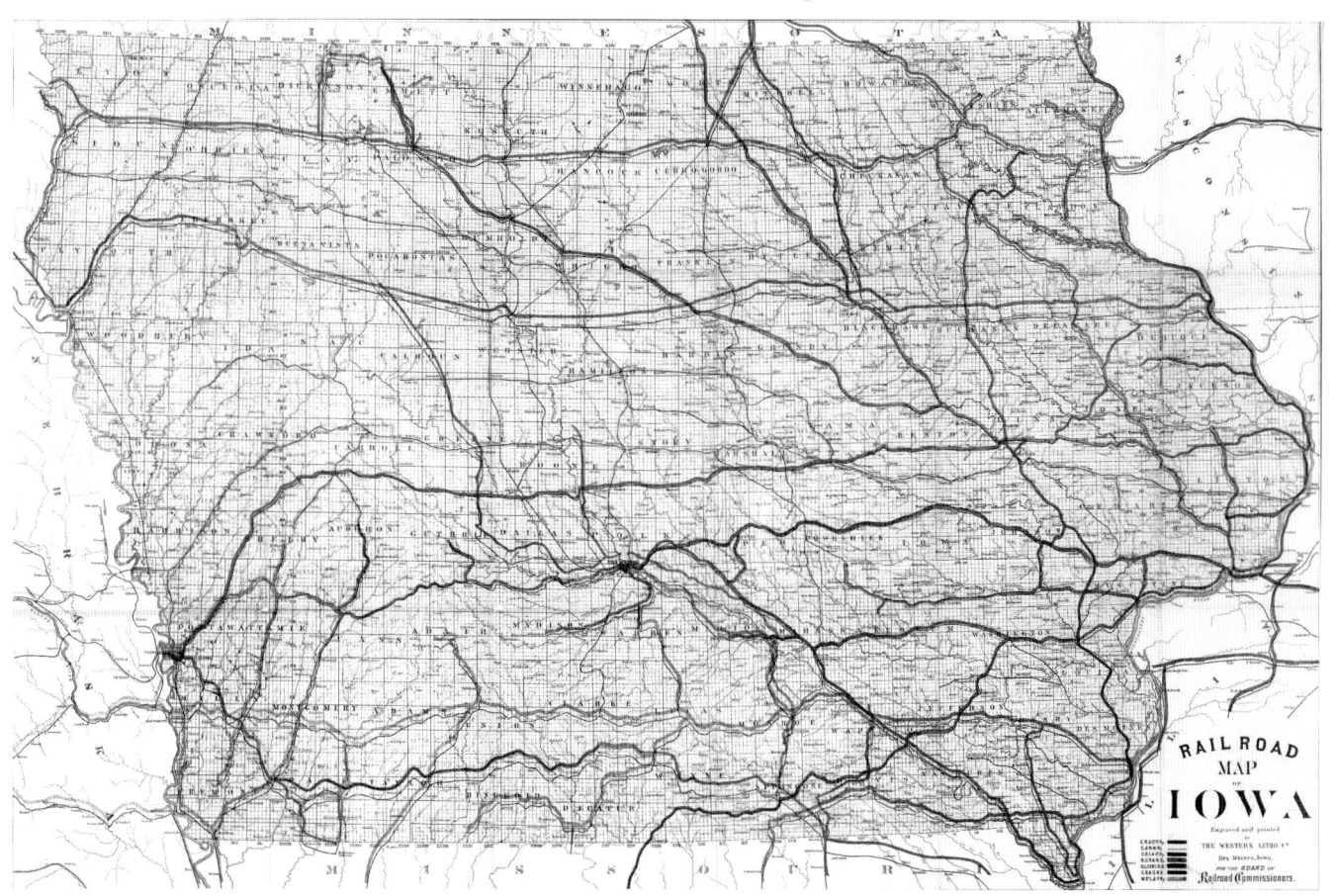

Iowa railroad map, 1881. Library of Congress

James Jordan: His Life and His Legacy

CHAPTER 34
Uncle Jimmy, "Good Old Boy"

As he got older, James Jordan was frequently referred to as "Uncle Jimmy," a congenial nickname bestowed on him for decades by friends and associates who had a fond yet respectful regard for him.

For over two decades Uncle Jimmy had been firmly entrenched as a part of the Des Moines "establishment." He had met the test and proven himself many times over as a politician, a statesman, an astute and successful businessman, and a knowledgeable stock trader and farmer. Even though his residence was a farm five and a half miles out in the country, he may as well have been living in the middle of Des Moines, as for years he had to come into town almost every day to pick up his mail.

As one of the establishment, James rubbed elbows regularly with the city's most respected citizens. When someone wished to start a new business venture that needed a prosperous and stable board of directors, James Jordan was one of the men asked to serve.

Equitable of Iowa

One new venture was conceived by a Des Moines newcomer, twenty-eight-year-old Frederick M. Hubbell, who had the inspiration to start a life insurance company. Hubbell felt the concept of insuring one's life would be well-received in the aftermath of the Civil War when so many husbands had died with little or no financial support or security for the widows and children remaining.

Starting the business was a risky challenge; at that time life insurance was a novel and unusual commodity for a pioneer, especially in the new prairie towns in Iowa and the Midwest. The huge toll of death from the Civil War, however, showed people it might be a good idea. As it turned out, Hubbell's company was the genesis of what would become the premier industry of Des Moines—an industry that from then on would bring millions of dollars into the city and the state.

The people of Iowa wanted cash flowing in their state, too. Surely Iowans could be shown they needed life insurance. If they would buy it from an Iowa company, the dollars they paid for their insurance premiums

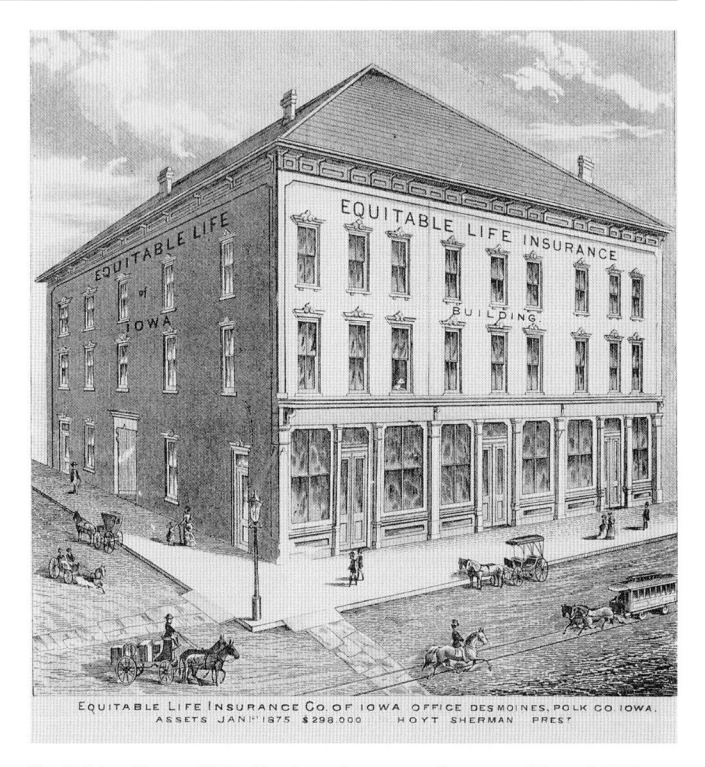

Equitable of Iowa, 1875. *Hawkeye Insurance Company Atlas of 1875*

would remain in Iowa instead of going elsewhere. Hubbell historian George Pease explained:

> Iowa desperately needed capital. Settlers from Ohio, New York, and New England continued to pour into the state lured west by eloquent blandishments of the railroads; Civil War veterans were reestablishing homes, clearing land, and breaking sod in valiant efforts to turn the state's rich black loam into gold.
>
> However, money was tight all over the US. It was difficult to finance new ventures locally in Des Moines, and eastern banks charged exorbitant interest rates because money was tight there as well. One way to get money was through life insurance companies. People would "pay in" on their policies for years and years. The company kept the money and invested it so that when it had to "pay out" on the death of an insured, they could have enough funds available, as well as make a profit for the company.

160   Pursuit of a Dream

Lending money and charging interest just like a bank was one way to get money flowing into the economy, and several New York life insurance companies were doing this. However, the life insurance companies domiciled in New York—Equitable Life Assurance Society of the United States, New York Life Insurance Company, and Mutual Life Insurance of New York, to mention three of the largest—were then compelled by law to restrict their investment to the State of New York and not lend to outside their state.

It was important this new company look stable, honest, and trustworthy, as it would accept money from subscribers and not pay out until decades later when the subscribers died. Therefore, the founding board of directors needed to be impressive, both locally and nationally. The year was 1867, and Hubbell's challenge was to sell his concept to the "good old boys" of Des Moines whose financial credibility and distinction were needed to get the company off the ground.

At the invitation of Hubbell on the afternoon of January 21, 1867, James Jordan, age fifty-four, came into the city of Des Moines by horse-drawn sleigh. He joined such notable Des Moines businessmen as Judge Phineas Casady, Hoyt Sherman, Isaac Cooper, Captain Francis West, Dr. Henry Whitman, Peter Myers, Robert Tidrick, Wesley Redhead, General James Madison Tuttle, Lampson Sherman, Jefferson Scott Polk, and B. F. Allen. This meeting was the beginning of the Equitable of Iowa Insurance Company, the cornerstone company of F. M. Hubbell's future business empire.

The group of businessmen agreed to the premise, "Who will build Iowa if her own people do not," and straightaway the group of men endorsed Hubbell's plan and organized a life insurance company. Pease continued:

> As he had promised Hubbell, Judge Phineas M. Casady accepted the Board presidency. Dr. Whitman agreed to establish and supervise enforcement of medical standards; B. F. Allen took the post of Treasurer; Wesley Redhead that of Vice President; Jefferson Polk agreed to serve as counsel. The promoter of the enterprise, Hubbell, assumed the title of Secretary.

> Hoyt Sherman was made Actuary Manager. He and Hubbell would run the business. All present save Lampson Sherman were elected to the Board of Trustees including James Jordan, and Lampson was added in 1871. Authorizing Judge Casady and Hubbell to draw up the necessary Articles of Incorporation, the group adjourned.

After the articles of incorporation were signed, an announcement of the company was released to the press. One newspaper commented, "A glance at the names affixed to the advertisement is all that is necessary to show the stability of the company."

By the end of the company's first year, December 31, 1867, Sherman reported $210,700 of life insurance in force and premium receipts of $17,458.73. From this modest beginning, Equitable of Iowa would eventually bring millions of dollars into the Iowa economy—dollars which were invested and used to finance further progress of the state.

Brotherhood of Early Settlers . . . and Many More

Underscoring once again James' involvement as one of Des Moines' oldest and most-established citizens, a year later, in 1868, he joined the Brotherhood of Early Settlers. That same year the Old Settlers' Association was formed. To qualify as a member, the applicant had to have been a local resident by 1856. James exceeded the requirement by ten years.

Other members of the group were W. W. Williamson, Isaac Cooper, J. M. Griffiths, J. A. Nash, H. H. Griffiths, P. M. Casady, David Norris, Frank Nagle, Thomas Boyd, J. S. Cook, John Hays, R. L. Tidrick, C. S. Spofford, Mr. and Mrs. S. F. Spofford, Madison Young, R. W. Sypher, Ezra Rathbun, William Baker, Thomas McNullen, W. A. Galbraith, C. W. Cleveland, William DeFord, Hoyt Sherman, M. R. Sypher, J. B. Bausman, Peter Myers, H. H. Saylor, R. P. Peters, Thomas Mitchell, and Thompson Bird. Thomas Mitchell was elected the chairman of the group, and James Jordan was elected one of the association's vice presidents.

One of the first social functions the Early Settlers organized was a festival to bring together old settlers' family members, as well as others who might not have been

Emily Hanawalt. Jordan Family Collection

George Hanawalt. From *Portrait and Biographical Album of Polk County, Iowa*, 1890

there quite as long as the original pioneers. The festival was held on October 12, 1868, in Capitol Square and the four hundred in attendance enjoyed a picnic lunch while listening to speaker J. M. Thrift reminisce about the past.

The association met periodically after that—once in 1869 to eulogize Presbyterian minister and former mayor of Des Moines Reverend Thompson Bird. The last recorded festival took place on August 20, 1873, on a day where the temperature rose to 102 degrees. On this day James was again elected as one of the vice presidents of the group.

In addition to being part of the Early Settlers Association, during his lifetime James was a member of several other civic groups, including the Tippecanoe Society, Pioneers Society, the Octogenarian Society, and Pioneer Law Makers Society.

George Hanawalt Arrives in Des Moines

Jordan's network of friends was probably the source of matrimonial prospects for his oldest daughter, Emily, an intelligent, spirited, and fashionable young woman. In 1868 the twenty-six-year-old completed her studies at Northwestern University in Evanston, Illinois, and returned to Walnut Township.

Not long afterward, Emily was introduced to Dr. George Hanawalt, who had just arrived in Des Moines. Hanawalt was a "genial, whole-souled gentleman in whom his patients had total confidence." Emily became interested in this newcomer. The fact he was a Republican interested her father.

Originally from Ross County, Ohio, Hanawalt was born in 1836 to John and Mary Jefferson (Hill) Hanawalt. George's mother was a lineal descendant of Thomas Jefferson. He was raised and educated in Ohio and in 1859 began a two-year program to study medicine under two Ohio doctors.

Shortly after the Civil War began in February 1862, Hanawalt enlisted in the Seventieth Ohio Infantry. Because of his medical background, he was transferred in August 1862 to Washington, DC, as a hospital steward. He completed his studies in the Medical Department of Georgetown University, graduating in March 1864, at which time he was promoted to acting assistant surgeon in the Union Army. Hanawalt served in this post for the next four years, resigning on May 22, 1868, to come to Des Moines as the physician for several railroads.

After a period of time, Hanawalt became part of the Des Moines "establishment," enjoying a reputation as a fine doctor and an excellent surgeon.

CHAPTER 35
James Jordan, Cattle Baron

In 1868 Cynthia Jordan, at age thirty-seven, gave birth to son Edward, the last of Uncle Jimmy's children. The living children in the Jordan family by this time numbered nine, and James and Cynthia also had a couple of grandchildren. Benjamin and Mary were the parents of grandchildren Charles and Hattie.

No longer living in the Jordan farmhouse, by 1874 Benjamin and Mary had built their own house immediately south of the Jordan homestead on two hundred acres of land that crossed over the Raccoon River. This land had been a gift to the young couple from Benjamin's father.

Emily (twenty-six) was just completing her studies at Northwestern University in Evanston, Illinois. James (twenty) was a college student, attending Simpson College in Indianola where he was training to be a teacher. His brothers Henry (twenty-four), John (twenty-two), and George (eighteen) were all working for their father as cowboys, business partners, and farm hands. Thirteen-year-old Ella, nine-year-old Eva, and six-year-old Calvin were in grammar school. Then there was baby Edward, the darling of the family. His sister Emily fell in love with him and treated him as if he were her own child for his entire life.

Life had changed after the Civil War. The stark puritan pioneer lifestyle was being replaced by one with visible signs of prosperity. It had been difficult to transport goods upriver or across the state since the early years when Fort Des Moines was built. Now, reliable railroad service to the city facilitated the steady influx of goods into the area. Sometime after the Civil War, Cynthia had convinced James to add a piano to the front parlor. He bought her a used one, a Chickering square grand piano made in 1845 in New York. James had it shipped in on the railroad.

Prior to the Civil War, music was considered frivolous and not part of the conservative, puritanical pioneer lifestyle. However, the songs, the drums, and the hymns that became popular during the Civil War initiated a change that brought music into homes. With the arrival of the piano, the younger Jordan children were given lessons, and Ella became an accomplished pianist. No doubt the major part of her repertoire was hymns, but nevertheless music became part of the Jordan family scene.

Besides a postwar shift in the family's lifestyle, James experienced a change in how he conducted his business. The US cattle industry, always profitable, took a decisive turn after the Civil War. Joe McCoy opened the Texas Range in 1867 when he commissioned an army of cowboys to drive massive herds of wild Texas Longhorn cattle north on the Chisholm Trail to Abilene, Kansas. From there, at the railhead of the Kansas Pacific Railway, the cattle were shipped by rail to packing plants in Chicago, Illinois.

While James was not personally involved with Longhorns, he was very interested in these new developments in the cattle industry. However, he focused his energies on Shorthorns. He was not alone. His friend Frederick M. Hubbell would also enjoy a reputation as a premier breeder of Shorthorn cattle, as would neighbor Pressley Bennett and another landowner living north of him, Martin Flynn, who had introduced Shorthorn cattle to Iowa in 1867, bringing the breed from his farm in Kentucky.

Shorthorn and Longhorn Cattle

Shorthorn cattle have a rectangular shaped body and are one of the larger beef breeds, weighing at maturity from 1,400 to 2,200 pounds. A favored breed of stockmen, they are an excellent source of meat.

Shorthorn cattle were imported to the Eastern Seaboard from Great Britain beginning in 1783. These animals were crossbred with domestic cattle which created hardier herds. In the early 1820s British stockman began to breed the milking Shorthorn of England with the beef-producing Shorthorn of Scotland. Crossbred herds appeared first in 1822 in England where they were perfected. Then they were exported to the United States.

A Longhorn steer. Author's personal collection

A Shorthorn steer. Author's personal collection

During his childhood, James observed his great-uncles in the Cunningham branch of his family raising Shorthorn cattle on their South Fork Valley plantation in western Virginia. Perhaps that is where he became interested in the breed.

Volume imports of crossbred Shorthorns occurred after the Civil War. At this time, James and other stockbreeders considered adding these dual-purpose cattle to their herds—Shorthorns were raised for milking as well as for beef.

James' primary goal was to sell his livestock in the Union Stock Yards in Chicago. However, it is very probable he also bred Shorthorns to sell breeding stock to the ranchers in the western states of Montana, Idaho, Wyoming, and the Dakotas, where cattlemen were starting to establish cattle ranches.

Initially these western ranchers raised Longhorns, Spanish in origin, which were brought up from Texas. Shorthorns were eventually introduced to improve the Longhorn herds. In subsequent decades, Shorthorn cattle were replaced by Herefords to breed with the Longhorns because Shorthorns produced too much milk.

The End of "The Range" in Western Iowa

The sudden and immense growth of the cattle industry was the result of two coincidental events: the growth of the railroad west of the Mississippi River after the Civil War years and the tremendous increase in the supply of cattle from the enormous Texas herds. Soon beef became a common item on dinner tables in the eastern states. By 1875, US shipment of beef to Europe had begun.

The invention of barbed wire occurred in 1874, enabling farmers in the western rangeland of Iowa to fence off land, thereby ending easy access to free pasturage of livestock owned by stockmen living in the more populated areas to the east. Before that, according to Iowa historian Eugene Hastie, "cattle ran the open range, all bearing the private mark of the owner." The use of barbed wire severely limited James' opportunities to pasture his large cattle herds out in the western Iowa prairie. That land was being purchased, fenced, and farmed.

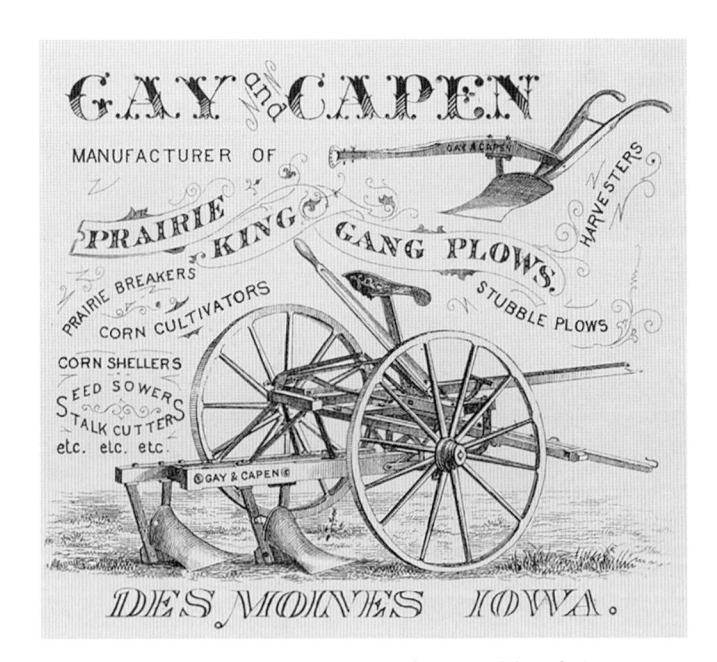

Modern plow, 1875. *Hawkeye Insurance Company Atlas of 1875*

164   Pursuit of a Dream

Elegant homes were built in Atlantic as the range disappeared. *Hawkeye Insurance Company Atlas of 1875*

Stationary letterhead for James Jordan. Jordan Family Collection

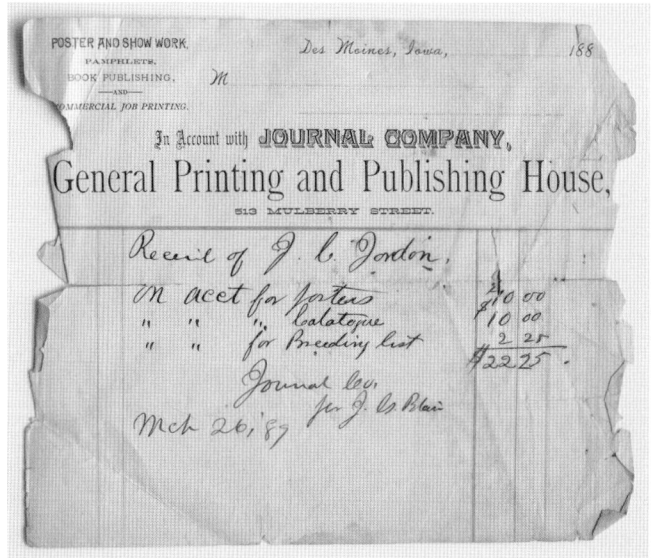

Receipt from the Jordan business enterprise. Jordan Family Collection

James Jordan, Cattle Breeder

Although Jordan lived in Iowa, not Texas, he nevertheless saw opportunity for a shift and potential profit in his own cattle business. Instead of exclusively focusing on stock production—ranging herds in western Iowa and selling them to the stockyards in the East—he began to shift to the breeding of excellent Shorthorn herds. Uncle Jimmy was soon well-known as a superior stockbreeder in the region. Being a member of this livestock-breeding network, he traveled by train to Texas and elsewhere in the country to transact business deals. As a member of the American Shorthorn Breeders Association, which was headquartered in Chicago, he also was involved in showing cattle, and this, of course, helped him network his reputation nationally.

Examples of James' breeding stock are found in the February 1883 *American Shorthorn Herd Book*, a several-hundred-page volume containing the pedigrees of top quality US Shorthorn cattle. Members of the Jordan herd are mentioned numerous times throughout the book in the categories of both bulls and cows.

Reflective of his passion for cattle, on one of his Texas trips he purchased a chair made of cattle horns. He put it in his office and it became his favorite piece of furniture. It could be said that in his later years James replaced his earlier zeal for politics and railroads with a passion for the finest bred Shorthorn cattle he could produce.

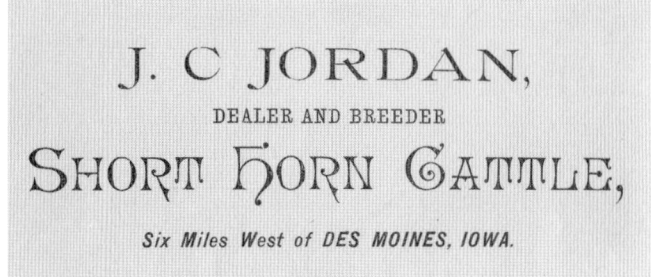

Horned furniture similar to a chair Jordan owned. Courtesy of West Des Moines Historical Society

James Jordan: His Life and His Legacy   165

Uncle Jimmy also enjoyed a reputation locally as a man to respect when dealing with conventional Iowa livestock. In one story, a Mr. Cunningham from Winterset brought a cow up to Polk County to sell at market in Des Moines. On his way, he stopped at the Jordan farm to ask Uncle Jimmy what he'd give for the cow. James offered a price, but Cunningham didn't think it was enough so he went along to Des Moines. At market in Des Moines, Cunningham was offered exactly the same price as Uncle Jimmy had said he'd pay, so he took his tired cow back to the Jordan farm and sold it to Jimmy.

LIST

OF

BREEDERS AND OWNERS,

WITH

POST-OFFICE ADDRESS; ALSO, REFERENCE, BY FIGURES, TO THE PAGES WHEREON THEIR NAMES MAY BE FOUND; THE PARENTHETIC FIGURES AFFIXED TO NUMBER OF PAGE INDICATING THE NUMBER OF TIMES SUCH NAMES OCCUR ON THAT PAGE.

FANNY EIGHTH,

Red, calved June 28, 1877, bred and owned by J. C. Jordan, Des Moines, Ia., got by Red Airdrie 46852, out of Fanny 7th (vol. 13) by Plumwood Lad 8797—Fanny 2d by Major Duncan 5926—Bourbon Belle 2d by Duke of Southwick 450—Bourbon Belle by Malcolm 1830—Butterfly by Sir Henry (5158)—Mary Tilford by imp. Symmetry (5382)—imp. White Rose by Publicola (1348)—Fanny by Premier (1331)—by Pilot (495)—by Agamemnon (9)—by Marshal Beresford (415).

1879, Oct. 28, red c. c., Fanny Jordan (vol. 24) by Red Airdrie 46852—J. C. Jordan.

FANNY NINTH,

Red, calved May 21, 1879, bred and owned by J. C. Jordan, Des Moines, Ia., got by Red Airdrie 46852, out of Fanny 7th (vol. 13) by Plumwood Lad 8797—Fanny 2d by Major Duncan 5926—Bourbon Belle 2d by Duke of Southwick 450, &c., as above.

1882, Nov. 16, red c. c., Lily (vol. 24) by Peri Constance Duke 2d 48914—J. C. Jordan.

FANNY TENTH,

Red, calved May 16, 1880, bred and owned by J. C. Jordan, Des Moines, Ia., got by Red Airdrie 46852, out of Fanny 7th (vol. 13) by Plumwood Lad 8797—Fanny 2d by Major Duncan 5926, &c., as in Fanny 8th, above.

FLORENCE DUCHESS,

Red, calved April 8, 1882, bred and owned by J. C. Jordan, Des Moines, Iowa, got by Royal Duke of Bloomfield 44874, out of Fanny Jordan (vol. 24) by Red Airdrie 46852—Fanny 8th by Red Airdrie 46852—Fanny 7th by Plumwood Lad 8797—Fanny 2d by Major Duncan 5926—Bourbon Belle 2d by Duke of Southwick 450—Bourbon Belle by Malcolm 1830—Butterfly by Sir Henry (5158)—Mary Tilford by Symmetry (5382)—imp. White Rose by Publicola (1348)—Fanny by Premier (3331)—by Pilot (495)—by Agamemnon (9)—by Marshal Beresford (415).

RED THORNDALE FOURTH,

Red, calved Aug. 14, 1882, bred and owned by J. C. Jordon, Des Moines, Iowa, got by Royal Duke of Bloomfield 44874, out of Red Thorndale 2d (vol. 14) by 2d Compton Lord Wild Eyes 10954—Red Thorndale by 8th Duke of Thorndale 8030—La Petite by Dill's Derby 9755—Rowena by Atholson 9455—Stella by Value 1061—Lily 2d by Jake 593—Lily by Frederick 515—imp. Milk Spring by Leander (4199)—Blossom by Brigade Major (817)—Old Blossom by Planet (1325)—Blyth by Wellington (681)—by grandson of Favorite (252).

Jordan cattle were featured in *America's Short Horn Herd Book* in 1883.

CHAPTER 36
The Farmhouse Becomes a Mansion

In 1869 Benjamin R. Allen and his wife, Arathusa, opened their home in Des Moines to Iowa's elite in celebration of their fifteenth wedding anniversary. No doubt Senator James Jordan and his wife, Cynthia, were included on the guest list, as, according to Terrace Hill historians Goettsch and Weinberg, "More than 1,000 invitations were mailed, some to New York City," some to Chicago and most, of course, to their friends in Des Moines. There was only one residence in Des Moines which at that time could accommodate those numbers, and that home was Allen's newly constructed Terrace Hill mansion

The period of economic growth and prosperity after the Civil War, plus the completion of Terrace Hill, sparked a building boom of smaller imitations of that mansion around Des Moines, including Hoyt Sherman's home, which was completed in 1877 on Sherman Hill, as well as the Flinn farm located west of the Jordan House on the road to Booneville.

Hoyt Sherman's residence, 1875. *Hawkeye Insurance Company Atlas of 1875*

Likewise, a building boom was occurring in Chicago. It was at this time the Chicago Water tower was built, as well as many other lovely Victorian buildings. Emily Jordan, while she was attending Northwestern University in Evanston, reported back to Des Moines about the architectural progress occurring in Chicago and its suburbs. Her father, who did his banking there and sent his livestock to the Chicago market, undoubtedly observed it himself. Chicago was only a train ride away, and James and Emily traveled there often.

Magazines like *Godey's Lady's Book* provided information and often inspiration to the women of these times, and every month they featured a new house plan. The time was ripe to show the world how successful fifty-nine-year-old James Jordan had become. No doubt fashionable Emily, back home from college and in hopeful anticipation of a wedding, dreamed of ceremonies in a renovated and enlarged home rather than the cramped old family farmhouse. Cynthia and the rest of the family had the same desire, and eventually they convinced Uncle Jimmy.

Terrace Hill at 2300 Grand Avenue in Des Moines. Library of Congress

James Jordan: His Life and His Legacy   167

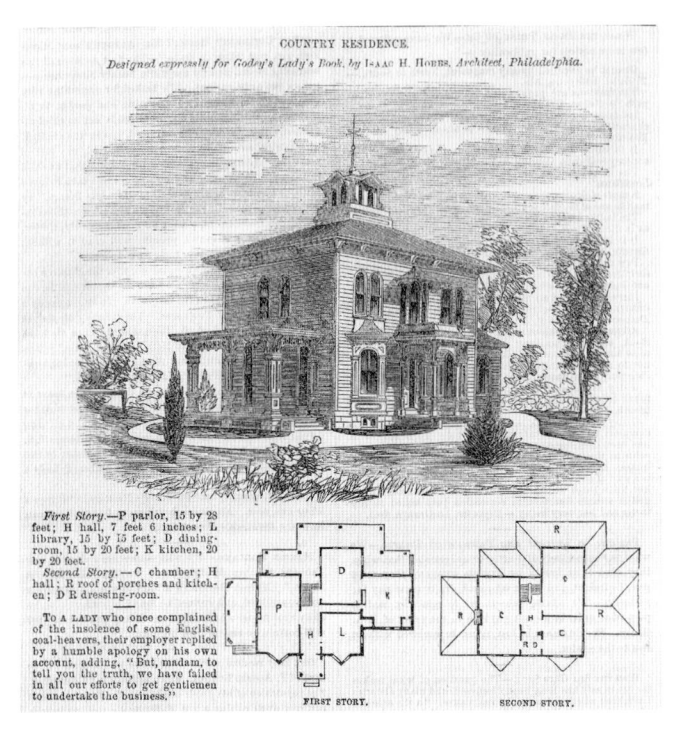

Plans like this inspired the renovation of the Jordan farmhouse into a mansion. From *Godey's Lady's Book and Magazine*

The Jordan House. Courtesy of West Des Moines Historical Society

The Flinn farm located west of the Jordan farm, 1875. *Hawkeye Insurance Company Atlas of 1875*

The plan was to add onto the back of the house, joining it with the kitchen/office building. The office and kitchen building had been previously enlarged with the addition of a second floor, so the second floor of the addition would have to merge the second floors of the two existing buildings.

The breezeway between the kitchen and the house was torn down and the ancient oak tree that for many decades had provided shade and shelter behind the house was cut down; its giant stump would serve as a foundation for the south side of the new wing. The stump was leveled off and provided support for the floor joists.

When building the new wing, James clearly reflected back upon his southern heritage in Virginia. The addition transformed the home by utilizing a typically southern scheme. It was only one room deep with a central hall. This is called the "I" house. (If it had been two rooms deep it would have been considered "Georgian.") The "I," however, was expanded with the additions.

Cynthia and James chose to adorn the exterior of their home in an Italianate Gothic motif which was popular at the time. On the ground level, open porches were added on either side of the old front doorway and on the entire south side of the house. All of the porches featured "gingerbread" ornamentation in the shape of swans, again reminiscent of the Old South. Above the porches were balconies accessible through the upstairs bedrooms.

The original front door on the east and a newly added entryway on the south were "fancied up" with Gothic arches, ornate trim, and impressive double doors. Decorative Italianate brackets were affixed below the eaves. The house was painted a creamy color, and dark green shutters were added to each window. The immediate grounds—a half acre around the house— were surrounded by a fancy white picket fence, probably replacing a more rustic one built previously.

168   Pursuit of a Dream

Nature inspired Victorian décor. Courtesy of West Des Moines Historical Society

An example of typical Victorian decor. From *Godey's Lady's Book and Magazine*

The interior was transformed as well. New furniture was purchased, and Victorian-style wallpaper with dark backgrounds and large, busy patterns was hung on the walls. Heavy, dark drapes with lace sheers were hung at the windows. Oriental rugs and runners graced the floors. New chandeliers fueled by kerosene were hung from the ceilings.

An impressive black walnut staircase was added to grace the new entry hall on the south, reflective of the long, dramatic entry hall with graceful stairs so typical of southern plantations. The original staircase on the east side of the house was adorned with a new walnut railing.

The "master" of a southern plantation typically had a locked room just inside the front door of the house. Again echoing the antebellum era, on the first floor James retained and incorporated his office into the renovation, keeping the small locked nook still containing his big desk and safe. The home's only fireplace was in his office, which for many years had served as a warm, cozy gathering place for Uncle Jimmy and his political cronies and business associates.

Cynthia was undoubtedly delighted with her renovated "modern" kitchen, to which a pantry was later added. Now inside the house, she would no longer have to traverse the breezeway to get to her stove. However, no indoor plumbing was installed; water still needed to be drawn by hand from the well outside the back door, baths would still be taken in the kitchen, and the toilet continued to be an outdoor privy.

A large dining room was adjacent to the kitchen and furnished with a beautiful, ornate hutch with glass doors. Displayed inside the hutch were the Jordan silver, a multitude of china, and other serving pieces.

The silver service Cynthia chose was uniquely suited to the house. In keeping with the Jordan cattle farm motif, the legs upon which each piece stood were actually shaped like hooves of animals. Victorian in design, each piece was engraved with an East Lake border around the top. This service was given to Cynthia's oldest daughter, Ella, when she married. Cynthia collected many sets of Havilland china over the years, and these she stored in the hutch. One beautiful set, her blue Havilland pattern, is still intact and belongs to one of the Jordan descendants. A large ornate buffet server also stood in the dining room.

Through a door from the dining room was a new back parlor, which was also accessible through another door from the formal front parlor and the southern entryway to the house. The back parlor became a comfortable family sitting room with horsehair settees and chairs, bookcases, and books.

The front parlor was redecorated with beautiful new wallpaper on the walls and ceiling. The piano, which had been added after the Civil War, remained and was surrounded by new furniture, rugs, and drapes reflecting all the impressive elegance that a front parlor should display.

The 1870s addition also added four much-needed rooms to the second floor. If all of these rooms were

Restored master bedroom in the Jordan House with original furniture. Courtesy of West Des Moines Historical Society

used for sleeping, the total number of bedrooms in the house would have been nine. Probably both family and hired help occupied the bedrooms; the help slept in the tiny bedrooms on the second floor of the new addition.

New bedrooms meant new furniture, and Cynthia purchased a splendid master bedroom suite. Their three-piece burled walnut bedroom set—with an enormous double bed, a dresser, and a commode—was brought out from Des Moines but was probably made elsewhere. A special feature in the dresser was the secret compartment at the bottom of the dresser where the Jordans may have kept private papers and letters. On either side of the dresser mirror were two shelves that held kerosene lamps or candles. These enabled Cynthia to comb or braid her hair at night by the light of the lamps.

Cynthia probably changed bedrooms and moved herself and James from the first-floor northeast room to the spacious southeast bedroom on the second floor, a room formerly occupied by all of the boys. A handy boudoir adjoined this room, a perfect respite from a snoring spouse.

James undoubtedly thought the best part of his "new" house were the porches. After the porches were built, the family spent a great deal of time on them, especially on the upper balconies where one could sit and rock in the evenings, enjoying a cool summer breeze and a pleasant glimpse of the distant, meandering Raccoon River.

By Christmas of 1870, the interior and exterior renovations were complete. James and Cynthia had built an "addition" to their home that was larger than the original structure and had created an impressive Victorian mansion out of their plain country farmhouse. The transformation of the Jordan House proclaimed the accomplishment and prosperity of James Jordan—a former state senator, wealthy landowner, livestock breeder and shipper, founding father of his community, devoted family man, and church supporter.

A Wedding in the New House

Cynthia and James decided their newly renovated home was the perfect place to celebrate the wedding of daughter Emily and her fiancé, Dr. George Hanawalt. For the past two years the family had been observing the very proper Victorian courtship between now twenty-nine-year-old Emily and thirty-five-year-old Hanawalt. On October 31, 1871, they were finally joined in marriage at the home of the bride.

Etiquette books of the time describe home weddings as "much less trouble, fatigue, and expense than fashionable church weddings." No doubt puritan James Jordan appreciated this. His role was to give away

Typical Victorian bridal attire. From *Godey's Lady's Book and Magazine*

Emily Hanawalt. Jordan Family Collection

the bride, which was to simply bow his affirmation when asked by the clergyman.

As a Victorian bride, Emily would have worn a simple, white wedding gown unadorned with jewelry but with flowers crowning her head. She probably wore a sheer veil or one of beautiful, old lace. In her gloved hands she may have carried a bouquet of flowers, either roses, orange blossoms, or perhaps lilies. It was customary for the bride, but not the groom, to wear a wedding ring. In the fashion of the day Emily's ring would have been a gold band. When Hanawalt proposed she received an engagement ring, and while diamonds were appropriate, other stones, even turquoises and opals, were also considered acceptable for engagement rings at that time.

Because Emily had several siblings, including her younger half-sisters Ella and Eva and her favorite and darling three-year-old brother Edward, she may have included some family members as her attendants. The ceremony took place in the flower-filled front parlor where a stirring wedding march was played on the grand piano. Afterwards supper was served to the family and guests. In keeping with the splendor of the newly decorated home, as well as the Jordan reputation for being generous hosts, the meal was probably quite elegant and may have included such treats as lobster and salmon salads, rolled turkeys and chicken salad sandwiches, beef bouillon, and ices.

Most likely dancing did not take place after the supper because James did not approve of such. However, the couple did participate in the ritual cutting of the cake. Rather than one large cake, they probably offered a selection of fancy cakes, such as macaroons, white bride's cakes, and groom's fruitcake.

At the close of the festivities and after mingling with her guests, Emily slipped upstairs to change into her traveling clothes. She then came back down the long stairway and was met at the foot of the stairs by her family, through whom she passed to join her new husband. After quick goodbyes, the newlyweds entered their carriage and rode away as the guests and family showered them with rice and cast-off slippers.

After their honeymoon, Dr. and Mrs. Hanawalt made their home at George's 816 Pleasant Street residence in Des Moines. As time went on, they would take up residence further west at Twelfth and Walnut Streets, a gift to them from Emily's father, who held the mortgage, and finally they would move permanently to a Tudor-style home at 4027 Ingersoll Avenue.

Soon after the Hanawalts' wedding, Benjamin, James' oldest son who had been his chief cattle hand and business partner, left the Jordan livestock enterprise and settled with his wife and two children on a farm near Gilmore in Pocahontas County. Western Iowa was becoming more and more settled, and the Iowa cowboy days were coming to an end. Benjamin stabled his horse, hung up his spurs, and became a farmer. Uncle Jimmy had turned increasingly to breeding rather than raising cattle. The cattle business as they had known it since the 1850s would eventually disappear.

That winter, the Jordan family experienced sadness at the death of ten-year-old Eva. She was the twin sister of Eda, who had died after sliding down the front hall banister. Eva died of natural causes—probably an illness, possibly diphtheria. She was buried in the family plot near her twin in the burial ground north of the house.

Post-wedding traveling attire. From *Godey's Lady's Book and Magazine*

James Jordan: His Life and His Legacy   171

CHAPTER 37
The Jordan Cemetery

At the Jordan farm, it was a full house. In 1875 six Jordan sons lived there: bachelors Henry (thirty), John (twenty-eight), James (twenty-six), George (twenty-four), and youngsters Calvin (twelve) and Edward (six). Besides the boys, Cynthia and James only had one daughter to keep them company, seventeen-year-old Ella, and they all had a wonderful time together.

Fun-loving Ella often played the piano in the front parlor while friends and family came in and rolled up the rug so they could dance in the adjoining back parlor. Often one of Ella's friends, probably one of the Cook girls, would come over for the fun. They all knew Ella's puritanical father forbade dancing and had only recently been "coaxed" into allowing a piano in his home. He did not approve of this type of frivolity and merrymaking, so it took place only in his absence.

Family legend states that when these parties were held, Cynthia would stand at the outside door acting as a look-out for her children. If she heard her husband coming she would begin loudly singing hymns, a signal for the dancing to stop.

The old Jordan schoolhouse was relocated, re-sided, and converted into a storage building. Courtesy of West Des Moines Historical Society

The new Jordan Schoolhouse. Jordan Family Collection

172   Pursuit of a Dream

The old log school was deteriorating and the schoolhouse needed to be enlarged, so after the renovation of the Jordan home was completed, they took on the project of building a brand-new schoolhouse. The old building was torn down and moved to a nearby farm to serve as a storage building. In its place, they built a traditional, white, one-room schoolhouse on the same spot as its predecessor—northeast of the Jordan House and across the creek. Calvin and Edward Jordan were thus able to complete their elementary education in the new, modern Jordan School.

With their home redone and the school replaced, it was time to think about how the surrounding grounds might complement their splendid new home. James and Cynthia decided the small family burial grounds near the house should be moved. There was also an Indian burial site on the Jordan property. A number of mounds were located together about one-fourth mile northwest of the Jordan home on a secluded knoll. James and Cynthia decided to leave them undisturbed, out of respect for the Indians who had helped the family when they were pioneers. The mounds are still there to this day.

In 1880 Jordan deeded eight and a half acres of his land for a cemetery, located about a half-mile from the Jordan home, along the former wagon trail that ran through his property (about a quarter mile west of what is now the intersection of Fuller Road and Grand Avenue). Also included was the land upon which the abandoned Jordan Chapel parsonage stood. The cemetery was named Jordan Cemetery.

The first graves in Jordan Cemetery were those which until then had been located in the small family plot northwest of the Jordan House. The bodies were all exhumed and reburied in Jordan Cemetery. This included the caskets containing the bodies of Jordan's first wife, Melinda; her niece, Mary; James' and Cynthia's twin daughters, Eda and Eva; and James' first grandson, John Cunningham Jordan. The graves of several pioneers remained on the property. The headstones of Ethelinda Downs and J. M. Rosecrants are the only ones still legible.

Gate to Jordan Cemetery, West Des Moines. Courtesy West Des Moines Parks and Recreation

The Jordan Cemetery Association was given the deed for administration purposes, and John Q. Jordan, son of James Jordan, was elected president of the association. He remained president and caretaker until he himself was buried in the cemetery.

Senator Jordan, his two wives, and all of their children eventually would be buried in Jordan Cemetery, with the exception of two Jordan daughters. Emily Hanawalt is buried next to her husband, George, in one of the most impressive monuments in Woodland Cemetery in Des Moines, and Ella Cook, her husband John, and their children are also buried in Woodland Cemetery.

Beginning in 1880 Jordan Cemetery was governed by a board of trustees. In 1920, the board asked the City of Valley Junction for financial assistance with cemetery upkeep. Finally, in 1926, Valley Junction acquired the cemetery, providing an initial contribution of $200.

Municipal funds were periodically provided by Valley Junction and later West Des Moines (when that area of Walnut Township was incorporated into the City of West Des Moines). Upkeep for the cemetery eventually became a line item in the City of West Des Moines' annual budget when the Cemetery Board voted to give the property to West Des Moines as a municipal cemetery.

CHAPTER 38
The Victorian Lifestyle

By late 1881, central Polk County included the bustling commercial and residential areas of the city of Des Moines, plus many smaller unincorporated communities surrounding it. These communities, such as Sevastopol, North Des Moines, Greenwood Park, Capitol Place, University Place, and others, each had their own commercial center and surrounding residential areas. By 1890, they were all incorporated into the city and became part of Des Moines.

The Des Moines city limits grew to include over fifty-six square miles, and its population also increased. From an 1860 census count of 3,965 residents, the number rose to 12,035 in 1870 and to 22,408 in 1880. By 1890 the number of people living in incorporated areas of Des Moines more than doubled to 50,093. The communities out west like Valley Junction and Clover Hills, immediately north of Valley Junction, would not have been considered for incorporation into Des Moines. They were too far away.

The city of Des Moines by this time had over a dozen operating coal mines. It had poultry plants, foundries, machine shops, oil wells, furniture factories, lumber mills and yards, woolen mills, brick factories, gristmills, carriage factories, packing companies, banks, insurance companies, and all the supporting service industries of a large city and seat of government.

If a person was not able to find a product or service in Des Moines, they could take the train to Chicago and find it and buy it there. Many people, including George and Emily Hanawalt, made frequent trips east to Chicago for just that reason. Emily loved beautiful dresses and fancy hats, and she had an extensive collection of both. She also had all the other trappings of the wife of a successful and prosperous husband: a lovely large brick home at an excellent address—Twelfth and Walnut—and all the appropriate furnishings, china, crystal, and other accouterments.

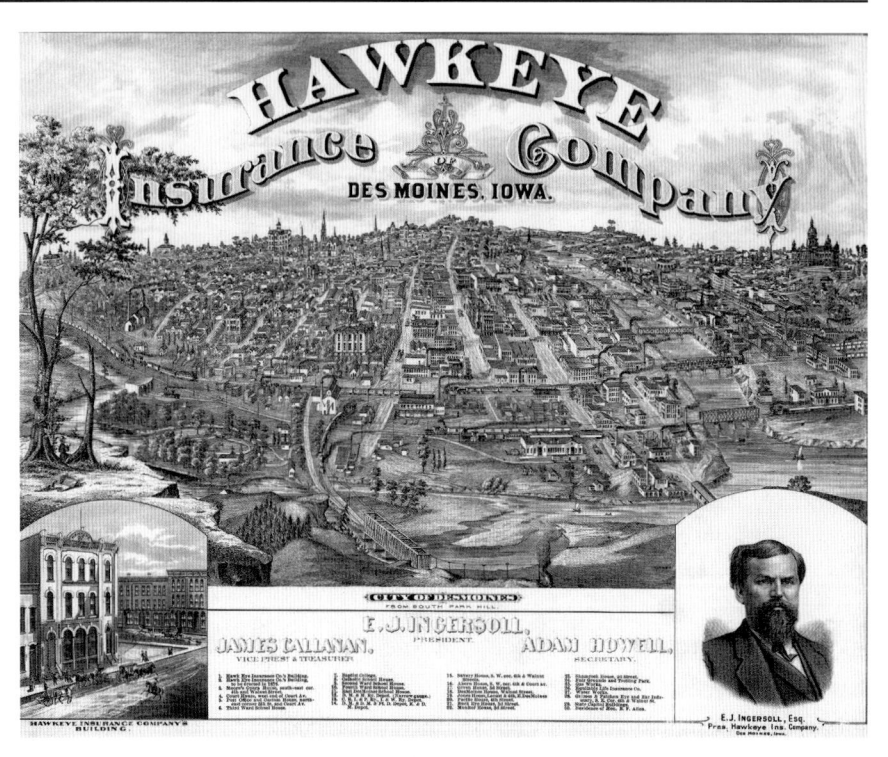

Aerial view of Des Moines, 1875. Library of Congress

The Victorian Lady

Emily's lifestyle was typical of well-to-do women of those times whose day revolved around socializing with friends. Much of this was done in homes. In the post-Civil War years of the Victorian era, entertainment in the home became much more sophisticated because supplies from the East as well as those manufactured locally were more plentiful. Unlike the harsh pioneer days, people were now able to afford some luxury in their lives. Immigrants arriving from Europe were available as servants in homes. They made life easier for those who hired them to cook and keep house. This afforded well-to-do women more time to engage in social activities.

As time went by, streets and roads improved and many in Des Moines were paved. Travel became easier.

Emily and her friends were able to participate in the custom of "calling" on one another. Calling involved a formal ritual of arranging visits to each other's homes, usually in the late morning or afternoon, by leaving calling cards. They responded to the cards by either visiting or not and entertaining visitors to one's home on the afternoon in which the lady of the house was "in."

On their calling cards they would write their name and under it their availability to entertain guests. For example:

> *Mrs. George Hanawalt*
> *Thursdays in February*
> *Tea Four o'clock*

Or, if for a single occasion:

> *Four o'clock Tea*
> *Tuesday February Fifth*
> *The home of Dr. and Mrs. Hanawalt*

Or, with more than one hostess:

> *Mrs. George Hanawalt and Mrs. James Jordan*
> *Thursdays Four to Seven*
> *Jordan House*

The cards would be left by either Emily or one of her servants at the homes of those she wished to visit her. If Emily was out on calls and found no one at home, she would leave her card so the occupants of the house knew she had tried to pay a visit.

The cards announcing when a hostess could receive callers required no RSVP. If callers could come, they did and left their cards in a tray in the hall when they arrived. Men and women could both call, and generally visits were not long.

Men would typically be attired in morning—not evening—dress, and women wore walking or carriage costumes. Emily and Cynthia Jordan would have on an attractive reception gown, never an evening dress. Teenaged Ella Jordan would wear a pretty dress in fabrics suitable for the season. The younger Jordan sons might be present, but the older ones, already grown, were generally absent as in the early years they were cowboys on the western Iowa range and in later years busy with their own farms.

During the time visitors came to call, tea and a light snack of cakes and sandwiches with only the freshest ingredients would be served. In the early days it was acceptable for women to do fancy needlework while they

Jordan hall tree, a place for visitors' calling cards. Courtesy of West Des Moines Historical Society

Iconic swan located in the Jordan House entry hall. Courtesy of West Des Moines Historical Society

James Jordan: His Life and His Legacy 175

visited with their guest, but later on, as society became more affluent, it was deemed inappropriate.

Aside from afternoon tea, if guests were entertained in Emily's home during the decade after the Civil War, it would *not* be for lunch. Dinner was the acceptable time to entertain guests. Recipes Emily used may have been ones she read about in women's magazines of the day, like *Godey's Lady's Book*, a monthly publication from Philadelphia.

Women all over the country studied *Godey's* or other women's magazines to learn about the latest trends and recommendations of how to live "in style." Recommended recipes included potted salmon, carrot soup, ham omelet, baked minced mutton, scotch eggs, German cream biscuits, or custard fritters.

In the later 1800s, the type of entertaining changed when luncheons—for ladies or occasionally for ladies and gentlemen—became the mode. Transported by horse and carriage, guests would often gather for the purpose of being entertained by a musician or speaker.

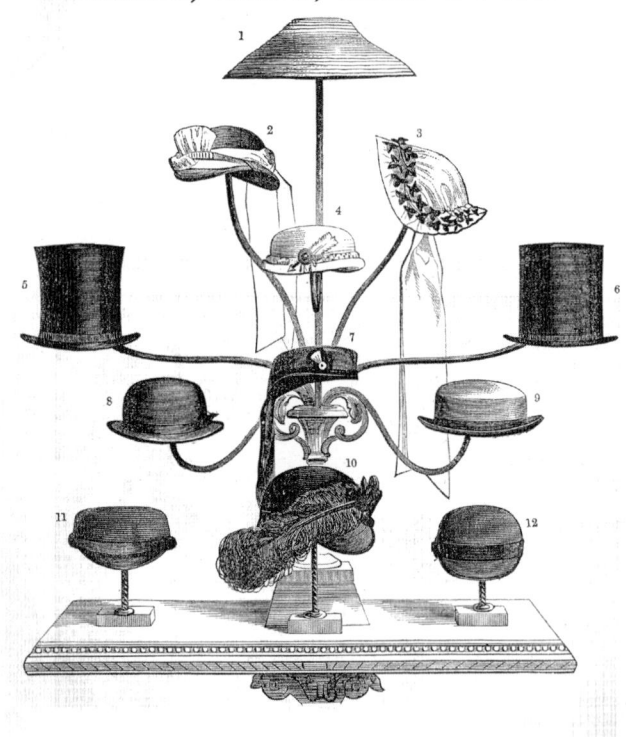

Hats typical of the ones worn by Emily. From *Godey's Lady's Book and Magazine*

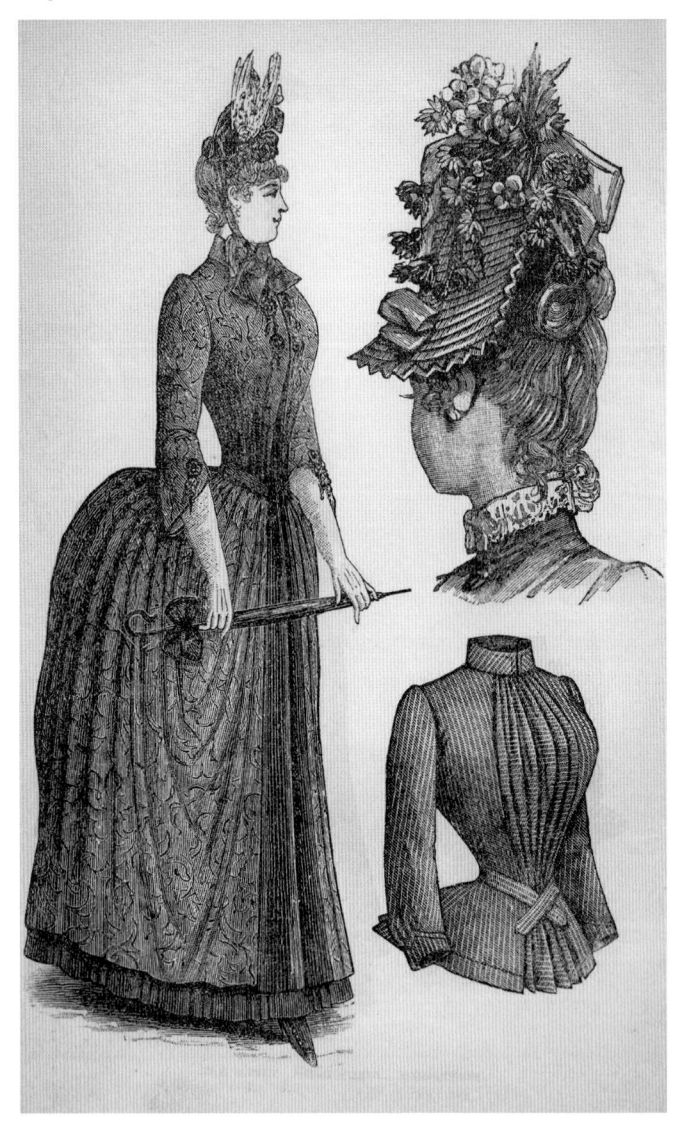

From *Godey's Lady's Book and Magazine*

From *Godey's Lady's Book and Magazine*

176   Pursuit of a Dream

Luncheons might center around a decorative theme, and typically favors would be given to each of the guests as they left. Emily Hanawalt and Cynthia Jordan both took enormous pride in their large and exquisite collections of crystal, silver, and china and would use these luncheons to display their finery. Many lovely and unique silver pieces were beautifully displayed in a massive china cabinet in the Jordan House dining room.

Visiting the Jordan Farm

In later years the Hanawalts often journeyed west out into the country to visit Emily's parents' farmstead, now being referred to as "Greenwood." They would take their own horse and buggy, or Emily might choose the option of riding public transportation, at that time a horse-drawn hack. The hack service operated between Forty-second Street and Grand Avenue in western Des Moines and traveled to Fifth Street and Railroad Avenue in the emerging town of Valley Junction. The approximately one-and-a-half-mile route took passengers through heavy timber on sometimes muddy roads. If roads were in poor condition, it could take several hours to travel the seven miles from their home at Twelfth and Walnut Streets in Des Moines to Valley Junction and then on out Wagon Trail Road to the Jordan House.

Once out in the country, the Hanawalts could call on Emily's sister Ella and her husband John or some of Emily's old neighbors at their farms. Unlike the busy city life of Des Moines, out at her parents' house it was rural, slower-paced, and quiet.

Silver service featuring animal hooves reflect the Jordan cattle enterprise. Courtesy of West Des Moines Historical Society

The Jordan farm had undergone a transformation during the 1880s. Rather than a farm whose main purpose was to provide sustenance for a large and growing family, responsibilities had shifted and James delegated many of the farming operations to his sons and hired hands rather than doing them himself. This gave him more time to manage his lucrative and very profitable agribusiness.

Dr. George Hanawalt. Jordan Family Collection

In 1888 James bought and sold over $33,000 worth of hogs and that year fed seven hundred head of steer and fifteen hundred head of hogs. Of the eighteen hundred acres he owned in Walnut Township, James and his sons had six hundred acres under cultivation.

Focusing on his passion for raising and breeding Shorthorn cattle, he indulged himself during those years, occasionally traveling by train to places like Texas, which was a source of Shorthorns, or to Chicago where the Shorthorn Cattlemen's Association was headquartered. Ranchers who were opening up the western plains could purchase good Shorthorn stock in Chicago to start herds in western states such as Montana, Idaho, and Wyoming.

Rather like the old mule-running days in Independence and St. Joe, Missouri, Uncle Jimmy enjoyed the art of the deal. He entertained himself in his later years with the creative pastime of buying and selling livestock in the big markets in Chicago. At the same time, George and Emily Hanawalt were developing an eye for thoroughbred trotting horses.

The Iowa State Fair

By the late 1880s, farming had become more of an occupation and less of a means of survival as it had been in the early pioneer days. This occupation was annually showcased at the Iowa State Fair. In its first twenty-five years the fair had been held in various cities around the state—Muscatine, Oskaloosa, Iowa City, Dubuque, Clinton, Keokuk, Burlington, and Cedar Rapids—but in 1879 it finally found a permanent home in Des Moines. Increasing settlement in western Iowa and the growing population of the capital city was enough to warrant a permanent state fair site.

The first fairgrounds in Des Moines were located at Brown's Park near Grand Avenue and Tonawanda Drive on the western edge of the city. Families who came to the fair camped outside the fairgrounds, much like the old church revival meetings.

The fair featured livestock exhibits, an amphitheater, and a race track. George and Emily Hanawalt were starting to become involved in thoroughbred harness racing, and the Iowa State Fair horse races inspired their interest. The fair also gave James and his friends F. M. Hubbell and Martin Flynn and other stockbreeders a convenient opportunity to showcase their finest Shorthorn cattle.

In 1886 the Brown's Park fairgrounds site was replaced by a bigger and better one at its present location on the east side of Des Moines. A few years after the move, Des Moines merchants initiated a downtown street carnival which would be held annually during the state fair to showcase the commercial center of the city. They named their carnival Seni Om Sed, which is "Des Moines" spelled backwards.

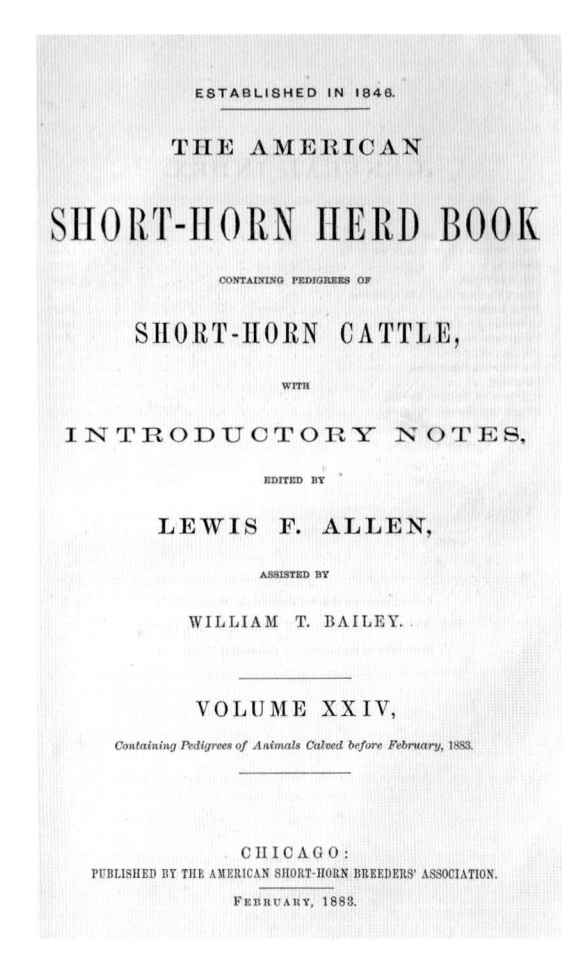

Book featuring prize Shorthorn cattle.

Horse racing was popular at state and county fairs. Currier and Ives

178   Pursuit of a Dream

CHAPTER 39
A Beloved Son-in-Law

When James Jordan's future son-in-law Dr. George P. Hanawalt arrived in Des Moines on May 22, 1869, there were no established hospitals in the capital city. During the next forty-four years Hanawalt would work diligently to provide quality health care to his many patients, initiate the establishment of hospitals in Des Moines, and become a leader in the state's medical community. As a physician, Hanawalt was reputed to be a caring person and an exemplary caregiver, as illustrated by one of his contemporaries, presented by Iowa historian Johnson Brigham, in a biographical sketch:

> It was as a physician at the bedside of those who were ill that his tenderness and sympathy naturally shone most strongly forth, inspiring confidence and hopefulness in his patients and winning for him the loving gratitude and enduring friendship which are after all the most valuable possessions of life. He was a great lover of flowers and it was his custom when visiting his patients to give them a bouquet as part of his cheery greeting. The expense of this gift was often greater than the fee which he would obtain, but that fact never entered his mind.
>
> He was genial, warm-hearted and enjoyed the respect of all. His kindly spirit went out in hearty sympathy and helpfulness to those who needed aide professionally or otherwise. He never sought notoriety but was content to lead a quiet and unostentatious life.
>
> One of his strong points was devotion to duty and he seemed to derive his greatest pleasure from the relief he could afford his patients. No exactions or demands were too great for him and were always met with patience and cheerfulness.

According to William Porter, Polk County medical historian, another biographer wrote that Dr. Hanawalt was "studious and attentive and always prompt and reliable . . . he is emphatically a worker and never neglects a patient . . . he soon made his mark, not only as a physician but also as an accomplished surgeon."

Still another account by the Polk County Medical Society reveals that George Hanawalt was "a most indefatigable laborer and his efforts, both as a physician and surgeon, have been crowned with the greatest degree of success. In surgery he is especially distinguished and enjoys a statewide reputation in the profession."

Two years after he arrived in Des Moines, he and Emily Jordan were married. They did not have children, and that may have been one reason why he displayed such compassionate care for his patients, whom he considered his family. Emily was supportive of her husband's attentive treatment of his patients. Family legend states that in addition to Hanawalt bringing his patients flowers, he would also often bring them homemade soup—no doubt sent by Emily.

Hanawalt initially came to Des Moines as a division surgeon for the Rock Island and Pacific Railroad Company. Later he added many other railroad lines to his emerging practice, securing appointments as railroad surgeon of the following railroads: the Des Moines and Fort Dodge; the Great Western; the Des Moines and Northern; the Chicago, Des Moines and Kansas City Railroad; the Des Moines Street Railway Company; and the Interurban Railway Company.

An Early Version of the "HMO"

Dr. Hanawalt operated like a later-day health maintenance organization (HMO) for the railroads, with him serving as the primary health-care provider. As an employee of the railroads, Hanawalt was expected to provide care for local railroad employees, their families, and for railroad employees and passengers who were passing through Des Moines who were injured or became ill.

Hanawalt's practice grew rapidly, and his reputation extended far beyond the Des Moines city limits and even Polk County. The same year he opened his practice he was elected to membership in the Iowa State Medical Society and within two years was voted to be the organization's treasurer. Ten years later, in 1879, he would be elected president. A veteran of the Civil War,

Hanawalt maintained an ongoing relationship with the US Army and in 1877 was commissioned as the surgeon general of the Iowa National Guard. He served in this position for the next sixteen years, finally retiring with the rank of brigadier general.

Addressing Medical Needs in Early Des Moines

In order to meet the medical needs of the patients in his practice as well as others in the community, it was important to Hanawalt to consider new ways to convey care to patients. During the Civil War, hospitals were a part of every battlefield. As a surgeon in the army, Hanawalt knew these to be unsanitary, makeshift affairs. On the pioneer prairie, hospitals were nonexistent; the custom, born of necessity, was to care for sick people in the home. If a doctor was available, he would come to the patient's home and, if necessary, perform surgery there. Rather than exacerbate their health problems by traveling long distances to see a doctor, it was actually better for sick people to remain at home for treatment and recuperation. Homes, even pioneer cabins, were generally more germ-free than the hospitals of the day.

However, with the advances made during the Civil War in the practice of medical surgery and the more sophisticated care patients required afterwards, hospitals were ultimately deemed necessary and the preferred place to conduct surgery. They also provided the community with a place to harbor patients afflicted with highly communicable diseases, such as typhoid fever, cholera, yellow fever, diphtheria, influenza, scarlet fever, and small pox.

The First Hospital in Des Moines

In the late 1860s there were very few hospitals in the state of Iowa, and those that existed were located in the eastern regions, generally along the Mississippi River. A fledgling hospital was established in Des Moines in 1868 with the purchase of a brick building on Market Street located on the east side of the Des Moines River. This hospital lasted for about five weeks and successfully treated approximately thirty Swedish immigrants suffering from typhoid. Only two patients died. No further attempts at starting a hospital took place during the next seven years.

On December 15, 1875, the Ladies of the Helping Hand Society of St. Paul's Episcopal Church opened a hospital at 923 Seventh Street. They called it the Seventh Street Hospital. With the support of their rector and parish, these women gathered resources to equip the hospital. This church and these women would pioneer the hospital movement in Des Moines until conventional hospital services were ultimately established.

The Seventh Street Hospital opened in anticipation of a recurring outbreak of diphtheria, which consistently happened during the winter. The problem faced by the founding board members (Mrs. Crocker, Mrs. Annie B. Tracey, Mrs. Monroe, Mrs. Jewett, Mrs. Porter, Mrs. Savery, Ms. Mitchell, and Ms. Griffith) had been to find a suitable location to care for people with contagious diseases. They first had tried to open their hospital at 1322 Locust Street but were unsuccessful in doing so

Hanawalt's sword and epaulets. Courtesy of West Des Moines Historical Society

because of protesting neighbors. Eventually they found a location at the Seventh Street address.

Soon after the hospital opened, however, it became apparent that not everyone saw the creation of this hospital as a good thing for Des Moines. The hospital was filthy, smelly, and objectionable to the surrounding neighborhood. On August 16, 1875, a letter to the editor appeared in the *Daily Iowa State Register* stating the Seventh Street Hospital was "a disgrace to the good intentions of the founders of the enterprise." A neighbor had written the complaint saying the hospital "was overcrowded and the smell was unbearable."

No doubt George Hanawalt, a member of St. Paul's along with his wife, was aware of the poor conditions. Hanawalt met with Annie B. Tracey and the Seventh Street Hospital Board of Directors, and together they made a new plan authorizing Mrs. Tracey to purchase a lot and building located at 1105 Sherman Street between Ascension and Ridge Streets, north of the downtown area in the vicinity of present-day Mercy Hospital. She did so in early August 1876. The new building was fitted out as a hospital, and the board voted to name it Cottage Hospital.

In this new venture, Hanawalt was in put charge of medical services and Mrs. Tracey served as the hospital administrator. The challenge of establishing a permanent hospital in Des Moines was finally being met. There is no doubt Hanawalt enlisted the financial support of his father-in-law, James Jordan, to keep this valuable community asset operating.

Rescue at Four Mile Creek

In the summer of 1877 Des Moines and its environs were waterlogged with significant flooding in the creeks and rivers of Polk County. On August 28 rain fell steadily all night long—so much so that Little Four Mile Creek, nine miles east of downtown Des Moines, became a raging torrent.

About one and a half miles southwest of Altoona, the tracks of the Rock Island Railroad crossed the creek. A Rock Island passenger train was due to come down the tracks that evening with another train scheduled to come through later. This later train included P. T. Barnum's Greatest Show on Earth's advance car and a few other circus cars on their way to Des Moines to make arrangements for a September 9 show.

The train wreck at Four Mile Creek. Courtesy of West Des Moines Historical Society

The tracks appeared safe to a Rock Island Railroad engineer driving a train over the bridge earlier that night. However, at 2:30 a.m. when the *next* train approached the Little Four Mile Creek bridge, its engineer had no way of knowing the swollen waters had torn out the stone supports anchoring the bridge. The engine suddenly lurched and sank as the rails gave way. The engine plowed ahead and came to a crashing halt, partly buried in the west bank. When the passenger cars and circus cars approached the bridge, they smashed into each other as one by one they toppled into the creek. George Mills of the *Des Moines Register* reported:

> Seventeen people were killed including the engineer and several circus employees. Thirty-eight others were injured, three of whom died later. The death toll of 20 still stands as the greatest loss of life in any Des Moines area railroad wreck.
>
> A number of the wreck victims drowned in the creek, which was an estimated 20 feet deep in places. Others were crushed to death. The mail and express car landed on top of one of the Barnum cars, grinding it to matchwood. Two passenger cars were so broken up that rescuers weren't sure whether they were working with one or two cars. There was only three feet left between the roof and floor of one car. The train might have come to grief even if it succeeded in crossing the Little Four Mile Creek bridge closer to Des Moines as the track was washed out that same night.

James Jordan: His Life and His Legacy

Circus tents and parade. Library of Congress

The east Des Moines medical community, citizens in the immediate Four Mile Creek area, and volunteers from the city of Des Moines all worked together in a frantic rescue attempt. Injured passengers were taken to Cottage Hospital in Des Moines as fast as possible. According to a Hanawalt biography, "Dr. Hanawalt took charge at the hospital and labored along with other physicians for many hours ministering to the victims."

Two of the deceased were a seven-year-old girl and her father from Boone. The mother survived. One of the circus men escaped death by grabbing a tree as he was swirled downstream. He had been badly scalded by escaping steam from the locomotive but lived.

The Barnum Circus advance car was filled with posters, tickets, and even some clowns. The posters and tickets were scattered all over the countryside and lost to over four thousand curiosity seekers who swarmed into the area afterwards.

P. T. Barnum was deeply appreciative of the efforts of Hanawalt, the other physicians, Cottage Hospital, and all the citizens who had worked so hard to rescue his employees and the other victims of the crash. To show his appreciation, he offered to deliver a Sunday night lecture at Moore's Opera House on September 9 to benefit Cottage Hospital.

On that night, all Des Moines clergymen cancelled their Sunday evening services so their parishioners could attend Barnum's talk for the price of $0.75 for a reserved seat or $0.50 general admission. George Mills, *Des Moines Register,* provided this description:

> Barnum didn't talk about either the wreck or his own gaudy life. He was an outspoken foe of liquor and he spent 1 ½ hours discussing the problems of strong drink. A newspaper report of the lecture said: "He believes in pledges and local temperance effort. He expressed his faith in the power of women to save men from the evil habit of drinking alcoholic stimulants, and especially in the influence of young ladies over their companions and sweethearts! The self-declared Prince of Humbug departed from his typical cynicism and declared his belief in the power of Christianity to unlock the fetters of the inebriate!"

There is no doubt Dr. Hanawalt's prohibitionist in-laws, James and Cynthia Jordan, were seated front and center for the lecture, listening in rhapsody to a subject dear to James' teetotaling heart.

Barnum's talk generated $300.00. In addition, Barnum donated the proceeds from a special circus performance the following day, which brought the total donations to more that $12,000.00. Hanawalt turned all of the money over to Mrs. Tracey, and she used it to expand and update Cottage Hospital into a larger, "modern," thirty-bed facility.

Cottage Hospital and Tracey Home Hospital

Dr. Hanawalt and Mrs. Tracey continued to run Cottage Hospital together, accepting donations of money and useful items from St. Paul's Episcopal Parish. This parish, which had provided major support for Cottage Hospital since its inception, was asked in 1887 by Hanawalt and Tracey to appoint their vestry as a hospital advisory board. The vestry took over the control of hospital finances and set up an endowment fund. They also revamped the administration of Cottage Hospital, allowing Mrs. Tracey to end her business relationship and start a new venture.

In 1890, Cottage Hospital, under the guidance of Hanawalt, formed a partnership with the Drake University Medical School. Hanawalt supervised the Drake/Cottage Hospital collaboration and also continued to treat patients at Cottage Hospital.

By then Mrs. Tracey had opened a new facility, Tracey Home Hospital, located in a large, converted, brick home just south of Cottage Hospital. Tracey Home was an assisted-living and rehabilitative facility providing state-of-the-art care to invalids. Hanawalt provided the medical care in this facility as well. Patients like Fort Dodge resident Dana Savery were grateful to be cared for in the Tracey Home Hospital, with excellent medical care available from Hanawalt and Mrs. Tracey's staff. The following letter is an illustration:

Fort Dodge

October 24, 1889

Dear Dr. H.,

After thinking the matter over carefully, I have decided to put myself in your care once more.

I hate to go to the hospital and won't do so unless I can have the room I had before. I saw Mrs. Tracey, but she may not have received my letter.

Won't you please telephone Mrs. Tracey to be sure and keep the room for me. I shall leave here next Monday at noon, get to Des Moines about five o'clock and if convenient for you will be ready at nine, Tuesday morning for the hospital.

I can't tell you how I dread it but I'm so anxious to be well.

If I don't hear from you in the meantime, shall conclude the appointment suits your convenience.

And will be on time.

Your friend,

Mrs. George Savery

"Positions of Trust"

In 1891, Dr. George Hanawalt was appointed chief medical director for Equitable Life Insurance Company. His father-in-law had been an investor and founding board member of that enterprise. This appointment occurred in the same year James Jordan passed away. Hanawalt had firmly established his reputation as an excellent doctor and also a community leader. In addition to having a fine man associated with the company, perhaps F. M. Hubbell and the Equitable Board of Directors wanted to express their loyalty and respect to James Jordan by continuing a relationship with his family through his son-in-law.

Before James Jordan died in 1891, he appointed Hanawalt as the principle executor of his estate. Because of the complicated nature of how the probate was carried out, the estate was not completely settled until after Hanawalt died. However, Hanawalt did his best to manage the complex financial affairs and assets of his deceased father-in-law.

Conventional Hospitals Emerge in Des Moines

In 1895 Mercy Hospital was opened by the Sisters of Mercy who had come from Dubuque, and not long afterward in 1901, Methodist Hospital opened its doors in the former buildings of Callanan College, located at 1200 Pleasant Street.

Prior to the opening of Methodist Hospital, the Cottage Hospital Board of Directors had decided in August 1899 to close its doors for lack of maintenance funds and also because Mercy and Methodist Hospitals would be better equipped. The closing of Tracey Home Hospital probably occurred at the same time. Cottage Hospital was absorbed into Iowa Methodist Hospital where a Cottage Hospital ward was established, financed by the sale of the Cottage Hospital buildings.

Dr. Hanawalt's Later Years

Dr. Hanawalt's office was always located in downtown Des Moines—for many years on the northeast corner of Seventh and Walnut Streets, close to his first two residences, and in later years on the eleventh floor of the Equitable Building. A friendly and popular gentleman, he belonged to a myriad of civic and fraternal organizations, many of the same ones as his father-in-law. They included the Octogenarian Society and the Old Settler's Association. Hanawalt was a founding member of both the Tippecanoe Club and in 1878 the G.A.R. Crocker Post No. 12. However, because of his busy practice, he was not able to give these organizations much of his time. Like his father-in-law he was also a member of the Republican Party, the political party of the railroads, but unlike his father-in-law, he was not politically active.

Dr. George P. Hanawalt died on July 6, 1912, at the age of seventy-six. He was eulogized as: "A man who probably held more positions of trust than any other medical man in Des Moines. He was not regarded merely as a physician by those who employed his services but as a friend, and all who knew him honored him for his genuine worth of character. He was an indefatigable worker, ever ready to respond to the calls from the poor and the needy, satisfied with a knowing that he was helping them. His motto, which clearly illustrated the composition of his life was, 'If it has to be done, I want to do it.'"

Hanawalt's burial was arranged by his wife, Emily, in a magnificent crypt in Woodland Cemetery. A year after his death, the Des Moines School Board voted to honor his contributions to the community by naming a new school in his memory. The school, Hanawalt Elementary, is located at Fifty-sixth Street and Robertson Drive on the very western edge of Des Moines.

Hanawalt School, Des Moines. Photographer, Scott Little

CHAPTER 40
The Junction in the Valley

Out in Walnut Township—and in particular in the little community becoming known as Valley Junction—life couldn't have been more different from the bustling pace of downtown Des Moines. However, as the 1890s approached, James Jordan would shrewdly seize the opportunity to make his last fortune. In doing so, he would initiate the transformation of the quiet community of little Valley Junction into a prosperous "boom town." He would do this by cashing in on his decades-old real estate investments. These properties would be sold to the Rock Island Railroad and to developers who would quickly transform Valley Junction into a thriving railroad center.

No stranger to making railroad deals, James was a twenty-year veteran of maneuvering the various lines he had dealt with over the years. In 1866 he had successfully led the final push for the Des Moines Valley Railroad to complete tracks into Des Moines and had facilitated railroad transactions as a board member of the Iowa Railroad Company.

In 1876, Uncle Jimmy cleverly maneuvered the Rock Island and Des Moines Fort Dodge Railroads to reinstate a shipping junction by the Raccoon River near *his* home instead of moving it to Waukee. James had accomplished this by offering the railroad companies "incentives" in the form of cash and other favors and by putting up a station house and establishing a small community near the Raccoon River at the junction. Since then, the community had been referred to as "Valley Junction."

The station was located in the vicinity of what is now the corner of Eighth Street and Railroad Avenue. James would build cattle and hog pens there, probably south of the railroad tracks. Early residents of "the Junction" recalled cattle and hogs being driven down the hill on what is now Eighth Street into pens along the tracks to await shipment to Chicago. This happened as late as 1888, when it was reported that Jordan had bought and sold over $33,000 worth of hogs and fed seven hundred head of steer.

Increasingly, people were coming out and settling in this little village and in the areas around it west of Des Moines. Since 1887, letters to James Jordan were no longer addressed to Des Moines but instead to "Valley Junction, Iowa," which by that year had grown to a population of nearly five hundred with its own post office.

In addition to the Rock Island, other railroads laid tracks through Valley Junction: the Sibley, the Winterset and Indianola branch of the Rock Island, and the Minneapolis and St. Louis Railroad all crossed the main east-west Rock Island line in the junction. This, of course, contributed to the growth of the little village.

From 1846, when James Jordan and his family first settled in the area, to the mid-1880s, his holdings expanded to eighteen hundred acres of land in Walnut Township (much of it around Valley Junction) and a

James C. Jordan. *From Portrait and Biographical Album of Polk County*, 1890

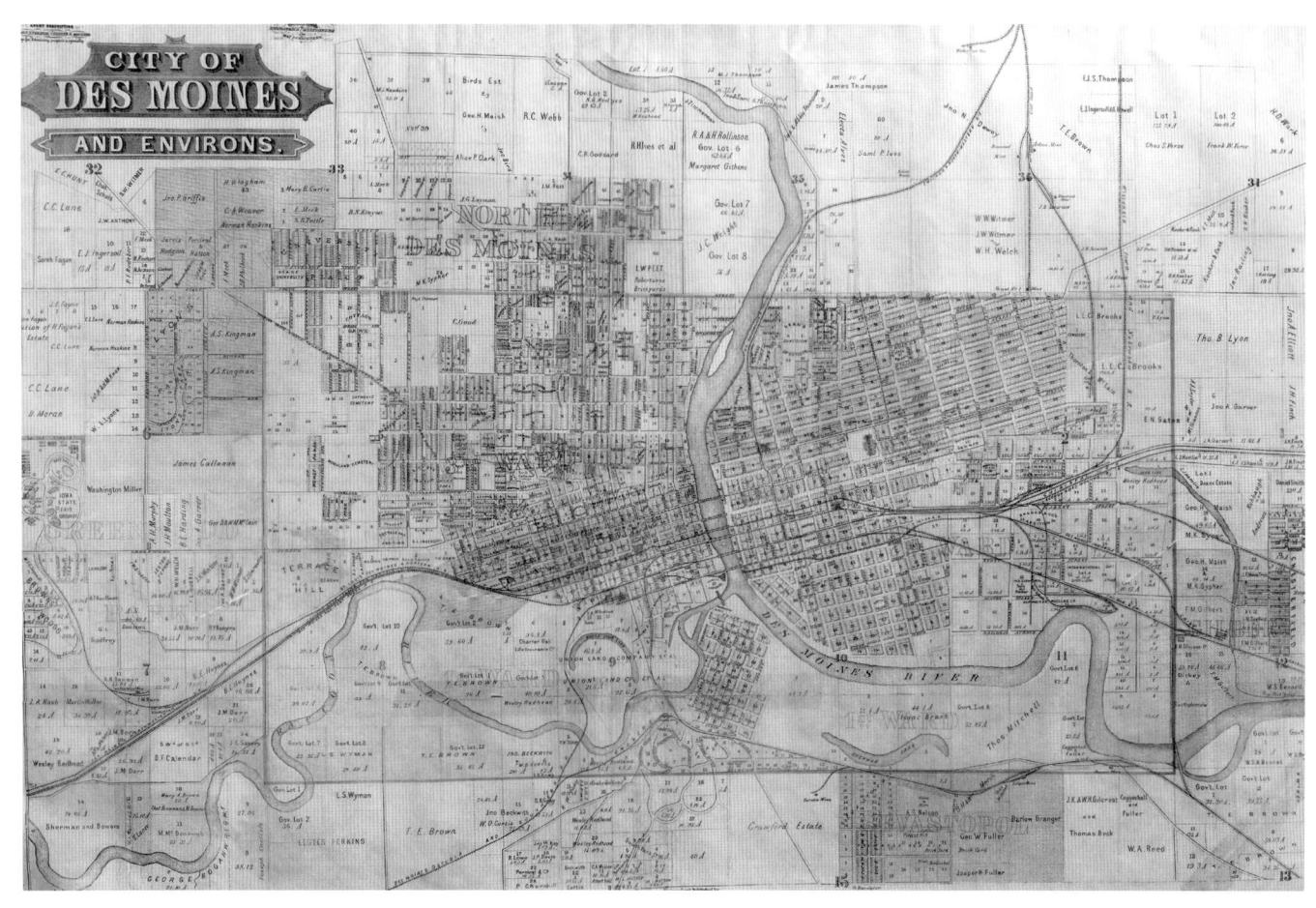

Map of Des Moines, 1882. Author's personal collection

myriad of farms and properties in adjacent counties, in Des Moines, and elsewhere in the state.

In 1884, James negotiated a sale of $28,000.00 worth of his Walnut Township holdings—land along the Raccoon River east of his farm. This land would become the property of the Rock Island Railroad.

Coincidental to this transaction, on March 22, 1884, James signed his last will and testament. At that time, he also executed and delivered to his wife and each of his nine living children a promissory note payable after his death.

The Hawkeye Investment Company Plats Valley Junction

Not long after James sold this tract of land, two Des Moines businessmen, Simon Casady and Conrad Youngerman, began a business association that ultimately led to the formation of the Hawkeye Investment Company in 1890. Youngerman became president and Casady was secretary/treasurer. Uncle Jimmy and Casady's father, Phineas, had settled Des Moines together. Casady had known James Jordan and his family all his life. In 1891 Casady and Youngerman began to buy up land in Valley Junction. They bought forty acres of the Collard farm east of Eighth Street, as well as property from L. Mott, H. S. Butler, Martha A. DeFord, and John P. Cook.

There had been a small community in this vicinity along Eighth Street near Railroad since 1876 when James platted out its first few lanes. The village kept growing, but it was nothing like the growth which was about to take place. In 1891 Hawkeye Investment platted a new town on their property, which was east of the original Eighth Street Valley Junction community. They initially built five two-story houses, and contractor John Mott added several more cottages.

This development would radically shift the focus of the railroad junction town. For almost twenty years it had been a livestock shipping point. Now it was being transformed

The Rock Island Railroad came to Valley Junction. Courtesy of West Des Moines Historical Society

into a town fully engaged in meeting the needs of the railroad transportation industry. Jordan's livestock business as he had known it would come to an end.

The Rock Island Railroad Arrives!

Also in 1891, the giant Rock Island Railroad announced their choice of this little hamlet as the site for their Iowa Terminal Division Station. There they planned to build a machine shop, blacksmith and boiler shops, a car shop, a roundhouse, and administrative offices for the Rock Island line in Iowa. This would catapult Valley Junction from a small village into a viable and thriving "boom town."

While the Rock Island decision sounds like a "stroke of luck" for Walnut Township, no move was made by any railroad without considerable wheeling and dealing. There is no doubt James Jordan played a significant role in getting the Rock Island to Walnut Township, just as his friend F. M. Hubbell was making deals with the railroads on the river bottomland he owned in Des Moines.

As he had done over a decade earlier with the Rock Island and Fort Dodge Railroads, Uncle Jimmy probably convinced the Rock Island to choose his "valley junction" with the promise of providing adequate housing for their workers. This he coordinated with the Hawkeye Investment Company which bought up land to get the town started. Of course, no stranger to a deal, James had also profited with the $28,000.00 land sale.

His health was beginning to fail, and he was slowing down. It is probable that the financially comfortable James Jordan, knowing his sons and grandsons were more farmers and civil servants than business developers, gave folks outside the family the opportunity to handle the complicated endeavor of creating a town by the Raccoon River Valley railroad junction.

With the advent of the Rock Island operation, James probably felt his efforts and those of others who had settled in Walnut Township were finally coming to fruition. Walnut Township had spawned a real town! Supported by the railroad, this town would most assuredly be successful and prosper.

James Jordan: His Life and His Legacy   187

Plat Map — Walnut Township (Ashawa / Commerce)

Section 6
- King 63.09 / 70.08
- Crumm
- 66½
- Mrs. S. C. Harrison 105.65
- W. W. Morris 81.76
- H. H. Rosecrants 160
- S. Snyder 42.52
- Dora B. Miller 80 / 40 — SCHOOL No. 5
- 42.83

Section 5
- 55.30 / 54.82 / 54.33
- E. T. & R. Day 120
- Daniel Fidler 120
- C. H. Good 160
- B. Rosencrans 40
- Dora B. Miller 40

Section 4
- Prof. W. Cr... 53
- John Fly 40
- P. J. Fly 40
- James McK... 53
- B. Murray 53.94
- J. T. & C. H. Ashworth 160
- **CLOV**[ER]
- D.
- J. T.
- 120

Section 7
- Sarah Day 39.52 / 42.69
- Robert P. Thurtle 240
- W. Davis 42.41 / 76.80
- R. P. & R. P. Thurtle, Jr. 104
- 48.73
- MINNEAPOLIS

Section 8
- R. A. Rosencrants 40
- Marg't M. Bayes 120
- R. P. Thurtle 104.91
- L. M. & W. C. Barnett 104.54
- N. Cope
- **ASHAWA**
- M. E.
- 15.18
- ST. LOUIS

Section 9
- C. A. Ashworth 130¼
- John Fisher 80
- Nerxes Clegg 80
- J. T. & C. H. Ashworth 160
- M. F. Kingman
- PARTITION PLAT
- Eddy
- 29
- R. R.
- 201.14

Section 18
- 42.60
- Musetta Bennett 96.7
- Maggie Brown 80
- W. & H. P. Newman 120
- W. H. Brown 40
- PARTITION PLAT
- F. G. Davis 60
- M. & W. A. Fuller 64
- 14.10
- SCHOOL No. 6

Section 17
- E. A. Irwin
- **W A L N U T**
- 120 / 80
- CLOVER DALE FARM
- L. P. Bennett 200 / 80½
- J. T. & C. H. Ashworth 39½
- Carrie E. Youtz 40
- H. L. Youtz 40
- A. F. Johnson 39

Section 16
- Benjamin Bennett 180
- John Husher 60
- Emily A. Hannawalt 60
- A. Jordan 44
- Fran...
- SCHOOL No. 7
- Cem.
- J. C. Jordon Est. 89¼
- F. N. Gilbert 37.26
- B. 163.4
- 2.74
- 40

Section 19
- Sarah E. Lewis 14.16
- Nelson A. Fuller 14.67 / 14.8
- Lewis Horman 15.10
- James H. Windsor 80
- L. P. Bennett 80 / 120
- J. A. Carlson 160
- H. B. Nicholson 80
- L. D. Youtz 80

Section 20
- C. C. Prouty 80
- A. F. & P. Johnson 80
- L. P. Bennett 160
- James Nugent 160

Section 21
- H. L. Youtz 80
- F. N. Gilbert 80
- Alice C. & Colgate Gilbert 66.56 / 56.28
- John P. Cook 40 / 93.6
- 61.68
- ROCK ISLAND R. R.
- RAC...

COMMERCE
- CHICAGO
- CHANNEL 242.64
- F. S. Davidson / A. F. Johnson 229
- L. D. Youtz
- J. Vantoon
- Ashaway
- B. F. ... Est. 149.05
- W. H. Mc... 187.30

CASS COUNTY (left margin)

Part Six

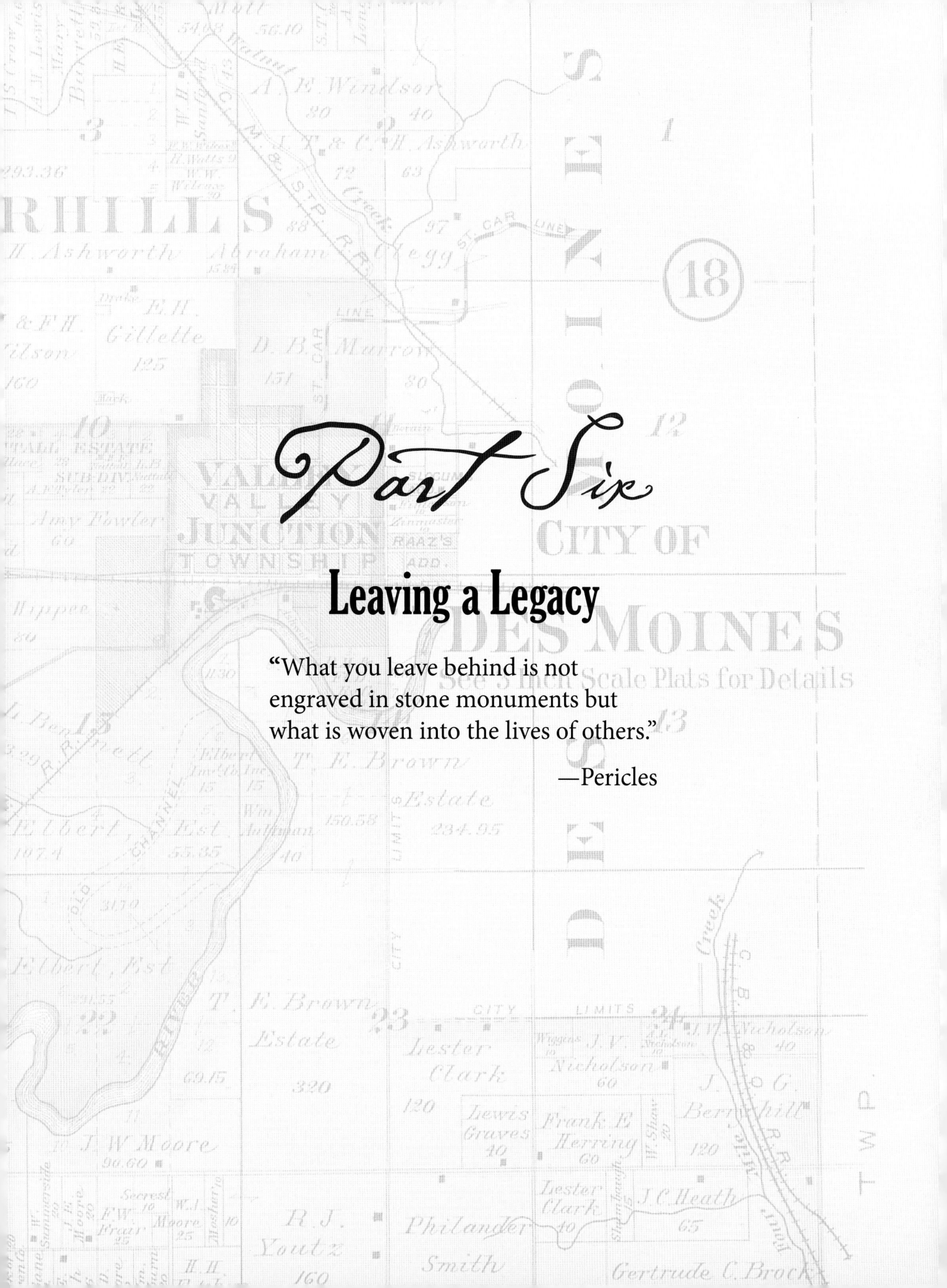

Leaving a Legacy

"What you leave behind is not engraved in stone monuments but what is woven into the lives of others."

—Pericles

CHAPTER 41
The Later Years

At the end of the 1880s James, in his late seventies, was a very old man for those times. He and Cynthia probably took time to relax at the end of the day, sitting out on the porch of their lovely home, now referred to as Greenwood, reflecting upon their lives and their family.

All of James' brothers and sisters had long since moved on. Sister Anna, brother George, and their families were settled in Cass County, Nebraska, where they had moved in 1860 just prior to the Civil War. Sister Phoebe and her husband, Joseph Cannon, joined them in Nebraska at the war's conclusion in 1865. Brother John and his wife, Mary, and their brood had taken off for California in 1859, had more children, and then joined sister Cynthia Babar in Oregon in 1871. John and Mary finally settled in the state of Washington in 1886. Sister Agnes and her husband, Calvin Smith, were nearby in Kansas. Smith, in fact, often came to Des Moines to visit the Jordans. Sister Margaret Eiler, who had lived near the Smiths, had died in 1881.

James' health was declining. Between 1886 and 1890 he had two strokes. These had only *temporarily* affected his brain, and he regained his mental faculties soon after each. However, his heart was beginning to fail, which was the more serious problem and concern. His large farm business continued to worry him, and because of that, George Hanawalt persuaded his father-in-law to sell off most of his livestock. James had already sold hundreds of acres of land in 1884 to Simon Casady and Conrad Youngerman, who were in the process of transforming it into the village of Valley Junction. Already the area around the railroad tracks was spawning taverns and other rowdy establishments designed to entertain railroad workers and those traveling through on the trains. No doubt this development greatly upset Uncle Jimmy, who had worked so diligently thirty-five years earlier to pass prohibition laws in his state. His sentiments would be voiced later, at the time of his death.

Health and business concerns aside, James' nine children were a major focus of his reflections. In 1890, son Henry, the Civil War veteran, was forty-six. Twelve years earlier he had married Alice Warner, the daughter of Benton and Nancy Warner who, in 1850, had come to Iowa and, like James, had settled a homestead. Theirs was over in Jasper County.

When Henry and Alice were married, per their tradition, James and Cynthia gave them a farm located near the Jordan home. Henry spent about five years working the farm and then sold it. With the money, he purchased two hundred acres of nearby timbered bottom land where he operated a sawmill for the next five years, probably milling all the trees on that parcel into lumber. He and Alice then moved to Pocahontas County, near Gilmore, where his brother Benjamin had bought a farm a decade earlier. Henry and Alice purchased ninety-six acres of unimproved land, cleared it, and farmed it for six years, raising potatoes, onions, and cattle on the side. They sold that and moved into the town of Gilmore where they purchased and ran the general store and Henry became Gilmore's postmaster. Henry was probably the only Democrat in the family, which is how he got the post office job, as the US president at that time was a Democrat. Politics aside, James was pleased that Henry had at least married a Methodist. Henry and Alice had four children: Kasson, Pauline, Ralph, and Rupert.

Son George, now forty, and his wife, Louise Wayne, also had four children: William, (Robert) Roy, George, and James. They lived in Pocahontas County, probably in Gilmore near brother Henry and his family. They had some financial trouble in 1889 and had a second mortgage on their farm. They were about to be foreclosed, but James covered them and saved the farm. Eventually they would move closer to Walnut Township and buy a farm in DeSoto.

James' oldest son, fifty-two-year-old Benjamin, and his wife, Mary, had two grown children, Charles and Hattie. Benjamin and his brother Henry were in the same business, as Benjamin and Mary were also running a grocery store. Theirs was in the village of Commerce, about two miles west of the Jordan farm. They had moved back to Walnut Township from Gilmore in Pocahontas County. Commerce, a small village on the

190 Pursuit of a Dream

Raccoon River, boasted a dam and flour mill which had been constructed in 1872, as well as a railroad stop and other commercial establishments.

Daughter Ella lived almost within shouting distance of her parents' farmhouse. She had married into an old-time Walnut Township family, the Cooks. Ella's father-in-law, Jeheil Cook, tilled hundreds of acres a couple of miles north and west of the Jordan farm. After he got the farm started, he departed for Colorado and bought a silver mine. He eventually returned to Iowa, but in the meantime Jeheil's wife, Catherine, stayed behind to raise their five children, one of whom was John, Ella's husband.

Ella, thirty-three, had given her parents three grandchildren—Emma, John, and Fred. Like Henry and Alice, Ella and John Cook had been given their farm by James and Cynthia when they married. It was located on the southwest quadrant of the intersection of Fuller Road and Grand Avenue.

James' son James Finley Jordan, the first pioneer child born in Walnut Township, followed in his father's footsteps, being a Methodist and a Republican. Unlike his father he was a member of the Knights of Pythias. These affiliations—plus his father's connections—had served him well when, a decade earlier, he decided to end his ten-year career as a teacher and accept a Republican political appointment from the US Secretary of the Treasury as the gauger and storekeeper at the International Distillery in Des Moines. James held this position for about eight years until 1889, when Democrat Grover Cleveland was voted in as US president. At that time, James Finley returned to his teaching career and was also elected as the Walnut Township supervisor. James, forty-two, a bachelor, was still residing at the Jordan House with his parents and unmarried brother John, forty-six, caretaker of Jordan Cemetery.

Brother Calvin, in his late twenties, was single and had gone to seek his fortune in Oklahoma in the cattle business and in speculating for oil.

Edward, twenty-two, was studying medicine under his brother-in-law, Dr. Hanawalt, and lived in Des Moines at the Hanawalt's residence at Twelfth and Walnut Streets. This was a perfect situation for both Edward and Emily, who adored her little brother since the time he was born.

Emily, forty-seven, James' oldest daughter, came out often to visit the family at the Jordan House. Later on, she and her husband would use the farm to raise and breed thoroughbred horses.

As with most families, the Jordan clan had its ups and downs. Some of the children were more successful than others. Many had adventures away from their roots. Always sensitive to their patriarchal father, they never strayed far enough or long enough to lose touch with him, and if they had problems, they always came to him for assistance, support, and sometimes rescue. As parents, James and Cynthia demonstrated commitment to their children and a real pleasure in their family—family connections had always been and continued to be very close.

Jordan Methodist Church

When James and Cynthia married in the mid-1850s, they became two of the early members of the First Methodist Church, which was the first church to be organized in Des Moines, in 1846. Its original location was a small frame building on Fifth Street. Because transportation at that time was by horse-drawn sleigh in the winter over frozen rivers or icy ground (not roads), and by horse and carriage in spring when rains would turn the ground to mud, it was not very practical for the Jordans to attend services every Sunday in Des Moines. It was much more convenient to hold services in their home or at a neighbor's, and later on in a local schoolhouse or church building.

This was accomplished first by inviting itinerant preachers into their home, followed by attempts to establish Methodist churches in the immediate vicinity of the Jordan House. One such attempt, Jordan Chapel, located where Jordan Cemetery now stands, failed. Another Methodist church was built in the little community of Ashawa, a few miles north and west of the Jordan House. As with the ill-fated Jordan Chapel, this church was too far away for its members to conveniently attend and was abandoned.

In 1881, after roads were somewhat improved, a group of Methodists began to hold Sunday services at Clegg Schoolhouse, located near the banks of Walnut Creek on the western boundary of the Des Moines city limits. They eventually became dissatisfied with Clegg School for church services, and in 1887 the congregation decided to raise funds to build a new Methodist church

The Clegg House, west of Walnut Creek, was surrounded by an orchard.
Library of Congress

on Walnut Hill, near Fifty-third Street and Grand Avenue in Des Moines. (Grand Avenue came as far west as Walnut Creek by that time and then diverted south along Walnut Creek and then west into the Valley Junction area.)

A one-half acre parcel of land was donated for the church by longtime Walnut Township residents the Shaw brothers. Along with Charles Ashworth, attorney A. H. Denman, and others, James' son John Jordan was appointed to the committee which oversaw the construction. John was the designee to collect funds and keep track of donations. They estimated they would need a total of $2,926. Two years later, on August 26, 1889, John was elected chairman of the board of trustees and appointed custodian.

By October 1890, there were outstanding bills and unfinished work, with uncollected subscriptions totaling $1,480.00—roughly half of the entire cost of construction. John must have appealed to his father to help with the shortfall, which James Jordan generously provided. At this time James was divesting some of his real estate holdings which were, in effect, his retirement fund. He probably raised money for the church by selling off some land. Before completion, Walnut Hill Church had a new name. The congregation voted to rename the church in honor of James Jordan, in appreciation of his large and much-needed contribution to finish construction.

Jordan Dies in Church Named for Him

Jordan Methodist Church was not yet completed when son James Finley, forty-five, married Anna Augusta Jackson, twenty-five, at the Jordan House on January 15, 1891. The newlyweds were happy the elderly Jordan was still alive and able to bless their union in spite of his failing health. One thing that kept Uncle Jimmy going was the thought of attending Jordan Church, and soon after his son's wedding the church was finally completed.

The dedication date was set for Sunday, March 1, 1891, three days before his birthday. When the big day arrived, James had to be coaxed to attend; he was not feeling well. However, once he and Cynthia were settled in the front pew, Uncle Jimmy became immersed in the rhetoric of Dr. Newman, Dr. Rees, and Pastor Louch, who were in charge of the dedication services.

Dr. Newman declared, "The people are here to dedicate a house of God, not a theater, or a concert hall, nor an amusement or dance hall . . ." whereupon James with an overflowing heart suddenly jumped up and cried, "Nor a saloon!"

Almost before the congregation could respond with an "Amen," James' head fell forward, and before anyone could reach him, he collapsed and dropped over dead. "Paralysis of the heart" was announced as the cause of death. He was three days short of his seventy-eighth birthday and had died exactly thirty-six years after his first wife, Melinda.

George Hanawalt was called to the scene and, according to local accounts, he said "it was the hardest task in all my life to go back and tell my wife Emily the news."

Uncle Jimmy's Eulogy

At his funeral, held at Jordan Methodist Church at 2:00 p.m. on Wednesday, March 4, 1891, the date of his seventy-eighth birthday, James Jordan was eulogized as follows:

> He had lived through a most momentous period in American History and on more than one occasion his influence was directly beneficial along lines of public improvement. The cause of education and religion as well found in him a stalwart champion. His home was always open for the reception of ministers and their families, and he did much to further the up building of the Methodist Church in pioneer times.
>
> The circle of his friends grew as the circle of his acquaintance broadened. He achieved distinguished success in the several fields of effort which engaged his best thought, and his life was an exemplification of the loftiest patriotism and the truest conception of the American idea of the common brotherhood of man.

Mr. Jordan, well-endowed in mind and heart by nature and discipline, struggled with zeal for independence and few in his day and in his sphere have been so successful. His honesty and integrity closely adhered to the Golden Rule which made for him a name highly honored throughout this section of the state. His sound judgment was always in demand.

For 50 years Mr. Jordan has been a member and earnest worker in the Methodist Episcopal Church. His roof has sheltered many a preacher and his hospitality has been extended to hundreds of poor but worthy people. To "Uncle Jimmy Jordan," the prosperity of the Methodist Church in Polk county and the state is largely indebted.

He was a true man. Beneath his rather gruff speech lay a tender man of charity and love which constantly cropped out and made his friends feel that, in him, they could place utmost confidence. Mr. Jordan could number his friends by the thousands and, with them all, there will remain a deep shadow of heart-felt grief and they will extend to the widow their greatest sympathy.

He has led a remarkably active and useful life. Indefatigable energy, enterprise and sagacious business foresight have characterized his progress while promptness and the strictest integrity have made his name respected and his word as good as his bond.

His acquaintance throughout the state among public characters is extended to a degree seldom acquired by one employed in agricultural pursuits, and all who knew him recognize him a man of superior intelligence, great force of character and sterling worth.

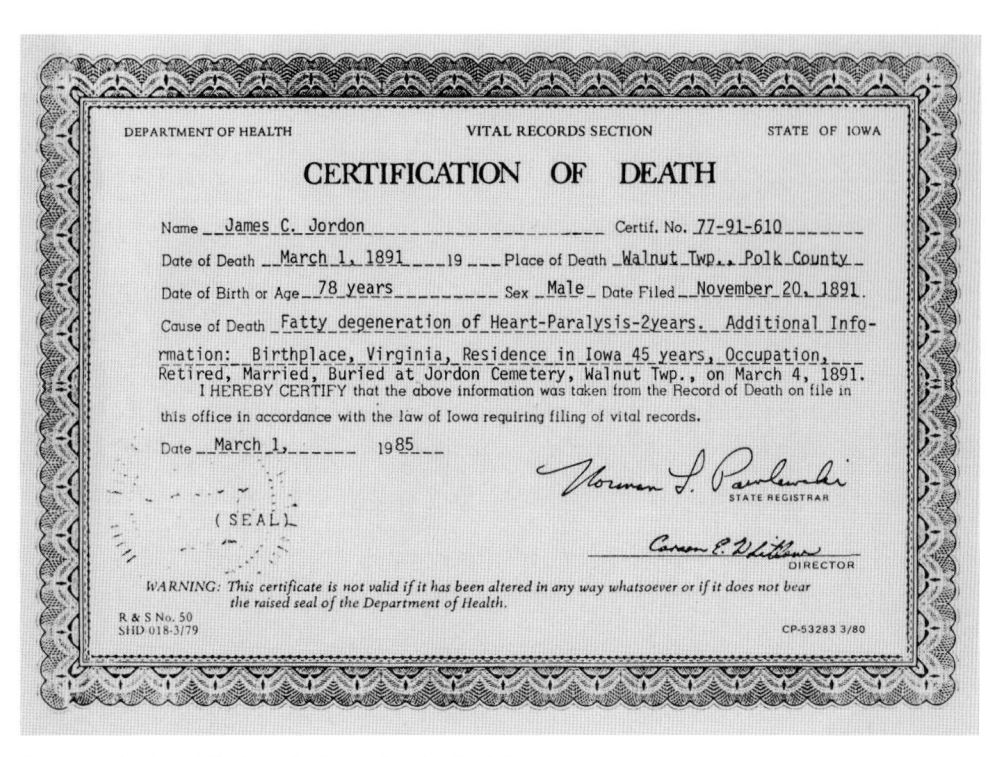

James Jordan's certificate of death. Jordan Family Collection

James Cunningham Jordan was laid to rest in Jordan Cemetery, about a mile west of his beloved home and the beautiful land which so many years earlier he had prized and purchased. The land had once been wilderness, and with his hands, he had transformed it into productive cropland, a grazing place for his livestock, and eventually a community for his children and grandchildren to grow and flourish.

James was survived by his wife, Cynthia, who was sixty years old, his nine living children and their spouses, and twelve grandchildren.

People continued to worship in Jordan Methodist Church for several more years, and a school was built next to it known as "Jordan School," part of the Valley Junction School District. Children who attended Jordan School would then go to Valley High School. In 1978 Margaret Mellor, at the age of eighty-two, remembered Jordan School and Jordan Church next door, where she and her friends would play on the organ, as the church was never locked. In 1920 the church was remodeled as a private residence. Later, it was torn down to make way for the building of Merrill Junior High School at 5301 Grand Avenue in Des Moines.

James Jordan: His Life and His Legacy

CHAPTER 42
Valley Junction, Iowa

Life didn't stand still after James Jordan's death, and that is exactly what Uncle Jimmy would have wanted. In Valley Junction, all of the buildings the Rock Island Railroad had planned to build were completed by 1892 and opened for business on February 23, 1893. The sleepy little junction in the valley was now wide awake. Lots available for construction and newly built housing were offered for sale to the hundreds of railroad employees who were being transferred there.

On October 9, 1893, when the population topped five hundred, papers were filed for incorporation of the area of Walnut Township near the railroad junction, under the name of "Valley Junction." The junction in the valley had officially become a town.

The year Valley Junction was incorporated there was no plumbing, no telephone system, no fire department. There were no sidewalks and no paved roads, not even on Fifth Street, the main street in the town. However, a modicum of progress was made when the *Valley Junction Express* newspaper opened for business. The newspaper office was located on the corner of Fourth and Maple Streets where the paper was written. It was then taken by train to Colfax where it was printed and returned to Valley Junction where it was read.

In April 1893, Valley Junction separated from Walnut Township School District in order to create their own. The newly formed district immediately began serving about 180 students with three teachers. During the next decade, Valley Junction students would attend one of two schools: one at the present site of Phenix School (which also contained the high school) or the Walnut Hill School (also called Jordan School) at Fifty-third Street and Grand Avenue in Des Moines. Walnut Hill School was located on the same site as the Jordan Methodist Church, which rented space to the school. The school was eventually abandoned and absorbed by the Des Moines School District, as Valley Junction expanded westward.

In 1890 a meat market opened in Valley Junction, and in 1893 fire protection began as a bucket brigade. The first bank was established, as well as the town's first hotel. In 1894 growth really took off, and downtown Valley Junction offered residents a potpourri of commercial establishments: two bakeries, two barbers, a billiard hall, two lumberyards, four grocery stores, three doctors, three restaurants, three painters, a tailor, two milliners, three drugstores, a dressmaker, a jewelry store, a tobacco shop, a coal and ice company, a livery and fuel company, and others.

In 1894 the city ordered downtown businesses to install sidewalks. While the new sidewalks were sufficient during dry weather, they proved to be

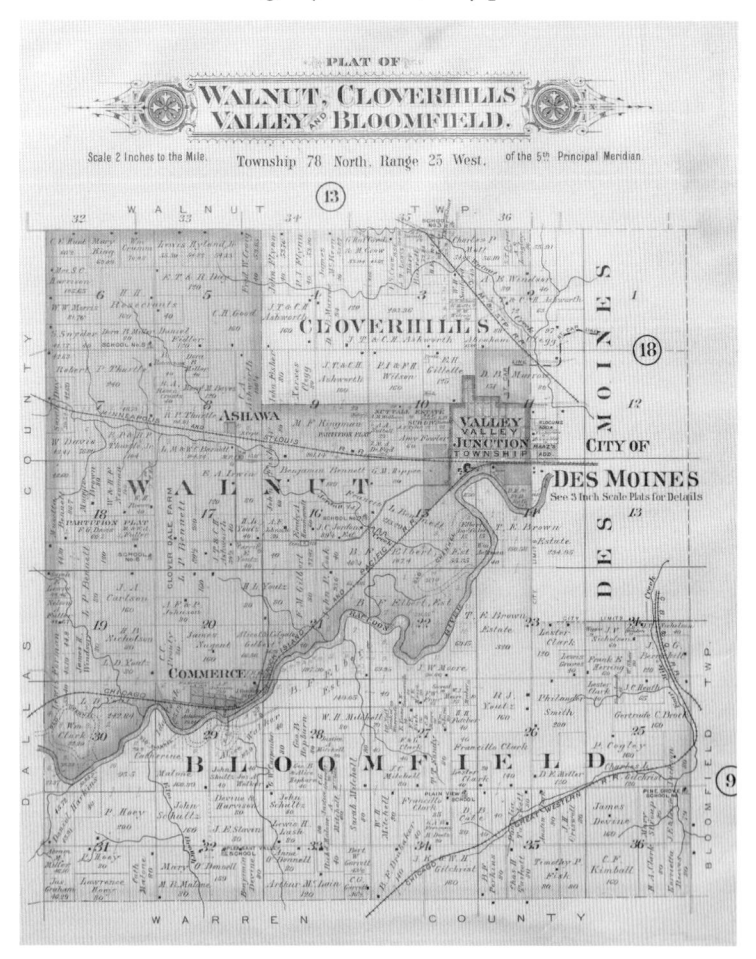

Map of Walnut Township, 1907. Author's personal collection

194   Pursuit of a Dream

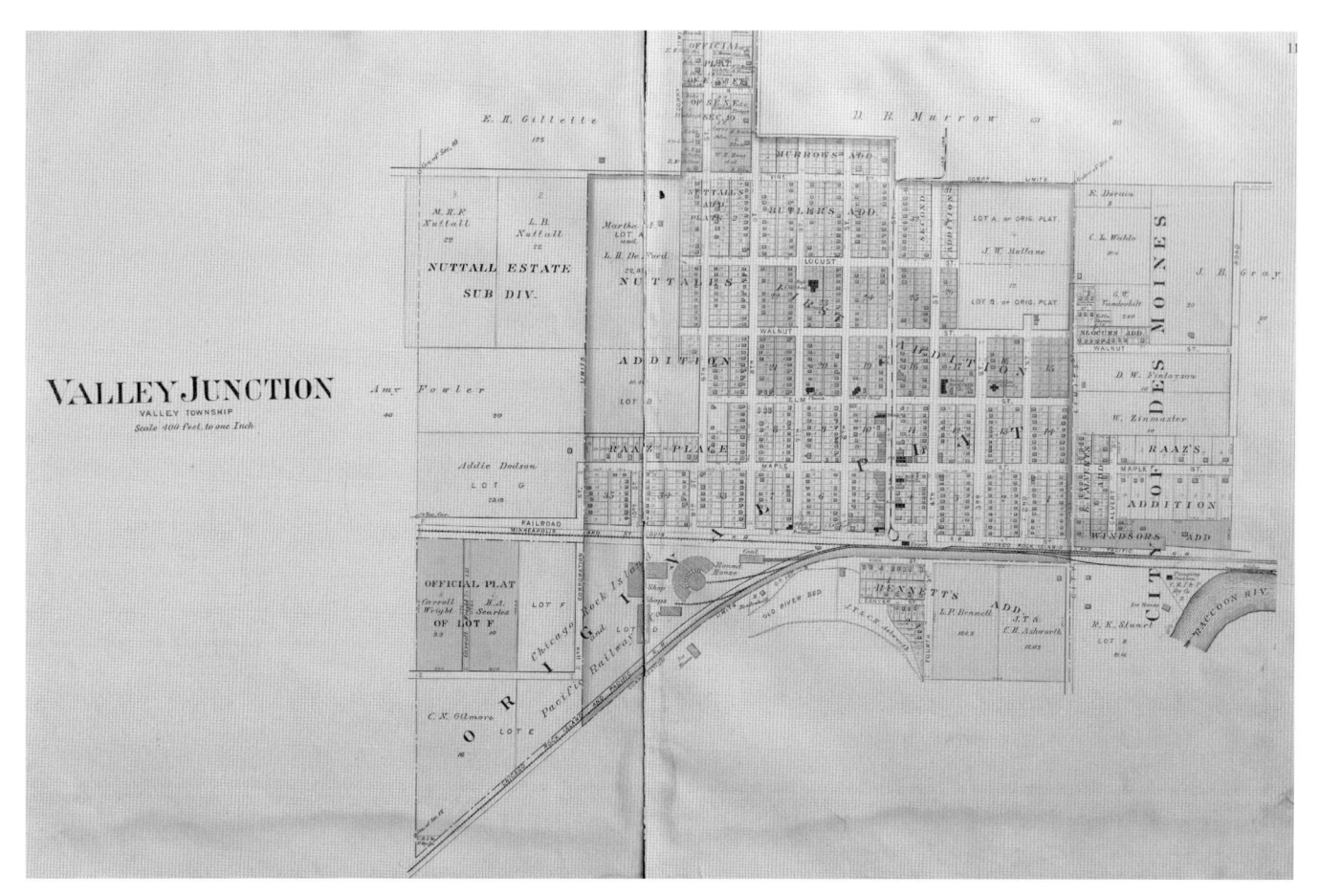

Map of Valley Junction, 1907. Author's Personal Collection

This trolley provided transportation to Valley Junction from Des Moines. Courtesy of West Des Moines Historical Society

inadequate during times of heavy rains and floods. In 1896 the business streets were graveled and gas mains were extended. In 1898 the electrically powered Interurban Railway streetcar trolley linked Valley Junction to Des Moines with twenty-four-hour service. Per Valley Junction authors Terri Fredrickson and Aldo Past, "The route began at 47th Street in Des Moines coming west on Ingersoll Avenue. The line curved at 59th Street to cross Grand Avenue and continued west along the south side of Grand Avenue, crossing the railroad tracks and a wooden trestle at Walnut Creek. The route continued into Valley Junction, turning south at 4th and Grand and following the east side of 4th Street. At 4th and Vine, the tracks moved to the center of Vine, then turned down 5th Street to Railroad Avenue."

James Jordan: His Life and His Legacy   195

James and Charles Ashworth, neighbors of the Cleggs. Courtesy of West Des Moines Historical Society

In 1890 the Disciples of Christ held worship services in Valley Junction, and in 1893 Hawkeye Investment Company platted and donated land at Sixth and Elm Streets for the erection of the first church building, which was called Valley Junction Christian Church. Within the next decade, Valley Junction would add congregations of Methodists and Roman Catholics. By the early 1900s, several impressive church buildings graced the city.

In 1898 Valley Junction got its first streetlights. At the turn of the century, the first telephone service was established, and work was started for the water mains. Electric light service for homes became available, but lights were turned on for only twelve hours per day. Charles Ashworth owned the first light company.

Valley Junction also had a rowdy side. It was a railroad town; people who worked on the railroads and passengers traveling through town took advantage of the many opportunities Valley Junction offered to carouse. Early court dockets reveal there was frequent public drunkenness, as well as other drinking-related infractions. Unruly activity in town occurred nightly, into the wee hours of the morning. In 1894 a jail was built on the south end of Eighth Street, appropriately near the railroad tracks, and it was always full of folks who "had enjoyed themselves too much."

On the 100 block of Fifth Street there were four saloons, two pool halls, and an open bowling alley. To pay for city services, intoxicated citizens were fined, and the city of Valley Junction assessed the saloons $25.00 per month. Pool halls paid $3.35 per month, and a shooting gallery license cost $7.50 per month.

Valley Junction continued to grow. By 1896 there were about 180 residences sheltering two hundred families with a total population of around one thousand. There were four church organizations and two new school buildings employing six teachers. The Rock Island Railroad was employing more than four hundred workers by the turn of the century, and every day twenty-six passenger trains and scores of freight trains passed through town.

In 1897 the Rock Island doubled the size of all their buildings, including the roundhouse. A new brick and rim carshop was added, and in 1898 a second roundhouse was built.

Two verses of a poem written in 1985 by Dudley Reid serve as an excellent illustration of Valley Junction at the turn of the century:

Valley Junction
Old Valley Junction
Just a place
That stood out in the weather
When fate and time
and two railroads
just chanced to come together.
A place of mud and board sidewalks,
And slush, of what a pity,
that anyone should ever think
It might become a city!

In 1938, Valley Junction was renamed West Des Moines.

CHAPTER 43
Home Sweet Home

With their father no longer guiding the family, the Jordan clan found new ways to carry on. Many of James' children who had ventured away from Walnut Township returned during the close of the 1800s.

George and Emily Hanawalt had taken up the hobby of breeding and racing thoroughbred trotting horses. After the death of Emily's father, his cattle and hog business had dissipated and they decided to make their equine hobby into a business. For twenty years, the Hanawalts and some of Emily's brothers were partners in the enterprise of breeding and trading thoroughbred horses at the Jordan farmstead.

One of many certificates of trotters owned by the Jordans and Hanawalts. Jordan Family Collection

In 1898 James Finley Jordan, a "hometown boy," was appointed postmaster of Valley Junction, a position he held until 1905. Previously he had held other civil service jobs and had also been a teacher. Obtaining the position of postmaster was accomplished through one's political connections. A member of the Republican Party like his father, James probably benefitted from the election of Republican President William McKinley and also the influence of his father's Republican legacy to get the job. James and his wife, Anna, had been happily

Thoroughbred trotters. Currier and Ives

James Jordan: His Life and His Legacy   197

Four generations of Jordan women including Cynthia and Ella. Courtesy of West Des Moines Historical Society

living in Valley Junction at the time of his appointment to the postmaster position.

Brother Henry moved his wife, Alice, and family back to Walnut Township from Gilmore, Iowa. His brother James' good fortune in getting the job as Valley Junction's postmaster was the opposite of what happened to Henry. With the election of Republican President McKinley, Henry, a Democrat, had lost his position as postmaster of Gilmore. Henry sold his grocery store there and returned to Walnut Township where he and his family lived in a farmhouse west of the Jordan farm. The house, across from Jordan Cemetery, was part of the Jordan estate and had always been referred to as the "Honeymoon Cottage." Henry stayed active in local and state Democratic politics and, during Iowa's twenty-sixth legislature in 1898, was chosen as doorkeeper of the Senate. He also took over responsibilities of what was left of the Jordan farming operation.

One sad outcome of his move back to Walnut Township was in 1894, Henry's son, (Henry) Kasson, age fourteen, drowned in the Raccoon River not far from the Jordan property.

John, still a bachelor, continued to live at the homestead with Cynthia and help Henry with the farm. From March 1891 to October 1893 John was paid $20.00 per month to serve as caretaker of the estate and Jordan Cemetery, where he tended his father's grave. After 1893, his brothers and sister who were executors of the estate rented the house to John for $100 per year. They always had a special fondness for their physically challenged brother John, who had fallen into a bonfire and had severely injured his right arm when he was a child. When Calvin moved back to the Jordan House from Oklahoma, he also was asked to pay rent in order to live in the home.

Edward, a bachelor like John and Calvin, had been a favorite of his sister Emily ever since he was born. He lived with the Hanawalts and continued in his "study" of medicine under Dr. Hanawalt. In actuality, Edward was more of a carriage driver and errand boy than a serious student of medicine.

George and Emily helped Henry and Calvin manage the Jordan estate, though they continued to live in their elegant brick home on the corner of Twelfth and Walnut Streets. There they provided convenient lodging for Emily's nephews Robert Roy and James Cunningham II while the boys were students at Drake University. Robert and James II had grown up in Gilmore in Pocahontas County. The family moved to the town of DeSoto in Dallas County where their parents, George and Louise, were now farming. James II eventually became an MD.

Ella, her husband John Cook, and their children continued to farm their land neighboring the Jordan farm. The oldest brother Benjamin and his wife, Mary, still lived just down the road in Commerce, running the village grocery store.

There is an amusing story about Ella and her mother, seventy-year-old Cynthia, which took place about this time. Everyone who was living at the Jordan House—Cynthia, John, and Calvin—had been invited to a party, and while sons John and Calvin were getting cleaned up and dressed to go, Cynthia was out in the yard chopping wood. She was still chopping when Ella's carriage arrived to take them to the party. Ella saw her mother splitting wood while the "boys," now dressed, were sitting around in their good clothes. The "boys" didn't help. While Cynthia hurried upstairs to dress, Ella, who was furious with her brothers, started splitting wood in *her* good clothes. Finally, they all left for the party.

198   Pursuit of a Dream

In 1903, Theodore Roosevelt became the president, and although he was a Republican, James Finley Jordan lost his job as Valley Junction postmaster. James and his wife moved from their house in Valley Junction into the Jordan House. John and Calvin were also still living there but by then Ella had moved her aged mother, Cynthia, into her house.

The Jordan Family Loses Cynthia

No doubt Cynthia's health was beginning to fail and she needed help. It was better for her to move in with her daughter so Ella could care for her mother and also tend to the responsibilities of her own family. James Jordan had provided for Cynthia's upkeep in his will, and Ella used the money for her mother's care. Emily visited Cynthia and Ella often, particularly now that she and George were involved with thoroughbred trotters who were kept nearby at the Jordan farm. Transportation from Emily's home out to Valley Junction had improved with the arrival in 1898 of the Interurban Trolley.

Cynthia Jordan passed away in 1908 at the age of seventy-seven. No doubt all of the Jordan children were very sad at her passing. She had accepted a tremendous responsibility when, at the age of twenty-five, she took on a ready-made family of six children, shared duties with her husband, and helped build their massive livestock, real estate, and farming enterprise.

For over thirty-five years she had been a hardworking and supportive wife to a man who, during the first years of their marriage, was immersed in state and local politics. She performed the role of social hostess with ease, as well as her role as mother to six stepchildren and her own five children. She had demonstrated the courage of her religious convictions by welcoming fugitive slaves into her home prior

Jordan "boys" at the old homestead in the early 1900s. Courtesy of West Des Moines Historical Society

James Jordan: His Life and His Legacy

"Honeymoon Cottage," located across from Jordan Cemetary on Fuller Road. Jordan Family Collection

to the Civil War and helping her husband establish several churches.

One of her most visible accomplishments was the transformation of the plain Jordan farmhouse into a beautiful and striking Victorian edifice, which has been appreciated by one and all for more than a century. After her death, Cynthia was laid to rest in Jordan Cemetery.

The Family Carries On

Always looking for an adventure, Henry, along with his wife Alice, and their three children, departed later that year from their home—the "Honeymoon Cottage" across from Jordan Cemetery—and set out for Colorado to enter into the land-development business. There they bought undeveloped parcels of land, improved them, and then sold them.

In later years, they returned to Valley Junction with their son, Rupert, leaving son Ralph and daughter Pauline in Colorado with the properties there. Eventually, Pauline, a teacher, returned to Valley Junction where she taught school at Rex Mathes Elementary School for many years.

James and Anna, who had moved into the Jordan House in 1903, continued to live there and run the farm. Most likely they helped out with the wedding festivities when James' younger brother, Calvin, forty-seven, married Grace Cook, twenty-three, the niece of his brother-in-law John and sister Ella Cook. Calvin and Grace were married on May 20, 1909. After their wedding they lived at the Jordan House. Later, they ran an orchard, which was located on the Jordan estate, north of Fuller Road past the Jordan Cemetery. At that time, they moved from the Jordan House to a home on the orchard property. Calvin and Grace had four children: Charles, George, Calvin Jr., and Clara.

Not long after Calvin and Grace's wedding, Ella, Cynthia's oldest daughter, passed away on September 3, 1909. She was buried in Woodland Cemetery. John and Ella Cook's farm was eventually sold to a dairy farming couple named Jim and Hazel Powers, who developed the farm into Powers Dairy.

CHAPTER 44
The Jordan Fortune

For thirty years after James Jordan died, there were problems with his estate. An exploration of these problems helps explain the often-asked question, "What ever happened to the Jordan fortune?"

James Jordan, Patriarch of His Family

Much of the real estate Jordan had owned over the years had been sold prior to his death, except for the farms on which his children resided, and all of those farms belonged to James Cunningham Jordan. He had paid for them and possessed the deeds. When one of his children married, or if for some other reason James Jordan decided to give a farm to one of his children, he simply gave him or her the deed but did *not* put the child's name on it. No official deed transfer was recorded at a courthouse. James Jordan, the patriarch of the family, remained the owner of record of all of his children's farms.

It was probably James' method of ensuring his children would always have means to a livelihood through a profession they all knew—farming. Most likely, James kept up the tax payments on these properties to protect the asset for his children. If any of his children fell upon hard times, and many of them did, they went to their father and borrowed against whatever their portion of the cash that would be given to them when he died, as stated in his will. James Jordan thus assisted his children in keeping their farms from any bank or tax collector.

Problems occurred for his children when James died. The exception to this was his daughter Emily, who was financially "set" because of her advantageous marriage to a successful doctor. Not one of his children owned their own farm; James' estate did. The children were not able to convert the real estate they were living on into cash. Nor could they borrow against it. All they could do was work their farms and derive income from the yield.

Emily Hanawalt. Jordan Family Collection

Assisting Children During "Hard Times"

Prior to James' death in 1891, he was frequently asked for financial assistance by those of his children who had fallen on hard times. James usually tried to help out. He made considerable financial advances to several of his children; the promissory notes were all in different amounts, ranging from $2,100.00 to $5,500.00 per person. These notes are part of the few financial records of James Jordan still in existence. The children were aware of these notes, and the fact that he saved them. What they may not have known was these notes ultimately became drafts against his will.

Other letters have been found which show James paying for second mortgages (to banks that took the risk of lending to a person who did not possess a deed to the property they were lending against), back taxes, etc., on properties owned by his children so they would not lose their farms. The financial assistance James rendered to his children gradually reduced the corpus of his estate.

By the time he died, he had sold off the cattle and used the money to live comfortably in his waning years. By then most of his cash reserves had been depleted; the assets listed in his will are modest, considering his enormous wealth in the past. Even though James had held a significant amount of real estate in the vicinity of his home (in the Valley Junction area), by the time he died most of it had been sold.

Though the Jordan children seemed to make modestly adequate incomes as civil servants, shopkeepers, or farmers, daughter Emily was a notable exception. She was college educated, socially prominent, and had made a good marriage to George Hanawalt. Their financial security was guaranteed. Unlike her siblings, at the time of her death, she had personal assets totaling $42,000.00.

James Jordan: His Life and His Legacy

James C. Jordan's Will. Jordan Family Collection

James Jordan's Last Will and Testament

"I, James C. Jordan of Polk County, Iowa, being of sound mind, but mindful of the uncertainty of life and the certainty of death do hereby publish and declare this my last will and testament, that is to say.

"1st— It is my desire that all my just debts, if any, and funeral expenses be first paid out of my estate.

"2nd—I devise and bequeath to my wife Cynthia D. Jordan in lieu of her rights under the statutes the sum of ($3,000.00) three thousand dollars, also all the kitchen and dining room furniture, all wearing apparel, beds, and bedding.

"3rd—I bequeath to Emma A. Hanawalt the sum of ($500.00) five hundred dollars in Trust to be paid by her for the education of my grandson James C. Jordan, son of my son George B. Jordan, as from time to time she may find it necessary, if the said James C. Jordan should die before the said five hundred dollars is expensed for the purpose above named, then the some or remainder thereof is to be applied by her to the education of his two other brothers, William W. Jordan and George E. Jordan, on education of the survivor of them, if the other be dead.

"4th—It is my will that the sum of ($500.00) five hundred dollars out of my estate be used and applied by my executors in the purchase and fitting of a suitable monument upon the family burying lot, which lot may be selected by my family after my decease.

"5th—And whereas I have heretofore, made considerable advances to several of my children out of my estate, and it is my desire that they should all share equally in my estate taking into account what has already been paid some of them and as I have a better understanding of all the sums heretofore advanced to any of them, and of what is right to be done to make them equal, then any other living person, I give and devise all the rest and rewards of my estate to them, in the following proportion, to:

"1st—To Benjamin P. Jordan the sum of ($2,700.00) Twenty-seven hundred dollars.

"2nd— To Emma A. Hanawalt the sum of ($2,100.00) Twenty-one hundred dollars.

"3rd— To Henry C. Jordan the sum of ($3,600.00) Thirty-six hundred dollars.

"4th—To John G. Jordan the sum of ($4,000.00) Forty hundred dollars.

"5th—To James F. Jordan the sum of ($4,000.00) Forty hundred dollars.

"6th—To George B. Jordan the sum of ($3,750.00) thirty-seven hundred fifty dollars.

"7th—To Ella Cook the sum of ($4,000.00) Forty hundred dollars.

"8th—To Calvin S. Jordan the sum of ($5,500.00) Fifty-five hundred dollars.

"9th—To Edward Jordan the sum of ($5,500.00) Fifty-five hundred dollars, if he be then of age, and if not to Dr. Hanawalt in first for him until he does become of age. In making this appointment I have not been unmindful that some of my children may and probably will receive more from my estate than others, as in the case of John G. Jordan and Emma A. Hanawalt, but I have taken into account some of the misfortunes of John G. Jordan in business and have also considered the many favors, and medical attentions to me personally and to my family rendered by Dr. G. T. Hanawalt, the husband of Emma A. Hanawalt, and how these accounts have not charged them with all the advancements heretofore made by me to them.

"6th—In case my wife does not survive me, the sums and property herein bequeathed to her I desire to go into my general estate and to be distributed to my children in the proportions named in the 5th item above and in case any of my children shall die before me without having transferred his interest in my estate, it is my wish that the share if such deceased child or children shall go to his or her heirs surviving at my death.

"7th—Unless my wife and children shall agree otherwise, it is my desire that my executors hereinafter named shall as soon as convenient and practicable, without sacrificing the estate in a dull market, after my death proceed to sell and dispose of my estate both real and personal at private sale for the purpose of paying off the legacies herein provided for and to pay debts, if any, and I hereby give any said executors ample power and authority to sell and dispose of and convey the same without being required to apply to any court for such authority at such prices and upon such terms as they may think most advantageous to the estate and to all parties interested.

"8th—I have simultaneous with the executors of this will executed and delivered to my wife and to each of my children who are of age and to Dr. G. T. Hanawalt in trust for Edward Jordan who is a minor, an instrument in the nature of a promissory note payable after my death for the sums respectively bequeathed to them in the 5th item above, and if anyone of my said children shall assign of transfer such obligation, it is my will and intent that the assignee on the proper holder of such obligation shall stand in the place of such child or of such children who may have thus disposed of their interest in any estate according to the tenor of such obligation.

"9th—I Hereby constitute and appoint my son-in-law, Dr. G. T. Hanawalt, and my sons, Calvin S. Jordan and Henry C. Jordan or the survivors of them to be executors of this my will and of my estate and it is my wish that they be not required to give any bond as such executors.

James C. Jordan March 22, 1884

The foregoing instrument signed in our presence by the above named James C. Jordan and witnessed by us at his request as and for his last will and testament. 22 March 1884."

This is not to say James' other children were irresponsible. Most were hardworking and industrious. They were, however, products of the patriarchal system within their family and perhaps expected to receive more money than they ultimately ended up with from a father who had always provided—and provided well. They probably were under the (mistaken) impression that, because their father had "come through" for them in the past, surely he would do so when he died, and they would henceforth live comfortable lives. That was not what happened. James was fair, but he had to divide up his now-somewhat-modest assets amongst a wife, many children, and some grandchildren.

The Executors of the Estate

At the conclusion of his will, he designated his son-in-law, Dr. George Hanawalt, and two of his sons, Henry and Calvin, to be the co-executors of his estate. James probably made Hanawalt the *principle* executor of his estate (along with Henry and Calvin, sons from each of his two wives) because Hanawalt had demonstrated he was financially astute.

When James Jordan wrote his will in March 1884, he stated in it that unless his wife and children agreed otherwise, the executors were directed to sell and dispose of the estate as soon as convenient and practical, without sacrificing the estate in a dull market. Further, the executors were given power and authority (without applying to the court for the authority) to sell and dispose of the estate at such prices and upon such terms as they thought most advantageous to the estate and to all parties interested. The purpose for selling and disposing of the real estate was to pay off the promissory notes provided in the will.

Family legend relates that when her father died, Emily sent her brother Edward around to all the brothers and sisters to collect the as yet unregistered deeds of the farms and properties their father had given them so they could be registered as part of the estate. These were taken to Hanawalt in order to assemble the estate into one package. They did this because they had all borrowed against the estate and were in debt to it. Relinquishing their farms was the easiest way to pay back the estate.

Most obliged, and George and Emily Hanawalt filed them all at the Polk County Courthouse. This supposedly put the Hanawalts and co-executors Henry and Calvin in control of all the Jordan property. All except one. Edward held out the deed for the Jordan House. He kept that one. Cynthia and all but two of the Jordan heirs (George and Ella's heirs) agreed to give a "quit claim deed" on their portions of the Jordan estate.

While the Hanawalts filed the deeds for various farms of Emily's siblings, the deed Edward kept—for the Jordan House and about forty acres surrounding it—was never filed. Decades later this would cause problems when the house and property were sold.

Recession Stalls the Financial Disbursement

Because of a financial recession in the early 1890s, James' principal executor, George Hanawalt, decided it would be wiser to hold on to the real estate assets listed in the will and not sell them until they rose in value. It would be at least another fifteen years before Hanawalt and the other two executors of the estate, Henry and Calvin, began selling some of the real estate, most of which Hanawalt eventually purchased.

In the meantime, some of the Jordan heirs, led by Ella and her husband John, were angry that action (and final disbursement) did not occur sooner. They filed a lawsuit asking for the estate to be immediately closed and any remaining funds disbursed. They were not successful and a split occurred in the family; those wanting the estate closed as soon as possible and the assets divided and those who did not mind waiting for the value of the assets to increase.

Many of the "impatient" offspring were land rich and cash poor. An illustration of how one family dealt with their financial situation is revealed in a vignette passed down, telling how, in the cash-poor John and Ella Cook household, John traded off the Jordan Family Bible to buy a set of encyclopedias. John had decided the encyclopedias were more valuable to his family than the old Jordan Bible.

Hanawalt had negotiated with the lawyers to buy some of the other real estate assets other than farms which were listed in the will. He eventually sold that real estate, converting property into cash, most of which was then dispersed to the family. However, when the family transferred the quit claim deeds from their farms to Hanawalt, it effectively put him totally in charge of most of the remaining Jordan assets.

Of course the situation infuriated those who wanted and in some cases *needed* the money; especially after George and Emily moved from their home in downtown Des Moines out to the leafy western suburbs in Greenwood Park. There they had built an elegant Tudor home at 4027 Ingersoll Avenue on vacated land that had once been the site of the Iowa State Fairgrounds.

Their brand-new home was located about a block away from a firehouse, which had been built in 1901 at 535 Fortieth Street and is still there today. To the west was Ingersoll Park, a privately owned amusement park, and according to an article in the *Des Moines Tribune*, it "had opened in the early 1900s with roller coaster, a little train, a merry-go-round, a bandstand, and three elephants. It offered concerts and topflight entertainment" and vaudeville acts. Sarah Bernhardt sang there. Teddy Roosevelt had given a speech at Ingersoll Park during a visit to Des Moines in 1903. The park closed a couple of years after the Hanawalts moved there in 1912. Further west was Des Moines' first golf course, Des Moines Golf and Country Club, located near Forty-ninth Street and Harwood Drive. Nearby was a golf and tennis club, called "Hyperion."

George Dies and Emily "Takes Over"

George Hanawalt died in 1912, and all of James Jordan's remaining assets and the responsibility for them transferred to Emily after her husband's death. Emily was now the principal executor of her father's estate along with her two brothers, Henry and Calvin. As a widow, Emily relied heavily on her brother Edward, who had always lived with her, to help her carry on. Edward supported Emily's reluctance to sell her father's assets before they had gained value; Edward's financial support came directly from Emily, and he was *always* complicit with her wishes.

From 1908 on, first George and then Emily Hanawalt and Calvin had managed the estate because Henry and his family had left Des Moines to live in Colorado. After Hanawalt died, Henry, his wife Alice, and their son Rupert returned from Colorado and moved back into the "Honeymoon Cottage" across from the Jordan Cemetery on Fuller Road and farmed twenty acres around their house.

Letter from Emily Hanawalt to Fred Weitz. Jordan Family Collection

By 1912 Benjamin and Mary also made a move, selling their grocery store in Commerce and moving out to DeSoto to live on a farm with brother George and his wife, Louise. George and Louise and their family had farmed out there for years. Their home was on the northwest edge of the town of DeSoto.

Emily and brothers Henry and Calvin continued to manage the Jordan estate, the majority of the assets of which were in Emily's hands. In 1914, at the age of seventy-two, Emily drafted her will. At this time her assets amounted to $42,000 of personal property, her inheritance from her husband, plus oversight of all of the remaining property in the Jordan estate.

James' wife, Anna, passed away in 1914, leaving bachelor brother John and widower James to live together at the Jordan House for the next two years until John died in 1916.

Family legend tells an interesting story about John's death. One day seventy-year-old John decided to trim a large branch off a tree in the Jordan House yard. In order to saw it off at a good angle he decided the best way to do it was to sit on the branch. He misjudged his ability to do the job, disregarding the fact his useless right arm might hinder him. He was not able to hang on when the sawed-off branch fell, and he went down with the branch. He did not survive the fall. John was buried in Jordan Cemetery, which he had tended for the last forty years.

That same year, George's wife, Louise, died out in DeSoto, leaving their home occupied by sixty-five-year-old George, his brother seventy-eight-year-old Benjamin, and Benjamin's wife Mary. Louise was buried in Jordan Cemetery.

Emily Dies and the Estate is (Finally) Settled

On January 21, 1918, Emily Hanawalt, aged seventy-six, passed away. Her seventy-four-year-old brother Henry died that same year. Henry was buried in Jordan Cemetery, but Emily, like her sister Ella, was interned in Des Moines in Woodland Cemetery. She was laid to rest next to her husband, Dr. George Hanawalt, in one of the most impressive vaults in the cemetery. Edward, who had been like a son to Emily, took care of her funeral arrangements.

Immediately following Emily's death, Edward applied to the courts as the executor of her will. The courts approved Edward's appointment, and he and Calvin finally wrapped up all the loose ends of the James Jordan estate and the disbursement of assets from Emily's will. It had taken twenty-seven years to put final closure on the James C. Jordan estate. In her will Emily assigned each of her living brothers places to live as well as making provisions for several of their children.

First of all, she gave her four-year-old house at 4027 Ingersoll to her brother Edward. Then she addressed the disbursement of forty acres of land west of the Jordan House and north of Fuller Road. The east twenty acres of this land included the "Honeymoon Cottage" across from Jordan Cemetery on Fuller Road. This parcel of land was designated for Henry, who lived and farmed there until his death. The west twenty acres, which included the orchard, were designated for Calvin and his wife, Grace.

Even though Henry died in the same year as Emily, her will, written two years earlier, appointed Henry with the responsibility of overseeing the entire forty acres and making sure the taxes were paid on them every year. She specified that when Henry died, all forty acres would go to Calvin's sons; however, both Henry and Calvin could live on their respective twenty acres during their lifetimes.

Next Emily assigned the old Jordan Homestead and adjacent property of approximately forty acres to her brother James, who was charged with the responsibility of overseeing and paying taxes on it. She also directed that John, a bachelor, be allowed to live in the homestead until he died. Since he had died two years earlier, the house and property went to James.

She directed when her brother James died, the Jordan House and the adjacent property would go to the sons of her brother George: William Henry, Robert Roy, George Ernest, and James Cunningham II. She did not leave property to her older brother Benjamin who was living out on the farm in DeSoto with George. Nor did she mention her deceased sister Ella's children. However, she did request that those of her personal possessions not bequeathed to dear friends be distributed amongst her brothers, nieces, and nephews.

Out of the eleven children of James Cunningham Jordan, only five were still living in the 1920s— Benjamin, George, James, Calvin, and Edward. Edward, a bachelor, had sold the house Emily had bequeathed to him, probably because he had no income source for upkeep and taxes, and moved back into the Jordan House with his brother James.

"The Ending of an Era"

By then, the farm was operated by three of George's sons, William, (Robert) Roy, and George, who also farmed the forty acres to the north across Grand Avenue. James II was practicing medicine. Calvin and his wife, Grace, were a little farther down Fuller Road, still running their orchard and raising their family. Grandchildren and great-grandchildren of James remember visiting the orchard and seeing Grace. Using apples from the nearby orchard, she would bake pies which one and all enjoyed.

In 1921 George died, but eighty-five-year-old Benjamin and his eighty-year-old wife, Mary, continued to live on the DeSoto farm. Not long afterward, Mary died in 1923. Benjamin, James Jordan's oldest child, lasted three more years and passed away in 1926 at the age of eighty-eight. They were all buried in Jordan Cemetery. James, Calvin, and Edward were the only three remaining living children of James C. Jordan.

By 1926, the Jordan House had fallen into disrepair. Seventy-eight-year-old James, a widower, and his brother Edward lived in the house until James died that year, leaving Edward alone in the dilapidated house.

Their brother Calvin's son, Calvin Smith Jordan Jr. recalled visiting his elderly uncles at the Jordan House where the old men had taught the boy how to make bows and arrows and hunt with them. It was the Depression and Calvin Jr. and his cousins recalled gypsies visiting the Jordan House, hoboes stopping in and asking for food, and vagrants living on the property.

New faces appeared for a time when young Robert Roy Jordan and his wife lived there with her parents, the Furmans, in 1927 and 1928. When they arrived they asked Edward to vacate. He did, moving west on Fuller Road to live with his brother Calvin and their family at the orchard.

Eventually, Robert and his wife moved out of the Jordan House, Edward returned and lived there until 1936, when George's son William, his wife Maud, and their only son, Max, moved in. A year later, Calvin died on May 20, 1937, and was buried in Jordan Cemetery.

Gate to Woodland Cemetery, Des Moines. Photographer, Scott Little

Edward, who had been employed as a janitor at St. Luke's Episcopal Church on Forest and Beaver Avenues in Des Moines, was the last living child of James Jordan. He passed away on December 8, 1942, and was buried with most of his other family members in Jordan Cemetery.

With the passing of Edward, the ownership of the Jordan homestead passed to George's three sons.

William and his wife, Maud, and son, Max, were the last of Jordans to reside in the Jordan House. The house was so big for the three of them they lived mostly on the first floor, using only the kitchen, office, and the room to the south of the dining room as William and Maud's bedroom. The only room used upstairs was one above the kitchen Max used as a bedroom. The front and back parlors on the first floor were shut off, as well as the rest of the house. Even in the modern 1940s, the Jordan House still had no running water or indoor plumbing. Water was still drawn from a well, and the toilet remained an outhouse. Maud would not move into the house until electricity was installed, so the house acquired rudimentary wiring, and with that came an electric pump to draw water out of the old well into the kitchen.

When Max married, he and his wife, Mary, lived in the house for a while, but eventually they moved out, leaving Will and Maud to live there alone. By then, living on limited means, Will and Maud decided to sell the house and land.

CHAPTER 45
James Cunningham Jordan's Impressive Legacy

The House and Property Are Sold

By 1946 the Jordan holdings, which once covered thousands of acres, had been reduced to a dilapidated old farmhouse standing on thirty-nine acres in Walnut Township. That year James Jordan's grandsons Will, George, and Rob Roy Jordan held a public sale to dispose of the contents of the house. What wasn't sold at auction or taken by family members was burned in a giant bonfire older residents still remembered decades later. An interesting family story is Cynthia's beautiful blue Haviland china was not given away to a family member as a complete set; Nancy Evjue, one of the descendants, recalled that each member who wanted one got a place setting. Nancy then located additional matching pieces to create her own impressive set.

A year later they sold the house and property to the Church of the Nazarene for the sum of $12,500.00. The church created a lovely campground on the property, and the old house, which had been the roost of so many Jordan children and grandchildren years before, was turned into a camp dormitory.

Renovation and "Rebirth"

By the early 1970s, the Jordan House had deteriorated so much that the Nazarene church considered demolishing it. However, at about that time the West Des Moines Historical Society was formed, and under the leadership of Board President Bonnie McFadden, the society saved the house from destruction by having it placed on the National Register of Historic Places in 1973.

Five years later, in 1978, the society was able to purchase the Jordan House and four acres of surrounding property for the sum of $20,000.00. In 1980 Vicki Baker became the president of the West Des Moines Historical Society Board of Directors, and under her leadership for the next decade the society focused on restoring and renovating the house.

The main floor, one basement room, and two upstairs bedrooms were refurbished as period rooms, typical of how they might have looked when James Jordan resided there. The West Des Moines Historical Society was fortunate to be able to acquire furniture and artifacts original to the house through auctions, estate sales, or through generous donations from the Jordan family. Several Jordan descendants were very supportive and active in the efforts to restore the house.

Photographer, Scott Little

Later, other rooms were restored and refurnished. One room in the basement is devoted to a display about the Underground Railroad. Some of the former bedrooms on the second floor focus on the history of Valley Junction and West Des Moines. There is also an office for the West Des Moines Historical Society on the second floor. All this was accomplished in time for the West Des Moines Centennial Celebration in 1993.

With the house restoration nearly complete, the historical society board, under the leadership of President Joyce Grabinski, began to focus on community outreach and education. New initiatives included the writing of this book, presenting history awards to West Des Moines students, and acquiring and renovating Bennett School—a vintage 1927 one-room school house, in many ways similar to the little white Jordan School built by James and Cynthia in the 1870s. From its original site near Fiftieth and Mills Civic Parkway, the

Pursuit of a Dream

THE JORDAN HOUSE HAS BEEN PLACED ON THE **NATIONAL REGISTER OF HISTORIC PLACES** BY THE UNITED STATES DEPARTMENT OF THE INTERIOR c. 1850-1870

Courtesy of West Des Moines Historical Society

THE JORDAN HOUSE has been selected as an official site on the **NATIONAL UNDERGROUND RAILROAD NETWORK TO FREEDOM** May 14, 2002

Bennett School building was moved to 4001 Fuller Road, two miles west of the Jordan House.

Subsequent leaders in the organization continued the renovation efforts, shifting to maintenance of the Jordan House after the renovations had been accomplished. This allowed the West Des Moines Historical Society to refocus on the man who built the building. In 2014 the Jordan Scholars program was initiated with the financial assistance of Jordan descendant Pat Jordan Berkley, who also organized a Jordan family reunion in the summer of 2016. Over seventy-five Jordan descendants from all over the United States attended the two-day event.

A family tree in the east entry of the Jordan House shows James Jordan's descendants and is updated regularly as new babies are born into the family.

A Remarkable Legacy

There are many visible reminders of James Jordan today in West Des Moines, a city which evolved from the little village of Valley Junction and at the time of this writing is the seventh largest city in the state of Iowa. Three notable examples are Jordan Creek, Jordan Creek Parkway, and Jordan Creek Elementary School.

Perhaps the most impressive is Jordan Creek Town Center, the largest shopping complex in the state of Iowa, the fourth largest in the Midwest, and the twenty-third largest in the United States. James Jordan would have been amazed to see this awesome commercial edifice featuring his name.

Jordan Creek Elementary, located in West Des Moines, Iowa. Photographer, Scott Little

Jordan Creek Town Center, the twenty-third largest shopping complex in the United States, is located on Jordan Creek Parkway. Photographer, Scott Little

James Jordan: His Life and His Legacy

However, grand as those places are, the Jordan House is the most nostalgic and sentimental reminder. A landmark in the area, the Jordan House and Museum have for years welcomed and enlightened visitors from the local community, all fifty of the United States, and dozens of nations. The Jordan House has become a place of pride for the citizens of West Des Moines and a tribute to the man who built it—James Cunningham Jordan.

James Jordan's memory survives today because his home remained intact despite the passing of over one and a half centuries. The house provided the impetus to uncover the fascinating and inspiring story of this remarkable man. The story unfolded to reveal an honorable, religious, and hardworking individual who did his best to nurture his family, build his farm, and serve his community.

His life is a shining example of how a person with ambition, fortitude, integrity, and intelligence can succeed and prosper. Highly regarded by his contemporaries, he became a leader and remained a leader until he died. He was a role model for the citizens of his community and across the state of Iowa, and he continues to serve as a role model today. He pursued his dreams, achieved them, and when his exemplary life ended, he left behind a remarkable and inspirational legacy.

The Jordan House, one of the oldest buildings in Polk County, Iowa, is an ongoing reminder of James Jordan.
Courtesy of West Des Moines Historical Society

FAMILY TREE

Jordan

John--**George**
(b. 1709, Palatine, Germany)   (b. ca. 1715, Palatine, Germany/d. ca. 1778, VA)
+ No Name

George Jordan, Jr. (b. January 26, 1754, Augusta County, VA/d. Mar 1, 1842, Anderson County, KY)
+ No Name (b. ca. 1753/d. New Design, IL)
(m. ca. 1773)
    John Jordan (b. January 14, 1775, Augusta, County, VA/June 8, 1832, Lewis County, VA)
    + Agnes Slater Cunningham (b. 1778, Randolph County, VA/d. September 29, 1854, in Smithville, Clay County, MO)
    (m. 1796, Pendleton County, VA)
        Mary (b.1797)
        Susan (b. 1802)
        Anna (b. 1804)
        George (b. 1806)
        Phoebe (b. 1808)
        Cynthia (b. 1810)
        James Cunningham Jordan (b. 1813)
        Margaret (b. 1815)
        John Slater (b. 1818)
        Agnes (b. 1821)
        SEE JORDAN/CUNNINGHAM TO CONTINUE THIS LINE
+ Martha Lightfoot (b. April 11, 1766, Culpepper County, VA/d. April 8, 1842, Anderson County, KY)
(m. ca. 1794, KY)

Cunningham

William (b. ca. 1690, Ayrshire, Scotland/d. ca 1750, South Branch Valley, VA)
+ No Name
(m. ca. 1709, Ulster Plantation, County Armagh, Northern Ireland)
    John (referred to as "Lord John") (b. ca. 1710, Ulster Plantation, County Armagh, Northern Ireland/d. 1758, South Branch Valley, VA/buried at Cunningham Plantation Homestead, South Branch Valley, Augusta County, VA)
    + Elizabeth (b. ca. 1710, Ireland/d. ca. 1745, Pennsylvania)
    (m. ca. 1732, Ireland)
        William II (referred to as "Irish Billy") (b. ca. 1733, Dublin, Ireland/d. 1790, Hardy County, VA/buried on Cunningham Plantation, Hardy County, VA)
        + Phoebe Scott
            William III (b. 1760)
            + Jemima Harness
                William IV (b. ca. 1782, Old Fields, Hampshire County, VA)
                +Sally Van Meter
        John Jr. (b. 1735, Dublin, Ireland/d. after 1755)
        +Rebecca Harness
            No children of record
        Robert (b. ca. 1740, PA/d. ca. 1801, South Branch Valley, VA/buried Hardy County, WV)
        + Prudence Parsons
            7 children
    +Mary Biedert Peterson
    (m. 1747, South Branch Valley, VA)
        James (b. ca. 1748, Augusta County, VA/d. September 28, 1810, Huttonsville, VA)
        + Agnes Slater
        (m. ca. 1764, PA)

    William (b. 1766)
    John (b. 1767
    + Francis Bland
        Jesse Cunningham
        +Mary Cunningham
    James (b. 1773)
    Margaret (b. 1774)
    Phoebe (b. 1776)
    Nancy (b. 1777)
    Agnes Slater Cunningham (b. 1778, Randolph County, VA/d. September 29, 1854, in Smithville, Clay County, MO)
    +John Jordan (b. January 14, 1775, Augusta, County, VA/June 8, 1832, Lewis County, VA)
    (m. 1796, Pendleton County, VA)
        SEE JORDAN/CUNNINGHAM TO CONTINUE THIS LINE
    Susanna (b. 1789)
    Stephen (b. 1790)
Mary (b. 1758, Chillicothe, OH)
+ Captain Isaac Henckle
    9 children

Jordan/Cunningham

John Jordan and Agnes Cunningham
(m. 1796, Pendleton County, VA)
   Mary Jordan (b. May 2, 1797, Pendleton County, VA/d. June 14, 1880, in Lewis County, W. VA)
   +Jesse Cunningham
   (m. 1816, Pendleton County, VA)
        Children: Frances, Elizabeth, John J., Enoch G., Phebe, Mary A.
   Susan Jordan (b. July 12, 1799, in Pendleton County, VA/d. June 14, 1880, in Lewis County, W. VA)
   +Abel Withrow
   (m. 1819, Nicholas County, VA
        Children: Mary Ann, Jane A., Abel Alderson, Susan
   Elizabeth Jordan (b. September 2, 1802, Greenbrier County, VA/d. 1829, Nicholas County, VA)
   +James Wood
   (m. 1828, Nicholas County, VA)
        No children
   Anna Jordan (b. February 2 1804, Greenbrier County, VA/d. December 4, 1876, Steele City, Jefferson County, NE/buried in Mount Pleasant Cemetery, Cass County, NE)
   +William Smith
   (m. 1826, Nicholas County, VA)
        Children: David Simpson, Margaret Elizabeth, Milton Marion, Lorenzo Waugh, William T., Armilda A.
   +William D. Gage
   (m. October 6, 1862, Cass County, NE)
   George W Jordan (b. February 26, 1806, in Greenbrier County, VA/d. ca. 1870, NE)
   + Marie Taylor
   (m. 1833, Fayette County, VA)
        Children: James Oliver, John, Susan J., George L.
   Phoebe Jordan (b. April 20, 1808, Greenbrier County, VA/d. October 9, 1871, Cass County, NE/ buried in Mt. Pleasant Cemetery, Nehawka, Cass County, NE)
   +Joseph Cannon
   (m. 1835, Berrien County, MI)
        Children: Enoch G., Mary A., Samuel L., William T.
   Cynthia Jordan (b. May 7, 1810, Greenbrier County, VA/d. Feb 18, 1882, Harrisburg, Lane County, OR/buried on their farm, Harrison County, OR)
   +Jordan Babar
   (m. 1831, Kanawha County, VA)
        Children: Richardson, Mary Agnes, Eliza
   + H. P. Oden
   (m. June 1 1876, Linn County, OR

James Cunningham Jordan (also referred to as "Jimmy" or "Uncle Jimmy") (b. March 4, 1813, Greenbrier County, VA/d. March 1, 1891 in Polk County, Iowa/buried in Jordan Cemetery, West Des Moines, IA)
+Melinda Pittman (b. August 5, 1819, Mount Vernon, Knox County, OH/d. March 1, 1855, Des Moines, Polk County, IA/ buried in Jordan Cemetery, West Des Moines, IA)
(m. 1837, Berrien County, MI)
    Benjamin Pittman Jordan (b. 1838, Niles, Berrien County, MI/d. 1926, Desoto, IA/buried in Jordan Cemetery, Polk County, IA)
    Emily Agnes (b. 1842, Platte County, MO/d. January 21, 1918, Des Moines, IA/buried in Woodland Cemetery, Des Moines, Polk County, IA)
    Henry Clay (b. 1844, Platte County, MO/d. 1918, Valley Junction, IA/buried in Jordan Cemetery, Polk County, IA)
    John Quincy (b. 1846, Platte County, MO/d. 1916, Valley Junction, IA/buried in Jordan Cemetery, Polk County, IA)
    James Finley (b. 1848, Polk County, IA/d. 1926, Valley Junction, IA/ buried in Jordan Cemetery, Polk County, IA)
    George Benton (b. 1850, Polk County, IA/d. 1921, DeSoto, IA/buried in Jordan Cemetery, Polk County, IA)
+Cynthia Disre' Adams Sheppard (b. 1831, Canandaigua, Yates County, NY/d. 1908/buried in Jordan Cemetery, Polk County, IA)
(m. May 21, 1856, Madison County, IA)
    Ella (b. 1857, Polk County, IA/d. September 3, 1909/buried in Woodland Cemetery, Des Moines, Polk County, IA)
    Eva (b. February 1860, Polk County, IA/d. ca. 1870, Polk County, IA/ buried in Jordan Cemetery, Polk County, IA)
    Eda (b. February 1860, Polk County, IA/d. ca. 1863, Polk County, IA/buried in Jordan Cemetery, Polk County, IA)
    Calvin Smith (b. 1862, Polk County, IA/d. 1937, Valley Junction, IA/buried in Jordan Cemetery, Polk County, IA))
    Edward (b. 1868, Polk County, IA/d. 1942, Polk County, IA/buried in Jordan Cemetery, Polk County, IA)
SEE "THE FAMILY OF JAMES CUNNINGHAM JORDAN" TO CONTINUE THIS LINE
Margaret Jordan (b. August 5, 1815, Greenbrier County, VA/d. February 4, 1881, Atchison County, KS /buried in Easton, KS)
+Jacob Eilers
(m. 1834, Berrien County, MI)
    Matilda T. (b. 1836, Berrien County, MI)
    Eliza E. (b. 1838, Platte County, MO)
    Daniel Wirt, Agnes C., Lavinia, George W., Nora M., Sara E., Mary E.
Reverend John Slater Jordan (b. March 1, 1818, Nicholas County, VA/d. November 4, 1891, Bickleton, Klickitat County, WA/buried in Cleveland, Klickitat County, WA)
+Drewsilla Pittman (b. ca. 1820, Knox County, OH/d. August 24, 1849, Fort Des Moines, Polk County, IA)
(m. 1837, Berrien County, MI
    Charles Green (b. 1838, Andrew County, MO)
    Jemima Jane (b. October 3, 1842, Andrew County, MO)
    Mary Melinda (b. July 4, 1849, Polk County, IA/d. October 1849, Polk County, IA)
+Mary Magdalene Worley (b. June 3, 1838, Grundy County, MO/d. February 8, 1916, Bickleton, Klickitat County, WA/ buried February 11, 1916, Cleveland, Kilckitat County, WA)
(m. November 29, 1855, St. Charles, Madison County, IA)
    Children: David Simpson, George Washington, Elizabeth Emma, Effie Alice, John James, William Arthur, Reverend Carol Lincoln, Evan Crawford, Edgar Milton, Franklin Ames
Agnes Jordan (b. August 2, 1821, Nicholas County, WV) d. January 5, 1884, Kansas City, MO/buried in Valley Falls, KS)
+Calvin Smith (b. December 23, 1813, NY/d. October 1, 1909, Kansas City, KS/buried in Valley Falls, KS)
(m. 1840, Platte County, MO)
    Children: Erastus, Almeda, Henry, Alice, Sebree, Marie, Ann, James G., Calvin Jr.

The Family of James Cunningham Jordan

James Cunningham Jordan (also referred to as "Jimmy" or "Uncle Jimmy") (b. March 4, 1813, Greenbrier County, VA/d. March 1, 1891, in Polk County, IA/buried in Jordan Cemetery, West Des Moines, IA)
+Melinda Pittman (b. August 5, 1819, Mt. Vernon, Knox County, OH/d. March 1, 1855, Des Moines, Polk County, IA/ buried in Jordan Cemetery, West Des Moines, IA)
(m. 1837, Berrien County, MI)
    Benjamin Pittman Jordan (b. 1838, Niles, Berrien County, MI/d. 1926, Desoto, IA/buried in Jordan Cemetery, Polk County, IA)
    +Mary Elizabeth Haines (b. June 24, 1841, Wayne County, IN/d. 1923, Dallas County, IA/buried in Jordan Cemetery, Polk County, IA)
    (m. December 15, 1859)

Harriett Ada "Hattie" (b. August 22, 1862, Walnut Township, Polk County, IA/d. March 8, 1922, Mexico, MO/buried in Mexico, MO)
+Franklin Burnett Cook (b. December 1, 1857, Walnut Township, Polk County, IA/d. February 26, 1945, Mexico, MO/buried in Mexico, MO)
(m. October 4, 1884)
    Children: Mildred, Mabel, Kate, Russell, Hobart, Ruth, Harry
Charles Jones (b. April 26, 1867, Walnut Township, IA/d. February 1950, Albuquerque, NM)
+ **Leota "Odie" Pritchard** (b. January 13, 1874/d. August 1915, DeSoto, IA/buried at Jordan Cemetery, Polk County, IA)
    Children: Veva, Henrietta
Ida Ann (b. November 25, 1860, Walnut Township, IA/d. June 11, 1902, DeSoto, IA/buried in Jordan Cemetery, Polk County, IA)
+ **John Phillips**
(m. November 22, 1887)
    Child: Marie Phillips
Emily Agnes (b. 1842, Platte County, MO/d. January 21, 1918, Des Moines, IA/buried in Woodland Cemetery, Des Moines, Polk County, IA)
+Dr. George P. Hanawalt (b. September 11, 1836, Chillicothe, OH/d. June 19, 1912, Des Moines, IA/buried in Woodland Cemetery, Des Moines, IA)
(m. October 31, 1871, Polk County, IA)
    Children: None
Henry Clay (b. 1844, Platte County, MO/d. 1918, Valley Junction, IA/buried in Jordan Cemetery, Polk County, IA)
+Alice Warner (b. 1860, Jasper County, IA/d. Marshalltown, IA)
(m. September 1878)
    Children: Rupert, Ralph, Pauline, (Henry) Kasson
John Quincy (b. 1846, Platte County, MO/d. 1916, Valley Junction, IA/buried in Jordan Cemetery, Polk County, IA)
James Finley (b. 1848, Polk County, IA/d. 1926, Valley Junction, IA)
+Anna Augusta Jackson (b. September 7, 1866/d. October 1, 1914, Walnut Township, IA/buried in Jordan Cemetery, Polk County, IA)
(m. January 15, 1891, Valley Junction, IA)
    Children: None
George Benton (b. 1850, Polk County, IA/d. 1921, DeSoto, IA/buried in Jordan Cemetery, Polk County, IA)
+ Charlotte Louise "Lou" Wayne (b. September 9, 1851/d. January 3, 1916)
(m. ca. 1870)
    Children: James Hanawalt, William H., George E., Robert Roy
+Cynthia Disre' Adams Sheppard (b. 1831, Canandaigua, Yates County, NY/d. 1908/buried in Jordan Cemetery, Polk County, IA)
(m. May 21, 1856, Madison County, IA)
    Ella (b. March 14, 1857, Polk County, IA/d. September 3, 1909, Valley Junction, IA/buried in Woodland Cemetery, Des Moines, Polk County, IA)
+John Peters Cook (b. January 4, 1856, Des Moines, IA/d. July 16, 1940, Corydon, IA/buried in Woodland Cemetery, Des Moines, IA)
(m. September 19, 1878, Walnut Township, IA)
    Children: Jeheil S. "Jay," Emily Agnes, John Calvin, Fred George
Eva (b. February 1860, Polk County, IA/d. ca. 1870, Polk County, IA/ buried in Jordan Cemetery, Polk County, IA)
Eda (b. February 1860, Polk County, IA/d. ca 1863, Polk County, IA/buried in Jordan Cemetery, Polk County, IA)
Calvin Smith (b. 1862, Polk County, IA/d. 1937, Valley Junction, IA/buried in Jordan Cemetery, Polk County, IA))
+ **Grace Irene Cook** (b. July 5, 1876, Des Moines, IA/d. March 18, 1966, Des Moines, IA)
(m. May 20, 1900, Des Moines, IA)
    Children: Charles Cunningham, George Hanawalt, Calvin Smith Jr., Clara Cynthia
Edward (b. December 5, 1868, Polk County, IA/d. December 8, 1942, Des Moines, IA/buried in Jordan Cemetery, Polk County, IA

Right: Family Photo Collage. Jordan Family Collection

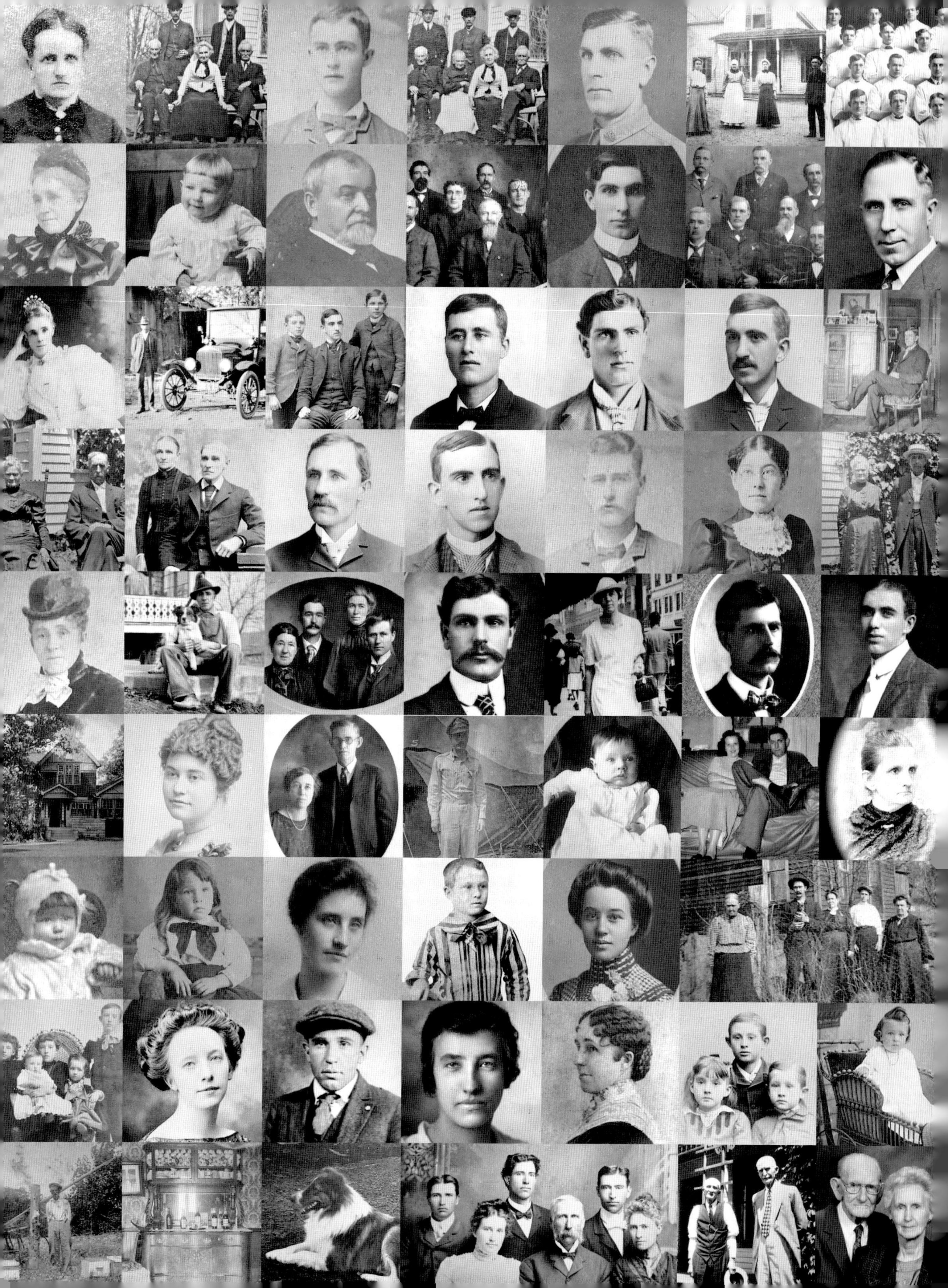

JAMES JORDAN DESCENDENTS

Barton	Dillon Joseph Barton		Glen John Cook	**Gannon**	Adam Gannon
	Dustin Lloyd Barton		Harry Peters Cook		Noah Gannon
	Lori Lynne Cleland Barton		Henrietta (Hattie)	**Gatewood**	Mildred Lucille
	Shane Michael Barton		Jordan Cook		Cook Gatewood
Berhow	Danny Berhow		Hobart Franklin Cook	**Glew**	Jay Jordan Glew
	Jake Berhow		Jehiel Cook		Jay Jordan Glew Jr.
	Keshia Berhow		John C. Cook		Mark Manly Glew
	Michael Berhow		John Cook		Veva Helen Jordan Glew
	Natashia Berhow		John Terrance Cook	**Goodson**	Morgan Jordan Goodson
	Rae Ann Jordan Berhow		John Terrance Cook Jr.		Regina Lynn Glew
Berkley	Jeffrey Arthur Berkley		Julia Cook		Hort Goodson
	Luke Jordan Berkley		Mary Mabel Cook	**Gray**	Ella Gray
	Lynn Cunningham Berkley		Max Cook		Emele Gray
	Patricia Irene Jordan Berkley		Nancy Jane Cook		Frankie Gray
	Scott Jordan Berkley		Russell Jordan Cook		Meghan Warhurst Gray
Blasco	Audrey Rose Blasco	**Cotton**	Nathaniel William Cotton	**Haage**	Rowen Haage
	Ian David Blasco		Nicole Christina Cotton		Sophia Haage
	James Jordan Blasco	**Crawford**	Danielle Halley		Theo Roxanna Joplin Haage
	Jared Douglas Blasco		Breman Crawford	**Hanawalt**	Emily Agnes
	Noelle Ann Blasco	**Crow**	Jeramiah Crow		Jordan Hanawalt
	Rachel Renee Blasco		Joshua Crow	**Hanstad**	Veva Helen Cleland
Blasco-Fogg	Carolyn Marie Blasco-Fogg	**Dabney**	James Augustus Dabney		Filmer Hanstad
Blasco-Pruitt	Claudia Kay Blasco-Pruitt		Susan Marie Cook Dabney	**Harris**	Bonnie Philipon
Blasé	Ruth Naomi Cook Blasé	**Daughtry**	Candace Jay Cline		Donahue Harris
Breman	Alexandra Halley Breman		Brewer Daughtry		Jordan Samantha Harris
	Cheyenne M. Breman	**Deroos**	Cameron Joseph Deroos		Ryan Andrew Harris
	Connor William Breman		Jennifer Rebecca	**Hartwell**	Christie Marie
	Cynthia Disré Breman		Jordan Deroos		Gorman Hartwell
	Roberta Cook Breman		Jordan Leigh Deroos		Michael Hartwell
	Stephen John Breman	**Donahue**	Natalie Hartwell Donahue	**Henderson**	Howard Wayne Henderson
	William Earl Breman		Spencer Donahue		Katherine Anna
	William R. Breman		Wyatt Hartwell Donahue		Cook Henderson
Caldwell	Dillon Anthony Caldwell	**Doyle**	Aiden Anthony Doyle		Marie Katherine Henderson
	Louise Ellen Renfro Caldwell		Constance Carolyn	**Highstreet**	Rebecca Artlette
	Morgan Elizabeth Caldwell		Ramer Doyle		Renfro Highstreet
Cleland	Joseph Henry Cleland		Elsie Marie Doyle	**Hitchcock**	Blanche Cook Hitchcock
	Kaleen Helen Cleland	**Entrop**	Jeremy Rumbaugh	**Jeshan**	Caroline L. Jeshan
	Sally Lynne Cline Cleland		Glew Entrop	**Johnson**	Crystal Victoria Johnson
	William Marion Cleland	**Evjue**	Nancy Alice Jordan Evjue		Jeffrey Lee Johnson
	William Robbins Cleland	**Faber**	Jordan Faber		Patty Jordan Johnson
Cline	Betty Jane Glew Cline	**Filmer**	Jaedyn Rae Filmer	**Jones**	Judith Ann Jordan Jones
Colman	Charles Colman		Sabrina Kaye Filmer	**Joplin**	Ella Belle Cook Joplin
	Emma Colman		Shawn Marie Filmer		Ted Joplin
	Pendance Jordan Colman	**Filmer-Brown**	Anthony James Filmer-	**Joplin-Haage**	Eric Joplin-Haage
Cook	Dean Russell Cook		Brown		Kirk Joplin-Haage
	Donna Colleen Cook	**Follett**	Clarissa Follett		
	Ella Jordan Cook		Debra Warhurst Follett		
	Emma Cook		Hannah Follett		
	Fred Hanawalt Cook				

216   Pursuit of a Dream

JAMES JORDAN DESCENDENTS
(continued)

Jordan
- Alyssa Jordan
- Amanda Jordan
- Ashley Jordan
- Austin William Jordan
- Benjamin Pittman Jordan
- Calvin Smith Jordan
- Calvin Smith Jordan Jr.
- Charles Cunningham Jordan
- Charles Jones Jordan
- Charles Jordan
- Charles William (Buddy) Jordan
- Connie Lea Jordan
- Dale Rupert Jordan
- Darryl Jordan
- Dennis Darrel Jordan
- Donald Eldin Jordan
- Donald Hartley Jordan
- Eda Jordan
- Edward Jordan
- Eva Jordan
- Gabriel Walker Jordan
- George Benton Jordan
- George E. Jordan
- George Hanawalt Jordan
- George P.H. Jordan
- Grantland Earl Jordan
- Guy William Jordan
- Henry Clay Jordan
- Henry Clay Jordan (II)
- Henry Kasson Jordan
- Jack D. Jordan
- Jacquita Louise Jordan
- James Cunningham Jordan (II)
- James Finley Jordan
- Jeremy William Jordan
- Jessie Jordan
- John Calvin Jordan
- John Cunningham Jordan
- John Quincy Jordan
- Kyle Matthew Jordan
- Lee Jordan
- Matthew Jordan
- Mickey Leigh Jordan
- Nicolas Jordan
- Ralph E. Jordan
- Robert Roy Jordan Jr.
- Robert Wayne Jordan
- Robery Roy Jordan
- Rupert James Jordan
- Sally Jordan
- Thomas Rehfield Jordan
- Tyler Jordan
- William Henry Jordan
- William Max Jordan
- Zoey Ann Crow Jordan

Kernaghan
- Ethan James Kernaghan
- Ryan Christopher Kernaghan

King
- Pauline Jordan King

Klotz
- Barbara Janelle Brewer Klotz
- Bradley Jordan Klotz
- Brody Dean Klotz
- Brynlee Drew Klotz

Knutson
- Ethel Marie Talmage Phillips Knutson

Leitzel
- Denise Philipon Leitzel
- Dillon Leitzel
- Dustin James Leitzel
- Gabriel Leitzel
- Haleigh Leitzel
- Liam Leitzel
- Malachi Leitzel
- Sadie Leitzel

Logan
- Alex Marie Logan

McNerney
- Sandra Sue Stevens McNerney

Nelson
- Patricia Jo Nelson

Nolten
- Mary Edna Jordan Nolten
- Noah Max Nolten

Partin
- Sabrina Kay Filmer Kernaghan Partin

Pena
- Eli William Pena

Philipon
- John Philipon

Pruitt
- Dionne Markell Pruitt

Ramer
- Jonathan David Ramer
- Nancy Michelle Ramer

Raridon
- Henrietta Scripps Jordan Raridon

Renfro
- Bonnie Merle Jordan Renfro
- Charles Eugene Renfro III
- "Charles Eugene Renfro, Jr."
- Louis Renfro
- Rebecca Renfro

Salagan
- Sandra Jeanne Jordan Salagan

Sanders
- Emily Cook Sanders

Schaner
- Kathleen A. Breman Schaner

Seiberling
- Michael Wayne Seiberling
- Scott Matthew Seiberling
- Shannon Lea Seiberling
- Susanna Grace Seiberling

Souik
- Benjamin Souik
- Erin Seiberling Souik
- Samuel George Souik
- Trevor Lea Souik

Stapel
- Casey Lea Stapel
- Grace Stapel
- Kristen Seiberling Stapel
- Matthew Stapel

Staver
- Clara Cynthia Jordan
- Nelson Staver

Stein
- Gage Charles Stein
- Jordan Patrick Stein
- Lance Christopher Stein
- Mary Lou Renfro Stein

Stevens
- Gwendolyn Cook Stevens

Warhurst
- Craig Eugene Warhurst
- Emily Cook Warhurst
- Julia Marie Warhurst
- Justin Warhurst
- Ryan Keith Warhurst
- Scott Warhurst
- Terrel Cook Warhurst
- Wyatt Warhurst

Wright
- Ida Ann Jordan Phillips Wright

BIBLIOGRAPHY

INTRODUCTION
Regarding James Jordan's character:
James Jordan obituary, *Des Moines Daily News*, March 2, 1891, p. 1.
Portrait and Biographical Album of Polk County, Iowa, James Jordan (Chapman Brothers, 1895, Lake City Publishing Co., 1890) pp. 169–171.

CHAPTER 1
Kercheval, Samuel, *The History of the Valley of Virginia*, 4th edition, (Strasburg Shenandoah Publishing House, 1925), originally published in 1833.

CHAPTER 2
Resources for land patents:
County Records for Augusta County, State of Virginia:
Augusta County Surveyor's Office and the Land Office of Virginia.
Bath County Surveyor's Records and the Land Office of Virginia.
Chalkley, Lyman, *Chronicles of the Scotch-Irish Settlement in Virginia, 1745–1800*, Vol. 1 (Mary S. Lockwood, The Commonwealth Printing Co., Rosslyn, VA, 1912), pp. 298, 435.
Davis, Virginia Lee Hutcheson, *Tidewater Virginia Families, A Magazine of History and Genealogy* (Vol. 8, August/September 1999), p. 71.
Hardy County Surveyor's Records and the Land office of Virginia.
Library of Virginia, Northern Neck Surveys, Northern Neck Plats and Certificates: Folders H & K, pp. 45, 49, 869, 1031–1032.
Morrison, Charles, "Early Fairfax Land Grants and Leases Along the South Branch of the Potomac," *West Virginia History* 38 (1976), p. 2.
Morrison, Charles, "Early Land Grants and Settlers Along Patterson Creek," *West Virginia Archives and History* Vol. 40 (1979), pp. 164–9.
Robinson, W. Stitt Jr., *Mother Earth, Land Grants in Virginia, 1607–1699*, Jamestown 350th Anniversary Historical Booklet No. 12, 1957, reprinted by Clearfield Co., Inc., Baltimore, MD, 1993, 1996, 2001.
Ward, Gae Grinnan and Nelson S. Kibler, *The New Hottel History— George Line*, The Shenandoah Germanic Heritage Museum, Hottle Memorial, Inc.
William and Mary College Quarterly Historical Papers, Vol. 1, No. 3, January 1893.
<u>August 28, 1750</u>
"(421) Benj. Skoot, John Knowles, Joel Hornback, John West, Thomas Crawford, George Baffenbarger, John Christian Carlock, David Craig, John Walker Jr. George Say, George Say Jr. Simon Say, John Cunningham, Wm. Cunningham, Henry Landcisco, John Colley, Burket Reager, Henry Carr, Daniel Richardson, Nathaniel Clearey, added to list of tithables."
Notes:
1. The South Branch Valley became part of Frederick County when Augusta County was subdivided. The Frederick County Courthouse in Winchester was only sixty miles away from Cunningham Plantation. In the early 1760s, the Cunninghams' county became a part of Hampshire County with the county seat thirty miles away in Romney. The last county subdivision took place in 1786 when the Cunninghams' part of Hampshire County became Hardy County. The county seat was Moorefield, a mere five-mile horseback ride from Cunningham Plantation.
2. Sara Stevens Patton, *Hardy County West Virginia Geneology Page, USGenWeb Project:* "Since leases for this land was considered a private transaction with Lord Fairfax, they were not generally recorded in the county deed books, though references can be found in Hampshire, Hardy, Frederick, and Augusta County records."
3. South Branch Manor was one of several subdivisions of Fairfax's South Branch Valley, as was Great South Branch where the Cunningham Homestead stood.
4. Mill Creek is a fourteen-mile-long tributary stream of the South Branch Potomac River and flows into the South Branch. Mill's Branch flows into Mills Creek.
5. There were other Jordans who were settling in Cowpasture and Calfpasture Valleys near South Branch Valley at about the same time—a married couple of Irish descent with the name of John and Ann Jordan and their offspring. These are *not* James Cunningham Jordan's ancestors.

Documentation on George Jordan:
Ruth Jordan Thoden, Jordan entry under "Surnames," Genealogy.com, December 15, 2009.
Note: George's brother may have been John Jordan with information from Ruth Thoden (see above) as follows: John Jordan: "Born in1709 in Germany. . . . He is on record as enlisting on May 15, 1760 in Capt. Jacobus Swartwout's Company of Dutchess County and was a weaver by trade. He was 5'5-1/2"; brown hair; brown eyes; fair complexion. John Jordan married Capt. Swartwout's daughter. Swartwout became a Brigadier General in the Continental Army during the American Revolutionary War under General George Washington. He was a close ally of many key Founding Fathers of the United States, and a delegate to New York State's convention for ratification of the US Constitution."
Chalkley, Lyman, *Chronicles of the Scotch-Irish Settlement in Virginia, 1745–1800*, Vols. I and II (Mary S. Lockwood, The Commonwealth Printing Co., Rosslyn, VA, 1912), Citations:Vol. I, pp. 170–179.
<u>February and March 1748</u>
"David Evans vs. George Jourdan—Attachment 18th June 1746. George has removed. On November 20, 1747, ordered to be served in hands of Fred Carlock, on South Branch."
<u>February 27, 1750</u>
"(531) David Evans summoned for not providing for his children in a decent and Christian like manner."
Vol. II, pp. 298, 435.
<u>August 28, 1750</u>
"(421) Benj. Skoot, John Knowles, Joel Hornback, John West, Thomas Crawford, George Baffenbarger, John Christian Carlock, David Craig, John Walker Jr. George Say, George Say Jr. Simon Say, John Cunningham, Wm. Cunningham, Henry Landcisco, John Colley, Burket Reager, Henry Carr, Daniel Richardson, Nathaniel Clearey, added to list of tithables."
<u>November 18, 1766</u>
"(337) These added to tithables—viz: Wm. Jordan, James Jordan, Anthony Johnston."

Notes:
1. In the citation above referring to David Carlock: "In 1745 Carlock sued Lawrence Washington, brother of George Washington, for non-payment of a bill." (It appears Carlock had sold to Washington.)
2. David Carlock was recorded as not having paid taxes on his land in 1756.

CHAPTER 3

Regarding the Indian capture of John, Mary, and James Cunningham:

Bosworth, Dr. A. S., *A History of Randolph County, West Virginia from Its Earliest Exploration and Settlement to the Present Time* (New York Public Library, Astor, Lenox and Tilden Foundations, 1932) p. 330.

Chalkley, Lyman, *Chronicles of the Scotch-Irish Settlement in Virginia, 1745–1800,* Vol. 2 (Mary S. Lockwood, The Commonwealth Printing Co., Rosslyn, VA, 1912), pp. 511–12.

Harter, Mary, *James Cunningham of Western Virginia* "The Preston Papers show, 19 March 1758, that John Cunningham was killed by Indians at South Branch and two persons, names forgotten, were taken prisoner."

Herda, Gertrude G., *My Jordan Family*, 1223 Cleveland Blvd., Caldwell, ID, June 1979.

Preston, William, *A Register of Persons Killed, Wounded, or Taken Prisoner in Augusta Co. VA. 1754–1758* (Draper MSS 1QQ 83, State Historical Society of Wisconsin).

Waddell, Joseph, *Indian Wars in Augusta County, Virginia, 1895,* reproduced in *The Virginia Magazine of History and Biography*, Vol. 2, p. 403.

Regarding John Van Meter and South Branch:

Kegley, Frederick Bittle, *Kegley's Virginia Frontier: The Beginning of the Southwest, the Roanoke of Colonial Days, 1740-1783* (Southwest Virginia Historical Society, Roanoke, VA, 1938), Forts: pp. 259–260; Weddings: pp. 266–269.

Kercheval, Sam, *A History of the Valley of Virginia*, 3rd Edition (W. N. Grabill, Woodstock, VA, 1902).

Regarding Governor Gooch:

Walton, Joseph Solomon, *Historic Pittsburgh Text Collection* (University of Pittsburgh).

Regarding Fort Pleasant:

Ferling, John E., "School for Command: Young George Washington and the Virginia Regiment," *George Washington and the Virginia Frontier*, Warren R. Hofstra, ed. (Madison: Madison House, 1998), p. 202.

Stoetzel, Donald I., *Encyclopedia of the French & Indian War in North America, 1754–1763* (Heritage Books, 2008).

Regarding Robert Cunningham and his property:

Chalkley, Lyman, *Chronicles of the Scotch-Irish Settlement in Virginia,* Vol. 2, (Roslyn, VA, 1912), pp. 459, 547.

Regarding John Cunningham becoming a lieutenant in the militia:

Gruber, Terry (HC 77 Box 16, Kirby, WV 26729), "Fort Pleasant: Soldiers and Civilians in the South Branch Valley: 1756–1762," p. 57.

Resources for the French and Indian War:

Abbot, W. W., *The Papers of George Washington: Colonial Series*, (University Press of Virginia, Charlottesville, VA, 1983–1997), Vol. 2, pp. 265–66; Vol. 3, pp. 30, 244–45.

Bosworth, Dr. A. S., *A History of Randolph County, West Virginia from its Earliest Exploration and Settlement to the Present Time* (New York Public Library, Astor, Lenox and Tilden Foundations, 1932), p. 33.

Miller, Jos. Lyon M.D., "Augusta Men in the French and Indian War," Source: *West Virginia Historical Magazine Quarterly*, The American History and Genealogy Project, August 2011–2017, (Original version Charleston, WV, April 1903).

Regarding Cunningham property purchases in 1762 and 1765:

Chalkley, Lyman, *Chronicles of the Scotch-Irish Settlement in Virginia, 1745–1800,* Vol. 2 (Mary S. Lockwood, The Commonwealth Printing Co., Rosslyn, VA, 1912), pp. 869, 1031, 1032.

Regarding Mary Biedert Peters/Peterson Cunningham Ward's remarriage, James Cunningham's marriage to Agnes Slater, and their residence in Pendleton and Randolph Counties:

Bosworth, Dr. A. S., *A History of Randolph County, West Virginia* (reprinted 1975, McClain Printing Co., Parsons, WV) pp. 330–331. "James Cunningham, the pioneer, was captured by the Indians in 1758. He was kept a prisoner for seven years and became nearly blind as a result of starvation while in captivity. After his release and return to his people he moved to Randolph."

Harter, Mary, *James Cunningham of Western Virginia* (The Virginia Genealogist, January–March 1985, Vol. 29, No. 1) p. 13. "It is not possible to tell from the tax lists just when our James Cunningham moved from Pendleton to Randolph County. There was another James Cunningham in Pendleton and by 27 Nov. 1781 our James was listed as a blind man when he had State Warrant 9409 for 2000 acres of land. Without quoting any more documents, it appears that our James Cunningham was the son of John Cunningham and Mary (Peterson), that his father was killed by Indians and that James and his mother were taken captive. It also appears that his mother Mary married Sylvester Ward sometime after 18 Aug. 1761 when she obtained land. As shown earlier, on the same dates, from the same grantor, Robert also got land. This surely suggests a relationship. Tradition says that James and Agnes were married in Pennsylvania."

Notes:

1. Mary Cunningham, half-sister of William Robert and James and wife of Sylvester Ward. Her children with Sylvester Ward: Levi (b. ca. 1763), Adonijah (b. ca. 1765), John (b. ca. 1767), Mary b. ca. 1768), William and Jacob (b. ca. 1769), Jemima (b. ca. 1779), Sarah (b. ca. 1773), and Phoebe (b. ca. 1783).

2. Bev, "Cunninghams of the Valley of Virginia—also how they lived, dressed, etc." (Geneaology.com, January 5, 2010). "According to extensive research conducted by many historians of the time, "there were nineteen distinctly separate families with the surname Cunningham living west of the Blue Ridge Mountains in Virginia."

3. Bev, "Cunninghams of the Valley of Virginia—also how they lived, dressed etc." (Geneaology.com, January 5, 2010). "During this early period of Cunningham families, with few exceptions, tended to remain on land they had originally settled: however, the jurisdictional bodies which governed them did change. As more and more settlers came into the Valley, the hardship of the distance required to travel to court and the increased volume of court business necessitated the formation of new counties. The formation of these counties changed the location of Cunningham court records. The records of the counties of Orange, Augusta, Frederick, Hampshire, Shenandoah, Rockingham, Rockbridge, Botetourt, Pendleton, Hardy, Monongalia, Harrison, Berkley, Highland, and others were involved."

CHAPTER 4

Background information:

Chalkley, Lyman, *Chronicles of the Scotch-Irish Settlement in Virginia, 1745–1800,* Vols. 1 and 2, (Mary S. Lockwood, The Commonwealth Printing Co., Rosslyn, VA, 1912).

Regarding the land purchase by Robert Cunningham in the Cheat River Valley:
Note: The area on the Cheat River Robert purchased was south of St. George, now in Tucker County, West Virginia.
Regarding James and Agnes Cunningham moving to Randolph County:
Bosworth, Dr. A. S., *A History of Randolph County, West Virginia* (reprinted 1975, McClain Printing Co., Parsons, WV) pp. 330–331.
Egan, Captain Michael, *The Flying Gray-haired Yank: Rural life in the Wilds of Virginia*, (Edgewood Publishing Company, 1888, by Hubbard Brothoki), digitized by Harvard University.
Smith, Edward Conrad, A.M., sometime teacher of history and civics at Weston High School, *A History of Lewis County, West Virginia* (The Morgantown Printing and Binding Co., Morgantown, WV, 1920), digitized by the New York City Public Library.
Note: Lewis County was formed from Randolph County, which was formed from Harrison County, which was formed from Augusta County.

CHAPTER 5
Chalkley, Lyman, *Chronicles of the Scotch-Irish Settlement in Virginia, 1745–1800*, Vol. 2, (Mary S. Lockwood, The Commonwealth Printing Co., Rosslyn Roslyn, Virginia, 1912),"List of Delinquents and Insolvents in the Revenue Tax for 1786 given in by Thomas Hughart, Sheriff, in Second Battalion. These removed, viz: Charles Ash, Jos. Bennett; Ephraim Beats, to Kentucky; Henry Baker, John Been, Henry Casebolt; Jno. Denison, to French Broad; Francis Graham, to Kentucky; James Hicklen, to Kentucky; John Jordan, to Kentucky"
Note: In 1786 John Jordan was eleven years old and would not be old enough to be a taxpayer; however, he did travel with his parents through Kentucky to New Design, Illinois. The family had left their Virginia property and probably did not pay taxes on it. Eventually John returned the to Jordan property in Harrison County, Virginia. They may have confused John with his father, George, who had fought in the Revolutionary War.
Regarding the Community of New Design:
Combined History of Randolph, Monroe and Perry Counties, Illinois (J. L. McDonough & Co., Philadelphia, 1883) pp. 330–332.

CHAPTER 6
Regarding Robert Cunningham's will:
Chalkley, Lyman, *Chronicles of the Scotch-Irish Settlement in Virginia, 1745–1800,* Vol. 1 (Mary S. Lockwood, The Commonwealth Printing Co., Rosslyn, Virginia, 1912) pp. 547, 459.
Hardy County, Virginia Courthouse Records, Book 1 (proved 16 April, 1802) p. 224.
Sage, Clara McCormick and Laura Sage Jones, "*Early Records, Hampshire County, Virginia, Now West Virginia*" (Clearfield 2013), p. 17.
Note: The properties may be originally listed at the time they were purchased in Frederick County. Over the years, population increases caused counties to divide and increase into more counties. This part of Frederick County changed into Hampshire County in 1753 and then it became Hardy County in 1785.
Regarding Germany Valley:
Whitaker, Carolyn, "My Paternal Ancestors—Virginia, North Carolina, Tennessee & Elsewhere."
Regarding James Cunningham after returning from captivity:
Bosworth, Dr. A. S., *A History of Randolph County, West Virginia*, (McClain Printing Company, Parsons, WV, reprinted 1975), pp. 330–331. "James Cunningham, the pioneer, was captured by the Indians in 1758. He was kept a prisoner for seven years and became nearly blind as a result of starvation while in captivity. After his release and return to his people he moved to Randolph."
Harter, Mary, "James Cunningham of Western Virginia" (*The Virginia Genealogist*, January–March 1985, Vol. 29), p. 13. "It is not possible to tell from the tax lists just when our James Cunningham moved from Pendleton to Randolph County. . . . by 27 Nov. 1781 our James was listed as a blind man when he had State Warrant 9409 for 2000 acres of land. Without quoting any more documents, it appears that our James Cunningham was the son of John Cunningham and Mary (Peterson), that his father was killed by Indians and that James and his mother were taken captive. It also appears that his mother Mary married Sylvester Ward sometime after 18 Aug. 1761 when she obtained land. As shown earlier, on the same dates, from the same grantor, Robert also got land. This surely suggests a relationship. Tradition says that James and Agnes were married in Pennsylvania."
Regarding James Cunningham's residency in Pendleton County in the late 1700s:
Toothman, Rick, "Deed Book Records, 1788–1813" (Pendleton County Courthouse, Franklin, WV).
Regarding James Cunningham's will:
"Deed Book 6" (Randolph County Courthouse, WV, Proved May 1813), p. 267.

CHAPTER 7
Garrison, Silor J., *The History of the Reformed Church in Virginia, 1714-1940* (Winston-Salem, NC, Clay Printing Company, 1948), pp. 44–45.
Gewehr, Wesley M., *The Great Awakening in Virginia, 1740-1790* (Durham, NC, Duke University Press, 1930), pp. 40–44.
Wust, Klaus, *The Virginia Germans* (Charlottesville: University Press of Virginia, 1969), pp. 34, 47, 94, 134–35.
Regarding how the churches reformed society:
Lindman, Janet Moore, "Acting the Manly Christian; White Evangelical Masculinity in Revolutionary Virginia" (*William and Mary Quarterly*, April 2000, Vol. 57, No. 2), pp. 393–416.

CHAPTER 8
(none)

CHAPTER 9
Regarding the schools and the schooling of children in colonial western Virginia:
Morton, Oren F., *A History of Rockbridge County, Virginia* (The McClure Company, Inc., Staunton, VA, 1920), pp. 184–186.
Smith, Edward Conrad, A.M., sometime teacher of history and civics at Weston High School, *A History of Lewis County, West Virginia* (The Morgantown Printing and Binding Co., Morgantown, WV, 1920), digitized by the New York City Public Library), pp. 125, 126, 268–272.
Note: Lewis County was formed from Randolph County, which was formed from Harrison County, which was formed from Augusta County.
Regarding the War of 1812 and to subjects studied in school:
Sparknotes Editors, "Sparknote on the War of 1812 (1809–1815)," SparkNotes. LLC.n.d. http://www.sparknotes.com/history/american/war of 1812/ (accessed March 1, 2017).
Regarding the Presbyterian Church:
Graham, James R., D.D., *The Planting of the Presbyterian Church*

in Northern Virginia Prior to the Organization of Winchester Presbytery December 4, 1794, (Geo. F. Norton PublishingCompany, 1904), Copyright 1998–2016 Grayson County Virginia, Heritage Foundation Inc. and New River Notes.

Herman, Arthur, "How the Scots invented the Modern World," (Random House/MJF Books, New York, NY) 2001.

"Records of the Presbyterian Church in the United States of America" (Philadelphia: Presbyterian Board of Publication, 1904), pp. 142,147, 138, 181–82, 193, 197, 199, 205, 215, 220, 226, 234, 237, 239, 247.

CHAPTER 10
Regarding Francis Asbury
Asbury, Francis, "The Journal and Letters of Francis Asbury, Vol. 2., October 21, 1800," Taken from: William Larkin Duren, *Francis Asbury, Founder of American Methodism and Unofficial Minister of State* (The Macmillan Company, New York, 1928), p. xiii.

Regarding the Second Great Awakening:
Scott, Donald, "Evangelicalism as a Social Movement" (Queens College/City University of New York, National Humanities Center).

CHAPTER 11
Regarding the village of Moorefield:
Heishman, Phoebe, "Moorefield," *The West Virginia Encyclopedia*, www.wvencyclopedia.org/articles/2036.

Moorefield and Hardy County, West Virginia, Chamber of Commerce.

Regarding James catching slaves:
Brigham, Johnson, *Iowa, Its History and its Foremost Citizens*, Vol. I (Clarke Publishing Co., Chicago, IL, 1916), pp. 268–269.

CHAPTER 12
Regarding Robert Cunningham's will:
Hardy County, Virginia, Courthouse Records, Book 1, p. 224 (proved 16 April 1802).

Regarding slavery:
Note: Hardy County had the sixth largest number slaves (1,073) among West Virginia counties. This substantial number contributed to conflict in the Valley in the mid-nineteenth century, since West Virginia was created as a Union state.

Coates, Ta-Nehisi, "The Case for Reparations," *The Atlantic Monthly*, June 2014, Vol. 313, No.5, p. 63, A quote from Walter Johnson, Department of African and African American Studies, Harvard University.

Gourley, Bruce T., Ph.D., "Racism and Inequality in the North Prior to the Civil War," (Archive: *This Day in Civil War History*, 2017).

James Jordan obituary, *Des Moines Daily News*, March 2, 1891, p. 1.

Morton, Oren F. B. L., A History of Highland County, Virginia (Monterey Publishing, WV, 1911), Chapter 21, pp. 211–215.

Morton, Oren F. B. L., *A History of Pendleton County, Virginia* (The Stone Printing and Manufacturing Company, Roanoke, VA, 1911), Chapter 13, pp. 103–106.

Newby-Alexander, Cassandra, "Underground Railroad in Virginia" (*Encyclopedia Virginia*, Virginia Foundation for the Humanities; First published: December 8, 2015. Last modified: December 10, 2015)

Tate, Thad W. Jr. "The Negro in Eighteenth-Century Williamsburg," Colonial Williamsburg Foundation Library Research Report Series—0121 (Colonial Williamsburg Foundation Library, Williamsburg, VA, April 1957).

CHAPTER 13
(none)

CHAPTER 14
Regarding getting the wagons ready and leaving home:
Riley, Glenda, *Frontiers Women, the Iowa Experience* (Iowa State University Press, Ames, IA, 1981), pp. 15–19, 27.

Regarding the settlement in Berrien County, Michigan
Johnson, Crisfield, *History of Berrien and Van Buren Counties, Michigan* (D. W. Ensign & Co./J. D. Lippincott & Co., Philadelphia, PA, 1880).

Regarding the pre-exemption rules:
Burlend, Rebecca and Edward, *A True Picture of Emigration* (University of Nebraska Press, Lincoln, NE, and London, 1987), p. 53.

Regarding traveling to Missouri:
Faragher, John M., *Women and Men on the Overland Trail* (Yale University Press, New Haven and London, 1979), pp. 24–25.

CHAPTER 15
Regarding traveling west to Missouri:
Faragher, John M., *Women and Men on the Overland Trail* (Yale University Press, New Haven and London, 1979), p. 24–25.

Regarding the meeting between Jordans and Calvin Smith:
Smith, Calvin, *The Autobiography of Calvin Smith of Smithville* (Sanford H. Robinson Jr. Philadelphia, PA, 1906), p. 9.

Regarding the frontier towns of Independence and St. Joseph:
Gilbert, Bill, "Westward Ho! And Never Mind the Indians," from *The Smithsonian*, Vol. 25, No. 2, May 1994, pp. 40–51.

Insert: Humphrey "Yankee" Smith
Conard, Howard Louis, "Smithville, Missouri," from the *Encyclopedia of the History of Missouri: A Compendium of History and Biography for Ready Reference* (The Southern History Company, Haldeman, Conard & Company, 1901), p. 10.

Coy, Roy E., "Little Dixie and the Mystic Land of Poosey" (St. Joseph Museum, St. Joseph, MO, 1954).

Crisler, Robert M., "Missouri's Little Dixie" (*Missouri Historical Review*, Columbia, MO, Vol. XLII, April 1948), pp. 130–139.

Pfannmuller, Susan, "From Smith's Mill to Smithville, this Clay County Town Continues to Grow," *Kansas City Star*, January 24, 2017.

"A Pictorial History of Smithville, Missouri," *The Smithville Herald*, now part of the *Courier-Tribune*, 2013.

Smith, Calvin, *The Autobiography of Calvin Smith of Smithville*, (Sanford H. Robinson Jr. Philadelphia, PA, 1906).

"The Story of Little Dixie, Missouri" (Missouri Division—Sons of Confederate Veterans, 2008).

Trombly, Albert Edmund, *Little Dixie* (Columbia, MO: University of Missouri Studies, 1955).

CHAPTER 16
Regarding family stages and emigration:
Faragher, John M., *Women and Men on the Overland Trail* (Yale University Press, New Haven and London, 1979), pp. 18–19.

Regarding J. B. Newhall's descriptions of early Iowa:
Newhall, J. B., *A Glimpse of Iowa in 1846 or the Emigrant's Guide and State Directory* (Iowa State Historical Society, Iowa City, IA, 1957 reprint).

Regarding the Dragoon Trace:
Palmer, John, *South Bend: Crossroads of Commerce* (Arcadia Publishing, 2003).

Regarding the Stagecoach Trails map:
Courtesy of the State Historical Society of Iowa.
Regarding the Fort Des Moines maps:
Courtesy of the Des Moines Centennial Commission.
Regarding early descriptions of Fort Des Moines No. 2 and James and John traveling to Iowa in 1844:
Porter, Will, *Annals of Polk County and Des Moines* (Jos. A. Miller Printing Company, Des Moines, IA, 1898), pp. 306–309 and 826–27.
Regarding dragoons in Iowa:
Wiggins, David, *The Rise of the Allens: Two Soldiers and the Master of Terrace Hill* (Historical-Midwest Books, Mt. Horeb, WI), p. 66.

CHAPTER 17
Regarding the quote about settlers:
Parker, George F., *Iowa Pioneer Foundations* (State Historical Society of Iowa, 1940), pp. 102–103
Regarding how common it was for settlers to first be squatters:
Petersen, Willian J., *The Story of Iowa, the Progress of an American State,* Vol. I (Lewis Historical Publishing Co. Inc., New York, NY, 1952), pp. 357–358.
Sage, Leland L., *A History of Iowa* (Iowa State University Press, Ames, IA, 1974), p. 68.
Regarding James Jordan settling on his property:
Brigham, Johnson, *Iowa, Its History and its Foremost Citizens*, Vol. I (S. J. Clarke Publishing Co., Chicago, IL, 1916), pp. 91–92.
Regarding the settlers waiting to claim land:
Beach, John, *Report to the Commissioner of Indian Affairs* (Washington: Government Printing Office, 1845), pp. 485–86.
Brown, Richard Frank, *A Social History of the Mesquakie Indians, 1800–1963* (Retrospective Theses and Dissertations. Iowa State University, 1964).
Hammer, Ilda M., *The Book of Des Moines* (Board of Education, Des Moines, IA, 1947), pp. 49–50.
Van der Zee, Jacob, "Forts in Iowa Country" (*Iowa Journal of History and Politics*, 1914), p. 194.
Regarding the Indian Agency house in Fort Des Moines:
Hastie, Eugene N., *High Points of Iowa History* (Perry, IA, 1966), p. 181.
Regarding Indian fur traders:
History of Polk County (Union Historical Co., 1880), p. 308.
Regarding the description of the night of October 11, 1845:
Turrill, H. B., *Historical Reminiscences of the City of Des Moines* (Redhead & Dawson, Des Moines, IA, 1857), pp. 16–17.
Regarding John Quincy Adams:
Nagel, Paul, *John Quincy Adams: A Public Life, a Private Life* (Cambridge, MA: Harvard University Press, 1999).
Insert: What Happened to the Indians in Iowa?
Notes:
1. The Sioux Massacre in northwest Iowa occurred in 1857, ten years after the Meskwaki's had been evacuated to Kansas. A Sioux Tribe was living on a reservation in Minnesota, suffering through a severe winter and starved for food. A group of Sioux braves came into the area in northwest Iowa from where they had been evacuated, which was part of their former hunting grounds. They were rebuffed when they went to pioneer cabins asking for help and sustenance. They were starving because the US government had not adequately supplied their reservation for the winter, as promised, nor had they fulfilled the terms of their treaty. Out of desperation, the Sioux returned to their old hunting grounds in northwest Iowa to find and hunt for food to feed their people.
2. Dragoon Trace from Fort Des Moines: to follow their route into Missouri, from Des Moines take US 169 and County Road J20 to Ellston, Iowa. The old trail picks up along the Grand River as it enters Missouri, following a southwest diagonal line leading to the Missouri River crossing at Fort Leavenworth.
3. Thanks to Jonathan L. Buffalo, historical preservation director, Meskwaki Nation, Sac and Fox Tribe of the Mississippi in Iowa, with whom I had a personal interview in 2013. He gave me an invaluable overview of the journey of the Meskwaki and the spiritual foundation that guided them.

Regarding the Meskwaki in Wisconsin:
Kellogg, Louise Phelps, *The French Regime in Wisconsin and the Northwest* (Madison: State Historical Society of Wisconsin, 1925), pp. 127–28.
Regarding the Meskwaki in the early 1800s:
Blair, Emma Helen, *The Indian Tribes of the Upper Mississippi Valley and Region of the Great Lakes* (The Arthur H. Clark Company, Cleveland, OH, 1912), Vol. II, p. 151.
Ewing, Donald Jackson, "Agricultural Agent to the Indians," (*Agricultural History*, XXXI, April 1957), p. 6.
Regarding the Meskwaki and Sac in the Black Hawk War:
Black Hawk, *Life of Black Hawk: Ma-ka-tai-me-she-kia-kiak*, Antoine Le Claire, translator (State Historical Society of Iowa, Iowa City, IA, 1932), p. 3.
Brown, Richard Frank, *A Social History of the Mesquakie Indians, 1800–1963* (Retrospective Theses and Dissertations, 1964, http://lib.dr.iastate.edu/rtd/10), p. 23.
Regarding the 1832 Treaty:
Aldrich, Charles, "The Acquisition of Iowa Lands from the Indians," (*Annals of Iowa*, 3rd Series, VII, January 1906), p. 286.
Regarding Thomas Forsythe's quote:
Blair, Emma Helen, *The Indian Tribes of the Upper Mississippi Valley and Region of the Great Lakes* (The Arthur H. Clark Company, Cleveland, OH, 1912), Vol. II, p. 236.
Regarding the quote from Chief Wapello when refusing to be relocated to Minnesota:
Grimes, James W., "Sac and Fox Council of 1841" (*Annals of Iowa*, July 1920), pp. 321–31.
Regarding the use of guns by the Indians:
Brown, Richard Frank, *A Social History of the Mesquakie Indians, 1800–1963* (Retrospective Theses and Dissertations, 1964, http://lib.dr.iastate.edu/rtd/10), pp. 38–40.
Regarding the Meskwaki agreeing to leave Iowa
Fulton, Ambrose Cowperthwaite, *A Life's Voyage*, 1898.
"The Sac and Fox Indians and the Treaty of 1842." *Iowa Journal of History and Politics*, Vol. 10, 1912.
Regarding the Indians returning to Iowa:
Brown, Richard Frank, *A Social History of the Mesquakie Indians, 1800–1963* (Retrospective Theses and Dissertations, 1964, Iowa State University Digital Repository. http://lib.dr.iastate.edu/rtd/10), pp. 52, 54–56.
Buffalo, Jonathan, *Meskwaki: A Brief History* (Meskwaki Nation Historical Preservation Department, Tama, IA, revised 2013).
Gearing, Fred, et al., *Documentary History of the Fox Project, 1948–1959: A Program in Action Anthropology* (Chicago: University of Chicago Press, 1960), pp. 208–209.
Palmer, John, *South Bend: Crossroads of Commerce* (Arcadia Publishing, 2003).

CHAPTER 18
Regarding how claims were marked:
Moeller, Hubert and Hugh, *Our Iowa, Its Beginnings and Growth,*

(Newson and Company, New York and Chicago, 1938), p. 129.
Regarding the winter of 1846:
Andrews, L. F., *Pioneers of Polk County, Iowa*, Vol. I (Baker-Trisher Company, Des Moines, IA, 1908), p. 182.
Regarding the description of the Jordan cabin:
Brigham, Johnson, *Iowa, Its History and its Foremost Citizens*, Vol. I (S. J. Clarke Publishing Co., Chicago, IL, 1916), p. 170.
Regarding the descriptions of a pioneer cabin:
Burlend, Edward and Rebecca, *A True Picture of Emigration* (University of Nebraska Press, Lincoln and London, 1987), pp. 47–50.
Note: Cellars were often dug to protect food, especially meat, from wild animals. It was impossible for the animals who had broken into the cabin to get through the trap door leading to the cellar.

CHAPTER 19
Regarding raising cattle and hogs:
Parker, George F., *Iowa: Pioneer Foundations*, Vols. I and II (Iowa State Historical Society, Iowa City, IA, 1940).
Regarding planting corn and harvesting hay:
Moeller, Hubert and Hugh, *Our Iowa, Its Beginnings and Growth* (Newson and Company, New York and Chicago, 1938), pp. 130, 133.
Regarding walleye:
Hammer, Ilda M., *The Book of Des Moines* (Board of Education, Des Moines, IA, 1947), p. 55.
Regarding planting the garden:
Faragher, John, M., *Women and Men on the Overland Trail* (Yale University Press, New Haven and London, 1979), pp. 52–53.
Regarding tobacco:
Burlend, Rebecca and Edward, *A True Picture of Emigration* (University of Nebraska Press, Lincoln and London, 1987), p. 95.
Regarding collecting plants for the garden:
Riley, Glenda, *Frontierswomen: The Iowa Experience* (Iowa State University Press, Ames, IA, 1981), p. 59.

CHAPTER 20
Regarding the 'coon story:
Andrews, L. F., *Pioneers of Polk County, Iowa*, Vol. I (Baker-Trisher Co., Des Moines, IA, 1908), the biography of James Jordan.
Union Historical Company, *The History of Polk County, Iowa* (Birdsall and Williams Company, Des Moines, IA, 1880), the biography of James Jordan.
Regarding the streets in early Fort Des Moines:
Hastie, Eugene N., *High Points of Iowa History* (Perry, IA, 1966), pp. 179–180.
Regarding the claims problems:
Hammer, Ilda M., *The Book of Des Moines* (Board of Education, Des Moines, IA, 1947), pp. 57–58.
Hussey, Tacitus, *Beginnings: Reminiscences of Early Des Moines*, (American Lithography and Printing Company, 1919).

CHAPTER 21
Regarding the quote of James Finley:
Scott, Donald, *Queens College/City University of New York* (National Humanities Center).
Regarding the 49er's traveling through Des Moines:
Hastie, Eugene N., *High Points of Iowa History* (Perry, IA, 1966), pp. 166, 301.
Regarding Ockerman School:
Union Historical Company, *The History of Polk County, Iowa* (Birdsall and Williams Company, Des Moines, IA, 1880).

Regarding the location of various school buildings:
Andrews, L. F., *Pioneers of Polk County, Iowa*, Vol. I (Baker-Trisher Co., Des Moines, IA, 1908).
McFadden, Bonnie, *Senator James C. Jordan* (West Des Moines Historical Society, 1981).
Regarding the description of the schools:
Moeller, Hubert and Hugh, *Our Iowa, Its Beginnings and Growth* (Newson and Company, New York and Chicago, 1938), pp. 137–138.
Parker, George F., *Iowa Pioneer Foundations*, Vols. I and II (Iowa State Historical Society, Iowa City, IA, 1940).
Riley, Glenda, *Frontierswomen: The Iowa Experience* (Iowa State University Press, Ames, IA, 1981), pp. 138, 139.

CHAPTER 22
Regarding itinerant preachers:
Andrews, L. F., *Pioneers of Polk County, Iowa*, Vol. I (Baker-Trisher Company, Des Moines, IA, 1908), p. 186.
Dixon, J. M., *Centennial History of Polk County, Iowa* (Polk County Board of Supervisors State Register, Des Moines, IA, 1876), found under the James Jordan Biography.
Regarding Methodism:
Sage, Leland L., *A History of Iowa* (Iowa State University Press, Ames, IA, 1974), pp. 54–55.
Regarding a description of services in the home and camp meetings:
Burlend, Rebecca and Edward, *A True Picture of Emigration* (University of Nebraska Press, Lincoln and London, 1987), pp. 144–147.
Faragher, John M., *Women and Men on the Overland Trail* (Yale University Press, New Haven and London, 1979), pp. 119–120.
Petersen, William J., *The Story of Iowa, The Progress of an American State* (Lewis Historical Publishing Co., Inc., New York, NY, 1952), p. 367.
Regarding the puritanical lifestyle of the settlers:
Parker, George F., *Iowa Pioneer Foundations*, Vols. I and II (Iowa State Historical Society, Iowa City, IA, 1940).
Regarding James Jordan's support of education and religion:
Andrews, L. F., *Pioneers of Polk County, Iowa*, Vol. I (Baker-Trisher Company, Des Moines, IA, 1908), p. 182.
Regarding the First Methodist Church in Des Moines:
Hussey, Tacitus, *Beginnings: Reminiscences of Early Des Moines* (American Lithography and Printing Company, 1919), pp. 62, 77.
Simbro, William, *Des Moines Register*, Monday, April 3, 1995, Vol. 146, No. 242, pp. 1, 2.

CHAPTER 23
Note: Information about the construction and design of the part of the house that was built in the early 1850s was obtained by the author during the 1990s from Bill Wagner, historical architect.

CHAPTER 24
Regarding the land offices and streets of Des Moines:
Hammer, Ilda M., *The Book of Des Moines* (Board of Education, Des Moines, IA, 1947), pp. 59, 75.
Regarding information and description of early Des Moines:
Perkins, Arozina, 1851 letter in "Teaching in Fort Des Moines, Iowa: November 13, 1850, to March 21, 1851." In *Women Teachers on the Frontier*, edited by P. W. Kaufman (Yale University Press, New Haven, CT, 1984) pp. 126–143.
Turrill, H. B., *Historical Reminiscences of the City of Des Moines* (Redhead & Dawson, Des Moines, IA, 1857), pp. 22, 87.
Regarding how the Methodist Church got its bell:

Hussey, Tacitus, *Beginnings: Reminiscences of Early Des Moines* (American Lithography and Printing Company, 1919).

Regarding the election of James C. Jordan to the Iowa Senate and the moving of the capital to Des Moines:

Andrews, L. F., *Pioneers of Polk County, Iowa*, Vol. I (Baker-Trisher Company, Des Moines, IA, 1908), pp. 183–184.

Moeller, Hubert and Hugh, *Our Iowa, Its Beginnings and Growth* (Newson and Company, New York and Chicago, 1938), p. 191.

Regarding the election of Jordan to the Senate, the moving of the capital to Des Moines, and the vignette of Dr. Hull:

Brigham, Johnson, *Iowa, Its History and its Foremost Citizens*, Vol. I (S. J. Clarke Publishing Company, Chicago, IL, 1916), pp. 239, 250, 254.

Note: The Iowa counties Senator Jordan represented during the fifth assembly were Jasper, Polk, Dallas, Guthrie, Greene, Boone, Story, Marshall, Hardin, Risley, Yell, Fox, Pocahontas, Humboldt, Kossuth, Palo Alto, Emmet, Bancroft, Winnebago, and Worth. The Iowa counties Senator Jordan represented during the sixth assembly were Polk, Dallas, and Guthrie.

CHAPTER 25
Regarding the pioneer woman's job description, food preservation, childbearing, and roles as doctors, etc.

Note: Many of these quotes were direct excerpts but transposed as if Melinda Jordan were doing them.

Faragher, John M., *Women and Men on the Overland Trail* (Yale University Press, New Haven and London, 1979), pp. 52, 58.

Riley, Glenda, *Frontierswomen: The Iowa Experience* (Iowa State University Press, Ames, IA, 1981), pp. 56–61, 75, 77.

Regarding the cause of Melinda's death:
Interviews with many Jordan descendants from 1986 to 2016.

Regarding Melinda's eulogy:
Brigham, Johnson, *Des Moines: The Pioneer of Municipal Progress and Reform of the Middle West, and the History of Polk County, Iowa*, Vols. I and II (S. J. Clarke Publishing Company, Chicago, 1911), p. 442.

CHAPTER 26
Regarding the stories about James and Cynthia's courtship and marriage remembered in the Jordan family:

Conversations with many family members in the 1990s.

Herda, Gertrude G., *My Jordan Family*, 1223 Cleveland Blvd., Caldwell, ID, June 1979.

CHAPTER 27
Regarding the Iowa Constitutional Convention to move the capitol to Des Moines:

Andrews, L. F., *Pioneers of Polk County, Iowa*, Vol. I (Baker-Trisher Co., Des Moines, IA, 1908), pp. 183–184.

Regarding the location of the capitol building on the east side of the river:

Wagner, William J., F.A.I.A., *Sixty Sketches of Iowa's Past and Present*, (Brown and Wagner, West Des Moines, IA, 1967), p. 108.

Regarding the constitutional convention, moving the capital to Des Moines, the two stories about the actual move, and "The Capital's Inaccessibility in Midwinter:"

Brigham, Johnson, *Iowa, Its History and Its Foremost Citizens*, Vol. I (S. J. Clarke Publishing Co., Chicago, IL, 1916), pp. 255–256, 267–268.

Petersen, William J., *The Story of Iowa: The Progress of an American State*, Vol. I (Lewis Historical Publishing Company, New York, NY, 1952), pp. 399–400.

Regarding the $100,000 contribution to Lee County and the Des Moines Valley Railroad:

Hussey, Tacitus, *Beginnings: Reminiscences of Early Des Moines* (American Lithography and Printing Company, 1919), pp. 164–166.

Portrait and Biographical Album of Polk County, Iowa, James Jordan (Chapman Brothers, 1895, Lake City Publishing Co., 1890), pp. 169–171.

CHAPTER 28
Regarding the legislation around the temperance issue:

Hastie, Eugene N., *High Points of Iowa History* (Perry, IA, 1966), pp. 211–212.

Wiggins, David, The Rise of the Allens: Two Soldiers and the Master of Terrace Hill (Historical-Midwest Books, Mt. Horeb, WI).

Regarding the decisions about the blacks in the Iowa Constitutional Convention of 1857:

Cross, Steven C., Secretary of the Senate, Iowa General Assembly, 1975–1978, "The Drafting of Iowa's Constitution," http://publications.iowa.gov/135/1/history/7-6.html.

Regarding the stories about banking in Des Moines in the 1840s and 1850s and the story about the express company:

Hussey, Tacitus, *Beginnings: Reminiscences of Early Des Moines* (American Lithography and Printing Company, Des Moines, IA, 1919), pp. 159–160.

Regarding the story about the merchant in St. Louis, the merchant who bought $100,000 worth of goods, the numbers of banks in Des Moines and Iowa, and general information about banking and B. F. Allen:

Goettsch, Scherrie and Steve Weinburg, *Terrace Hill: The Story of a House and the People Who Touched It* (Wallace Homestead Company, Des Moines, IA, 1978), pp. 10–12.

Regarding the amount of daily land sales in Des Moines:

Hammer, Ilda M., *The Book of Des Moines* (Board of Education, Des Moines, IA, 1947), p. 58.

Regarding the background on B. F. Allen and his banking practice:

Alex, Tom, "Founding Father who had it all—and lost it," *Des Moines Register*, May 30, 1995.

Regarding Grimes' role in banking and how the banks were legally established:

Sage, Leland L., *A History of Iowa* (Iowa State University Press, Ames, IA, 1974), p. 126, 135.

Regarding the Jordan quote, "financial cost is clear:"

Brigham, Johnson, *Iowa, Its History and its Foremost Citizens*, Vol. I (S. J. Clarke Publishing Co., Chicago, IL, 1916), p. 441.

Regarding Jordan's entwinement with the Des Moines business community and the "Missouri Bill" story:

Andrews, L. F., *Pioneers of Polk County, Iowa*, Vol. I (Baker-Trisher Co., Des Moines, IA, 1908), pp. 185, 186.

CHAPTER 29
Regading the Grimes election:

Petersen, William J., *The Story of Iowa: The Progress of an American State*, Vol. I (Lewis Historical Publishing Company, New York, NY, 1952), p. 391.

Regarding the development of the Republican Party in Iowa and Wisconsin, the election of Samuel Kirkwood, the domination of Republicans in Iowa politics, and descriptions of Tabor, Iowa:

Moeller, Hubert and Hugh, *Our Iowa, Its Beginnings and Growth* (Newson and Company, New York and Chicago, 1938), pp. 204, 223–224, 330, 217.

Regarding a description of Samuel Kirkwood's and James Grimes' background and all of the political background:

Sage, Leland L., *A History of Iowa* (Iowa State University Press, Ames, IA, 1974), pp. 86–89, and Chapter 7.

Regarding Jordan's relationship with Iowa politicians:
Andrews, L. F., *Pioneers of Polk County, Iowa*, Vol. I (Baker-Trisher Company, Des Moines, IA, 1908), p. 182.
Brigham, Johnson, *Des Moines: The Pioneer of Municipal Progress and Reform of the Middle West, and the History of Polk County, Iowa*, Vols. I and II (S. J. Clarke Publishing Company, Chicago, 1911).
Brigham, Johnson, *Iowa, Its History and its Foremost Citizens*, Vol. I (S. J. Clarke Publishing Company, Chicago, IL, 1916), section about James C. Jordan.
Porter, Will, *Iowa Annals of Polk County and the City of Des Moines* (George A. Miller Printing Company, Des Moines, IA, 1898), section about James C. Jordan.
Portrait and Biographical Album of Polk County, Iowa, James Jordan (Chapman Brothers, 1895, Lake City Publishing Co., 1890), pp. 169–171

Regarding the relationship of Republicans to Methodists:
Murray, John J., *The Heritage of the Middle West* (University of Oklahoma Press, Norman, OK, 1958), p. 159.
Parker, George F., *Iowa Pioneer Foundations*, Vols. I and II (Iowa State Historical Society, Iowa City, IA, 1940), p. 401.

Regarding James Jordan as a Polk County supervisor:
Portrait and Biographical Album of Polk County, Iowa, James Jordan (Chapman Brothers, 1895, Lake City Publishing Co., 1890), p. 171.

CHAPTER 30
Regarding Underground Railroad locations, associated religious groups, and information on John Brown:
Sage, Leland L., *A History of Iowa* (Iowa State University Press, Ames, IA, 1974), pp. 139–140.
Note: Regarding Ishmael and Mariam (Marmon) Lee's involvement in the URR in Polk County, Iowa, please see the Lois Craig Collection at the State Archives in Des Moines, Iowa. When the Lees were living in Michigan, Ishmael Lee and several other white abolitionists were sued in 1847 by Kentucky slave owners for harboring escaping slaves. This resulted in an action being brought against them in 1850 for violating the Fugitive Slave Act. They lost their Michigan farm because of the steep legal fees needed to defend their case. They moved to Iowa in 1852 where they settled in a Quaker community in Warren County. There they were known to have signed an antislavery petition. —Debian Marty, Associate Professor, California State University, Monterey Bay, CA.

Regarding John Brown's biographical information and Harper's Ferry:
Moeller, Hubert and Hugh, *Our Iowa, Its Beginnings and Growth* (Newson and Company, New York and Chicago, 1938), pp. 216–219.
Sanborn, Franklin Benjamin, editor, *The Life and Letters of John Brown: Liberator of Kansas, and Martyr of Virginia* (Roberts Brothers, Boston, MA, 1891), p. 482.
St. John's Congregational Church, 45 Hancock Street, Springfield, MA, web brochure, http://sjkb.org.

Regarding the Barclay Coppoc vignette:
Petersen, William J., *The Story of Iowa: The Progress of an American State*, Vol. I (Lewis Historical Publishing Company, New York, NY, 1952), p. 405.

Regarding visits by John Brown to the Jordan House:
Andrews, L. F., *Pioneers of Polk County, Iowa*, Vol. I, (Baker-Trisher Company, Des Moines, IA, 1908), p. 184.
Portrait and Biographical Album of Polk County, Iowa, James Jordan (Chapman Brothers, 1895, Lake City Publishing Co., 1890), p. 170.

Regarding Isaac Brandt, John Teesdale, Reverend Demas Robinson, and Jeremiah Anderson:
The Union Historical Company, *History of Polk County, Iowa, 1880*, (Birdsall, Williams and Company, 1880), pp. 347, 691, 708, 744, 774–776.

Regarding information about Isaac Brandt:
Brigham, Johnson, *Des Moines: The Pioneer of Municipal Progress and Reform of the Middle West, and the History of Polk County, Iowa*, Vols. I and II (S. J. Clarke Publishing Company, Chicago, IL, 1911), p. 1231.
Brigham, Johnson, *Iowa, Its History and its Foremost Citizens*, Vol. I (S. J. Clarke Publishing Company, Chicago, IL, 1916), pp. 442–443.
Hammer, Ilda M., *The Book of Des Moines*, (Board of Education, Des Moines, IA, 1947), pp. 79–80.

Regarding slaves escaping in western Iowa and Nebraska City:
Hastie, Eugene N., *High Points of Iowa History* (Perry, IA, 1966), pp. 138–140.

Regarding information on the Underground Railroad, John Brown's letter about the Kansas slave raid, visits of John Brown to the Jordan House, the Kansas War, the vignette about getting the slaves out of Iowa City, and information on Harper's Ferry:
Gue, Benjamin F., *History of Iowa from the Earliest Times to the Beginning of the Twentieth Century*, Vol. I, "The Pioneer Period" (The Century History Company, New York, NY, 1903), Chapter 29, pp. 373–383.
Hastie, Eugene N., *High Points of Iowa History* (Perry, IA, 1966), p.141.
Jordan Nancy Alice, Jordan descendant, story related at the Jordan Family Reunion in West Des Moines, Iowa, in 2016.
Katz, William L., *The Black West* (Doubleday and Company, Inc., Garden City, NY, 1971), pp. 106–110.
Linton, Calvin D., Ph.D., *The Bicentennial Almanac* (Thomas Nelson, Inc., Nashville, TN and New York, NY, 1975), pp. 155–156.

Regarding information on Harper's Ferry, young James Jordan being a slave catcher, and the Harper's Ferry vignette:
Brigham, Johnson, *Iowa, Its History and its Foremost Citizens*, Vol. I (S. J. Clarke Publishing Company, Chicago, IL, 1916), pp. 268, 269, 442.
Insert: James Jordan, A Friend to John Brown
History of Polk County, Iowa (The Union Historical Company, printed by Mills and Company, Des Moines, IA, 1880).

CHAPTER 31
Regarding the descriptions of Des Moines during the Civil War and Camp Burnside:
"Civil War left its Mark on City," *Des Moines Register*, March 31, 1993.

Regarding Des Moines through the years:
Brigham, Johnson, *History of Des Moines and Polk County* (S. J. Clarke Publishing Company, Chicago, IL, 1911), no direct quotes, just general information.
Dixon, J. M., *Centennial History of Polk County, Iowa* (Des Moines: State Register, print, 1876), no direct quotes, just general information.

Regarding drafting of soldiers and support of soldiers on the front:
Hammer, Ilda M., *The Book of Des Moines* (Board of Education, Des Moines, IA, 1947), p. 83.

Regarding the siege of Vicksburg:
Moeller, Hubert and Hugh, *Our Iowa, Its Beginnings and Growth* (Newson and Company, New York and Chicago, 1938), p. 231.
Sage, Leland L., *A History of Iowa* (Iowa State University Press, Ames, IA, 1974), pp. 153–155.

Regarding the result of the Vicksburg victory and medicine during the Civil War:

Cooke, Alistair, *Alistair Cooke's America* (Alfred A. Knopf, New York, NY, 1973), pp. 203–204.
Regarding the specific battles fought by the Twenty-third Iowa Infantry:
Gue, Benjamin F., *History of Iowa from the Earliest Times to the Beginning of the Twentieth Century*, Vol. II, "The Civil War" (The Century History Company, New York, NY, 1903) pp. 265–269, 368.
Regarding the letters from Henry Jordan and the "long-john story:"
Enjue, Nancy, late great-granddaughter of James C. Jordan, Gurnee, Illinois.

CHAPTER 32
Regarding Iowa's response to the Civil War:
Parker, George F., *Iowa Pioneer Foundations*, Vols. I and II (Iowa State Historical Society, Iowa City, IA, 1940).
Regarding the story about the freed slaves who came to Des Moines:
Hussey, Tacitus, *Beginnings: Reminiscences of Early Des Moines* (American Lithography and Printing Company, Des Moines, IA, 1919), p. 75.
Regarding the story about the freed slaves who came to Jordan House:
Interviews with family members.

CHAPTER 33
Note: The Des Moines Fort Dodge Railroad Company was later absorbed by the Milwaukee Road. The Mississippi and Missouri Railroad later became part of the Rock Island Line.
Regarding the railroad coming to Des Moines:
Baker, Vicki, *Valley Junction's Beginnings* (West Des Moines Historical Society, West Des Moines, IA, 1989).
Brigham, Johnson, *Iowa, Its History and its Foremost Citizens*, Vol. I (S. J. Clarke Publishing Company, Chicago, IL, 1916), p. 443.
Hammer, Ilda M., *The Book of Des Moines* (Board of Education, Des Moines, IA, 1947), pp. 75, 83.
Hussey, Tacitus, *Beginnings: Reminiscences of Early Des Moines* (American Lithography and Printing Company, Des Moines, IA, 1919), Chapter XI.
McFadden, Bonnie, *Senator James C. Jordan* (West Des Moines Historical Society, West Des Moines, IA, 1981).
Sage, Leland L., *A History of Iowa* (Iowa State University Press, Ames, IA, 1974), pp. 108–115.
Regarding the platting of the railroad junction:
McFadden, Bonnie, *Senator James C. Jordan* (West Des Moines Historical Society, West Des Moines, IA, 1981).
Insert: Crossing the Mississippi River
Donovan, Frank P., *Iowa Railroads* (University of Iowa Press, 2000), pp. 171–173.

CHAPTER 34
Regarding the beginning of Equitable of Iowa Insurance Company:
Goettsch, Scherrie and Steve Weinburg, *Terrace Hill: The Story of a House and the People Who Touched It* (Wallace Homestead Company, Des Moines, IA, 1978), pp. 22–23.
Pease, George S., *Patriarch of the Prairie; The Story of Equitable of Iowa, 1867–1967* (Appleton-Century-Crofts, New York, 1967), p. 13.
Regarding George Hanawalt:
Portrait and Biographical Album of Polk County, Iowa (Lake City Publishing Company, Chicago, IL, 1890), pp. 181–182.

CHAPTER 35
Regarding ranging cattle on the open range:
Hastie, Eugene N., *High Points of Iowa History* (Perry, IA, 1966), p. 58.
Portrait and Biographical Album of Polk County, Iowa, James Jordan (Chapman Brothers, 1895, Lake City Publishing Co., 1890), pp. 169–171.
Regarding Longhorn cattle:
Cooke, Alistair, *Allstair Cooke's America* (Alfred A. Knopf, New York, NY, 1973), pp. 229–233.
Regarding Shorthorn cattle:
Allen, Lewis F., *The American Short-Horn Herd Book*, Vol. XXIV (American Short-Horn Breeders' Association, Chicago, IL, February 1883), pp. 18322, 18524, 18526, 18527, 18755, 18804.
Sanders, Alvin H., *Red, white, and roan; stories relating to the origin of the shorthorn breed of cattle in Great Britain* (Chicago, American Shorthorn Breeders' Association, 1936).
Wilholm, Dr. Richard, a specialist in genetics at Iowa State University, Ames, IA.

CHAPTER 36
Regarding the Terrace Hill anniversary party:
Goettsch, Scherrie and Steve Weinburg, *Terrace Hill: The Story of a House and the People Who Touched It* (Wallace Homestead Company, Des Moines, IA, 1978), pp. 22–23, 25.
Regarding the architecture and accoutrement of the renovated house:
Wagner, Bill, Iowa historical architect.
Regarding the Haviland china pattern:
Evjue, Nancy, visit to Nancy's house in Gurnee, Illinois. Nancy was the Jordan descendant who kept the china pattern, inherited through her relative Henry Jordan, and enlarged the collection.
Regarding Victorian wedding customs:
Cooke, Maud C., *Social Etiquette, or Manners and Customs of Polite Society* (H. J. Smith and Simon Publishing Company, Chicago, IL, 1896), pp. 143–160.

CHAPTER 37
Note: The Jordan Schoolhouse was used until the 1940s. In the early 1980s, the building was relocated to Nineteenth Street in West Des Moines and was converted to a residence.
Regarding the story about the piano in the front parlor:
Berkley, Pat Jordan and her father Bob Jordan, Jordan descendants.
Regarding information about Jordan Cemetery:
Kraus, Carroll, "West Des Moines May Inherit Historic Cemetery," *Des Moines Register*, date unknown.
McLain, Mary, "Pioneer Cemetery Still in Use," *West Des Moines Express*, September 12, 1974, pp. 10–11.
Treeshakers of Valley Junction, "Jordan Cemetery, West Des Moines, Iowa" (Iowa Genealogical Society, Des Moines, IA, 1990), pp. 1–2.

CHAPTER 38
Regarding information about social customs of the Victorian era:
Cooke, Maud C., *Social Etiquette, or Manners and Customs of Polite Society* (H. J. Smith and Simon Publishing Company, Chicago, IL, 1896), p. 51107.
Godey's Lady's Book and Magazine (Philadelphia, PA, 1866, January–December issues).
Regarding the amount of land and livestock Jordan owned:
Herda, Gertrude G., *My Jordan Family*, 1223 Cleveland Blvd., Caldwell, ID, June 1979.

Regarding Shorthorn Cattle:
Sanders, Alvin H., *Red, white, and roan; stories relating to the origin of the shorthorn breed of cattle in Great Britain* (Chicago, American Shorthorn Breeders' Association, 1936).
Regarding the growth Des Moines and the Iowa State Fair:
Hammer, Ilda M., *The Book of Des Moines* (Board of Education, Des Moines, IA, 1947), pp. 87, 92.
Regarding information on Martin Flynn:
Banger, Linda, "Meet me on the Corner, N.W. 111th and Hickman," *Des Moines Register*, January 19, 1997.

CHAPTER 39
Note: The Iowa College of Physicians and Surgeons, founded in 1882, was absorbed into Drake University in 1886.
Regarding the character sketches of George Hanawalt:
Brigham, Johnson, *Prominent Iowans, Iowa: Its History and its Foremost Citizens* (Pioneer Publishing Company, Chicago, IL, 1916), pp. 73–75.
Polk County Medical Society, *Polk County Medical Bulletin*, Vol. 23, January 1952, p. 23–24.
Porter, William, *Annals of Polk County, Iowa, and City of Des Moines* (Geo. A. Miller Printing Company, Des Moines, IA, 1898), p. 1034.
Portrait and Biographical Album of Polk County, Iowa, James Jordan (Chapman Brothers, 1895, Lake City Publishing Co., 1890), pp. 181, 182.
Regarding the train crash:
Mills, George, "1877 Train Crash Worst in Des Moines History," *Des Moines Register*, September 28, 1988.
Regarding the establishment of the hospitals in Des Moines:
Bjornstad, Edith M., *Wings in Waiting, A History of Iowa Methodist Hospital 1901–1951* (Des Moines Register and Tribune Company, Des Moines, IA, 1952), p. 5.
Greiner, Loretta, "Sister Mary S. McMahon," *Those Who Come to Bless, 100 Years of Healing, Mercy Hospital, 1893–1993, Des Moines, Iowa* (Watt/Peterson, Inc., Plymouth, MN), pp. 26–29.
Iowa State Medical Society, *One Hundred Years of Iowa Medicine, Commemorating the Centenary of the Iowa State Medical Society, 1850–1950* (Athens Press, Iowa City, IA, 1950), p. 383.
Petersen, William J., *The Story of Iowa: The Progress of an American State*, Vol. II (Lewis Historical Publishing Company, New York, NY, 1952), p. 793.
Polk County Medical Society, *History of Medicine of Polk County*, No. 16.

CHAPTER 40
Regarding information about F. M. Hubbell:
Goettsch, Scherrie and Steve Weinburg, *Terrace Hill: The Story of a House and the People Who Touched It* (Wallace Homestead Company, Des Moines, IA, 1978), pp. 61–62.
Regarding the growth of Valley Junction and the Jordan will:
McFadden, Bonnie, *Senator James C. Jordan* (West Des Moines Historical Society, 1981).

CHAPTER 41
Note: Ella Jordan married into the Cook family. Part of their farm is the site of Resthaven Cemetery on Ashworth Road in West Des Moines.
Regarding building Jordan Church:
Portrait and Biographical Album of Polk County, Iowa (Lake City Publishing Company, Chicago, IL, 1890), pp. 169–171.
Regarding the disposition of Jordan's estate:
Herda, Gertrude G., *My Jordan Family*, 1223 Cleveland Blvd., Caldwell, ID, June 1979.
Last Will and Testament of James Jordan.
Regarding James Jordan's death:
Andrews, L. F., *Pioneers of Polk County, Iowa*, Vol. I (Baker-Trisher Company, Des Moines, IA, 1908), p. 182.
Brigham, Johnson, *Iowa, Its History and its Foremost Citizens*, Vol. II (S. J. Clarke Publishing Company, Chicago, IL, 1916), Section on James Jordan.
Regarding James Jordan's obituary:
"James Cunningham Jordan Obituary," *Iowa Daily News*, March 2, 1891.
Regarding Jordan School, Ingersoll Park, and places on the west side of Des Moines:
McLaughlin, Lillian, "A D.M. Area Rich in History," *Des Moines Tribune*, December 21, 1978.

CHAPTER 42
Regarding the growth of Valley Junction:
Fredrickson, Terri and Aldo A. Past, *West Des Moines: From Railroads to Crossroads, 1893–1993* (Acme Printing, Des Moines, IA, 1993), pp. 16–40.
McFadden, Bonnie, *Senator James C. Jordan* (West Des Moines Historical Society, 1981).

CHAPTER 43
Herda, Gertrude G., *My Jordan Family*, 1223 Cleveland Blvd., Caldwell, ID, June 1979.
Last Will and Testament of James Jordan.
Many interviews with descendants of James Jordan from 1985 to 2016. Robert Jordan, a West Des Moines lawyer and great-grandson of James Jordan was especially helpful.
McFadden, Bonnie, *Senator James C. Jordan* (West Des Moines Historical Society, 1981).

CHAPTER 44
Herda, Gertrude G., *My Jordan Family*, 1223 Cleveland Blvd., Caldwell, ID, June 1979.
Last Will and Testament of James Jordan.
Many interviews with descendants of James Jordan from 1985 to 2016. Robert Jordan, a West Des Moines lawyer and great-grandson of James Jordan, was especially helpful. Nancy Enjue, a descendant of Henry Jordan, collected antique china and expanded her one setting into an entire set, which she proudly displayed in her home, along with George Hanawalt's desk.
McFadden, Bonnie, *Senator James C. Jordan* (West Des Moines Historical Society, 1981).
Note: Thanks to Gary Gately for providing explanations, insight, and interpretation of the last will and testament, the execution of the Jordan estate, and the final business affairs of James Jordan.

CHAPTER 45
Herda, Gertrude G., *My Jordan Family*, 1223 Cleveland Blvd., Caldwell, ID, June 1979.
McFadden, Bonnie, *Senator James C. Jordan* (West Des Moines Historical Society, 1981).
The Jordan Creek Town Center website (www.jordancreektowncenter.com).
The West Des Moines Historical Society website (www.wdmhs.org).
The West Des Moines, Iowa, website (www.wdm.iowa.gov).

INDEX

A

Abilene, Kansas, 163
abolitionism, 117, 126, 129, 140
Adams, Cyrus, 117
Adams, John Quincy, 52, 78, 117
Adams, John, 116, 117
Agency City, Iowa, 19, 70, 73, 76, 77, 82, 83, 158
Allegheny Mountains, 12, 19
Allen, Arathusa, 167
Allen, B. F., 123, 125, 158, 161, 167
Allen, Captain James, 70, 72, 73, 122
Allen, Richard, 41
American Anti-Slavery Society, 133
American Party ("Know-Nothing Party"), 128
American Shorthorn Breeders Association, 165
American System, 53, 78, 125
Anderson, Jeremiah G., 135, 141
antislavery movement, 35, 53, 100, 128, 130, 133, 136
Armagh County, Northern Ireland, 211
Asbury, Bishop Francis, 41
Ashworth, Abraham, 146
Ashworth, Charles, 192, 196
Atlantic, Iowa, 134
Augusta County, Virginia, 16, 17, 20, 23, 26, 27, 47, 211, 212
Ayrshire County, Scotland, 13

B

Babar, Cynthia Jordan, 58, 60, 68, 78
Babar, Jordan, 51, 60, 68, 78, 212
Baker, Vicki, 7, 208
Baker, William, 161
Baltimore, Maryland, 35
Baptists, 32, 33, 38, 41
barbed wire fencing, 164
Barnum, P. T., 181–183
Battle of Black River Bridge, 147
Battle of Lake Erie, 35
Battle of New Orleans, 35
Battle of Point Pleasant, Virginia, 25
Battle of Port Gibson, 147
Bausman, J. B., 161
Beach, Major John, 71, 77, 83
Bennett School, 209
Bennett, Pressley, 163
Benton, Thomas Hart, 102
Berkley, Pat Jordan, 209, 216
Berrien County, Michigan, 53, 59, 60, 62, 212, 213
Bible, 40, 96-99, 111, 204
Big Yough, Virginia, 25
Bird School, Des Moines, Iowa, 97
Bird, Anna P., 97, 106
Bird, Reverend Thompson, 40, 97, 161, 162
Black Din, 137
Black Hawk Purchase, 81
Black Hawk War, 53, 80, 81, 83
Bleeding Kansas, 126, 140, 143
Blue Sulphur Springs, Virginia, 51, 58
Bonaparte, Iowa, 158
Bowen, Dr. Jesse, 120, 143
Boyd, Thomas, 161
Brandt, Isaac, 135, 138, 140
British Band, 80
British Durham Cattle, 89
Brooklyn, Iowa, 107
Brotherhood of Early Settlers, 161
Brown, John "Ossawatomie," 139
Brown, John, 126, 127, 132, 135, 136, 138–144
Brown's Band, 141
Bryan, Theophilus, 109
Buchanan, Michigan, 59, 60
Bucks County, Pennsylvania, 13, 14
Buena Vista, Iowa, 158
Burlington, Iowa, 92, 118, 132, 156, 177
Butler, David, 84
Butler, H. S., 186
Butler, Isaac, 84
Butler, Phillip, 84

C

Calhoun, John C., 35
California Gold Rush, 94, 115
California, 8, 61, 67, 86, 100, 114, 115, 126, 190
Callanan College, 184
Camp Burnside, East Des Moines, Iowa, 146
camp meetings, 99
Campbell, Dr., 83
Canada—Underground Railroad, 50, 117, 133, 134, 139, 141, 143
Canandaigua, Yates County, New York, 116, 213, 214
Cannon, Joseph, 60, 190, 212
Cannon, Phoebe Jordan, 60
Capitol Place, Iowa, 174
Carey Baptist Mission, Niles, Michigan, 53
Carlisle, Iowa, 73, 86, 92, 103
Carlock, David, 17, 18
Carlock, Fred, 17, 18
Carr, General, 146
Carroll County, Missouri, 65
Casady, Phineas, 9, 107, 158, 161, 186
Casady, Simon, 186, 190
Cass County, Michigan, 134
Cass County, Nebraska, 190, 212
Cass, Governor Lewis, 53
Catholics, 13, 41, 196
Cayuse Tribe, 61
Cedar Rapids, Iowa, 177
Central Presbyterian Church, 150
Chariton County, Missouri, 65
Charles II, King of England, 13
Cheat River Valley, 24, 25
Chesapeake Bay, 35
Chicago and Rock Island Railroad, 155, 156, 159
Chicago, Illinois, 163
Chicago, Rock Island and Pacific Railroad, 159
Chickasaw Tribe, 33
Chief Black Hawk, 80
Chief Hardfish, 83
Chief Keokuk, 81, 83
Chief Ma me nwa ne ke, 84
Chief Poweshiek, 83
Chief Wapello, 81
Chillicothe, Ohio, 21
Chippewa-Ottawa Tribe, 84
Chisholm Trail, 163
Church of the Nazarene, 208
circuit riders in Iowa, 94, 98, 99, 103
Civil Bend (Percival), Iowa, 137
Civil War, 8, 9, 48, 50, 53, 65, 89, 90, 97, 123, 125, 127, 135, 139, 141, 143, 145–148, 149, 150, 154, 156, 158, 160, 162, 163, 164, 167, 169, 174, 176, 179, 180, 190, 200
Claims Club, Fort Des Moines, Iowa, 77, 86, 93
claims jumpers, 91
Clark, William Penn, 143
Clay County, Missouri, 64, 65, 86, 211, 212
Clay, Henry, 35, 53, 68, 78, 125, 133, 136, 213, 214
Clegg House, 192
Clegg Schoolhouse, 191
Cleveland, C. W., 161
Clinton, Iowa, 92, 134, 177
Clover Hills, Iowa, 174
Colfax, Iowa, 194
Colony of Virginia, 12, 27
Columbus, Texas, 148
Commerce, Iowa, 190, 198, 206
common schools, 36
Company E, Iowa Twenty-third Regiment Volunteer Infantry, 146
Compromise of 1850, 102, 126
Congregational Church, 132, 134, 138, 140
Congregationalists, 31, 132, 133, 134, 138, 139
Cook, Catherine, 191
Cook, Ella Jordan, 150, 171, 173, 175, 191, 198, 216
Cook, Emma, 191, 216
Cook, Fred, 191, 216
Cook, Grace, 200, 214
Cook, Jeheil S., 161, 191, 216
Cook, John P., 186
Cook, John, 191, 216
Coon Point, Fort Des Moines, Iowa, 71, 73, 135, 145
Cooper, Isaac, 161
Coppoc, Barclay, 143, 144
Coppoc, Edwin, 143, 144
Cottage Hospital, Des Moines, Iowa, 181–184
Council Bluffs, Iowa, 94, 121, 157, 159
Cowles, Charles, 59
Crawfordsville, Iowa, 129
Crocker, Mrs., 180
Cunningham Homestead, 19, 21–23
Cunningham Plantation, 22-24, 29, 44, 45, 47, 49, 211
Cunningham, Agnes Slater, 25, 211, 212
Cunningham, Agnes, 23, 28, 30, 36, 212
Cunningham, Elizabeth, 13, 14, 25
Cunningham, James, 16, 23, 30, 38, 44, 58
Cunningham, Jesse, 36, 212
Cunningham, John "Lord John," 12, 13, 15, 16, 21, 22, 25, 26
Cunningham, John Jr., 16, 19, 22, 25
Cunningham, Mary (daughter of "Lord John" and Mary Peterson Cunningham), 21, 25, 30, 212
Cunningham, Mary Jordan, 36, 58, 212
Cunningham, Mary Peterson, 21
Cunningham, Phebe Scott, 21, 22, 25, 211
Cunningham, Prudence Parsons, 24, 25, 29, 211
Cunningham, Rebecca Harness, 29
Cunningham, Robert, 16, 22, 24, 25, 29, 34, 48
Cunningham, Sally Van Meter, 26, 29, 211
Cunningham, Virginia, 34, 64
Cunningham, West Virginia, 17
Cunningham, William "Old," 12, 13, 14
Cunningham, William II "Irish Billy," 13, 26, 44, 46
Cunningham, William III, 29
Cunningham, William IV, 26, 29, 211

D

Dallas County, Iowa, 198, 213
Davies, Samuel, 32
Davis, John M., 84
DeFord, Martha A., 186
DeFord, William, 161
Delaware Tribe, 21
Democrat Party in Iowa, 108, 120, 128, 132
Denman, A. H., 192
Des Moines Golf and Country Club, 205
Des Moines River Improvement Land Grant, 157
Des Moines River Valley, 157
Des Moines River, Iowa, 71, 72, 76, 90, 92, 106, 110, 119, 140, 142, 145, 157–159, 180
Des Moines Valley Railroad 119, 158, 159, 185
Des Moines, Iowa, 6, 8, 9, 71, 77, 86, 89, 90, 92, 94, 100, 107, 108, 110, 112–114, 118–121, 123–125, 127, 129, 132–135, 138, 145, 146, 148–151, 154–162, 166, 167, 170, 171, 173, 174, 177–187, 190–195, 205–207, 213, 214
DeSoto, Iowa, 190, 198, 206, 207, 213, 214
Dodge, Augustus C., 108
Dolly Ridge, Virginia, 30
Douglass, Frederick, 133, 140
Dragoon Trace, 73, 78, 83
dragoon, 71, 73, 83, 107
Drake University Medical School, Des Moines, Iowa, 183
Dubuque, Iowa, 81, 92, 177, 183
Duchess County, New York, 17

E

Earlham, Iowa, 134, 138
East Des Moines, Iowa, 134, 182
Eddyville, Iowa, 158
Education of slaves in western Virginia, 150
Edwards, Jonathan, 31
Eiler, Eliza, 62, 213
Eiler, Jacob, 60, 62, 63, 213
Eiler, Margaret Jordan, 60, 62, 63, 190, 213
Eiler, Matilda, 62, 213
Ellston, Iowa, 83
Emancipation Proclamation, 150
emancipation—slavery, 133, 134, 150
Emerson, Ralph Waldo, 144
emigration, 67, 68
end of "The Range" in western Iowa, 164
Episcopalians, 32, 41
Equitable Life Insurance Company, 183
Equitable of Iowa, 160, 161
Evans, David, 17
Evjue, Nancy, 208
Ewing, George Washington, 71
Ewing, Washington George, 71

F

Fairfax, Lord, 13, 15, 16, 21, 26, 29
Fairfax, Thomas, 13
Fairfield, Iowa, 92
Farmington, Iowa, 158
Fayette County, Virginia, 36, 51, 212
Financial Panic of 1857, 145, 156
Finley, Reverend James B., 42, 94, 100
First Great Awakening, 31, 33, 133
First Methodist Church, Des Moines, Iowa, 91, 117, 191
Flood of 1851, 145

228 Pursuit of a Dream

Florida, 34, 35, 51, 126
Flynn, Martin, 163, 178
Fontanelle, Iowa, 134
Forest Home Seminary, Des Moines, Iowa, 97, 145, 148
Forsythe, Thomas, 82
Fort Des Moines No. 2, Iowa, 6, 71–73, 77
Fort Des Moines, Iowa, 6, 8, 70–73, 76–78, 83, 85, 86, 91–95, 97, 98, 103, 106–108, 110, 111, 118, 119, 122, 124, 135, 145, 157, 158, 163, 213
Fort Hall, Idaho, 61
Fort Leavenworth, Kansas, 70, 73, 83
Fort McHenry, Baltimore, Maryland, 35
Fort Pleasant, Virginia, 15, 20, 21, 26, 44–46
Fort Van Meter, Virginia, 15, 45
Fort Walla Walla, Washington, 61
Four Mile Creek, 120, 138, 181, 182
Fox Tribe, 77, 79–83
Fox Wars, 79
Frederick County, Virginia, 45
French and Indian War, 19–21, 23, 25–27, 34, 44
Fugitive Slave Law, 129

G

G.A.R. Crocker Post No. 12, 184
Galbraith, W. A., 161
game chickens, 34
Garrison, William Lloyd, 133
George Jordan Family Cemetery, Anderson County, Kentucky, 28
Georgia, 31, 33
German Redemptionists, 22, 31, 47
Germany Valley, Randolph County, Virginia, 18, 21, 22, 25, 30
Gill, George B., 141
Gilmore, Iowa, 198
Glasgow, Scotland, 40
Glebe House, Romney, Virginia, 45
Godey's Lady's Book, 112, 167–169, 171, 176
Gooch, Governor William, 19
Grabinski, Joyce, 208
Grand River, 83
Grant, General, 146
Great Awakening, 31–33, 38
Great Neck Proprietary, 26
Greenbrier County, Virginia, 18, 36–38, 51, 58, 212, 213
Greenfield, Iowa, 117
Greenwood Park, Iowa, 174, 205
Griffith, Captain Henry, 125
Griffith, Ms., 180
Griffiths, H. H., 161
Griffiths, J. M., 161
Grimes, US Senator/Governor James W., 9, 84, 108, 109, 110, 118, 119, 120, 124, 126, 127, 128, 129, 132, 136, 148
Grinnell, Iowa, 134, 136, 138, 142
Grinnell, Josiah, 132, 136, 138, 142

H

hack service to Valley Junction, 177
Haines, Mary Elizabeth, 144, 213
Hall, Towne, 86
Hampshire County, Virginia, 16, 21, 22, 29, 44, 45, 212
Hanawalt Public School, Des Moines, Iowa, 184
Hanawalt, Dr. George P., 162, 170, 171, 173, 174, 175, 177–184, 190–192, 197, 198, 201, 203–206, 214
Hanawalt, Emily Jordan, 162, 170, 171, 173–175, 177–179, 197, 198, 201, 204–206, 216
Hardy County, Virginia, 27, 44, 45, 47, 211
Harlan, US Senator James, 9, 108, 109, 110, 118, 129, 131, 148

Harness, George, 45
Harness, Jemima, 29, 211
Harness, Rebecca, 22, 25, 29, 211
Harper's Ferry, Virginia, 138, 141–144
Harrisburg, Texas, 148
Harrison County, Virginia, 18, 23, 27, 28, 36, 51, 212
Harrison, William Henry, 80
Hawkeye Investment Company, 186, 187, 196
Hays, John, 161
Hazlett, Albert, 141
head rent system, 17
Hempstead, Governor Stephen, 123
Henkel, Jost, 30
herefords, 164
Higgins, Lieutenant Robert, 45
hill farmers of the western Virginia highlands, 49
Hiner, Samuel, 95
Hiner's Grove, Polk County, Iowa, 76, 86, 95, 115
Hinkle (Henkle), Jost and Maria, 30
Hinkle, Captain Isaac, 25, 30
Hinkle, Mary Cunningham, 25, 30
Hitchcock House, East Nishnabotna River, Lewis, Iowa, 138
Hitchcock, George B., 138
Holland's Fort (Town Fort), Virginia, 19, 21
Homestead Acts, 102
Honeymoon Cottage, 198, 200, 205, 206
Horseshoe Bend, Virginia, 18, 24, 25
Howard County, Missouri, 65
Hoxie, B. T., 91
Hoxie, Melville, 91
Hoxie, Ruth, 91
Hoxie's cornfield story, 91
Hubbell, Frederick M., 9, 160, 161, 163, 178, 183, 187
Hull, Dr. Andrew Y., 107, 110
Hull, John A. T., 107
Hunker Political Party, 128
Huttonsville, Virginia, 18, 30, 211
Hyperion Golf and Tennis Club, 205

I

indenture contract, 17, 18
indentured servants, 31, 47
Independence, Missouri, 61, 62
Indian Agency House, Fort Des Moines, Iowa, 71–73
Indian Agency, Marion County, Iowa, 76
Indian attacks, 19
Indian Council of 1842 at Agency City, Iowa, 82, 83
Indian Removal Act of 1830, 80
Indian Territory, 71, 73, 76, 77, 81, 92
Indianapolis, Indiana, 59
Indianola, Iowa, 138
Ingersoll Park, 205
Interurban Railway streetcar, 195
Iowa Banking, 124
Iowa Capitol Building, 110, 118–120, 146
Iowa City, Iowa, 92, 93, 108, 110–113, 115, 118–120, 124, 129, 130, 134–136, 138, 142, 143, 156, 177
Iowa Constitutional Convention of 1857, 110, 118, 119, 122, 132
Iowa Election of 1854, 108
Iowa House of Representatives, 6
Iowa Land Office, Fort Des Moines, Iowa, 92, 93, 107
Iowa Land Rush of 1845, 77, 85, 122
Iowa Legislative Session—Fifth (1854–55), 110
Iowa Legislative Session—Fourth (1852–53), 108
Iowa Legislative Session—Sixth (1856–57), 118
Iowa Pre-Exemption Act of 1841, 93

Iowa Railroad Company, 185
Iowa River, 81, 84, 118
Iowa State Fair, 177, 178, 205
Iowa State Medical Society, 179
Iowa temperance law, 122, 132
Iowa Terminal Division Station, 187
Iowa Territory, 8, 68 – 71, 73, 83, 92, 93, 123, 134
Iowa Thirty-ninth Regiment Volunteer Infantry, Des Moines and Davenport, Iowa, 146, 147
Iowa Twenty-third Regiment Volunteer Infantry, Des Moines, Iowa, 147
Iowa Wesleyan College, Mount Pleasant, Iowa, 108, 131
Iowa, 6, 8, 9, 26, 27, 40, 53, 68, 70, 71, 73, 75 – 95, 99, 100, 102, 103, 107–115, 117–120, 122–132, 134–150, 154–167, 175, 177, 179, 180, 185, 187, 190, 191, 194, 198, 202, 209, 210, 213
Iowa's Central Clearing House in Iowa City in the 1850s, 124
Ireland, 13, 15, 29, 40, 211
Ireland, James, 32
Itinerant preachers in Iowa, 33, 97, 98, 103, 191

J

Jackson, Anna Augusta, 192, 214
Jackson, Mississippi, 147
Jackson, President Andrew, 35, 52, 53, 80
Jasper County, Iowa, 109, 110, 190, 214
Jefferson, President Thomas, 34, 162
Jesse, B. F., 86
Jewett, Mrs., 180
John Brown's Raid, 142
John, George (son of Grace and Calvin), 200
Jordan Cemetery Association, 173
Jordan Cemetery, 6, 151, 172, 173, 191, 193, 198, 200, 205–207, 213, 214
Jordan Chapel, Walnut Township, Polk County, Iowa, 150, 151, 173, 191
Jordan Creek Elementary School, 6, 209
Jordan Creek Parkway, 6, 209
Jordan Creek Town Center, 6, 209
Jordan Creek, Polk County, Iowa, 6, 86, 88, 94, 96, 103, 111, 138
Jordan estate, 198, 200, 204, 206
Jordan farm, 51, 58, 88, 94, 95, 103, 114, 115, 141, 145, 146, 166, 168, 172, 177, 190, 191, 198, 199
Jordan House, 6, 7, 111, 114, 133, 134, 136–138, 140–142, 145, 150, 167, 168, 170, 173, 175, 177, 191, 192, 198–200, 204, 206–210
Jordan Livestock Enterprise, 171
Jordan Methodist Church, 100, 189, 192–194
Jordan Scholars program, 209
Jordan School, 96, 172, 173, 193, 194
Jordan, Agnes (daughter of Agnes Cunningham Jordan), 28, 51, 64, 65, 213
Jordan, Agnes Cunningham, 28, 36, 44, 49, 51, 57, 60, 62, 64
Jordan, Alice Warner, 190, 214
Jordan, Anna (James' sister), 60, 212
Jordan, Anna Augusta Jackson, 192, 214
Jordan, Benjamin Pittman, 59, 139, 213, 217
Jordan, Calvin Jr., 207, 217
Jordan, Calvin Smith, 217
Jordan, Charles (son of Benjamin), 141
Jordan, Charles (son of Grace and Calvin), 200
Jordan, Charles Green, 62
Jordan, Cynthia Disre' Adams Sheppard, 116, 117, 150, 151, 163, 175, 177, 183, 190, 198, 199, 212, 213, 214
Jordan, David Simpson, 115
Jordan, Drewsilla Pittman, 61, 95, 100, 213

Jordan, Eda, 151, 217
Jordan, Edward, 163, 171, 173, 203, 217
Jordan, Elizabeth, 212
Jordan, Ella, 150, 171, 175, 216
Jordan, Emily, 163, 206
Jordan, Eva, 171, 206, 217
Jordan, George Benton, 102, 202, 214, 217
Jordan, George Ernest, 202
Jordan, George Jr., 19, 26, 49, 211
Jordan, George Sr. (James' great-grandfather), 12, 26
Jordan, George, 17–20, 22, 27, 33, 49, 58, 102, 115
Jordan, Grace Cook, 200
Jordan, Hattie, 216
Jordan, Henry Clay, 217
Jordan, James C.—abolitionist, 8, 9, 27, 47, 49, 53, 117, 132, 136, 144
Jordan, James C.—antislavery candidate in the Iowa 1854 election, 109, 110
Jordan, James C.—as state senator, 86, 110, 112, 115, 118, 122, 125, 129, 130, 132, 158, 167, 173
Jordan, James C.—birth, 34–36
Jordan, James C.—Board member of the Iowa Railroad Company, 185
Jordan, James C.—cattle breeder, 40, 165
Jordan, James C.—Chief Conductor of the Underground Railroad in Polk County, Iowa, 8, 133, 135
Jordan, James C.—death in Jordan Methodist Church, 192
Jordan, James C.—elected Polk County Supervisor, 1858, 6, 132
Jordan, James C.—elected to the Iowa House of Representatives in 1878, 6
Jordan, James C.—elected Township Trustee of Fort Des Moines, 103, 106
Jordan, James C.—elected vice president of the Old Settlers' Association, 1868, 161
Jordan, James C.—Equitable of Iowa Board of Directors, 160
Jordan, James C.—funeral, eulogy, and burial, 192
Jordan, James C.—helping to form the Republican Party, 6, 9, 47, 129, 197
Jordan, James C.—Jordan Chapel builder, 151
Jordan, James C.—known as "Honorable" James C. Jordan, 106
Jordan, James C.—known as "Uncle Jimmy," 7, 46, 91, 98–100, 102, 103, 106, 107, 114, 125, 132, 158, 160, 163, 165–167, 169, 171, 177, 185–187, 190, 192–194, 213
Jordan, James C.—Last Will and Testament, 202, 203
Jordan, James C.—marriage to Melinda Pittman, 61
Jordan, James C.—member of the American Shorthorn Breeders Association, 165
Jordan, James C.—paying for and receiving title to his Iowa farm, 201
Jordan, James C.—Polk County Board of Supervisors, 145
Jordan, James C.—Polk County Poor Farm, 9, 132
Jordan, James C.—provides financial assistance for Cottage Hospital, 182
Jordan, James C.—re-elected vice president of the Old Settlers' Association, 1873, 162
Jordan, James C.—runs for Iowa State Senate as a Whig, 107
Jordan, James C.—sale of land to Simon Casady and Conrad Youngerman in 1884, 186, 190
Jordan, James C.—sells land to the Rock Island Railroad and plats an area by the tracks in, 185, 186

James Jordan: His Life and His Legacy 229

Jordan, James C.—showcase Shorthorn cattle at Iowa State Fair, 178
Jordan, James C.—State Bank of Iowa in Des Moines, Iowa—investor and Director, 125
Jordan, James C.—superintendent of local school, 95, 116
Jordan, James Finley, 94, 100, 139, 191, 197, 199, 217
Jordan, Jemima, 60, 93, 100, 102, 114, 213
Jordan, John (brother of George Sr.), 17
Jordan, John (son of George Jr.), 26, 27, 49, 51
Jordan, John Quincy, 78, 217
Jordan, John Slater (brother of James C.), 26, 28, 68, 73, 86, 96, 98, 114, 115, 116, 213
Jordan, Kasson, 190, 198, 214, 217
Jordan, Louise Wayne, 190
Jordan, Margaret, 62, 63, 213
Jordan, Marie Taylor, 51, 212
Jordan, Martha Lightfoot, 27, 28, 211
Jordan, Mary Elizabeth Haines, 144, 145, 213
Jordan, Mary Magdalene Worley, 115, 213
Jordan, Mary Melinda Dewitt, 100
Jordan, Mary, 36, 58, 212
Jordan, Maud, 207
Jordan, Max, 207, 217
Jordan, Melinda Pittman, 60–64, 67, 68, 78, 85–88, 90, 91, 94–96, 99, 100, 102, 103, 107, 111–114, 136, 139, 173, 192, 213
Jordan, Pauline, 190, 200, 214, 217
Jordan, Phoebe, 212
Jordan, Ralph, 190, 200, 214, 217
Jordan, Robert Roy, 190, 198, 206, 207, 217
Jordan, Rupert, 190, 200, 205, 214
Jordan, Susan (James' sister), 28, 36, 57, 58, 211, 212
Jordan, William Henry, 206, 217

K

Kagi, John Henri, 141, 143
Kanawha County, Virginia, 18, 51, 58, 212
Kansas border ruffians, 140
Kansas Pacific Railway, 163
Kansas-Nebraska Act, 126, 127
Kansas/Nebraska Territory, 63
Kaskaskia River, 27
Kasson, John, 129, 130
Kentucky, 18, 22, 23, 27, 29, 34, 35, 41, 42, 65, 100, 163
Keokuk, Fort Des Moines and Minnesota Railroad Company, 157, 158
Keokuk, Iowa, 76, 89, 106, 119, 145, 146, 157–159, 177
Keokuk's Reserve, 81
Keosauqua, Iowa, 119
Key, Francis Scott, 35
Kirkwood, Samuel, 9, 118, 129, 130, 136, 139, 144, 146, 148, 149
Knights of Pythias, 191
Knox, Iowa, 137

L

land patents, 16
land speculators in Iowa, 77, 93
Lee County, Iowa, 80, 119
Lee, Ishmael and Marion, 134
Lee, Jason, 61
Leighton, Calvin, 158
Leman, Joseph, 27
Lewis and Clark, 34, 61
Lewis County, Virginia, 18, 23, 24, 37, 51, 58, 211, 212
Lewis Mills, Iowa, 142
Lewis, Iowa, 138
Liberator, The, 133
Lightfoot, Goodrich, 27

Lightfoot, Martha, 27, 28, 211
Lightfoot, Susanna Elizabeth Slaughter, 27
Lincoln, Abraham, 53, 129, 130, 131, 145, 148, 149, 150, 155, 156
Literary Fund, 36
Little Dixie, 65, 68, 127, 134, 140
Longhorn cattle, 163
Lord Dunmore's War, 25, 34
Louisiana Purchase, 34, 35, 53, 126
Lynnville, Iowa, 134
Lyons, Hinton, 86
Lyons, Jacob, 86

M

Madison County, Iowa, 102, 114–117, 213, 214
Madison, President James, 35
Maine, 126
Manifest Destiny, 81, 110
Marion County, Iowa, 76, 82
Marion, Iowa, 92
Marshall County, Iowa, 84, 146
Marshalltown, Iowa, 110, 214
Mayhew Cabin Tunnel, Nebraska City, Nebraska Territory, 137
Mayhew, Allen B., 136
McCleary, George, 84
McCoy Creek, Berrien County, Michigan, 60
McCoy, Joe, 163
McCoy, Reverend Isaac, 53
McCoy, Russell, 60
McFadden, Bonnie, 208
McNullen, Thomas, 161
Mercy Hospital, 181, 183
Merrill Junior High School, Des Moines Public Schools, Des Moines, Iowa, 193
Meskwaki Tribe, 68, 79, 118
Methodism, 8, 9, 27, 33, 38, 39, 41, 42, 43, 47, 49, 51, 60, 61, 86, 91, 92, 94, 98, 99, 100, 108, 116, 117, 122, 127, 129, 130, 131, 132, 134, 136, 150, 151, 190, 191, 196
Methodist Church in Iowa, 91, 92, 94, 99, 100, 107, 116, 117, 122, 127, 130, 136, 150, 151
Methodist Church, Ashawa, Polk County, Iowa, 191–193
Methodist Hospital, Des Moines, Iowa, 184, 191
Michigan Farm, 61, 62
Michigan Road, 59
Michigan, 8, 40, 53, 56–62, 68, 78, 79, 88, 116, 134
Middle River, Carlisle, Iowa, 73, 117
Minneapolis and St. Louis Railroad, 185
Mississippi and Missouri Railroad (M&MRR), 156, 158, 159
Mississippi River, 8, 27, 35, 48, 53, 79–81, 87, 139, 147, 148, 155, 156, 164, 180
Missouri Bill, 125
Missouri bushwackers, 125
Missouri Compromise, 53, 126
Missouri Farm, 78, 85
Missouri River, 8, 63, 65, 67, 82, 83, 87, 127, 134, 136, 137
Missouri, 8, 40, 53, 61–68, 73, 76, 78, 79, 81, 83, 85–89, 100, 102, 114, 115, 117, 125–127, 129, 134, 136, 139–142, 146, 147, 156, 159, 177
Mitchell, Ms., 180
Mitchell, Thomas, 72, 73, 161
Mitchellville, Iowa, 73, 134, 138
Moccasin Bluff, Berrien County, Michigan, 60
Monroe City, Iowa, 110
Monroe, Mrs., 180
Montgomery County, Ohio, 60
Moorefield, Virginia, 18, 24, 29, 40, 44, 45
Mormon Trail, 94

Mott, L., 186
Mrs. Bird's Female Seminary, Fort Des Moines, Iowa, 106
Muscatine, Iowa, 177
Myers, Peter, 161

N

Nagle, Frank, 161
Nash, J. A., 161
Nat Turner Rebellion, 52, 53
National Bank, 53, 78, 125
National Banking Act of 1863, 125
National Register of Historic Places, 6, 208, 209
National Republican Party, 53, 129
National Road, 57–59
National Underground Railroad Network to Freedom, 6, 209
Nebraska City, 136–138
Nebraska Territory, 63, 136
Neutral Ground—Indian, 71, 80, 81
New Design, 26, 27, 33, 39, 49, 51, 211
New River Gorge, Virginia, 36
Newhall, J. B., 70, 75
Newton, Iowa, 110
Nez Pierce Tribe, 61
Nicholas County, Virginia, 35, 51, 212, 213
Niles, Berrien County, Michigan, 53, 59, 60, 213
Norris, David, 161
North Des Moines, Iowa, 174
Northern Neck Proprietary, 13, 14
Northwestern University, 97, 145, 162, 163, 167

O

Ockerman, Mrs., 95
Octogenarian Society, 162, 184
Ogle, Captain Joseph, 27
Oglethorpe, General George, 33
Ohio River, 19, 25, 27, 50, 57–59
Old Fields Church Cemetery, 29
Old Fields, South Branch Valley, Virginia, 26
Old Settlers' Association, 161
Old Stone Tavern, Moorefield, Virginia, 45
Oregon Trail, 8, 61, 62, 64, 67, 68, 87
Oregon, 61, 67, 86, 116, 190
Osawatomie, Kansas, 140
Oskaloosa, Iowa, 107, 110, 158, 177
Ottumwa, Iowa, 76, 119, 158

P

P. T. Barnum's Greatest Show on Earth Circus, 181, 182
Pa ta co to, 84
Page County, Iowa, 146
Palatinate, Germany, 17
Palo Alto County, Iowa, 84
Parmalee, John, 73
Parmalee's Mill, Carlisle, Iowa, 73, 86, 90, 103
Parsons Plantation, 24
Parsons, James, 24, 26, 29, 45
Parsons, Parthenia, 24
Parsons, Prudence, 24, 25, 29, 211
Parsons, Thomas, 29, 45
Parsons, Tom Jr., 24
Parsons, West Virginia, 25
Pearsall's Flats, Virginia, 21
Pella, Iowa, 110
Pendleton County, Virginia, 25, 28, 30, 48, 211, 212
Pennsylvania, 12, 13, 14, 19, 23, 25, 27, 50, 139, 211
Peters, R. P., 161
Petersburg, Virginia, 29, 30

Peterson, Hans Joggi Biedert, 16
Peterson, Mary Ursula Biedert, 16, 211
Peterson, Sarah Mohlerin, 16
Phelps and Company, 72
Phenix School, Valley Junction, Iowa, 194
Philadelphia, Pennsylvania, 13, 17, 176
Piedmont Virginia, 12, 47
Pinkerton, Allen, 143
pioneer cabins, 15, 16, 18, 19, 20, 21, 24, 25, 37, 38, 44, 45, 49, 60, 63, 73, 76, 85, 86, 87, 95, 97, 98, 102, 110, 115, 180
pioneer housewife, 111, 112
Pioneer Law Makers Society, 162
Pioneers Society, 162
Pittman, Benjamin, 60, 61
Pittman, Drewsilla, 60, 61, 213
Pittman, Jemima DeWitt, 60
Pittman, Melinda, 60, 61, 113, 213
Platte County, Missouri, 63, 64, 65, 68, 78, 85, 86, 213, 214
Platte Purchase, 64
Pocahontas County, Iowa, 171, 190, 198
Polk County Board of Supervisors, 145
Polk County Poor Farm, 9, 132
Polk County, Iowa, 6, 8, 73, 78, 86, 91, 92, 93, 94, 95, 102, 107, 108, 109, 110, 111, 115, 119, 125, 129, 132, 133, 134, 135, 141, 145, 166, 174, 179, 181, 193, 202, 204, 210, 213, 214
Polk, Jefferson Scott, 161
Pony Express, 114, 115
Porter, Mrs., 180
Pottawattamie County, Iowa, 146
Pottowatomie Tribe, 70
Powers Dairy, 200
Powers, Jim and Hazel, 200
prayer meetings, 33, 43, 99
Pre-Exemption Act of 1838, 62
Presbyterian Church, 32, 40, 150
primogeniture, 22, 29
pro-slavery, 65, 135, 140
prohibition, 9, 100, 108, 118, 122, 132, 190

Q

Qua ti bi ta—interpreter, 84
Quakers, 110, 134, 138, 139, 142, 143

R

Raccoon River, 6, 71, 73, 76, 85, 86, 88, 92, 96, 107, 110, 119, 145, 154, 159, 163, 170, 185, 186, 187, 191, 198
Randolph Academy, 38
Randolph County, Virginia, 21, 23, 24, 25, 29, 30, 38, 211, 212
Rathbun, Ezra, 161
Raynor, Reverend, 98
Red Rock Wall in Marion County, Iowa, 76
Redhead, Wesley, 135, 161
Republican Party, 6, 9, 47, 53, 122, 126, 129, 131, 133, 184, 197
revivals, 24, 41, 42, 96, 98, 99, 178
Revolutionary War, 26, 27, 30, 34, 38, 41, 45, 47, 51, 80
Rising Sun, Iowa, 138
Robidoux, Joseph—trading post, 62, 67
Robinson, Reverend Demas, 135, 138
Rock Island Railroad disaster, 181, 182
Rock Island Railroad, 143, 155, 156, 159, 181, 185, 186, 187, 194, 196
Rock Island, Illinois, 79, 81, 155, 156
Romney, Virginia, 16, 21, 44, 45, 46
Rotterdam, Holland, 17

S

Sac (Sauk) Tribe, 77, 79, 80, 81, 82, 83, 84
safe house, 136, 138

Salem, Iowa, 134
Salter, William, 132
Santa Fe Trail, 67
Saukenuk, Illinois, 79
Savannah Township, Platte County, Missouri, 63
Savery, Mrs., 180
Saylor, H. H., 161
Saylor, John B., 73
Saylorville, Iowa, 73
scalping, 19
Schotarie Valley, New York, 22
Scott, J. B., 73, 83
Scott, Phoebe, 21, 22, 25, 211
Scott, Wilson Alexander, 120
Scott's Purchase, 81
Second Fox War of 1728, 79
Second Great Awakening, 8, 41, 43, 47, 49, 53, 61, 133, 136
Seni Om Sed, 178
Sevastopol, Iowa, 174
Seventh Street Hospital, Des Moines, Iowa, 180, 181
Seward Whigs/Free Soilers Political Party, 128
Shasta County, California, 115
Shaw brothers, 192
Shaw, Samuel, 86
Shawnee Tribe, 21, 23
Shenandoah Valley, Virginia, 19, 22, 24
Sheppard, Cynthia Disre' Adams, 116, 117, 213, 214
Sherman Hill, 167
Sherman, General, 147, 148
Sherman, Hoyt, 9, 161, 167
Sherman, Lampson, 161
Shorthorn cattle, 39, 40, 89, 163, 164, 165, 177, 178
Sibley, Iowa, 185
Silver Grey Whig Political Party, 128
Simpson College, 97, 163
Sioux Tribe, 79, 80, 81
Sketches of Iowa, 70
Slater, Agnes, 23, 25, 211, 212
Slaughter, Goodrich, 27
Slaughter, Susanna Elizabeth, 27
slave bounty hunters, 136, 139
slavery, 8, 33, 46, 47, 48, 49, 52, 53, 63, 65, 78, 94, 100, 102, 108, 109, 110, 117, 118, 126, 127, 128, 129, 132, 133, 134, 136, 139, 140, 143, 144, 149
Smart, Joseph, 129
Smart, Josiah, 71
Smith Cemetery, Ridgely, Missouri, 65
Smith, Agnes Jordan, 190
Smith, Anna Jordan, 60, 68, 89, 114, 145, 212
Smith, Calvin, 64, 65, 140, 145, 146, 190, 213, 214
Smith, Humphrey "Yankee," 64, 65, 67, 136, 140
Smith, James, 27
Smith, John, 33
Smith, William, 51, 58, 60, 68, 89, 114, 211
Smith's Fork, Missouri, 64
Smith's Mill, 64
Smithville, Missouri, 64, 211
South Bend, Indiana, 59
South Branch Potomac River, 13, 14, 21, 24, 29, 39
South Branch Valley Farms Plantation, 29, 46, 48
South Branch Valley, Virginia, 13, 14, 15, 16, 17, 19, 21, 22, 23, 24, 25, 26, 29, 44, 45, 64, 211
Spanish Fort, Mobile, Alabama, 148
Spaulding, Henry H., 61
Spofford, C. S., 161
Spofford, Mr. and Mrs. S. F., 161

Springdale, Iowa, 134, 139, 142, 143, 144
Springfield, Massachusetts, 139, 140
squatters, 15, 76, 83, 91, 92, 93
St. Charles, Madison County, Iowa, 115, 213
St. John's Congregational Church, Springfield, Massachusetts, 140
St. Joseph River, Berrien County, Michigan, 53, 59, 60
St. Joseph, Missouri, 62, 67, 68, 73, 87
St. Louis, Missouri, 34, 70, 80, 89, 124, 145, 146, 155, 158
St. Paul's Episcopal Church—Ladies of the Helping Hand Society, 180
St. Paul's Episcopal Church, Des Moines, Iowa, 108, 181, 183
"Star Spangled Banner," 35
State Bank of Iowa, 6, 9, 53
state banks, 108, 118, 125, 149
State Road from Davenport to Council Bluffs, Iowa, 94
Statesman, The, 129
steamboat travel, 63, 71, 87, 90, 92, 108, 119, 120, 145, 154, 155, 157
Stevens, Aaron D., 141, 143
Story County, Iowa, 146
Stowe, Harriet Beecher, 133
Street, General Joseph, 76
Summers, US Marshall Laurel, 143
surgeon general of the Iowa National Guard, 180
Swift, Benton, 62
Sypher, M. R., 161
Sypher, R. W., 161

T

Tabor, Iowa, 126, 129, 132, 134, 136, 137, 138, 140, 142, 143
Tama County, Iowa, 84
Tama, Iowa, 84, 118
Taylor, Marie, 51, 53, 212
Taylor, Reverend John Wray, 51, 53, 60
Teesdale, John, 135, 138, 142
Teeter, George and Philip, 30
Terrace Hill Gala in 1869, 167
Terrace Hill, Des Moines, Iowa, 124, 167
Texas Longhorn cattle, 163
Texas Range, 163
Thirty-ninth Regiment Volunteer Infantry, Des Moines and Davenport, Iowa, 146
thoroughbred trotting horses, 177, 178, 191, 197, 199
Thrift, Hamilton, 83
Thrift, J. M., 162
Tidewater Virginia, 12, 32, 47, 50, 52
Tidrick, Robert L., 93, 161
Tippecanoe Society, 162
Tipton, Iowa, 134
Todd, C. P., 141
Todd, Reverend John, 132, 138, 143
Toledo, Iowa, 84, 118
Tracey Home Hospital, 183, 184
Tracey, Annie B., 180, 181, 183
Trading Post, Kansas, 141
Treaty of Fontainebleau, 27
Treaty of Lancaster (Pennsylvania), 19
Treaty of St. Louis, 1804, 80
treaty signing with the Sac and Fox Tribes at Agency City, Iowa, 82
Trough of South Fork Potomac, 15, 45
Trowbridge, Colonel, 143
Truth, Sojourner, 140
Tubman, Harriet, 117
Tuttle, General James Madison, 161
Tygart Valley, Randolph County, Virginia, 23, 39, 30

U

Ulster Plantation, Northern Ireland, 13, 40, 211
Ulster Scots, 13, 40
Uncle Tom's Cabin, 133
Underground Railroad (URR), 6, 8, 9, 47, 128, 129, 130, 132, 133, 134, 135, 136, 137, 138, 139, 140, 141, 142, 143, 144, 150, 208
Underground Railroad stations in Polk County, Iowa, 137
Union Stock Yards, Chicago, Illinois, 164
University of Iowa, Iowa City, Iowa, 110
University Place, Iowa, 174
US Senatorial and gubernatorial elections 1848–1932, 107, 108, 109, 110, 122, 129, 136, 197, 198

V

Valley Junction Christian Church, 196
Valley Junction Express newspaper, 194
Valley Junction, Iowa, 6, 7, 9, 96, 173, 177, 185, 186, 187, 190, 192, 194, 195, 196, 197, 198, 199, 200, 201, 208, 209, 213, 214
Valley of Virginia, 12, 14, 28, 38, 41, 47
Van Meter family, 15, 20, 21, 22, 26, 29, 44, 45, 46, 48, 64
Van Meter, Annetje (Hannah), 14
Van Meter, Benjamin, 13, 15, 16, 29
Van Meter, Garrett, 26, 29, 48
Van Meter, Isaac, 14, 18, 19, 26
Van Meter, Sally, 26, 29, 211
Vandalia, Illinois, 27, 58
Vicksburg, Mississippi, 146, 147
Victorian lifestyle, 167, 169, 170, 174, 200
Victorian weddings and rituals, 170, 171, 174
Virginia House of Burgesses, 13, 19, 51
Virginia, 6, 8, 12, 13, 14, 15, 16, 17, 19, 22, 25, 26, 27, 28, 29, 30, 31, 32, 33, 34, 35, 36, 37, 38, 39, 40, 41, 42, 44, 45, 47, 48, 49, 50, 51, 52, 53, 57, 58, 59, 60, 61, 64, 97, 99, 100, 103, 138, 141, 143, 144, 164, 168
Virginian's Burying Ground, Buchanan, Michigan, 60

W

Wagon Trail Road, Walnut Township, Polk County, Iowa, 177
wagon train, 8, 57, 61, 62, 64, 67, 115, 137
Walnut Creek Settlement, Polk County, Iowa, 86
Walnut Creek, Polk County, Iowa, 76, 86, 145, 191, 192, 195
Walnut Hill School, Valley Junction Public Schools, Valley Junction, Iowa, 194
Walnut Township, Polk County, Iowa, 8, 9, 76, 78, 86, 94, 98, 141, 145, 146, 150, 151, 162, 173, 177, 185, 186, 187, 190, 191, 192, 194, 197, 198, 208, 214
Wapello County, Iowa, 73
War Hawks, 35
War of 1812, 35, 38, 80
Ward, Mary Peterson Cunningham, 21, 22, 25, 30, 211
Ward, Sylvester, 21
Warner, Alice, 190, 214
Washington, DC, 35, 77, 108, 109, 126, 129, 130, 162
Washington, George, 19, 20, 28, 35, 71, 102, 144
Wayne County, Iowa, 146, 213
Webster Township, Polk County, Iowa, 145
Welton, William, 29
Wesley, Charles, 33
Wesley, John, 33
West Branch, Iowa, 139

West Des Moines Historical Society, 7, 208, 209, 232
West Des Moines, Iowa, 6, 9, 173, 196, 208, 209, 210, 213, 232
West Liberty, Iowa, 143
West Point, 97, 148
West Virginia, 12, 17, 25, 36, 38, 50, 59
West, Captain Francis, 161
Westport, Missouri, 64, 65, 67, 68, 87, 146
Westward Expansion, 99, 154
Wheeling, Virginia, 59
Whig Political Party, 53, 108, 109, 124, 128, 129, 130, 133, 136
White House, 35
Whitefield, George, 31, 32, 33, 54
Whitman Mission, 61
Whitman, Dr. Henry, 161
Whitman, Dr. Marcus, 41
Willamette Valley, Oregon, 61, 62, 116
Williamson, Colonel James A., 125
Williamson, W. W., 161
Winchester, Virginia, 45
Winnebago Tribe, 79
winter of 1846, 86
Winterset, Iowa, 89, 102, 114, 115, 116, 117, 134, 166, 185
Withrow, Abel, 36, 51
Withrow, Susan Jordan, 28, 36, 51, 57, 58, 211, 212
Wood, Elizabeth Jordan, 5, 212
Wood, James, 51, 212
Woodland Cemetery, Des Moines, Iowa, 173, 184, 200, 206, 207, 213, 214
Worley, Mary Magadalene, 115, 213
worm fence, 88
Wray, Hiram, 60

Y

Young, Madison, 161
Youngerman, Conrad, 186, 190

Louise Gately. Photographer, Scott Little

Jan Davison. Photographer, Scott Little

About the Author:

(Mary) **Louise Gately** was born in Milwaukee and raised in Delafield, Wisconsin. She graduated from Drake University, Des Moines, Iowa, with a BA in history and social science and also holds an MSE in higher ed. administration/development from Drake. She has held various jobs: college administrator in Germany and in the United States; communications director for several non-profit organizations; special education teacher; and grant writer. Throughout her life she has been a community volunteer—in Iowa and also in Minnesota. She served on the board of West Des Moines Historical Society for almost twenty-five years and is the Jordan historian in West Des Moines.

Her home overlooks Jordan Creek in West Des Moines, Iowa. She is married to Gary Gately. Her family includes her two children, three step-children, and eleven grandchildren.

About the Editor:

Janet M. Davison grew up in Owatonna, Minnesota. She earned a bachelor of fine arts degree from Drake University in Des Moines, Iowa, where she studied graphic design and journalism. For most of her working career she owned her own freelance graphic design business but also was employed as a director of communications for several years before retirement.

Jan now spends her time drawing, painting, writing poetry, volunteering, and enjoying her family, which includes her husband, Polk Davison, their daughter, son-in-law, and two grandchildren.

Map Labels

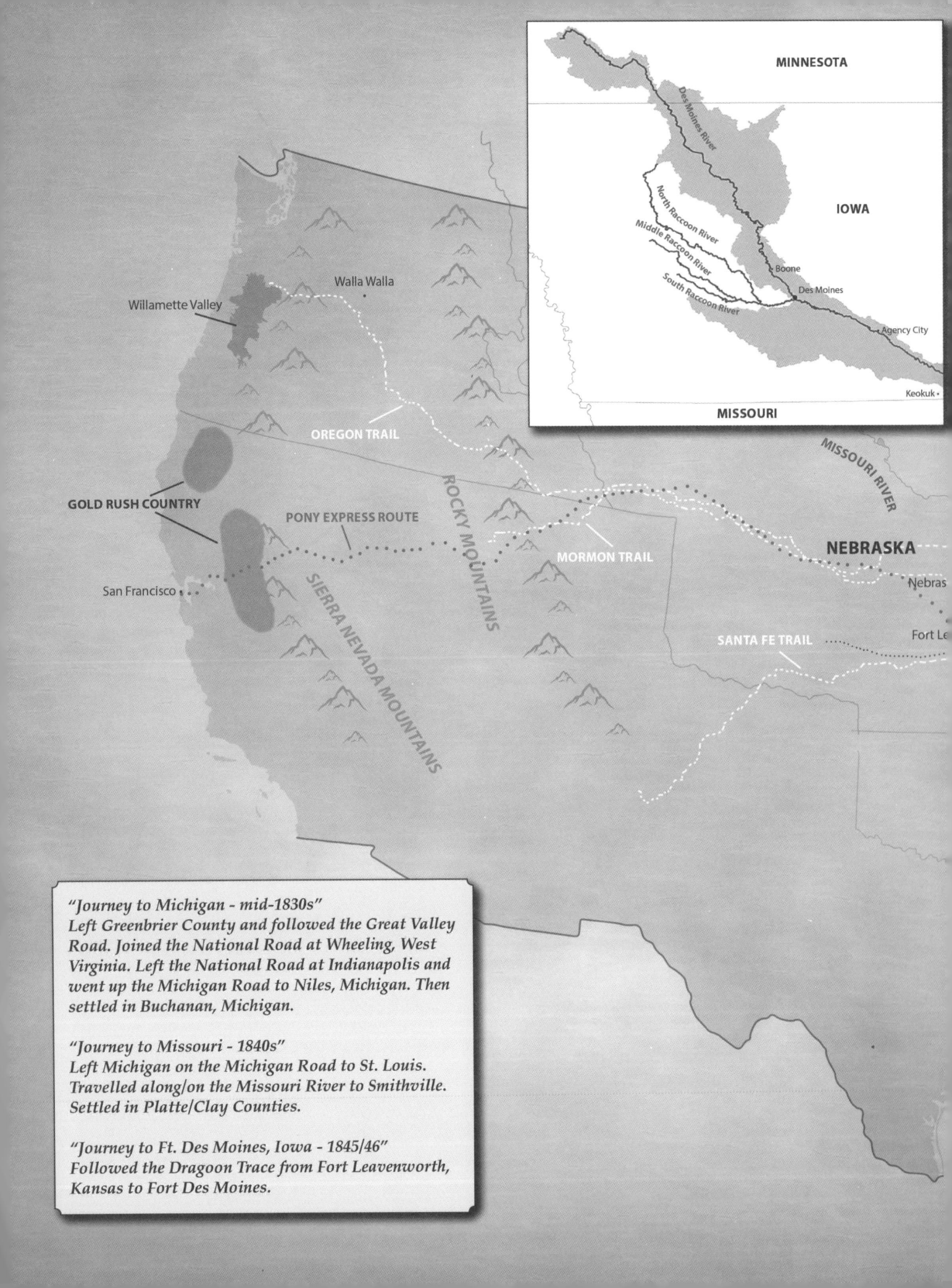

- Willamette Valley
- Walla Walla
- **GOLD RUSH COUNTRY**
- OREGON TRAIL
- PONY EXPRESS ROUTE
- San Francisco
- ROCKY MOUNTAINS
- SIERRA NEVADA MOUNTAINS
- MORMON TRAIL
- MISSOURI RIVER
- SANTA FE TRAIL
- NEBRASKA
- Nebras[ka]
- Fort Le[avenworth]

Inset Map
- MINNESOTA
- IOWA
- MISSOURI
- Des Moines River
- North Raccoon River
- Middle Raccoon River
- South Raccoon River
- Boone
- Des Moines
- Agency City
- Keokuk

Journey Descriptions

"Journey to Michigan - mid-1830s"
Left Greenbrier County and followed the Great Valley Road. Joined the National Road at Wheeling, West Virginia. Left the National Road at Indianapolis and went up the Michigan Road to Niles, Michigan. Then settled in Buchanan, Michigan.

"Journey to Missouri - 1840s"
Left Michigan on the Michigan Road to St. Louis. Travelled along/on the Missouri River to Smithville. Settled in Platte/Clay Counties.

"Journey to Ft. Des Moines, Iowa - 1845/46"
Followed the Dragoon Trace from Fort Leavenworth, Kansas to Fort Des Moines.